THE BRIGHTER SIDE OF HUMAN NATURE

By the Same Author

No Contest: The Case against Competition (1986)

THE
BRIGHTER SIDE
OF HUMAN NATURE

Altruism and Empathy in Everyday Life

ALFIE KOHN

BasicBooks
A Division of HarperCollinsPublishers

Library of Congress Cataloging-in-Publication Data
Kohn, Alfie.
   The brighter side of human nature : altruism and
   empathy in everyday life/Alfie Kohn.
     p. cm.
   Includes bibliographical references.
   ISBN 0-465-00665-5 (cloth)
   ISBN 0-465-00758-9 (paper)
   1. Altruism. 2. Empathy. I. Title.
BJ1471.K64 1990
171'.8—dc20   89-43102
                                  CIP

Those who dwell preponderantly upon the selfish aspect of human nature and flout as sentimentalism the "altruistic" conception of it, make their chief error in failing to see that our self itself is altruistic. . . . The improvement of society does not call for any essential change in human nature, but, chiefly, for a larger and higher application of its familiar impulses.

—Charles Horton Cooley (1909)

Contents

Acknowledgments

All books, even those with one name on the cover, are cooperative projects. Anyone who writes seriously soon comes to realize that authors express their indebtedness not because some federal law requires it but because they truly are indebted. This book, for example, literally would not exist without other people's labor, specifically that of the researchers and writers represented in the bibliography's six or seven hundred entries.

One of the lessons I learned a few years ago is that the best way to research any subject is to publish a book on it. Readers are only too happy to point out to you the sources you should have included but somehow missed. I have no doubts that this will happen again, and perhaps I should express my appreciation in advance to those who will send citations to me and complain about my oversights.

In the meantime, there are plenty of people who already have contributed to the book and to my thinking on the subjects it covers. I had conversations, in some cases lengthy and multiple, with a number of talented people. The willingness of Dan Batson, Ervin Staub, Nancy Eisenberg, and Martin Hoffman to share their insights and scholarship suggests a delightful fit between professional interest and personal character. I'm happy to report that there is no evidence of a trade-off between studying generosity and living it. Parts of the book are also richer for the talks I've had with Dick Lewontin and Leon Kamin, Ann Higgins and Bob Selman, Carol Gilligan and Martha Minow, Dennis Krebs, Paul Schervish, George and Barbara Morgan, Larry Blum, and Suzanne Gordon.

For an author nothing epitomizes what moral philosophers call supererogation—and the rest of us simply refer to as going beyond the call of duty—like reading and criticizing someone else's work. I'm very grateful for the critical comments on various chapters that I've received from Nancy Eisenberg, Larry Blum, Dick Lewontin, David Adams, Jeffrey Goldstein, Marian Yarrow, Bob Selman, Dennis Krebs, Eric Schaps et al., Martin Hoffman, and Tom Wiedman. Special mention goes to Dan Batson, Ervin Staub, and Phil Korman, who were positively heroic in their willingness to review and dissect excessive quantities of my prose. And let me spare any of these folks from having to say it out loud: It's true—I should have accepted more of their suggestions.

Then there is Bill Greene. Bill doesn't read my manuscripts: He sifts through them, line by line, idea by idea, pointing out awkward phrasings, inconsistent arguments, structural deficiencies, and unnecessarily provocative rhetoric until I want to strangle him with gratitude. He does this, astonishingly enough, with every single chapter. You want an operational definition of altruism? My sharing Bill with other authors would do nicely. I don't know what I did to deserve the time and care he invests in my writing, but I desperately hope he doesn't call it quits after two books.

The gratitude continues. It was George Morgan who introduced me a dozen years ago to the writings of Martin Buber and who gently challenged me to recognize the limits of any world view premised on the solitary individual. Jon Beckwith was kind enough to open his file cabinets to me. John Ware, my agent, worked his tail off to find a publisher for this project because he believed in its value. Finally, let me say that Jo Ann Miller at Basic richly deserves the praise lavished on her by other authors in *their* acknowledgment sections; this woman knows what she is doing.

I

NATURAL ASSUMPTIONS

1

On the Existence
of a "Human Nature"

*The wave of acceptance of genetic influence on behavior is growing
into a tidal wave that threatens to engulf the [message that] . . .
variability in complex behaviors of interest to psychologists and to
society is due at least as much to environmental influences as it is
to genetic influences. . . . The danger now is that the swing from
environmentalism will go too far.*

—Robert Plomin (1989)

Consider this curious set of facts about our culture: Someone who thinks
well of himself is said to have a healthy self-concept and is envied. Someone who thinks well of his country is called a patriot and is applauded.
But someone who thinks well of his species is regarded as hopelessly
naive and is dismissed.

The conventional wisdom has it that no one could look hard at the
particulars of human behavior and be pleased with what he sees. So
deeply held is this view that if some extraterrestrial intelligence were to
talk about us the way *we* talk about us, there would likely be an interplane-
tary war. Think, for example, of the expression "I'm only human." The
emphasis is on the middle word: it is what we fail to do or be that seems
to us most noteworthy. The phrase "human nature," meanwhile, is reserved, as if by some linguistic convention, for what is nasty and negative
in our repertoire. We invoke it to explain selfishness rather than service,
competition rather than cooperation, egocentricity rather than empathy.
On any given day we may witness innumerable gestures of caring, ranging from small acts of kindness to enormous sacrifices, but never do we
shrug and say, "Well, what did you expect? It's just human nature to be
generous."

Of course, this is no mere quirk of language. It is evidence of a widespread belief that our darker side is more pervasive, more persistent, and somehow more real than our other facets. Notice also that the most common modifier for *truths* is *unpleasant*. Or that *anarchy* is invariably intended as an epithet; we assume that the absence of state-controlled power is an invitation to murderous chaos. Conversely, *altruism* is a label reserved for extraordinary, self-sacrificing actions—thereby confirming our assumption that those who put the interests of others first are a rare breed indeed.

We raise our children, manage our companies, and design our governments on the assumption that people are naturally and primarily selfish and will act otherwise only if they are coerced to do so and carefully monitored. We assume that genuine generosity is only a mirage on an endless desert of self-interest; if we are lucky, that self-interest will occasionally be of the "enlightened" sort, but it will retain the same prefix.

My argument in this book is not that aggression and competition, selfishness and egocentricity, do not exist. Obviously they do, and the joyful squeals about human potential one hears from some quarters are all the more grating for their failure to acknowledge this. But the dominant sounds in this culture are grumbles of cynicism about human nature that issue from a grossly unfair and distorted view of our species. My aim is to present a more balanced perspective—an affirmation of what there is to appreciate about humankind without ignoring the reality that people sometimes act rotten. Clearly, the only species to invent for itself judgments of good and evil has frequent occasion to use both.

In any attempt to arrive at balance, the decision about what facts to emphasize will depend on the starting point, the way our attitudes are currently skewed. Thus, in response to a stubborn refusal to recognize what is heartening about humans, I am chiefly interested in showing that there is more to us than the negative qualities we have come to identify with human nature. Most of us have heard only half the story. Human beings *are* selfish and self-centered, looking for any opportunity to take advantage. But human beings are also decent, able to feel others' pain and prepared to try to relieve it. There is good evidence to support the proposition that it is as "natural" to help as it is to hurt, that concern for the well-being of others often cannot be reduced to self-interest, that social structures predicated on human selfishness have no claim to inevitability—or even prudence. In short, the cynical consensus about our species is out of step with the hard data.

In the course of defending the idea that there is a brighter side of human nature, I will take the time simply to explore some ideas and research findings that pertain to the side of human beings that is other-regarding. This exploration is useful even apart from advancing the central argument, but it has usually been confined to writings intended only for specialists in the field. Thus part 2 of this book, "Responding to Others," addresses the matter of helping behaviors, beginning with a description in chapter 3 of the sort of person who is likely to come to someone else's aid and the conditions that promote this. It is interesting, in this context, to ask just how early in life we begin responding to others' distress and what can be done to encourage this response.

Chapter 4 examines the nature of empathy and the act of imagining the world from another person's point of view, proposing a fresh theoretical framework for conceiving of these processes. What does it mean, I ask, to imagine someone else's emotional state without actually feeling it—and vice versa? Chapter 5 discusses the tension between seeing others primarily as members of groups and seeing them simply as humans—with a consideration of dehumanization and what can be done about it—followed in chapter 6 by a report about experimental school programs that can help children become caring people.

Part 3, "From Me to You to Us," looks into our attitudes about altruism and self-interest. Chapter 7 describes and tries to account for the common view that all of our actions, even helping others, can ultimately be explained as so many attempts to benefit the self. This assumption, I argue in chapter 8, is philosophically untenable and empirically unjustified: contrary to the dominant models in sociobiology, economics, psychology, and the culture at large, sometimes we help simply to help. Finally, chapter 9 explores the consequences—including the moral implications—of moving beyond the individualistic foundation on which the ideas of selfishness and altruism are constructed.

The first task, though, is to inquire more deeply into our tendency to think the worst of ourselves. Anyone who attributes certain unsavory characteristics to human *nature* means to say more than that some people have acted badly. What is meant is that we are born with a particular orientation. Built into our pessimism, in other words, is a kind of determinism. Thus, to ask whether there is evidence to substantiate the idea of a brighter side to our nature is to raise the question of what it means to talk about having a nature—any nature—in the first place. After considering why so many of us accept this restricted and restricting view, I will turn in the next chapter to the task of exploring some of our assumptions about the *content* of this putatively given nature of ours—specifically, the belief that it is (that we are) basically selfish and aggressive.

RETURN TO THE PLANET OF NATURE/NURTURE

Whether we are the way we are because of nature or nurture, biology or environment, is today generally viewed as a question that is not only tiresome but settled. Nearly everyone agrees the dispute rests on a false dichotomy. Even the most extreme sociobiologist pays lip service to the importance of culture; conversely, blank-slate, give-me-a-baby-and-I'll-turn-it-into-anything-you-want behaviorists are no longer listed in the phone book. As a 1987 editorial in *Science* put it, "The debate on nature and nurture in regard to behavior is basically over. Both are involved."[1]

But not so fast. Biological determinists are still around, and so are their critics. The abandonment of immoderate rhetoric on the issue should not be confused with the disappearance of the controversy itself. "While claiming an interactionist position, most writers emphasize either a biological or environmental position," one psychologist observes.[2] And from a leading geneticist: Although "the current scientific fashion goes against reviewing the 'old' and 'pointless' nature-nurture argument . . . [it is] still very much with us, and it is time to exhume it from the rhetorically satisfying but scientifically meaningless cliches and give it new life as a meaningful problem."[3]

Certainly biology influences behavior. No writer I know denies this, and it is not my intention to equate any and all hereditarian findings with determinism. "The issue," in Stephen Jay Gould's words, "is not whether biology is relevant but how. The debate is between biological determinism (a theory of limits) and biology viewed as a range of capacity"[4]—the raw material for an unimaginably vast number of possible behaviors from which to choose.

Determinism may be said to take three forms, holding, respectively, that (1) differences among particular groups of people (genders, races, and so on) are innate, which is usually to say, genetically based, (2) a particular behavior, attitude, or social arrangement is an unavoidable part of being human, or (3) characteristics of a given individual are innate. Thus, the first sort of determinist may assert that females are naturally less talented than males at mathematics; the second may hold that human aggression is inevitable because we are hard-wired to hurt others; the third may believe that she was destined from birth to be a teacher.

Distinguishing among these categories is a practical matter, not just a conceptual one. Behavioral geneticists, who are keen to show that individual differences are innate, do not generally argue that there is a genetically determined *shared* human nature.[5] This belief is, however, common in other quarters, and of the three varieties it is my primary focus here. Despite, or perhaps because of, the celebrated happy-medium resolution of the nature/nurture question, there is an astonishing readiness on the part of psychologists, other researchers, and the public at large to assume that our behavior is largely determined by our genes. In this chapter, I want to offer examples of this orientation, explain what might account for it, and then examine the validity of particular determinist claims.

"INNATE? NECESSARILY SO"

Just as Americans were preparing the paraphernalia of patriotism to celebrate Independence Day in 1988, a U.S. battleship in the Persian Gulf shot down a commercial airliner carrying 290 civilians, 66 of them children. The dissimilarity between this jet and the F-14 fighter plane for which it was said to have been mistaken was so embarrassingly obvious that other explanations for the event were quickly invented: the plane was descending as if to attack, moving with unusual speed, and located well outside of the international commercial air corridor. When each one of these turned out to be completely false, *Newsweek* readers were no doubt relieved to learn that to one "expert on perceptual bias, such mistakes are almost unavoidable in battle. 'We call it human error,' he says. 'In fact, it's human nature.' "[6]

Apart from the ideological uses of the human nature argument—and anyone who doubts the relevance of ideology need only consider the likelihood of the same explanation's being proposed and prominently published if 290 American civilians had been killed by the Iranian military—the fact is that we are primed to accept it. Experts have been telling us, and we have been reminding each other, that virtually anything can be accounted for by referring to our genes or invoking the talismanic phrase "human nature." Consider some examples.

Psychological disorders, especially serious ones, are taken, with some justification, as the strongest case for the genetic hypothesis in the fields that study behavior. Most mental health professionals now believe that schizophrenia and bipolar disorder (manic-depressive illness) have a biological component. This assumption was reached largely on the basis of twin studies—which, as we shall see, are seriously flawed—but let us grant the strong probability that some persons are more likely than others to become schizophrenic, holding the environment constant.

The problem is that it is often asserted not merely that a genetic component exists but that schizophrenia is simply "a brain disease, now definitely known to be such," as a well-known psychiatrist put it.[7] A full-page newspaper advertisement by the National Alliance for the Mentally Ill (and partly underwritten by the American Psychiatric Association) assured readers that not only schizophrenia but severe depressive disorders, too, "are real biological diseases as clearly as cancer, multiple sclerosis, and diabetes are biological diseases. Like these disorders, mental illnesses are 'no fault' illnesses."[8] Even a modest familiarity with the relevant literature is enough to demonstrate how truly extraordinary this claim is,[9] but such statements are typical of our society's view of the nature/nurture dispute.

We expect and accept biological accounts of behavioral problems even where there is no supporting evidence at all. Take the case of hyperactivity.[10] The medical journals are littered with the remains of discarded theories purporting to explain how children more restless or distractible than most are really suffering from a disease (currently called Attention-Deficit Hyperactivity Disorder). It was held for quite some time that stimulant drugs have a "paradoxical effect" on hyperactive children; the very fact that they—and only they—were quieted by this sort of medication was said to prove that their troubles were biochemical. In the late 1970s, however, it was demonstrated that stimulants had precisely the same effects on the motor activity and attention of normal children.

For a while it was thought that the nervous systems of hyperactives were overaroused. Then it was thought they were underaroused. No reliable differences have been found in either direction, however. Indeed, the overwhelming majority of studies have shown that most hyperactive children have no discernible brain damage or neurological abnormalities; their EEG readings are not distinctive. Yet most researchers continue to assume that hyperactivity is biologically based; ask one whether there is any evidence to support this assumption, and a typical response is, "Not yet."[11]

This approach determines how the issue is framed and thereby manages to perpetuate itself, and what the psychologist Gerald Coles says about the study of learning disorders applies to a great many other topics in human behavior:

> The overwhelming majority of research is *not* a disinterested examination of a scientific question but a collection of tracts intent on making the child or the child's neurology responsible for his or her learning problems. . . . [The theory thus becomes] a research agenda . . . [that] carries with it a methodology in which brain structure and function are considered to be the primary, and usually the only, causal influences that need to be examined.[12]

Alcoholism is viewed by many researchers as likely to have a genetic component, although even those who hold this view—let alone those who do not—concede that no unequivocal proof exists that the major cause of excessive drinking is genetic. The psychologist John Searles of the University of Pennsylvania reviewed a Swedish adoption study said to show that heredity plays a significant role in alcoholism—the best piece of evidence that hereditarians have on this issue, incidentally—and found that it actually showed environmental pressures counted for more.[13] Even if one's tolerance to liquor turns out to have a heritable component, moreover, this does not mean—nor have good data shown—that hereditary factors have anything to do with how much one drinks. But such distinctions and reservations are often blurred; with the notable exception of a few dissenting monographs on the subject, alcoholism is usually described simply as a disease, something that happens to one—and (according to many) a disease that cannot be cured unless one acknowledges one's own helplessness in its presence.

Crime, in the determinist's view, is something particular individuals are born to get involved in. The most recent apology for a connection between crime and human nature was a book of that name by James Q. Wilson and Richard J. Herrnstein, the methodological shortcomings of which have been described by Leon Kamin.[14] (Kamin is the psychologist who exposed the fraudulent data on which Cyril Burt's claims of inherited intelligence were based.) The book was nonetheless discussed widely and appreciatively in the popular press, even as another new study, Elliott Currie's *Confronting Crime,* was being ignored. Currie's rigorous analysis considered the social and economic context of criminal behavior, showing, for example, that claims of universal increases in violent crime obscure the ten- or twentyfold differences between the murder rate in the United States and in most European countries,[15] making it very difficult indeed to defend any argument that relies on human nature.

Various personality features are regularly attributed to neurotransmitters, one improbable notion after another being published without any trace of irony. A leading professional journal not long ago included an assertion by the authors of the much-publicized Minnesota Twin Study that "personality differences are more influenced by genetic diversity than they are by environmental diversity"—the numerous personality characteristics in question ranging from achievement to "traditionalism."[16] The mere mention of dopamine or serotonin seems to paralyze the critical faculties of magazine and newspaper science writers, causing them to take seriously virtually any claim about how our behavior is chiefly a function of our biochemistry. One recent article gave credence to a neurological theory of why some people enjoy riding roller coasters. A Harvard psychiatrist, meanwhile, was quoted in the *New York Times Magazine* as explaining that people who stick others with the check at restaurants can best be understood in terms of "constitution, genetics, temperament. We think of the temperamental part of the person . . . someone who is just *naturally* tight, constricted, orderly, as opposed to someone who is more effusive, outgoing, open, expressive." He concedes that the environment, too, plays a role, but emphasizes a second time— and, of course, without evidence—that he is talking about "genetic differences."[17]

If specialists are rarely challenged on breezy pronouncements of this sort, it should surprise no one that laypeople leap to similar conclusions. In a recent newspaper profile of a movie actor, we read this: " 'I think it's just something that's genetic,' he said of his choice of career. 'It hits you and you know it's what you've got to do.' "[18] Helping to disseminate this type of thinking is the redoubtable Ann Landers. When "Meant Well Parents" sighed that "many of our children are on drugs, unemployed dropouts, migrants, drifters, angry with the world, hostile toward us and out-of-joint with society," Landers reassured them that they "did the best [they] could with the tools at hand. . . . I have come to believe in the genetic factor which has been ignored by many behavioral 'experts.' "[19]

It is no easy matter to determine the identity of these "experts" allegedly guilty of ignoring the genetic factor. In fact, so eager have psychologists (to say nothing of psychiatrists) become to explain behavior as genetically determined that the behavior geneticist Robert Plomin, himself no radical critic of the hereditarian position, has lately begun to sound a warning about excesses in that direction, as this chapter's epigraph suggests.[20] That his assessment may be described as charitable is clear from the fact that Plomin refrains from accusing his colleagues of having gone too far already—a conclusion I believe would be amply justified. The reliance on genetic explanations, moreover, is a hardy one, virtually impervious to data. In his book about intelligence, *Frames of Mind,* the Harvard psychologist Howard Gardner observed:

Not even the demonstrations that a normal college student can increase his short-term memory tenfold, or that most differences in school performance can be virtually eliminated by tutoring, or that seemingly average Japanese children can become violin virtuosos, suffice to convince the committed hereditarian that individual differences can be fully dissolved by judicious intervention.[21]

Notwithstanding the reputation Americans have acquired for disbelieving in limits, for a charmingly naive faith in self re-creation, committed hereditarians are everywhere on this continent. Perhaps our famous cultural character extends only as far as championing the cause of the individual against social forces, political obligations, and environmental determinants. In any case, it does not seem to have been translated into the language of skepticism toward biological determinism. Indeed, from psychiatry departments to the daily newspaper to bars and kitchens across the country, the word has gone out: experience may play a role, but our personalities were essentially fixed before we were born. If some people drink or write poetry, look to their genes for the reason. If we cheat or steal or shoot down airplanes, blame human nature. This is very nearly the conventional wisdom of late twentieth-century America.

BEHIND THE APPEAL OF DETERMINISM

As with any other belief system in a complex culture, no single cause can be identified for this determinism. To begin with, "human nature" is simply the easiest and most direct way of making sense of what we see around us. If a particular attitude or way of living is common to virtually everyone we know, it seems a matter of common sense to attribute it to our nature, to life itself. The early insights (and excesses) of cultural relativists in the field of anthropology seem by now to have evaporated—or, more likely, never to have seriously jeopardized the assumption that if some practice is present in our society, it must be present everywhere, and indeed it must finally be a consequence of being human.

Those who reach for this explanation, the closest to hand, are in good—or at least influential—company. The dark portrait of our species first painted by the seventeenth-century philosopher Thomas Hobbes—an image of violent, competitive, self-interested creatures locked in unceasing struggle—was inspired by similar intellectual carelessness. C. B. MacPherson, in his influential study, *The Political Theory of Possessive Individualism,* shows how Hobbes's "state of nature" not only was not intended as a historical hypothesis, a speculative anthropology of primitive people, but was not even really about human nature as such. Rather, MacPherson argues, Hobbes began with what he knew of Western civilization, of individuals already shaped by an ethic of egoism, and then imagined how they would act if the enforcement apparatus of the state suddenly vanished. He has told us nothing about the nature of the organism. "To get the state of nature, Hobbes has set aside law, but not the socially acquired behaviour and desires of men," MacPherson writes, adding that "Hobbes offers, as a confirmation of the 'natural' tendency of men to invade and destroy each other, the observable behaviour of men in present civil society. . . . The nature of man is thus got primarily from observation of contemporary society."[22] In short, by attributing observable features to a postulated underlying nature, Hobbes not only presented us with a theory that wound up corroborating and legitimating our own determinism, but he actually based that theory on the same sort of facile equation that many people resort to today.

The simplicity of a human nature account, however, cannot alone explain the tenacity of this theory. To summon the specter of genes or neurotransmitters is also to call on the comforts offered by any version of determinism: an escape from responsibility. Observe that it is groups like the National Alliance for the Mentally Ill—composed of parents and other relatives of people with psychological disorders—which insist most strenuously that these disorders are no-fault diseases. Read again that poignant letter to Ann Landers, pleading for a genetic theory that will exempt the parents from any complicity in raising children whom they now regard as social misfits. Consider an article in *Playboy* that advised readers: "If you get caught fooling around, don't say the Devil made you do it. It's the Devil in your DNA."[23] And reflect on the fact that each time a new claim is offered to the effect that violent behavior can be explained in terms of brain chemistry, nowhere is the excitement greater than among defense attorneys.[24]

Of course, it is not only guilty parents, adulterers, and lawyers who make use of deterministic assumptions. By virtue of living in a desperately competitive society, most Americans at some point find themselves working against the interests of other people, and this promotes feelings of hostility. Why take personal responsibility for these actions or raise troubling questions about the social system when one can just hold biology responsible? Jerome Kagan observes:

In order to rationalize the blizzard of cruelty and aggression in contemporary society, it is helpful, and occasionally therapeutic, to believe that it is not always possible to control open anger, rivalry, and jealousy. This rationalization mutes feelings of guilt and dilutes a continuing sense of personal responsibility for hurting others. The Japanese, by contrast, believe that each person can control his or her anger, and the differential frequency of violence in Tokyo and New York implies that if people believe they can tame their aggressive impulses they often do.[25]

The issue of responsibility suggests a third reason for the popularity of biological determinism, and that is a desire to preserve the status quo. Those who are well served by the present social and economic arrangement have an interest in justifying that arrangement as not merely advantageous but inevitable. The dogma that people are naturally acquisitive and lazy, Erich Fromm pointed out, is "little more than an expression of the wish to prove the value of our social arrangements by imputing to them that they follow the needs of human nature."[26] As I have argued elsewhere,[27] the easiest way to head off social change is not to argue that reformers are wrong but instead to dismiss the very idea of change as naive.

The relation between one's politics and one's views on the nature/ nurture question was explored forty years ago by Nicholas Pastore. After examining the writings of two dozen leading American and British scientists, he found that eleven of the twelve whom he classified as environmentalists were politically liberal or radical, while eleven of the twelve hereditarians were conservative. "It would be as reasonable to classify the nature-nurture controversy as sociological in nature as it is to classify it as scientific in nature," he concluded.[28]

This, of course, is a double-edged sword, and determinists have made much of the political affiliations of their critics. But it is worth focusing attention on these determinists themselves—first, because they are particularly likely to wrap their findings in the mantle of Science, effectively denying that political considerations play any role in their thinking, and second, because their orientation is the dominant one in American intellectual life. Apart from the evidence that can be cited for or against the view that crime is a matter of genetics, or that women are better suited than men to care for children, or that war is just part of the human condition, it is worth reflecting on who benefits from these widely held assumptions.*

Such psychological and political explanations probably play a role in constructing institutional supports for determinism, but these supports can also be understood as causes in their own right. Consider, for example, how the social sciences view themselves. Still relatively new as academic disciplines, and still sensitive to charges that they are "soft," practitioners are anxious to prove their legitimacy. In the academy, legitimacy frequently is measured by one's proximity to the natural sciences—more accurately, to an outdated, mechanistic model of the natural sciences. "The promised biologization of social studies is precisely a realization of the desire of sociologists, anthropologists, and economists to be *scientists.* "[29] This is manifested in a preoccupation with technique, an emphasis on precision in measurement that often edges out questions about the importance of what is being studied. (Freud reminded us of the man who spent all his time polishing his spectacles without ever putting them on to look around.)

The collective insecurity of social science shows up not only in the choice of method but in the conclusions that are reached about why we act the way we do. These two are integrally connected, of course, with a hereditarian position far more likely to emerge from the work of an investigator who looks at a self and sees an organism, who watches people interacting and collapses this into demand curves or exchange theory. From sociologist Alvin Gouldner's formal analysis of reciprocity norms it is only a short walk to biologist Robert Trivers's evolutionary reduction of reciprocal "altruism."

In psychology one hears a particularly defensive tone—"We are *too* scientists!"—that prepares the way for biological explanations. Psychiatrists, long regarded with condescension by other medical specialists who do not see them as practicing "real medicine," have over the last decade or two been remedicalizing their discipline, turning to neurobiological models and medical (usually pharmacological) treatments. The structuralist bias of developmental psychology and the increasing popularity of heritability studies and physiological measurement in personality theory

---

*The biologist Richard Lewontin (personal communication, December 1988) argues that those committed to making social change actually have a powerful incentive to know whether determinism has any basis in fact because if it did their efforts would be in vain. If anything, their research should thus be *less* ideologically driven than that of the determinists.

are other tiles in this same mosaic. Psychologists may reason that if their methods and hereditarian conclusions are akin to those of biologists, then perhaps they will be taken seriously in the world of science.

For whatever reason a discipline might shift in this direction, the orientation soon becomes incorporated into the curriculum of training institutions and the criteria employed by the agencies that fund research. If you are schooled to look at nature rather than nurture, drilled in a methodology that overlooks familial or social influences on behavior, then your findings (to say nothing of your world view) will be predictable. Abraham Maslow once wrote that "it is tempting, if the only tool you have is a hammer, to treat everything as if it were a nail."[30] This metaphor is all too apt for the behavioral sciences. According to the psychologist Lois Wladis Hoffman, "Greater support has emerged for the genetic than for the environmental position, I think, because the bulk of the relevant research is being conducted by behavioral geneticists who, though very sophisticated in their own area, are not familiar with environmental theory or with socialization models."[31]

Research is expensive, and those who do it cannot help but be influenced by the viewpoint of those who support it. If it is fashionable to study anxiety or obsessive-compulsive disorder these days, this may have something to do with the fact that the drug companies are busy underwriting experiments and symposia on these topics.[32] (The question thus becomes, for both researchers and clinicians, not "How can we best deal with this problem?" but "What is the best *drug* to deal with this problem?") Or, to take another example, one of the major recent collections of experts' views on the value of electroconvulsive (shock) therapy, an anthology appearing as a volume of the *Annals of the New York Academy of Sciences,* was partly underwritten by a corporation that manufactures ECT machines.[33]

Even more disturbing are instances where the financial and political issues seem to dovetail—that is, where investigators accept funding from organizations that not only have a strong hereditarian bias but another, darker agenda as well. The Minnesota Twin Study, for example, has been partly supported by the Pioneer Fund, a foundation apparently committed to promoting theories of black inferiority and other racist doctrines.[34] (Among the proponents of such Pioneer-supported doctrines, incidentally, is J. Philippe Rushton, a psychologist at the University of Western Ontario who was hitherto a respected researcher of altruism.)[35]

The larger point, though, is not just that conclusions will be colored by the source of the grant money, but that the topics to be studied in the first place—topics inclining toward biological explanations—are largely determined by the grantor. If a psychiatrist or psychologist is in need of support from the National Institute of Mental Health—and most researchers in the field must depend on this agency at some point—it is my impression that her proposal stands a far better chance of being approved if it talks about neurological abnormalities or genetic predispositions as opposed to, say, patterns of child rearing. Broadly speaking, pharmaceutical companies and other grantors open their wallets to nature, not nurture; universities like to appoint faculty members with grants already attached to them; these instructors then teach what they know, reinforcing the orientation among their students and reproducing it in the next generation.

Finally, as already indicated, the mass media also play a significant role in perpetuating the assumption that we are what our genes have made us. This is clear from the determinedly deterministic slant of stories on human behavior in newsweeklies and women's magazines. On the subject of aggression in particular, Jeffrey Goldstein, a professor of psychology at Temple University, remarks, "If all one knows is what one sees on TV or reads in the newspaper, what one knows is nineteenth-century biology."[36] Explanations that invoke biological necessity are relatively easy to describe and make for a snappy news story. Thus, no major news organization in the United States was interested in reporting on the Seville Statement, a declaration to the effect that aggression is not an inevitable part of human nature, which was signed in 1986 by leading natural and social scientists from twelve nations. One reporter told an organizer of the international conference, "Call us back when you find a gene for war."[37]

Even when more serious attempts are made in the media to address the issue of aggression, the results are distressingly predictable. Take, for example, a relatively highbrow documentary called *The Mind,* which aired on public television in late 1988 and was partially funded by the National Science Foundation. The final episode, "The Violent Mind," was as remarkable for what it did not include in its treatment of aggression as for what it did. Not one word was addressed to the effects of parenting practices, violent entertainment, competitive sports, political propaganda, and so forth. Instead, for ninety minutes viewers saw profiles of people whose violent behavior was allegedly caused by hypoglycemia, pesticide exposure, progesterone imbalance, epilepsy, and bipolar disorder, respectively. One man, a former sociopath who now works as a volunteer social worker, is given time to say, "I'm accountable for my behaviors . . . but I believe that . . . when we place people in dehumanizing . . . institutions, facilities, what we do is we foster and we nurture antisocial violent behavior." An expert is quickly brought on screen to correct this misapprehension by explaining that "the psychopath is an individual who's wired up differently." The narrator concludes as follows:

There's a little of Mr. Hyde in each of us. Science is beginning to show how brain disease and brain damage can on occasion release that Mr. Hyde. . . . From a widely accepted scientific point of view, *all* our thoughts derive from electrical activity in nerve cells, themselves influenced by messages from our genes, chemicals in our blood, and information from the outside world—and we have little control over any of these factors.[38]

What is true of aggression is also true of what we are taught about gender differences. With respect to whether these differences "owed more to hormones and cerebral hemispheres than to manners and mores," the author Beryl Lieff Benderly found conflicting and ambiguous research in the scholarly literature but "near unanimity reported in magazines" in favor of the biological view:

The skeptics' ideas, though, made singularly poor feature copy. "Re-analysis Faults Finding of Differences" or "Painstaking Attempt Fails to Replicate Influential Study" headlined no late city editions. "What We Still Don't Know About the Brain" and "Faulty Assumptions Weaken Chain of Evolutionary Reasoning" enthralled the readers of no slick magazines. "Scientists Urge Caution in Interpreting Statistical Data" blared from no Sunday supplements.[39]

Indeed, a 1988 article in *U.S. News and World Report,* tellingly titled "Men vs. Women," claims that determinist studies are "savagely attacked" and that feminist scholars "fear" the consequences of publicizing them—as if the only criticism that existed was shrill and politically motivated. Repeatedly in this article (and others), a sympathetic description is offered of the biological position, after which one paragraph of strawman challenges is included for balance, followed by "But . . ." and a rescue of the original position.[40]

TAKING LIBERTIES WITH BIOLOGY

For someone attempting to give serious and fair-minded consideration to the nature/nurture question, these proposed explanations for the popularity of biological determinism—simplicity and common sense, relief from responsibility, conservatism, academic respectability, research training and funding, and the influence of the mass media—do not speak directly to the truth or falsity of the position itself. On the other hand, they are indirectly relevant, in that a satisfactory account of why a given view has been accepted calls into question the assumption that it has been adopted strictly on its merits.

Technically speaking, there is no single "human nature" argument; there are only individual behaviors and issues that are believed to be dominated by innate forces. In the following section I will review a few of these specific controversies, but let me first frame the discussion with a few general observations about the nature/nurture dispute.

1. *There is no nature without an environment.* It is senseless to proclaim, as Robin Fox does, "It is not that man is as culture does, but that culture does as man is."[41] To think that we can ever identify something called man outside of a culture is specious. There is no distilled essence of human being onto which a series of cultural norms have been grafted; rather, the very idea of humanness depends on cultural context.

I am not arguing merely that the role played by our natural or social environment is of X percent greater significance than we normally assume,[42] but that human nature itself is a social product. In fact, biological determinism is faulty long before we arrive at issues peculiar to our species. First, no genetic instruction can be meaningfully evaluated without knowing something about the environment in which an organism must function; what is adaptive in one setting may be maladaptive in another. Birds with long beaks, perfectly evolved for extracting bugs from tree bark, may go hungry on a savanna where the insects are to be found on the ground. (It is important to keep in mind, incidentally, that it is the organism as a whole, rather than its genes, that interacts with an environment.)

Second, the relation between even very simple organisms and their environment is reciprocal: the individual both reacts to and actively transforms the world around it.* The instincts of most animals are invariably

---

*A preliminary but provocative piece of new research suggests that evolution may not depend exclusively on the blind forces of random mutation. Challenging this version of determinism is a study indicating that bacteria apparently can "choose" which mutations

a product of experience,[44] and this instinctive behavior then shapes the environment, which in turn affects the organism. Ants, for example, have recently been shown to live in flexible social systems that interact with the environment; they cannot usefully be understood as a collection of individuals, each behaving according to the imperatives of a static genotype.[45] It hardly needs mentioning that humans are uniquely able to transcend biological forces, but even the discovery of a genetic marker for a given human behavior or disease should not incline us to adopt a simple-minded determinism. As two scientists recently pointed out, such a discovery

does not determine how a genetically linked behavior might be expressed by other individuals or in different environments. For instance, the strong moral code of the Amish may have a significant influence on the development of MDI [manic-depressive illness]. The Amish environment either may be more likely to induce this condition or, alternatively, might reduce the likelihood of its appearance.[46]

Third, not only does the environment shape the development of an organism, but the organism's biology is *itself* a product of an interaction between heredity and environment. The status of a newborn, for example, is affected not only by genetic instructions but by what happened to its mother during pregnancy. In short, no biological reality exists in a vacuum.

2. *The real alternative to biological determinism is human choice.* Those who urge caution in talking about human nature usually do not resort to environmental determinism instead.[47] The assumption that our behaviors are entirely a function of genes or of environment (or of some blend of these two) remains pervasive, however. I vividly recall attending a graduate school class in which the instructor drew a diagram on the blackboard to represent the balance of genetic and cultural determinants of behavior. When a student asked about the omission of freedom—the realm of nondetermination—from this tidy model, the professor reacted

_____

to produce, based on environmental contingencies. A study by John Cairns and his colleagues at the Harvard School of Public Health found that when mutant versions of these one-celled organisms, unable to digest a particular kind of sugar, were introduced to an environment containing that sugar, they rapidly (and apparently "deliberately") mutated in such a way that some of their offspring could metabolize it. These results should be qualified by noting that this mutation was nowhere near universal and that it consisted of returning to the "natural" genotype of the species.[43]

rather as if someone had corrected his spelling and said he supposed that, yes, there was this, too. It is interesting to observe that the most over-heated biological determinists are willing to temper their doctrine only by acknowledging that we are also at the mercy of cultural forces, rather than by taking human freedom seriously.[48]

3. *"Universal" does not mean "biologically based."* This is true, and a point worth emphasizing, in both directions. Many elements of our culture, such as aggression and competition, by no means exist all over the world. But even if they did, we could not automatically conclude that they were therefore rooted in biology. Virtually all Finns may be Lutherans and virtually all cultures may make some form of pottery, but that does not mean there is a gene for Lutheranism or for pottery-making.[49] (Among those who fail to grasp this distinction is the biologist E. O. Wilson, who announces that "men hunt and women stay home . . . in most agricultural and industrial societies and, on that ground alone, [the prac-tice] appears to have a genetic origin.")[50] Moreover, we frequently draw the wrong conclusion from cultural similarity. The fact that most societies have some sort of incest taboo indicates not that a biologically based revulsion to incest exists, but rather that it apparently does not exist—else why would social sanctions be necessary?[51]

Conversely, the fact that a given phenomenon can be said to be biological does not imply that it is universal. Obviously a feature—say, a disease—can have a genetic basis without being present in all members of a species.

Biology is as full of subtle diversity and variability as any culture. . . . For Darwin, individual variation was a central fact of life; and species possessed no ideal or essential natures at all. On this view, then, Darwin ought to have ended the quest for a fixed human nature, in opposition to human nurture, once and for all.[52]

4. *Biological correlates are not necessarily causes.* The distinction between correlation and causality is emphasized in all introductory statistics and methodology courses, yet it is striking to see how many published papers continue to confuse the two.

The correlation of a behavior with some genetic factor may camou-flage more than it reveals. For instance, it is undoubtedly true that the presence of at least one inherited characteristic tends to predict the likelihood of arrest for property crimes. That characteristic is skin color. Now obviously a greater concentration of melanin does not predispose people to commit crimes, but it does affect the way such people are perceived and treated by those with lighter skins, which in turn can affect economic status or the likelihood of being suspected of criminality, and so on. Thus the fact of a statistical relation to an inherited trait only raises questions about how environmental forces are involved. In other instances, the role of the environment may not be so apparent, yet it still may be misleading to assume that a mere correlation—say, between nearsightedness and mathematical ability—has taught us something important about the role of genes in human behavior.

Genes aside, the fact that physiological changes may correspond to a given behavior pattern tells us absolutely nothing about *why* an individual engages in these behaviors. Altered neurotransmitter levels are not particularly surprising in light of the interactive relation between the self and brain chemistry. But the two events may coincide not because our actions are mere by-products of that chemistry but because both are the results of a third, unsuspected cause. This is a pattern we come across all the time: instead of assuming that temporary impotence resulted from a bout of heavy drinking, we might consider that both the impotence *and* the drinking were responses to having lost one's job.

Alternatively, a behavior may have caused, rather than been caused by, the physiological change. This possibility is at least as plausible as its opposite, but experts and laypeople alike rarely take it seriously. Both testosterone and serotonin levels, in point of fact, can be dependent variables—affected by aggression or position in a social hierarchy.[53] That people with psychological disorders are distinguished by unusual neurotransmitter activity does not mean their behavior is a *result* of the chemical abnormality any more than finding mucus in the nose of someone with a cold proves that mucus causes colds.[54]

In the early 1960s, the experimental psychologist Mark Rosenzweig and his colleagues discovered that giving rats objects to play with changed not only their brains' enzyme activity but the weight of their cerebral cortexes.[55] More recently, Gerald Edelman's theory of "neural Darwinism" has proposed, inter alia, that the function and structure of the brain "depend on context and history and not on localized functions and fixed memories"; only some of the possible neural connections develop, depending on environmental stimuli.[56] Or, to cite still another illustration, when females live together, their menstrual cycles often come to coincide.[57] In each example, experience is the actor and biology the reactor, as well as the other way around.

Biological determinists cannot consider this possibility because their position is grounded in reductive thinking—the same sort that assumes the only way to understand a whole is by analyzing its component parts. One maverick observes that some scientists reason

> like a child who, because turning the knob on the television set makes the picture appear, concludes that the knob "causes" or "programs" the picture, and then goes the next, more absurd step of trying to understand the mechanism of television by chemically analysing the knob.[58]

5. *"Innate" does not mean "fixed."* Even sociobiologists will concede that "it is a fallacy—incidentally a very common one—to suppose that genetically inherited traits are by definition fixed and unmodifiable."[59] A gene may be fixed, but its behavioral effect often is not, as behavioral geneticists, too, point out. A common example is a metabolic defect called phenylketonuria, which produces signs of mental retardation: there is no doubt that it is inherited, but its effects can be counteracted by a change in diet. Problems with a genetic cause may, practically speaking, be less resistant to change or control than many learned behaviors.

Even from an evolutionary perspective, the social behaviors of a species are to some degree plastic. If a sudden change in the environment demands flexibility, an organism must adapt or die. "Biochemical and physiological mechanisms are the servants of social adaptation, not the other way around," Robert Cairns has written. "Furthermore, the same genetic-biological stuff can be organized differently in the course of development to bring about drastically different patterns of social adaptation."[60] The possibility of change, in other words, is built into biology itself. For humans in particular, the word *genetic*—even when the data do support its use—need not be heard as having a ring of finality to it.

DETERMINISM IN ACTION: FROM SEX TO TWINS

Sociobiology

After fifteen years, the idea that contemporary human social behavior can be adequately explained by appealing to natural selection and genetics continues to claim a following across many disciplines. I should emphasize that sociobiology in its strict sense is not at issue here: the label is worn by some good scientists who investigate, say, how bees interact and would not presume to force humans onto the Procrustean bed of their method. When I refer to sociobiology, I mean to denote what is sometimes called vulgar or pop (or, what may amount to the same thing, human) sociobiology. It is this variety, championed by Wilson, Richard Dawkins, David Barash, and others, that the distinguished anthropologist Clifford Geertz had in mind when he referred to the field as "that curious combination of common sense and common nonsense."[61]

Such sociobiologists assert that evolutionary imperatives mean that certain propensities are part of human nature. Thus, it is no brash graduate student but the father of inclusive fitness theory* himself, W. D. Hamilton, who announces that "some things which are often treated as purely cultural in man—say racial discrimination—have deep roots in our animal past and thus are quite likely to rest on direct genetic foundations."[62] What, then, do we make of individuals who fail to display the trait in question? Assuming that we do not take the absence of racism as prima facie evidence against membership in our species, we are left with two choices. Either the evolutionary imperative can be overridden, in which case we need to ask just how useful the theory is in the first place for predicting behavior, or else a new subtheory will have to be invented to account for exceptions.

Most evolutionary biologists point out that the idea of natural selection, however heuristic, can be overused. It is not necessarily true that *any* individual (or gene or group) will benefit from evolution. Nor is it the case that all traits and behaviors have been selected for. While it may be entertaining to pick a particular feature of a particular animal and ask why it evolved, many such features are not so neatly explained as the giraffe's long neck, which we learned about in junior high school science class. Many features are selectively neutral—either epiphenomenal (merely accidental consequences of other changes that were adaptive) or else entirely random.

Many sociobiologists, however—and this includes some who write about species other than ours—seem to proceed on the assumption that there must be a biological basis for all characteristics and behaviors. They invariably succeed in coming up with explanations for them. Dawkins was remarkably candid about the purely conjectural, even whimsical nature of this enterprise, with special reference to the exact application of sociobiology with which we will be concerned:

*That many people think first of sociobiology when they see the word *altruism* is due largely to this theory, which I will take up in chapters 7 and 8. Briefly, it refocuses natural selection to take account of the genes shared by an organism and its relatives.

There is no end to the fascinating speculation which the idea of reciprocal altruism engenders when we apply it to our own species. Tempting as it is, I am no better at such speculation than the next man, and I leave the reader to entertain himself.[63]

Thus we are presented with contrived, often ingenious theories to account for everything—including why you gave a quarter to a homeless man last night and why you ate at McDonald's.[64]

One result of this tendency to create what Gould, borrowing from Kipling, calls "Just So" stories, is that sociobiology is unfalsifiable—that is, it has been set up in such a way that no fact could ever refute it. (This is nowhere more painfully obvious than in Trivers's famous paper on reciprocal altruism. Citing one example after another of complex, apparently culturally informed, nonself-maximizing behaviors—widespread acts of genuine altruism—his refrain is that this is just the sort of thing one would expect selection to favor. Whatever we come across, however unexpected or apparently devastating to the theory, is simply construed as further evidence for that theory.) In his book, *The Battle for Human Nature,* Barry Schwartz writes:

Pair bonding is fitness maximizing where it occurs; promiscuity is fitness maximizing where it occurs. Multiple spawnings are fitness maximizing, as are single spawnings. Brute selfishness maximizes fitness, but so does self-sacrifice. . . . There is no possible finding—no pattern of animal behavior in nature—that can embarrass sociobiology. . . . Any activity at all can be shown to be maximizing fitness if the constraints are drawn carefully enough. . . . Theories with this much flexibility can explain everything; as a result, they explain nothing.[65]

Another consequence of the assumption that everything is adaptive is a sort of conservatism in the broadest sense; taken to its logical conclusion, the implication is that whatever is, is right. For years, charges of a reactionary political agenda lurking within sociobiology have been made and heatedly denied, but I want to emphasize that the theoretical suppositions of the field already contain political implications.

The anthropologist Marshall Sahlins has shown how the idea of natural selection has been reconfigured as exploitation, greed, and competition by sociobiologists, turned into something remarkably like the dogma on which our economic system is based.[66] Michael Ghiselin has made this connection explicit, stating baldly that nature runs according to the precepts of laissez-faire capitalism.[67] And some social scientists have wasted no time in taking advantage of this newest version of the human nature argument: "Once we can derive the genetic basis for human desires," says conservative economist Gary Becker, "we can determine which policies will work and which will not." (This quotation appeared in a *Business Week* article that included the following two sentences consecutively: "And there is no hard evidence to support the theory. Yet, bioeconomics provides a powerful defense of Adam Smith's laissez-faire views.")[68]

Readers can decide for themselves whether there are political implications to the particular behaviors and attitudes said to be biologically based (setting aside the motives and affiliations of the writers themselves). Certainly it does not take a conspiratorial sensibility to find in Hamilton's pronouncement a purportedly scientific justification for racism, or in Wilson's comments about gender-based divisions of labor a biological basis for sexism.

There is more that could be said about sociobiologists—the way they overlook the culture-boundedness of concepts said to be simply biological; the way they slip from neutral descriptions of animal behavior (bonding, self-sacrifice, dominance) into words like *love, altruism,* and *slavery* as if the equation had in each case been proved rather than simply asserted; the way they defend themselves against charges of vulgar determinism by agreeing that cultural forces pull against our biology, but then proceed to insist that culture is really just an extension of that biology, playing out its evolutionary agenda.[69] Suffice it to say that Geertz's pithy dismissal of the field—suggesting that its findings are all either obvious or ridiculous—seems more apt the more familiar one is with sociobiological writings.

Gender Differences

As I shall show later, researchers have taken a lively interest in the extent to which gender differences exist in helping behaviors and empathy. In light of this, I want to pause here to question whether one is permitted to conclude, where these differences have proved robust, that they are biological in origin.

This conclusion is simply taken for granted by many of us: we observe that girls and women in our culture seem more caring or less violent than males, more nurturing with babies or less inclined to enter the fast track of the business world, and we promptly assume that some inborn factor is responsible. Several recent books have debunked these assumptions in detail,[70] and it should be sufficient here to touch briefly on only a few points.

Anyone who has read studies in social or developmental psychology will recognize the sentence "No sex differences were found." It appears frequently but usually in passing, directly after a brief reassurance about the reliability of the measure being used in the study. The reader is inclined to glide over the phrase since sex differences are typically neither expected in, nor germane to, the study. Yet the cumulative significance of these nonfindings is not to be dismissed. Over and over again, with different attributes, different measures, and different populations, males and females seem to act and react, reason and feel, in pretty much the same way. Moreover, it often turns out that even where there is a statistically significant difference between the sexes, the variation *among* women and *among* men is even greater.

This, then, is the context in which occasional findings of gender difference should be located: the white noise of "no difference" in the vast majority of studies. But where men and women do not turn out the same, distinctive patterns of socialization usually are adequate to account for the differences.

Apart from the fact that only women can become pregnant and lactate, is there reason to think that they are biologically better prepared than men to care for children? If there is any support at all for this idea, it is applicable only to the first few months of an infant's life. Even here, though, says Nancy Chodorow,

women who have just borne a child can be completely inadequate mothers, just as adoptive mothers can be completely adequate. We do not know what the hormonal bases of caretaking in humans are, or whether there are any at all. . . . Nor is there anything biological or hormonal to differentiate a male "substitute mother" from a female one. The biological argument for women's mothering is based on facts that derive, not from our biological knowledge, but from our definition of the natural situation as this grows out of our participation in certain social arrangements.[71]

The hypothesis that socialization makes the difference here is supported by at least two studies finding that boys and girls at the toddler stage are equally interested in looking at, touching, and otherwise interacting with infants. At about age four or five, though, the boys' proclivity to play with babies falls off dramatically. There is no "natural" disparity in the ability or inclination to be nurturant, these researchers conclude; rather, boys in our society eventually get the message that caring for children is not a fit activity for males.[72]

What about aggression? The issue here turns out to be substantially more complicated than many people assume. Whether gender differences are found depends on whether one is concerned with aggression that is physical or verbal, direct or indirect, aimed at men or women, group-based or individual, observed in field settings or in the laboratory, and so on. These distinctions are relevant because the sort of behavior in which gender differences do appear turns out to be so strictly circumscribed that it is impossible to conclude sweepingly that women are less "aggressive" or "violent" than men.* For example, a study of two-year-old children at the National Institute of Mental Health found no gender differences on measures of overall interpersonal aggression, even though boys engaged in more destruction of property. When the children were observed at home instead of in the laboratory, there were no gender differences at all in frequency or style of aggression.[74]

So many environmental factors play a part in mediating aggression— and, indeed, can have the effect of wiping out gender differences—that biology seems either an unlikely explanation or functionally meaningless. According to the authors of a major review of the relevant research, "If sex differences were due to differences in the wiring, it would not seem likely that mere situational or attitudinal changes could erase them."[75] Along with other researchers, they point out that a significant proportion of the sex differences that do exist with respect to aggression in adults are due to the fact that women are more likely to feel guilty about hurting others. (Stipulate that the act of aggression is permissible, and sex differences virtually vanish.) Someone who favors nature-based over nurture-based explanations is thus in the position of having to devise (and prove) a biological account of gender differences in guilt.

Much has been made in the popular press about how testosterone levels determine aggressive behavior.[76] To begin with, it is interesting that Anke Ehrhardt, one of the researchers whose work is frequently cited in support of this conclusion, has written that "sex hormones . . . only

---

*Sometimes the assertions one hears are even more sweeping. The fact that men get into more fistfights than women is captured by the shorthand of "aggression," and this word is then widely interpreted as also including assertiveness, achievement, and other desirable qualities. If men in the United States score higher on measures of such traits, or are more successful according to other societal standards, it is important that we do not use aggression research to invoke a biological explanation for these facts.[73]

play a limited part in a whole network of factors. . . . there is no evidence
that [they] have a major or predominant influence."[77] Second, as the
biologist Anne Fausto-Sterling and others have shown, "Elevated testosterone levels may, in fact, *result from* aggressive behaviors" rather than the
other way around.[78] Third, there are methodological problems with some
of the studies purporting to show that aggressiveness (and tomboyism,
in particular) is a function of hormone levels.[79]

Women and men have also been said to differ with respect to spatial
and mathematical ability, and these assertions have been trumpeted in
the popular press, with little or no attention given to the weaknesses of,
disclaimers to, or critiques published after, such research. Hypotheses
about differences in brain size and structure to account for male superiority in spatial skills have been proposed for some time. A 1982 study, based
on exactly fourteen autopsies, concluded that the rear portion of the
corpus callosum, the bundle of nerves connecting the left and right
hemispheres of the brain, was slightly larger in women. This was
promptly interpreted as supporting the idea that women's brains are less
specialized and therefore less fit for doing spatial tasks.[80] Much less
publicity attended the release of no fewer than seven subsequent and
much larger studies, all of which found no statistically significant sex
difference in this area of the brain.[81] Brain size aside, gender differences
on most tasks measuring spatial ability have by now declined to the point
of insignificance.[82] Studies have also demonstrated that certain toys—
coincidentally, the ones usually given to boys—can markedly improve
visual-spatial skills.[83]

Even more interest was generated by the claim in 1980 that because
a group of boys did better than girls on math tests, even when they had
all taken the same classes, some innate factor must be at work.[84] ("Do
Males Have a Math Gene?" asked *Newsweek.*) Largely overlooked were
several criticisms subsequently raised by specialists, including the possibility that boys and girls have different learning experiences even though
they sit through the same lectures.[85] In fact, a study of 74,000 adolescents
from twenty nations released in 1988 showed that boys and girls did
equally well on most tests of mathematical ability, suggesting that the
differences that do exist are more likely to reflect cultural training than
different hardware.[86]

In yet another illustration of dubious research in support of inborn
differences—and the uncritical media coverage to which such claims are
treated—fluctuations in women's estrogen levels were said not long ago

to account for significant differences in women's performance on verbal, spatial, and muscular coordination tasks. The study's authors explicitly asserted that if estrogen levels affect a given woman's performance, then sex differences in cognitive abilities are also likely to be based on biology. Unfortunately, the research was fatally flawed by a failure to quantify the hormone levels or to keep subjects blind to the study's purpose, by the use of trivial measures of performance and minuscule samples.[87] Nevertheless, coverage of this research appeared on the front pages of both the *New York Times* and the *Los Angeles Times,* the article in the latter going so far as to suggest that girls would now have to consider taking standardized tests at certain times of the month.[88]

The various declarations about natural differences between the sexes in all of these areas overlook the demonstrated fact that boys and girls are not socialized in the same ways. Moreover, these distinct socialization patterns start at birth. A study at Tufts University found that the parents of newborn boys described them as stronger, firmer, larger, better coordinated, and more alert than did parents of newborn girls— even though objective data indicated no differences by sex.[89] In a Cornell University study, people watched a videotape of a diapered nine-month-old. Those told that the baby was a boy were more likely to interpret the baby's crying as reflecting anger (rather than fear) than were those told the baby was a girl.[90] (The implication here is not merely that gender differences are caused by the social environment, but that the very *existence* of many of these differences, derived from previous research and common-sense observation, is dubious.) Other research has shown that parents ask their eighteen-month-old girls how they are feeling—and talk to them about emotions—more often than parents of same-aged boys.[91] All of these studies, along with other accounts of the significance of sex-differentiated parental and peer socialization,[92] seem to suggest that we perceive and raise boys and girls so differently that biological explanations scarcely seem necessary to account for the separate paths that they sometimes take.

Twin Studies

By showing that identical (monozygotic or MZ) twins, who share all the same genes, are more likely to be similar to each other than are fraternal (dizygotic or DZ) twins, who share only half of their genes, researchers have concluded that a substantial proportion of human behavior must be genetically determined. On the basis of these studies, claims are routinely offered that half of the variance in human intelligence is a function of genes, that schizophrenia is just a brain disease, and so on.

These claims should be put in perspective, first of all, by keeping in mind the challenges to biological determinism raised earlier. Moreover, even the most resolute hereditarian on the question of schizophrenia has to acknowledge that environmental factors are at least as critical as genes in determining who is diagnosed as having the disorder: when an MZ twin is schizophrenic, the odds are at best only 50-50 that his or her co-twin will be similarly diagnosed—even though their genes are identical.[93] A number of twin studies, in fact, have been noteworthy precisely for *challenging* hereditarian conclusions; over and over again, they offer examples of genetically identical siblings whose lives are radically different in various respects.[94]

The fact that MZs are more similar than DZs on a variety of measures should not really be startling, in any case. Since a raft of studies has shown that physical appearance affects the way people perceive and respond to us, two children who look alike are apt to be treated alike and, *presumably as a result of that similar environment,* develop similar personalities. Other environmental factors, too, can help to explain why identical twins might grow up to resemble each other psychologically more than other siblings do. A case in point was provided after several studies found that MZ twins are more similar with respect to such characteristics as dietary habits or extroversion than are DZs. It happens that identical twins spend more time together than do fraternal twins,[95] and once investigators controlled for this variable, the number of genes shared with the sibling no longer mattered as much. Environment, in other words, accounted for much of the difference that had reflexively been attributed to genes. In 1988, a reanalysis of data based on a study of Finnish twins was published. It found "a significant association between the personality similarity of MZ cotwins and the frequency of their social interactions . . . [that] cannot be explained by age or gender differences in twins' patterns of social contact . . . [or by] genetic variation within pairs."[96]*

---

*Just as siblings who spend time together are more likely to be similar than those who do not—for reasons having nothing to do with genetics—so does the fact that children inevitably have different experiences with the same parents help to explain why they may grow up to be very different from one another. Our inclination is to take such differences as evidence of inborn factors, but "siblings in the same family experience considerably different environments in terms of parental treatment and their interaction with one another and with their peers," in Robert Plomin's words.[97]

Compounding one's doubt about the significance of the genetic factor are schizophrenia studies demonstrating that DZ twins show a higher concordance rate—that is, are more likely to be similar to one another—than are other siblings.[98] DZ twins are, from a genetic point of view, no different from ordinary siblings, so any such differences must be due entirely to environmental factors.

Even to the extent that MZ twin similarity might be due to shared genes, though, it may be improper to make generalizations to other people on this basis. Two researchers raised this crucial, and widely overlooked, caveat:

The finding of behavioral similarities between twins may be peculiar to the situation of two people who carry identical genes at all loci. Extrapolations from identical twin behavioral genetic data to estimates of the extent or origin of behavioral variation in the general population is problematic.[99]

More promising than these twin studies, of course, are adoption studies, regarded with some justification as the ideal natural laboratory for examining the nature/nurture question. In these much rarer studies, MZ twins raised apart from each other are compared to see whether genes or environment matters more. Unfortunately for investigators, though, children who are put up for adoption generally are not placed with families on a random basis. The adopted family may be related to, live in the same town as, or be unusually similar in other respects to the family of origin—all of which leaves the door open to environmental hypotheses about why adopted-away children are similar to their biological twins. Leon Kamin's reanalysis of some of Seymour Kety's data found that adopted children turned out to be suspiciously similar to their stepsiblings and nonbiological parents, a fact that obviously cannot be explained on the basis of genes. A significant proportion of schizophrenic adoptees had *adopted* parents who had spent time in a psychiatric hospital; this was true of none of the nonschizophrenic subjects who were used as controls.[100]

There is yet another possibility to be considered: parents may treat an adopted child differently from a natural child and make less of an effort to raise him or her in their own image. Lois Hoffman points to a study finding that intelligence scores were just as highly correlated between two children who were both adopted (by the same parents) as between two natural siblings in the same home. When one child was adopted and the other was not, however, the correlation was lower, suggesting that parental treatment made the difference.[101]*

In principle, adoption studies provide a promising mechanism for distinguishing genetic from environmental factors. But taken together, these criticisms appear to raise troubling, perhaps fatal, questions about the way these studies have actually been conducted. Because their data have been swallowed whole by both specialists and laypeople, the broader hereditarian conclusions are, of course, likewise called into question.

Heritability

Chiefly on the basis of twin studies, psychologists have come to publish and treat seriously claims about trait heritability. Despite the frequency with which one sees this word, however, it does not mean what it is typically taken to mean. In fact, if researchers in the field were to remember only one sentence from the present chapter, it should be this one: *Heritability estimates tell us virtually nothing about the extent to which genes determine a given trait.* It is difficult to understand how this rather basic point could be lost on so many people publishing papers on various aspects of human behavior. Heritability is only a measure of how much genes account for *differences* in a population with respect to a trait, not the absolute level of genetic contribution to the trait.

The distinction is critical. If nearly everyone is characterized by the same trait—even a trait with an obvious genetic basis, such as having toes—this does not mean that its heritability is high.[103] (If most people who are missing toes lost them in accidents, then the heritability for this trait is actually quite low.) Conversely, where heritability levels *are* reasonably high, as some researchers claim they are for particular measures of aggression or altruism, the hereditarian position is not supported at all. Again, heritability tells us what proportion of variance in a trait is

---

*Hoffman goes on to make another intriguing point: adoption studies of intelligence often measure the extent of environmental effect simply by comparing the respective IQ scores of parent and child rather than by gauging the richness of intellectual stimulation offered in the household. Similarly, she writes, "If I were looking for a family effect on personality, I would not seek trait similarity between parents and children. I would study child-rearing patterns and the family environment, and see if these predicted to the child variables. Children do not develop as clones of the parent. To explain dependency in a child, I would not expect to find a dependent parent but rather an overprotective one. . . . So the relative absence of parent-child similarity on such traits does not provide for me an indication of the absence of an environmental effect in the adopted families."[102]

explained by genetic variance. If the qualities in question were really established features of human nature, almost everyone would have them (that is, the total variance would be low) and there would be no reason to expect a high heritability level. More to the point, even if heritability *were* high, this would not mean very much in light of the fact that total variance is low.

Apart from the fact that heritability does not tell most of us (unless we happen to be behavioral geneticists) what we really want to know, the concept is so limited, even when properly understood, as to be almost meaningless. A heritability statistic refers to the variance of a trait *only for a particular population in a particular environment at a particular time.* Regardless of how staggeringly high a heritability estimate might be, all bets could be off after a simple change in the environment. Some behavioral geneticists readily concede this,[104] yet one is left puzzled as to why researchers continue to be awed by high heritability figures.

This, of course, recapitulates the earlier point about how *genetic* (in this case, referring merely to the role of genes in variance) does not mean fixed. We would also do well to recall another qualification mentioned above: there is no nature without an environment. Studies of individual differences in personality routinely offer breakdowns on the nature/nurture question, asserting, for instance, that sociability is 37 percent determined by heredity. Unfortunately, the idea that purely environmental or genetic components can be isolated—that "every behavior can be factored into a percentage attributed to each—is just as wrong as determinism and in reality merely an adjunct to it," as Gould puts it.[105] Or, in Lewontin's words, "the appearance of the separation of causes is a pure illusion."[106] This point is not terribly controversial, yet the pastime of artificial division into nature- and nurture-based causes continues in the social science journals as though the objection were trivial instead of something that vitiates the whole enterprise.

Consider a child who grows up to be unusually helpful and solicitous of others' feelings. The very idea of quantifying the degree to which this is a matter of genetics is nonsensical. The way infants are treated by parents varies enormously, depending not only on their gender and appearance, but also on how many siblings they have, the state of the parents' marriage, whether Mom happens to be anxious over a promotion at work, whether Dad is thinking of having an affair, and hundreds of other variables. It may well be that some basic temperamental inclinations are inborn—some neonates seem more reactive to the environment than others, for example—but such a difference immediately affects the extent and style of nurturing. A cycle, vicious or auspicious as the case may be, is thereby created, the impact of which is twofold: first, it is easy to overemphasize the significance of vague temperamental qualities that serve primarily to shape environmental forces, and second, it is impossible to assign exact measures of responsibility to nature and nurture, respectively.

My point in this chapter has not been that biology should or can be excluded from a study of human behavior, but that it is relied on too heavily and too casually. Sloppy thinking and questionable methodology in support of biological determinism have often been excused because of a widespread tendency to accept and even seek out "human nature" explanations. The next task is to inquire why many of us have assumed not only that we have a fixed nature but that this nature is a nasty one.

2

On the Nature
of "Human Nature"

To state quite simply what we learn in a time of pestilence: . . .
there are more things to admire in men than to despise.
—Albert Camus (1947)

WE'RE ONLY HUMAN

Every day people near your home steal wallets, and every day other
people go out of their way to return lost wallets to their owners. Schools
are vandalized and blood is donated. On the one hand, "I've got to look
out for Number One"; on the other hand, "What can I do to help?"

Whether one's point of reference is the broad sweep of world history
or last Saturday's visit to the shopping mall, the range within our species
is utterly remarkable. Our dual (or, really, multifarious) nature is a source
of wonderment. But so, too, as I pointed out at the start of the last
chapter, is our tendency in Western culture to tell only half the story, to
dismiss half the evidence. We see the seamier sorts of human behavior
as being at the core and our capacity for generosity and goodness at the
periphery—incidental and out of the ordinary.

Rather than being welcomed as evidence for a more balanced perspective, moreover, anything hopeful about our species is likely to be
received suspiciously, a tendency that suggests a peculiar, defensive attachment to the gloomy viewpoint. As I have begun to write about a
more hopeful side of human nature, I have noticed, as others have
before me, that the reception given this perspective in the publishing
world is less than enthusiastic. A well-known magazine, initially interested in an article about a successful program to foster children's

prosocial behavior, seemed to require that the project be described in skeptical, even smirky, tones. One publisher dismissed a proposal for the book you are now reading on the grounds that it seemed "too well-meaning to be engaging."

What gets written about is only one index of the *Zeitgeist.* How we use the phrase "human nature"—whether it is normally employed to explain selfishness or generosity—is another. What we tell pollsters is a third. A national survey taken in 1983 asked 649 people, all of them employed, to agree or disagree with statements such as "Most people are just out for themselves" and "Most people are not really honest by nature." A book-length review of the results concluded that "cynicism" seemed an apt label for fully 43 percent of the respondents.[1]

To some extent, this world view may reflect concrete experience with mendacity. It is important to acknowledge that humanly caused horrors have shattered countless lives; nothing said here should be construed as an attempt to trivialize them. But while the habit of locking one's door in a big city is simply good sense, the inclination to write off our species— to assume that what is contemptible is more real than what is commend-able—strikes me, above all, as something that needs explaining. Thus, the premise of this chapter is not that such cynicism is incomprehensible or based on delusion. (Illustrations can be found for almost any sweeping generalization, including the one that "people are no damned good.") The premise, rather, is that the belief that we are defined principally by what is ignoble—that such tendencies are universal, inborn, and inevita-ble—is so frequently expressed, and so much at variance with evidence about our other tendencies, that the question is worth pursuing further.

While most of this book makes the affirmative case for a brighter view of human nature, this chapter challenges the dark view. It does so by building on the argument already presented about biological determi-nism, which is to say, by trying to refute the specific versions of the human nature argument that assert certain disagreeable features are givens and are more real than other features. What follows also might be understood this way: Even if there is no human nature in the strong, deterministic sense, it is still important to inquire into the ways by which humans can and do distinguish themselves. Thus I begin by proposing several expla-nations for our habit of assuming the worst about ourselves.

BEHIND THE APPEAL OF CYNICISM

Just as repeated exposure to a particular behavior leads some people to assume that it reflects human nature, so does exposure to bad news affect one's qualitative assessment of human nature. Two thousand years ago, Cicero put it this way: "If we are forced, at every hour, to watch or listen to horrible events, this constant stream of ghastly impressions will deprive even the most delicate among us of all respect for humanity."[2] Harvey A. Hornstein and his colleagues at Columbia University conducted a series of experiments in the 1970s showing that subjects who "accidentally" heard a radio news broadcast about a particularly cruel act—compared with those who heard a report about an act of charity— were subsequently less likely to behave cooperatively in a game, to expect cooperation from others, to judge a defendant innocent and recommend a more lenient sentence, and to express a belief that people in general are honest and helpful.[3] The implication seems to be not only that a sour view of our species can be explained partly by exposure to unpleasant events, but also that we are sufficiently malleable so as to change our general outlook on the basis of hearing about heartening actions on the part of our fellows. (Hornstein himself proposed that bad news has the consequence of sharpening the dividing line between in-groups and out-groups, "us" and "them," and also of shrinking the group with which we identify and toward which we are favorably disposed.)[4]

Why, though, would we come to regard human egoism or evil as more real than other dimensions of human nature? Perhaps we are for some reason attending selectively to these elements, or perhaps evil is more often brought to our attention. Let us pursue the latter possibility for a moment. Some people, by virtue of where they live or with whom they associate, are struck full in the face with evil. But anyone who turns on a television set is confronted with a lopsided lesson that has a comparable effect. This is not to haul out the stale complaint that the mass media do not report enough good news; it is rather to inquire into, among other things, what we learn from entertainment programming.

For more than two decades, George Gerbner and his colleagues at the Annenberg School of Communications at the University of Pennsylvania have been exploring this question. More striking to them than the customary connection between TV viewing and violence is the finding that "television's mean and dangerous world tends to cultivate a sense of relative danger, mistrust, dependence, and—despite its supposedly 'entertaining' nature—alienation and gloom." Specifically, according to data from questionnaires, the more TV a person watches, the more likely he or she is to believe that most people are just out for themselves and would take advantage of you if given a chance.[5] The stories and characters in one's living room—and let us remember that the average American television set is on for about seven hours a day—support a dismal view of human nature, so it should not surprise us that people repeatedly exposed to those stories and characters would internalize just such a view.

Another possible explanation is suggested by one of Dostoyevsky's characters when he declares that "the higher the stage of development a man reaches, the more prone he becomes to cynicism, if only because of the increasing complexity of his make-up."[6] Instead of assuming that a sophisticated man is one who can see, we assume he is one who can see *through.* The assumption is that nothing ought to be taken at face value, that it is invariably more sensible to doubt what appears to be worth admiring. To be cool, in the sense of fashionable, is also to be cool in the sense of disdainfully skeptical. Since we, ourselves, aspire to sophistication, we take pains not to be taken in. We adopt the attitude that only an innocent could be trusting or cooperative—could be naive enough, that is, to deny the unpleasant reality of basic human self-centeredness and aggression.

This cynicism, of course, is never called by its right name; it is labeled realism. It counsels us smugly that however much we might wish humans were not selfish or competitive, we must nevertheless Face Facts (that is, those facts that corroborate this view of the world). Just such a posture has been codified in the social sciences, as the psychologists Michael and Lise Wallach see it: "Cynicism is encouraged in the name of scientific accuracy. . . . The possibility of concern for and commitment to another person's welfare as an end in itself, rather than as a presumptive means to some personal benefit, seems not to be taken seriously."[7]

While it is not immediately clear *why* cynicism should be valued, we get a clue from the fact that the rhetoric of negation is less likely to put one's intellectual reputation at risk than is affirmation. One of the most important lessons learned in college, in fact, is that it is safer to be dubious. Brandeis psychologist Teresa Amabile observed that "if a film buff asks us what we thought of a French movie we just saw, the less sure we feel discussing foreign films, the more inclined we may be to resort to complaints about the director's self-indulgence or the film editor's lack of eloquence."[8] (Likewise, to respond to an admirer of some work by asking, with a faintly incredulous tone and patronizing smile, "You *liked* it?" is to quench the other's enthusiasm in a hurry and call forth defensiveness in its place.) In its most exaggerated expression, the indiscriminate negativism of the academy recalls that of the punk movement, whose motto is Everything Sucks. Certain scholars have merely transformed that vulgar oppositional impulse by honing their critical skills and polishing their erudition until virtually any idea laid on their plate can be summarily deconstructed and dismissed.[9]

The idea here is that the tendency to assume the worst about a given product may reflect some personal or institutional insecurity, even if the criticism is communicated with intimidating certitude and expressed in mystifying, arcane language. Amabile conducted two simple, rather mischievous studies to test her hunch that students made to feel doubtful about their academic status would tend to be extremely critical of others. She and a colleague asked subjects to evaluate some written work (supposedly written by other students) on the basis of such criteria as intelligence and clarity. Those who were told that the quality of their evaluations would determine whether they would be kept on as experts for another task, and those who were told the experimenter was a visiting professor (rather than a first-year graduate student) were indeed more negative in their judgments.[10]

Amabile then set out to determine whether this sort of critical posture really does get interpreted as an indication of higher intelligence in the way that the critics apparently assumed. She presented a hundred subjects with two book reviews, one very positive about the book in question and the other very negative. (The reviewer was the same in both cases to ensure that the style would be similar.) When each subject was asked to rate the reviewer on a range of traits, "the negative reviewer was seen as more intelligent and competent, with higher literary expertise than the positive reviewer."[11]

If one feels less vulnerable and is judged as more competent for saying something unflattering about a book or film, this effect is even more evident (for those within and without the academy) when it comes to the question of human nature. There is no danger of being perceived as credulous or fluffy if one knowingly refers to ulterior—that is, self-serving—motives in every person and every act. In this connection it is worth reflecting on Rollo May's observation that some of his patients "did not repress their sexual, aggressive, or 'antisocial' urges . . . [but] their needs and desires to have responsible, friendly, and charitable relations with other people."[12]

I noted above that repeated exposure to offensive behaviors could help to explain the assumption that these define the core of human beings—just as repeated exposure to any behavior might lead an observer to conclude that it was innate. So it is that other explanations for cynicism are parallel to those for biological determinism. Consider the matter of fending off change. It is theoretically possible to defend any feature of the status quo on the grounds that it simply reflects the underlying tendencies of human nature, but it can hardly escape notice that we hear this line most often in connection with those aspects of our system that turn on triumphing over or doing harm to others. Leon Eisenberg said it well:

To believe that man's aggressiveness or territoriality is in the nature of the beast is to mistake some men for all men, contemporary society for all possible societies, and, by a remarkable transformation, to justify what is as what needs must be; social repression becomes a response to, rather than a cause of, human violence. Pessimism about man serves to maintain the status quo. It is a luxury for the affluent, a sop to the guilt of the politically inactive, a comfort to those who continue to enjoy the amenities of privilege.[13]

Once again, political motives blend with attempts to excuse one's actions—or one's inaction, as the case may be. You can hardly be faulted for lying to a friend, omitting a few items on the tax return, spreading a bit of gossip about a rival, losing your cool, turning a deaf ear to someone else's misery, or any of a hundred other peccadilloes if it can be said that virtually everyone does these things. Informing the belief that such actions are widespread is the larger conviction that humans are simply flawed. This is not an example of a personal shortcoming, then, but of the limitations built into human nature.*

A friend of mine told me recently about an experience she had in Japan. She was standing in line to buy a fare card for the subway and noticed a pile of money lying on a counter unattended. She also noticed that others in the area noticed it, and she watched with mounting incredulity as each person left it right where it was. "Finally," she said, "I was glad to see one woman walk over and pick up the bills. But she just took them to someone else to ask if that person had left them there. When he said no, she put the money back."

---

*To duck responsibility is simultaneously to duck difficult value questions, as Barry Schwartz has keenly observed: "If the pursuit of self-interest, be it preference (economics), fitness (biology), or reinforcement (behavior theory) is a law of human nature, then arguing about whether people *ought* to be this way loses much of its force."[14] Playing the human nature card, we might say, is one more mechanism by which a resolutely relativist—or, more accurately, antinormative—society functions.

"Glad?" I said. "Why were you glad to think she was going to take the money?"

"Well, you know, that at least *someone* there was 'normal.' " My friend smiled and pronounced the last word with the appropriate note of irony. But many of us have a tendency to regard the norms of our own culture as normal in this universal sense. At the same time we recognize a discrepancy between some of our practices and how we know people ought to behave. This is why we take a kind of perverse pleasure, a self-serving relief, from thinking that people in other cultures do as we do. After all, if the Japanese woman had stolen the money, an American could be reassured that it is just natural to do so. And if it is indeed part of our nature, then there is no need to feel guilty when we act accordingly. As Jerome Kagan put it:

Rather than acknowledge that the structure and philosophy of our society invite each of us to accept self-interest as the first rule, many Americans find it more attractive to believe that this mood, along with jealousy, hatred, violence, and incest, is the inevitable remnant of our animal heritage and so we must learn to accept it.[15]

This sort of thing is, not coincidentally, a staple of American comedy. I recall a skit in which a man harasses someone eating dinner at a restaurant by describing to him in detail the agony of the animal that was slaughtered and even the plaintive cries of the vegetables as they were plucked up to make his salad. The diner finally gets up and leaves, his appetite gone, and after a precisely timed interval, the other man breaks into a triumphant grin and dives into the abandoned dinner. The humor emerges from our enjoyment, arguably malicious, in seeing apparently principled people unmasked as greedy, selfish folks like the rest of us.

Harold Schulweis, chairman of a foundation to honor Europeans who rescued Jews during World War II, makes a correlative point here:

Paradoxically, confronting goodness may be more painfully challenging than confronting evil . . . [because it] presents us with a hard mirror. Would I rescue a pregnant woman, a hungry and homeless child, an aged, frightened couple . . . knowing that doing so might bring disaster upon my family and myself . . . ? The rescuers' goodness shakes the foundations of my claims to virtue.[16]

Just as assumptions of "natural" wickedness allow us to justify our own slimy behavior, so evidence to the contrary threatens to pin responsibility on us for what we do—and for what we dimly recognize we might not have the courage to do.

A number of well-articulated belief systems sustain, and in some cases probably generate, our assumptions about the nature of human nature. The best known of these is, of course, Original Sin, the doctrine in Christian theology that all of us since Adam require divine redemption since we are born impure and thus are naturally inclined to commit evil acts. (Although this idea owes its current form to St. Paul, it did not originate with Christianity; the fifty-first Psalm tells us: "Behold, I was brought forth in iniquity; and in sin did my mother conceive me.")

Even many people who scoff at the idea that the virtue of contemporary humans could be compromised by (or would be seen by a merciful divine being as compromised by) the actions of some character in prehistory seem to adopt a pseudoscientific version of the same belief. When Freud wrote that "children are completely egoistic; they feel their needs intensely and strive ruthlessly to satisfy them," and, thirty years later, that "the inclination to aggression is an original, self-subsisting instinctual disposition in man,"[17] he had no need for a mythical Eden from which we were banished, nor of a redemption which we might achieve. When the late Konrad Lorenz referred to human nature as "unreasoning and unreasonable,"[18] it was on the basis of ethology rather than theology. When a sociobiologist described us as "survival machines—robot vehicles blindly programmed to preserve the selfish molecules known as genes,"[19] this allegedly morally neutral vision is just as damning as any hellfire Sunday sermon.

From the traditionally opposed quarters of religion and science, then, we receive instruction on our innate wickedness. This instruction also takes diverse forms. There are some who view our unique humanity as inspiring but believe it is a mere overlay on the vicious animal nature beneath—a conception that, like Freud's notion of a veneer of civilizing influences barely covering the unruly horrors of the id, does not speak well for us on balance.

Others may have arrived at their assessment of human nature on the basis of a simple confusion of self-interest with self-centeredness (see chapter 8). Looking out for one's own needs—choosing the meal from a restaurant menu that one finds most appealing, for example—is not in itself objectionable. It only becomes so when it excludes consideration of others' needs. To observe that we often act so as to please ourselves, and to defend doing so, is not to draw up an indictment of the species. It may well be that many people who argue that humans are self-regarding and therefore tainted are conflating something neutral or necessary with something more ominous.

There are still others whose estimation of humans as evil is influenced by their concern about the practical consequences of assuming otherwise. "The one advantage of believing that man is base by nature is that you cannot be taken in by the brutes who promise to perfect him at a reasonable cost in deaths," is how one writer puts it.[20] This position, of course, takes for granted that acceptance of human baseness is the only alternative to utopianism—that is, to a faith in human perfectibility and the will to slaughter people in the name of that vision. (It also proceeds from the highly debatable premise that a society is most likely to impose its will ruthlessly if its central ideology maintains that people are basically good.)

Political utopianism aside, the assumption that people are either good or evil, a construction no less silly or sophomoric than the nature versus nurture polarity, continues to color our thinking. Even those who have resisted outright cynicism may regard talk of the brighter side of human nature as reflecting a simple-minded "Man Is Good" dogma that seems starry-eyed and untenable in a century pockmarked by genocide. I am suggesting that the error lies not in being skeptical of that position but in creating a false dichotomy. To insist that there is more to our species than egoism or aggression is not necessarily to cast one's lot with Carl Rogers or TV's Mr. Rogers. Confronted with the kaleidoscopic variation of human behavior, some humanistic psychologists and other neo-Rousseauvians have argued that the good in us is essential and the loathsome is contingent; without a corrupting environment, we would individually and collectively be admirable. This leap of faith, cogently criticized even from within the humanistic tradition,[21] is simply the mirror image of the unsupported assertions on the subject to come from Hobbes, Freud, and other partisans of Original Sin (in its original or pseudoscientific versions). To wince at the naiveté of "we're all beautiful creatures deep down" need not bring us to assume that we must be fundamentally corrupted, self-serving creatures—or vice versa.*

Clearly, there is no calculus for determining where we are on that

---

*The relationship between these two diametrically opposed outlooks often amounts to no more than a matter of time. Just as doctrinaire Communists frequently become doctrinaire anti-Communists, so does excessive credulity beget cynicism. Psychologically speaking, it is not surprising to realize that he who used to trust everyone now trusts no one, as though atoning with a kind of free-floating bitterness for the naiveté of his younger days.

hypothetical continuum that stretches between good and evil, no way to tally up the praiseworthy and objectionable actions of our fellows. There are grounds for denying our perfectibility (whatever *perfection* means in this context), and also grounds for an unsentimental observer to agree with Albert Camus's pronouncement about humans being more admirable than not. Moreover, there are grounds for repudiating the idea of such a continuum to begin with, in favor of a dialectical account of our nature[22] or an affirmation of the idea that we have no given nature at all in the moral realm.[23]

That I am skating quickly past these ponderous issues does not mean that they can be dispatched with a few phrases or that they do not warrant serious treatment. That we cannot simply choose up sides—Good, Bad, Both, Neither—and have done with it should be obvious. Interestingly, even those thinkers whose names we associate with a jaundiced view of human nature have given mixed signals. Even Adam Smith, descriptively and prescriptively a philosopher of self-interest in *The Wealth of Nations*, began his other major book, *The Theory of Moral Sentiments*, as follows:

How selfish soever man may be supposed, there are evidently some principles in his nature, which interest him in the fortune of others, and render their happiness necessary to him, though he derives nothing from it, except the pleasure of seeing it. . . . That we often derive sorrow from the sorrow of others, is a matter of fact too obvious to require any instances to prove it.[24]

Even Thomas Hobbes is not a strict psychological egoist since he does not insist that people are always and exclusively concerned with their own interests.[25] And even Herbert Spencer, coiner of the term "survival of the fittest," also insists that "self-sacrifice . . . is no less primordial than self-preservation," that real gratification can be had only by "unstinted benevolence"—a benevolence that may foster, but is not motivated by, egoistic pleasure.[26]

The story of our nature, if indeed it makes sense to speak in this context of having a nature, must be told without relying on tired formulas and uncritical assumptions that emphasize only the worst in our collective repertoire. Freud and Nietzsche, among others, saw themselves as debunking romantic illusions about the species, ripping off the reassuring deceptions that blocked out bad news.[27] But Freud also said that it was not his "intention to dispute the noble endeavours of human nature"; he tended to emphasize "what is evil in men only because other people disavow it."[28] This correction may have been sensible at one time, but today the dominant view has slid to the other extreme. Anyone concerned with restoring balance is now more likely to be working at debunking the debunkers. There are two steps to this enterprise: attending to the admirable features of the human race and challenging the conclusions hastily drawn from the fact that people sometimes hurt and even kill each other. Let us proceed with the latter.

HUMAN AGGRESSION

Is aggressive behavior part of human nature? Yes, in the sense that virtually all of us have the capacity to respond in this way to a perceived threat. But neither that fact nor any evidence of which I am aware permits us to say that aggression is an innate tendency of our species or anything close to an inevitability in the life of any given individual. It is not any more real or integral a response than reacting to the same threat by fleeing, embracing, laughing, weeping, or writing.

In saying this, I join a number of investigators who have come to dismiss explanations appealing to innateness. In his 1977 book, for example, the psychologist Robert A. Baron cited more than three hundred studies, including two dozen of his own, before concluding that

contrary to the views espoused by Freud, Lorenz, Ardrey, and others, aggression is *not* essentially innate. Rather, it seems to be a learned form of social behavior, acquired in the same manner as other types of activity and influenced by many of the same social, situational, and environmental factors.[29]

Even more impressive, some of the world's leading psychologists, neurophysiologists, ethologists, and others from the natural and social sciences signed a declaration in 1986, the Seville Statement, that makes essentially the same point (see Appendix).

To understand the logic of this conclusion, let us begin by observing the indisputable fact that aggressiveness, as we normally understand the concept, does not describe everyone we know. In order to maintain that it is a response toward which humans naturally incline, we must therefore stretch the term almost beyond recognition. Once Gandhi's commitment to nonviolence is understood to reflect nothing more than a form of displaced aggression, we have entered the realm of unfalsifiable argument: no piece of evidence could conceivably disprove the theory because it has been set up in such a way that any sort of data serves only to confirm it.

I do not propose to discard such ideas as the classification of "passive aggressive" personality patterns. There is good reason, moreover, to peer beneath the surface when someone loudly describes himself as completely free of hostility while simultaneously grinding his teeth together and shredding his napkin. But there is no good reason to imagine that unconscious aggressive impulses lurk behind every expression of disagreement or every vigorous bite of an apple or every dream. The question is not whether aggression can sometimes manifest itself indirectly; of course it can. It is whether we are justified in having an a priori commitment to believing in its universality (much less its inevitability), a blind faith in the naturalness of wanting to hurt, a confidence in the existence of ulterior motives anytime someone remains unperturbed in response to a stimulus to which *we* might have reacted with rage. (Theories of universal aggression may well tell us more about the theorist than about the human mind as such.) Nothing approaching traditional standards of empirical proof has ever been offered by an orthodox psychoanalyst, an ethologist, a sociobiologist, or anyone else in support of the prejudice that behaviors apparently devoid of aggression must have originated as, or otherwise symbolize, an invisible urge to harm.

For the sake of the argument, though, let us entertain the possibility that it is indeed sensible to explain the personality of an introverted, nonviolent political activist by conjuring up an underlying aggressive drive. This is done not only by Freudians but by humanistic psychologists like Abraham Maslow, who spoke of aggression's being transformed into "righteous indignation," a "passion for justice," or "healthy self-affirmation."[30] What are we to make of this? If our aggressive brew has been watered down to this point, it may be drinkable, but there is no point in walking to a bar and paying good money for it. The substantive conclusion remains that it is possible to avoid what we would then have to call Aggression$_1$ (the hurting kind) in favor of Aggression$_2$ (the healthy, self-affirming kind).

Ah, replies the aggression theorist, but there is predictive utility in the notion that even the latter is a type of aggression. It suggests that one must inhibit or transform an urge to aggress; the fact that this can be, and often is, done does not disprove the existence of the urge or its primacy.

Yet what is the point of such an assumption? Where is the evidence that individuals who most successfully "disguise" their putative aggression will be more likely to erupt—or to do so with deadly consequences? Or, if individual differences are not the point, where is the evidence that the universality of aggression means that every individual will sooner or later lash out? (As I hope is becoming clear, the common-sense assumptions about aggression in this post-Freudian age eventually collapse into the old catharsis model which, as we shall see, today commands the loyalty of almost no theorists or researchers.)

If our nature "at bottom" is to be aggressive—a nature which we can only struggle to inhibit—then why are so many hunter-gatherer cultures apparently devoid of aggression? Erich Fromm has pointed out that "the most primitive men are the least warlike and that warlikeness grows in proportion to civilization. If destructiveness were innate in man, the trend would have to be the opposite."[31] Why, for that matter, are severely mentally retarded people, whose inhibitions are also presumably low, so rarely characterized by aggressiveness?[32]

These examples aside, we would do well to reconsider our assumptions about the very idea of inhibition—specifically, the premise that an inhibited behavior represents the genuine inclination of the individual onto which an artificial restraint has been stapled. This we take for granted, just as we assume that we are witnessing someone's true self when she has had a lot to drink: the obnoxious or flirtatious behavior is thought to have been freed from its usual restraints, permitting us a look at Sue as she really is.

This, however, reflects our own theoretical construct rather than the reality before us. It is by no means clear that Sue-after-three-whiskey-sours is in some way ontologically prior to Sue-before-three-whiskey-sours, or, to put it differently, that alcohol is more an agent of revelation than simply a psychoactive drug. Likewise, hurting someone does not reflect any truer or deeper part of oneself than not hurting someone. An individual's inhibition—perhaps we ought to say her decision to avoid acting on an urge—is as much a part of her as the (environmentally elicited) urge itself or her occasional decision to act on it.

Of course, even if aggression is taken to be innate, and inhibitions are understood in their usual sense, the very fact that the latter exist or can be taught reminds us again that what is innate is not inevitable, what is biological is not fixed. The fact that people voluntarily fast or remain celibate or commit suicide shows that even drives like hunger, sex, and survival can be overridden. In the case of aggression, where the existence of such a drive is doubtful to begin with, our ability to choose is even clearer.[33]

Are We Natural Warriors?

We can go further: the more serious the act of aggression, the more often its commission seems to require overcoming a deep-seated repulsion rather than liberating our natural instincts. Let us consider the organized killing of other human beings. Polls have shown that roughly 60 percent of American adults, undergraduates, and high school students believe that wars can never be eliminated because fighting them is an inevitable consequence of human nature.[34]

Now this assumption is in trouble to begin with because the aggression ascribed to that nature has very little to do with war, which, as Rousseau put it, is "not a relation between man and man, but between State and State, and individuals are enemies accidentally."[35]* Moreover, even casual reflection on what happens before, during, and after wars exposes the human nature view as specious. While there are exceptions, the first thing that strikes an observer is the fact that those who declare and direct wars apparently must make extensive use of propaganda to elicit and solidify support on the part of the populace. Sam Keen has reviewed the graphic forms that such propaganda has taken over the last century. He concludes as follows:

We continually visualize our enemies in a demeaning way precisely because we are *not* instinctually sadists. If anything, we have a natural inclination not to kill our own kind, and therefore we have to make them horribly unlike us before we can overcome our instinctual compassion and kill them.[36]

If propaganda depicting the other side as barbaric aggressors who threaten Our Way of Life does not adequately stimulate young men to kill, the state will resort to coercion. The frequency with which nations draft its citizens into combat (and invoke stiff penalties for those who resist it) qualifies as powerful evidence against the idea that wars reflect natural human aggressiveness. Once drafted, the process of military training is characterized by remaking human beings into soldiers, dehumanizing the draftees themselves as well as the enemy, replacing critical thought with mindless obedience ("In war men are more like sheep than wolves"),[37] and trying to replace an abhorrence for taking a life with

---

*The conceptual chasm between aggression and war yawns even wider in the case of nuclear war, the strategic plans for which have nothing to do with hostility and everything to do with a chilling, hypertrophied rationalism.

either indifference or positive enthusiasm. These procedures have their analogue in the ritual preparations for warfare in primitive tribes, all of which leads us to ask: Why the universal need for this deliberate and involved process if we are innately disposed to kill?

The difficulty of killing someone who has not first been dehumanized has been observed by a number of writers. André Malraux said you cannot aim a flame-thrower at a person who is looking at you.[38] George Orwell described his inability to pull the trigger at an enemy soldier whose pants were falling down: "A man who is holding up his trousers isn't a 'Fascist,' he is visibly a fellow creature, similar to yourself, and you don't feel like shooting at him."[39] In his plays, Camus refers several times to the inability to kill people one can see, regardless of the ideological reason for wanting them dead,[40] and empirical research has confirmed that being able to see one's victims usually reduces the aggressive actions one is willing to take against them.[41]

More remarkable than the need for propaganda, the draft, and basic training, than the fact that no one will kill until the identified victim has been painstakingly stripped of his humanity, is the fact that *even then* most people will refuse to take another's life. In 1947, the military analyst S. L. A. Marshall, who had been appointed chief historian of World War II and was later to serve as a general in the Korean War, wrote a book called *Men against Fire,* in which he discusses the results of interviews with hundreds of infantry companies in the central Pacific and European theaters. These findings are nothing short of astounding and are worth quoting at length:

On average not more than 15 percent of the men had actually fired at the enemy positions or personnel with rifles, carbines, grenades, bazookas, BARs [Browning automatic rifles], or machine guns during the course of an entire engagement. Even allowing for the dead and wounded, and assuming that in their numbers there would be the same proportion of active firers as among the living, the figure did not rise above 20 or 25 percent of the total for any action. The best showing that could be made by the most spirited and aggressive companies was that one man in four had made at least some use of his fire power. . . . A commander of infantry will be well advised to believe that when he engages the enemy not more than one quarter of his men will ever strike a real blow unless they are compelled by almost overpowering circumstance or unless all junior leaders constantly "ride herd" on troops with the specific mission of increasing their fire. The 25 percent estimate stands even for well-trained and campaign-seasoned troops. I mean that 75 percent will not fire or will not persist in firing against the enemy and his works. These men may face the danger but they will not fight.[42]

Several points about this passage are noteworthy. First, Marshall does not mean that 15 or 25 percent of soldiers in a company were firing at any given time; he means that only that proportion of the men would use their weapons *at all.* Even that figure, he emphasizes, is generous: soldiers who so much as fired a rifle once during a battle are included in it. Second, this reluctance to kill was not true only of novices. It persisted even after soldiers had been through three or four battles, which "appeared to indicate that the ceiling was fixed by some constant which was inherent in the nature of the troops."[43] Third, Marshall is talking about an unwillingness to kill, not a fear of being killed. Some of the men who refused to use their weapons did not back away from danger, and he notes also that psychiatric studies of combat fatigue found that

fear of killing, rather than fear of being killed, was the most common cause of battle failure in the individual. . . . It is therefore reasonable to believe that the average and normally healthy individual—the man who can endure the mental and physical stresses of combat—still has such an inner and usually unrealized resistance toward killing a fellow man that he will not of his own volition take life if it is possible to turn away from that responsibility.[44]

These cannot be dismissed as the tendentious findings or interpretations of an antiwar activist or even a humanistically inclined psychologist. Marshall was a lifelong military man, writing in this case to other military men about a situation that he viewed with alarm, about what he referred to as a handicap of most soldiers, not a sign of health.[45] It should also be noted that he was not interviewing participants in the Vietnam War, about which many soldiers had profound moral doubts. This was World War II, to which virtually everyone was ideologically committed. But commitment apparently is not enough when this sort of aggression is involved. There are multiple and variable social pressures at work here, but on balance it would seem that resistance to killing is at least as "natural" as killing.

Is Aggression Unavoidable?

In order to regard as plausible the idea that humans innately tend toward aggression, it is first necessary to collapse a great number of diverse behaviors and motives into that single word. As we have seen, the discovery of gender differences in this realm depends on whether we are speaking of direct or indirect aggression, and so forth. Similarly, careful students of the subject have distinguished between aggression and violence and between positive destructiveness and the defensive use of force. To use a single word to refer to killing a deer for food, taking part in a religious ritual involving cannibalism, smacking one's child, and shooting a security guard in the course of a robbery invites sloppiness of the highest order. Then to treat this word as a single concept that admits of a single explanation is to accept the invitation. Just such reductionism is required, in fact, to drum up evidence for the innate view. As one group of scholars put it, it is false to assume that

there is a single ("instinctive") motivational source for all the things that people customarily term aggressive. . . . Aggression is not a natural category of analysis; rather, it is a more-or-less useful construct that we impose upon nature. . . . Aggression is not "located" in particular genes, hormones, or brain "centres"; rather, various kinds of aggressive behaviour are the developmental consequences in specific environments of multiple and diverse interactions within and between social animals or humans.[46]

This is worth keeping in mind as we review several arguments in favor of the idea that aggression is unavoidable.

The idea that we have within us a naturally occurring reservoir of aggressive energy, a force that builds up by itself and must be periodically drained off lest we explode into bestial violence, is appealing because it is easy to visualize. It is also false. One is hard-pressed to name another model concerning any aspect of human behavior that is so widely accepted by the general public and has been so thoroughly repudiated by specialists in the area. Freud and Lorenz notwithstanding, there is absolutely no evidence from animal behavior or human psychology to suggest that individuals of any species fight because of spontaneous internal stimulation. We may be acquainted with people who have come to react violently to a wide range of environmental stimuli, but this proves neither that the violence is spontaneous rather than reactive nor that it is innate rather than learned. Likewise, writes the physiologist K. E. Moyer, the so-called hydraulic metaphor is inappropriate even when we come across

the *appearance* of a build-up of aggressive energy . . . [since this] is no more than a lowering of the response threshold which may change as a function of alterations in the individual's physiological status. There is no aggressive energy which continues to accumulate, and there is no *necessity* for the expression of hostility.[47]

The existence of nonaggressive individuals and societies[48]—without any trace of the inexorable build-up of pressure that the theory would predict—clearly refutes the idea of spontaneous aggression, as does the demonstrated relevance of the environment in eliciting all aggressive acts (discussed below). The theory also predicts that venting aggressive energy should make us less aggressive—an effect known as catharsis, following Aristotle's idea that we can be purged of unpleasant emotions by watching tragic dramas. It has been repeatedly shown, however, that participating in, or even observing, aggressive activities—such as competitive sports, which Lorenz recommended—not only is unnecessary for curbing violent behavior but actually exacerbates it.[49] Taking part in such activities does not "discharge" some mythical internal force; it reduces learned inhibitions against aggressive behaviors and reinforces them.

This failure of the catharsis effect is also relevant to a revisionist version of the theory to be found in certain newer, humanistic traditions in psychotherapy and counseling. Rather than positing that aggression is inborn, these schools argue that disagreeable experiences, particularly early in life, are the source of later emotional difficulties. But they go on to prescribe various cathartic techniques to "discharge" or "work out" hostility, thus drawing on the discredited premises of the hydraulic model, the same simplistic belief that there exists within us a repository of unwanted feelings that can be reduced by giving them expression.

Such theories seem to offer an attractive and accessible means of explaining why it is that the chap who one day picks up a gun and begins firing at innocent people in a school or post office is invariably described on the evening news as having been a shy loner. We say: You see? He kept his aggression bottled up inside until it finally had to burst out. But apart from overlooking all the other shy loners who will go to their graves without having harmed anyone—and, conversely, the less newsworthy sorts who have been episodically violent over many years—we are ignoring the possibility that it was not an endogenous force but the social circumstance of isolation that contributed to sociopathic behavior. Or, more likely, there may have been other variables that caused both the isolation *and* the violence.

Some people who know enough to dismiss the catharsis theory nevertheless point to other data as supporting the innateness of aggression. First, there are the neurological and hormonal factors. Electrical stimulation of the section of the brain known as the amygdala has been experimentally linked to acts of violence, as has exposure to high levels of testosterone. But this tells us nothing about inevitability or our true nature; it merely helps us to identify more precisely the biological corre-lates—as distinct from causes—of aggression. We have already seen that testosterone levels can be the consequence rather than the cause of behavior. Similarly, "It is not that the brain is 'wired' for aggression, but that neural elements in certain parts of the brain can be readily organized by experience to function in behavior we call aggressive," as Montagu has written.[50] The role played by experience is important for all species. Even when the neural system in question has been activated, aggressive behavior will occur only if there is a target available, as Moyer and others have shown.

For humans, of course, the social environment as subjectively per-ceived and interpreted is not merely relevant but decisive, giving the lie to biological determinist claims. We might recall the classic study by psychologists Stanley Schachter and Jerome Singer in the early 1960s. They gave experimental subjects an injection of adrenalin, which causes the heart to pound, the hands to shake, and the face to flush. Those who were told to expect these effects felt little emotion as a result. But subjects who were told they had only been given a vitamin found their mood dramatically affected—with the direction of the effect dependent on who was around them. The adrenalin enhanced their anger if someone hostile was in the vicinity but not when they were in the company of a person acting giddy and playful.[51] The physiological arousal, in other words, meant little without a social context, and so it is that the neurochemical basis of aggression is meaningful only with respect to a given environ-ment. In light of this, to talk of an innate tendency to be aggressive makes about as much sense as asserting that because there can be no fires without oxygen, and because the earth is blanketed by oxygen, it is therefore in the nature of our planet for buildings to burn down. Obvi-ously, a given building would remain standing if it contained no flamma-ble material to feed the fire, if no carelessly (or feloniously) dropped match had started it, or if a smoke detector had warned us at an early stage. Each of these elements has its analog in the case of human aggres-sive behavior.

Aggression is also said to be innate in humans by virtue of its pres-ence in other species. This method of reasoning, which Jeffrey Goldstein wittily summarizes as taking "one giant leap toward mankind," is, unhap-pily, not restricted to laypeople. Apart from the conceptual pole vaulting of some sociobiologists, the generous funding of animal research on the topic proceeds from the implicit belief that we can better understand wars and wife battering by studying cats and rats—despite the fact that most forms of human violence are not analogous, let alone homologous, with animal aggression.[52] Only human behavior is saturated in cultural meanings, organized around symbols, conceived in terms of long-range, rationally devised purposes, and so on. Even where our species is at its most violent, we cannot look to others for an explanation: organized group aggression is rare outside of the realm of Homo sapiens, and war is a distinctively human phenomenon.[53]

Even if the naturalistic and experimental findings with other species *were* accepted as apposite to our own, the reality is that they do not support a simple-minded view of built-in aggression. This is true, first, because of the role of the environment, not only as a supplier of targets for aggressive behavior but as a potential modifier of that behavior. Altering the way an animal is reared—even an animal bred to fight—can virtually eliminate its aggressiveness.[54] Recent experiments at the University of North Carolina found that changes in the environment "were sufficient to mask or eliminate the heritable effects in social behavior" of mice. These findings of "great plasticity" in social behavior, particularly aggression, "do not fit very easily with the presumption that there is an isomorphic correspondence between genetic units and behavioral units that is invariant across development, as is implied by the notion of an 'aggressive gene.' "[55]

Second, the truth is that few species are as aggressive as most casual watchers of nature documentaries assume. I have discussed this matter elsewhere, with special reference to the predominance of interspecific and intraspecific cooperation,[56] and so will simply note here that just as migration is one of the many methods by which animals seem to go out of their way to avoid competing, so it is that dominance hierarchies and ritualized threatening postures are adaptive precisely by virtue of how they *limit* genuinely aggressive encounters. When such encounters do occur, students of primates have observed an elaborate mechanism by which the disputants make peace afterward in order to forestall further aggression. (A recent book on this subject argues that little attention has been paid to conflict avoidance and reconciliation on the part of animals or humans, with the result that we falsely assume violence is more natural than peace.)[57]

With nothing in neurobiology or animal behavior to support them, believers in unavoidable human aggression may resort to pointing to the simple prevalence of violence in human history—as though the frequency of a behavior in the past constituted a reason for assuming it can never be changed. Yet here we must repeat that war, the phenomenon most often cited in this context, has very little to do with aggression as such. Participants in wars are characterized less by aggressive energy in search of an outlet than by carefully socialized obedience. The fact that fiercely warlike societies can become peaceful in a matter of a few centuries—witness Sweden—also corroborates the importance of social and political rather than biological factors. Moreover, evidence is accumulating that war is a relatively recent event in human history: there appears to be little evidence of warfare among Pleistocene people,[58] and even since that era it has not been the rule. In a provocative synthesis of data from archaeology and other disciplines, Riane Eisler argues that the bloodiness we have come to see as a dominant feature of history in fact describes only the last five thousand years or so, less than 1 percent of the time our species has existed. War and other sorts of oppression, according to Eisler, constitute the historical exception, a detour from the main road of cultural development in which none of the landmarks have to do with destruction.[59]

What Is the Source of Aggressive Behavior?

The preceding section has been concerned with theoretical and empirical deficiencies in the schools of thought seeking to argue that human nature is necessarily aggressive. The case against this position is not exclusively negative, however; one can choose from among numerous persuasive accounts of our aggressiveness—mechanisms of learning, psychological conditions, and environmental variables—that do not invoke biological explanations. I will not attempt to describe these in any detail, let alone adjudicate among them. The point here is merely to review the range of possibilities that lead many observers to conclude with Leon Eisenberg: "Learning may not account completely for human aggression, but the social forces in contemporary society that encourage its development are so evident that preoccupation with hypothesized biological factors is almost quixotic."[60]

One of the signal advances in learning theory was the recognition that we need not be reinforced directly in order to engage in a given behavior: we may imitate an action simply after observing others do it. Aggression may be reinforcing to a child if it yields approval, but it may be enough for adults (on TV programs, on the football field, or at home) to model such behavior. By now, of course, there is an enormous literature on this.

The question of what distinguishes aggressive from nonaggressive

individuals has occupied researchers for many years. The traditional
position on people so violent as to be classified sociopathic is that they
are unable to empathize or take the perspective of others,[61] an issue on
which I will spend considerable time in chapter 4. More recently, it has
been argued that aggressive individuals may have the capacity to empathize but cannot interpret others' behavior correctly in emotionally
arousing situations; the problem lies in an inappropriate attribution of
hostility to nonhostile others.[62] In either case, it appears that one way we
cannot account for differences in aggressiveness is by appealing to genes.
The latest evidence against that hypothesis comes from Robert Plomin.
In a 1981 study of more than two hundred children, he found that correlations for identical twins on a widely used measure of aggression were
no greater than those for fraternal twins: individual differences clearly
result from environmental rather than genetic factors, he concluded.[63]

There are good data by now to justify the conclusion that physical
punishment[64]—and, even more compellingly, abuse[65]—produces children who are more aggressive than their peers. There is less certainty,
however, and more varied hypotheses concerning the nuances of a situation and of an individual's personality dynamics that predict aggression.
The classic theory about the role of frustration, offered half a century ago
by John Dollard and his colleagues, has been revised rather than discarded. First, the fact that aggression can invariably be traced to some
sort of frustration—that is, interference with the fulfillment of one's
goals—does not imply that *any* instance of frustration will necessarily
produce an aggressive response. (It is more likely to do so if an individual
is already emotionally aroused.) Second, psychologists have come to
understand that the relevance and potency of frustration depend on how
it is construed by the individual subject.* A situation that frustrates me
to the point of rage may fail to disturb your equanimity; what I found
frustrating last week may not ruffle my feathers today.

First cousin to this more flexible, subjective conception of frustration
is the idea that people are aggressive when they or something about them
is challenged. The psychologist Ervin Staub sums up the relevant literature this way: "Threat to existence, to the self-concept, and to fulfillment

---

*Almost in spite of themselves, psychologists gradually have had to abandon the
assumption that objective, quantifiable phenomena such as frustration or stress operate on
people in uniform and lawful ways. Importing this natural science paradigm into the study
of human behavior did not take account of the individual as subject—as perceiver, meaning
maker, existential agent. The paradigm has been discarded less out of distaste on the part
of researchers than because of a recognition that its naive objectification simply makes for
poor science.

of goals all appear to increase the probability of aggressive responses. These conditions at times directly and physically, at other times potentially or symbolically, threaten a person's existence."[66] The threat posed by a noisy, crowded environment can promote violence—depending, again, on whether one is inclined to perceive that environment as threatening. (Violence is extremely rare in Tokyo, after all.)

War and other particularly egregious sorts of violence cannot be explained in terms of hostility or hatred, as we have seen. Herbert Kelman, who has written widely on evil and violence, rejects these affective explanations, along with references to sadism, proposing that "we can learn more by looking, not at the motives for violence, but at the conditions under which the usual moral inhibitions against violence become weakened."[67] Those conditions, he goes on to argue, typically take the form of *authorization,* in which someone seen to be in charge relieves the actor of responsibility; *routinization,* which turns the commission of violence into a normal, even bureaucratic, operation; and *dehumanization,* in which victims are made faceless and impersonal, stripped of personal identity and connection to a community.[68]

Just as dehumanization of an other may be required in order to kill him, so can we better understand the killer by inquiring into the dehumanizing circumstances in which *he* has lived. Turned into an object, argues the well-known social psychologist Philip Zimbardo, a person may resort to violence in order to be taken seriously, to assert a sense of agency. "In one sense, violence and destruction transform a passive, controlled object into an active, controlling person."[69] This idea has been expressed in other words by a number of writers: vulnerability and powerlessness—perhaps as imposed on us by crushing political or economic forces, perhaps as a function of the human predicament itself— move us, paradoxically, to turn to power and aggression as a response (or as a means of denial).[70] Whichever of these theoretical approaches strikes one as credible or particularly appropriate to a given instance of aggression, all of them share the feature of rendering "human nature" accounts superfluous.

Why Do We Believe Aggression Is Innate?

Just as the pervasiveness of apparent evil can lead us to conclude that this must be our natural state, so the frequency with which we are exposed to acts of violence may lend plausibility to the view that aggression is unavoidable. Something on the order of twenty thousand murders are reported each year in the United States (to say nothing of ninety thousand rapes and about three-quarters of a million cases of aggravated assault). These numbers are, even on a per capita basis, astronomical from the perspective of other Western industrialized nations. Also anomalous is the existence of capital punishment: while almost all countries we view as civilized have come to regard its moral status as akin to that of slavery, many of our states persist in electrocuting, gassing, or shooting people to death for failing to understand the sacredness of human life. Moral considerations aside, there is evidence that the death penalty, so far from deterring criminals, actually encourages some of them to imitate the state. Thus is the society made more dangerous and the climate of violence, from which conclusions are drawn about human nature, worsened.[71] Likewise, if "people in a highly warlike society are likely to overestimate the propensity toward war in human nature,"[72] then it must be noted that the United States is one of the most warlike societies on the face of the planet, having intervened militarily around the world more than 150 times since 1850.[73] Within such a society, not surprisingly, the intellectual traditions supporting the view that aggression is more a function of nature than nurture have found a ready audience.

Like other beliefs about the intrinsic unsavoriness of our species, such an assumption about aggression can also be explained in terms of the responsibility it lifts from our shoulders ("Yeah, I punched him out, but when somebody insults you, it's just human nature to fly off the handle"), in terms of images presented to us by the mass media, and in terms of the powerful interests who are benefited by just such an assumption. The last of these may be the most troubling for us to consider, but it seems plausible that citizens would be more likely to accept the need for intervention abroad and draconian "antiterrorist" measures if they have first been persuaded that these tactics are required to cope with people's innately violent instincts. Similarly, in light of aggression on the part of other citizens, such a view helps to divert attention from the actions of the policy makers themselves and from oppressive economic and social conditions that might be identified as contributors to such violence, focusing our gaze instead on a biological "reality" to which one must be resigned.

Finally, and most insidiously, there is the phenomenon of the self-fulfilling prophecy. To assume that humans are bound to be aggressive (or egoistic or competitive) is to act in such a way as to provide evidence for the assumption. Thus, by virtue of believing that humans are naturally aggressive, one may be relatively unlikely to oppose particular wars or to become involved in the peace movement. For some, this belief undoubtedly just functions as a rationalization for their unwillingness to become active for other reasons. But there is some limited empirical support for the proposition that the attitude itself has an impact. In a 1985 Finnish study of 375 young people, Riitta Wahlstrom found that those who considered war to be part of human nature were less inclined to support the idea of teaching peace or of personally working for it.[74] Two American researchers got similar results in a smaller U.S. study: college students who said they thought war was "intrinsic to human nature" proved less likely than others to work on a peace-related activity, according to a follow-up questionnaire.[75] A survey of students during the Vietnam War revealed that "those who believed wars to be inevitable were more likely than others to view the U.S. military involvement to be justified and to express the opinion that the involvement should be escalated."[76] Indeed, the sociologist C. Wright Mills has argued that the most important cause of World War III will be the preparation for it.[77]

The simple assumption that we cannot help being aggressive helps us to continue being aggressive. No circle is more vicious than the one set up by the fallacious assumption that we are unable to control an essentially violent nature. Aside from the respect in which it proves itself true, then, this belief is not only inaccurate for all the reasons reviewed here, but also deadly. While the various other psychological and social factors that contribute to aggressive behavior cannot simply be wished away, assumptions about the nature of our species can be—and, given the stakes, must be—reconsidered.

II

RESPONDING TO
OTHERS

3

Prosocial Practices:
Prediction and Promotion

*It is a feeling common to all mankind that they cannot bear to see
others suffer. . . . This feeling of distress (at the suffering of
others) is the first sign of Humanity.*
—Mencius (fourth century B.C.E.)

GENEROUS HELPINGS

It should not be surprising, in light of this society's widely shared assumptions about human nature, that helping, caring, rescuing, and sharing
were not systematically studied until the mid- to late 1960s—and even
then were investigated chiefly so that we might understand the reasons
for their absence.[1] The examination of what would later be called prosocial behavior* was prompted generally by the disturbing growth of violent crime and specifically by what might be called the Genovese 38. The
latter refers to those neighbors who, despite hearing a New York City
woman, Kitty Genovese, scream for help over the course of more than
half an hour while she was being stabbed to death, nevertheless failed to
come to her aid or even call the police. This celebrated case led psycholo-

---

*The term *prosocial*, introduced in the early 1970s to contrast with *antisocial*, is awkward,
jargony, and very nearly indispensable. It refers to actions undertaken voluntarily and
intentionally to benefit someone else, but, unlike the word *altruism*, it does not address the
question of ultimate motivation. (It seems important not to decide this question by means
of terminology in light of the fact that one may very well be thinking of one's own benefit
even while deliberately acting to help another. Whether helping is ever truly altruistic will
be the central question of a later chapter.) But the word *prosocial*, by virtue of standing for
such diverse actions as helping someone pick up a pile of papers, donating money to charity,
sharing one's possessions, and extending sympathy or protection, remains problematic
inasmuch as each of these actions actually may be quite distinct, both conceptually and
empirically.[2]

gists to inquire why bystanders sometimes continue to stand by. Only within this conceptual framework did investigators eventually begin to collect data about how we *do* help.

When they did begin to turn their attention in this direction, researchers became theater directors, staging an assortment of accidents and waiting to see how many people would come to the rescue. Stooges collapsed on subway floors, made choking sounds in the next room, set fires in the hall, and otherwise feigned crises while their confederates busily took notes. We will want to look carefully at the consequences of manipulating some of the situational variables, but let us first notice the overriding truth that emerges from these studies: people of all ages usually do go out of their way to help, particularly when the need is clear and when they believe that no one else is in a position to get involved. Of course, some people help more reliably than others, just as some circumstances are more likely to elicit help, but the horror of the Genovese death, while unfortunately not unique, made its impact partly because it was exceptional. Ordinary people often lend a hand, and sometimes, when the situation seems to require it, they act positively heroically.

It is the heroic acts that turn up in the newspaper ("Man Dives into Pond to Save Drowning Child") and upstage the dozens of less memorable prosocial behaviors that each of us witnesses and performs in a given week. In my experience, cars do not spin their wheels on the ice for very long before someone stops to offer a push. We disrupt our schedules to visit sick friends, stop to give directions to lost travelers, ask crying people if there is anything we can do to help. According to polls, nearly 90 percent of Americans give money to charitable causes and nearly half take the time to do some sort of volunteer work.[3] In one study, 83 percent of blood donors indicated a willingness to undergo anesthesia and stay overnight in a hospital in order to donate bone marrow to a complete stranger.[4] And if we, like some researchers, choose to expand the idea of prosocial behavior to include cooperative activities—working with others for mutual benefit, such as in structured collaboration at work—we would find even more evidence of prosocial inclinations. All of this, it should be stressed, is particularly remarkable in light of the fact that we are socialized in an ethic of competitive individualism. Like a green shoot forcing its way up between the concrete slabs of a city sidewalk, evidence of human caring and helping defies this culture's ambivalence about—if not outright discouragement of—such activity.

As striking as the frequency of prosocial actions may be, and as informative for someone in search of data about our species, the picture becomes even clearer once we introduce the behavior of children. While Freud was still grousing about ruthlessly egoistic tots, his countryman William Stern was observing in an early book on child psychology, "Even the two year old child has the power of feeling another's sorrow."[5] In 1948, an American psychiatrist complained that "the emphasis on the inborn or instinctive features of hostility, aggression, death wishes, and the negative emotional experiences represents a one-sided approach which has led our students of child psychology astray."[6] Such remarks were, however, at least until recently, quite unusual: the frequency and significance of early prosocial behavior was generally lost on professional specialists in child development.

Today, psychologist William Damon can write: "Most scholars believe that moral emotions are a natural component of a child's social repertoire, and that the potential for moral-emotional reactions is present at birth."[7] Indeed, just as psychoanalysts were wrong about children's egoism, so were many cognitive-developmentalists wrong about their egocentrism. (Well before the age of seven and the arrival of Piaget's concrete-operational stage, children apparently can regard the world from other people's perspectives [see chapter 4].)

That there is more even to toddlers than selfishness and self-centeredness will hardly seem astonishing to anyone who has watched, say, a twenty-month-old burst into tears upon seeing a cut on her daddy's knee or a thirty-month-old retrieve his favorite stuffed toy to console a weeping visitor. Still, the idea that concern for others must be forced down the throats of naturally egocentric creatures has not departed gracefully. It has persisted despite study after study substantiating Damon's assertion.

To start at the beginning, research has established that newborns are more likely to cry—and to cry longer—when they are exposed to the sound of another infant's cry than when they hear other, equally loud, noises. The sounds used for purposes of comparison have included a computer-generated synthetic cry and a burst of white noise carefully designed to be as sudden in onset, as long-lasting, and as loud as the stimulus newborn's cry. The infants in these studies ranged from thirty-four to seventy-two hours old, and their cries seemed to be spontaneous reactions rather than mere vocal imitations. These findings were published in two papers that described five studies with a combined total of more than 250 infants.[8]

One might object that the infants were simply confusing the cries of

others with their own. (One of the studies had found that each infant
cried for a few seconds longer upon hearing a tape of his or her own cry
than when someone else's was played, but only twenty infants were used
in this experiment, and the difference was not statistically significant.)
Even if this interpretation was accurate, of course, the fact that we are
predisposed to make this confusion and become distressed in the face of
another person's distress seems significant in itself. But two researchers
conducted another study in 1982 with infants just eighteen hours old, and
found that they were more likely to cry upon hearing a tape of another
infant's cry than upon hearing a tape of their own. What's more, those
who were already crying continued doing so when they heard someone
else's cry and *stopped* crying when they heard their own.[9] Taken together,
these findings suggest, in the view of Abraham Sagi and Martin Hoffman,
who conducted one of the studies, the existence of "a rudimentary empathic distress reaction at birth," a primitive precursor to what we think
of as empathy.[10] Our species may be primed, in other words, to be
discomfited by someone else's discomfort.

As an infant grows, this discomfort continues and takes more sophisticated forms. Marian Radke-Yarrow, Carolyn Zahn-Waxler, and their
associates have been studying toddlers for the better part of two decades,
having in effect deputized mothers as research assistants to collect data
in the home instead of relying on brief (and possibly unrepresentative)
observations in the laboratory. A ten- to fourteen-month-old child, they
have found, can be expected to show signs of agitation and unhappiness
in the presence of another person's distress, perhaps crying or burying
her head in her mother's lap. As the child develops the capacity of pur-
posive behavior, in the period between eighteen and twenty-four months,
her response to distress will become more active: patting the head, fetch-
ing a toy, offering verbal expressions of sympathy, finding an adult to
help, and so forth. The ability to be of assistance seems to build on a
preexisting sense of concern and responsibility for others. "Complex
prosocial responses occur long before there is a high level of cognitive
development" or the capacity to turn the reactive distress into helping
behavior.[11] This developmental progression has been replicated in several longitudinal studies.

By the time children are of preschool age, comforting, sharing, and
helping are regular occurrences. One study of preschoolers during free
play discovered that sixty-seven of the seventy-seven children shared
with, helped, or comforted another child at least once during only forty
minutes of observation.[12] Researchers who simply count the number of

prosocial behaviors occurring per unit of time have come up with widely varying figures—depending in part on how broadly the concept of prosocial behavior is defined—but virtually any such finding is likely to understate the children's inclination to help for two reasons. First, "the benign environment of the nursery school is probably not filled with occasions for sympathy and generosity";[13] and second, since not all children at this age feel competent to help, their failure to do so should not be construed as a failure to react with empathy and sensitivity to the plight of others.

Like all parents, researchers have also observed hostile and selfish actions on the part of children. To say that sympathy or helping behavior is pervasive and precocious is not to replace a demonic portrait with an angelic one, or to deny that toddlers—particularly in a society suffused with norms of possessiveness—will sometimes snatch back a toy truck ("Mine!") or throw it across the room. But the antisocial is neither logically nor chronologically prior to, nor more natural than, the prosocial. We are disposed to reach out to others from our earliest years.

WHO HELPS AND WHEN

Psychologists have looked into the questions of how often prosocial behavior occurs and why it occurs, but the overwhelming majority of the research has concerned the factors that make its occurrence more or less likely. Some of these factors have to do with the environment—that is, the situation in which people find themselves—while others pertain to the characteristics of the individuals themselves. This classification recalls the personality versus social structure debate that has, in one form or another, dominated the social sciences (and social psychology in particular) for decades. To sort out the predictive research on prosocial behavior, it might be useful to further subdivide each set of factors, leaving us with four categories arrayed on a continuum from the general to the specific: environmental factors, interactive elements of the situation, the person's state of mind, and enduring traits of the person. I will address each of these in turn.

Environmental Factors

Probably the best known and most thoroughly researched aspect of helping behavior concerns the effect of the presence of bystanders. More than

one hundred studies have been published on this topic since the Genovese killing, most prominently by the psychologists Bibb Latane and John
Darley.[14] The key finding from this research is that any given individual
is most likely to come to another person's aid if she believes no one else
can do so. The presence of other witnesses, that is, reduces the probability of helping. Apart from the obvious fact that we may, in some situations, assume someone else has already done something, our inaction is
said to occur for any of several reasons: first, a crowd of people failing
to attend to someone's distress can distract us, too, from noticing it;
second, even if we do notice what is going on, the fact that other people
are not helping can lead us to conclude that the situation does not
constitute an emergency requiring our intervention; third, we fear appearing foolish in the eyes of others if it turns out no help was actually
needed; fourth (and most famously), the duty to act is shared by everyone
present, diffusing the responsibility and thereby reducing our own obligation; and, finally, if it turns out something should have been done,
there will be other people to share the blame, too.

Ironically, the bystander theory may not be of much use in explaining
the episode that inspired it. As Melvin Lerner has pointed out, the people
awakened by Genovese's screams at 3 A.M. were alone (or at least
removed from bystanders) in their apartments and could have called the
police anonymously. That they failed to do so cannot easily be explained
in terms of a model relying on cost-benefit analysis.[15]

The psychoanalyst Arno Gruen proposes that we begin with the
assumption that the default condition of humans—including these bystanders—is a tendency to empathize, sympathize, and help. The question to ask, then, is what could compel us to override this proclivity. He
suggests that cultures such as ours compel us to deny our own basic sense
of helplessness, and that being confronted with someone else's helplessness threatens to unmask us, forcing a painful recognition of our own
psychological state. This hypothesis, Gruen argues, can explain the psy-
chosomatic symptoms sometimes exhibited by those who refuse to help;
the cost of ignoring our prosocial inclinations is high. (In a well-known
experiment by Darley and Latane, subjects who thought there were others present were less likely to aid someone they heard having an epileptic
seizure. But those who failed to help were not apathetic or indifferent:
"They often had trembling hands and sweating palms. If anything, they
seemed more emotionally aroused than did the subjects who reported the
emergency.")[16] As a variation of conventional behavioral analysis, the
bystander theory not only proves to be inadequate by virtue of missing

the significance of this phenomenon, according to Gruen, but it is also positively dangerous: "If our refusal to come to the aid of a fellow human being is translated into terms of a purely geometric relationship between bystanders and victim, the ability to maintain our own integrity will be shattered . . . thereby precipitating the downfall of our ability to think, to respond to reality, and to behave morally, as well as to pass moral judgments."[17]

For reasons likely related to the bystander effect, several groups of researchers have also found (to no one's surprise) that some varieties of prosocial behaviors are less common in larger cities. In one experiment, a six- to ten-year-old child stood on a busy street and said to passersby, "I'm lost. Can you call my house?" On average, nearly three-quarters of the adults in twelve small towns did so, compared with less than half in big cities (New York, Philadelphia, Boston, and Chicago).[18] Other studies, using different measures of helpfulness and responsiveness, have found much the same thing. It also seems clear that cooperativeness is more likely to characterize the residents of rural societies, and competitiveness those of urban societies.[19]

Theorists steeped in the egoistic premises of social science have asserted that if people are more helpful in small towns it must just be because they know their kindness (or their unkindness, as the case may be) is likely to be reciprocated. But we do not need this assumption of self-interest as sole motivator: the fact that one knows the other residents of a small community simply makes their humanness harder to avoid. The philosopher Thomas Nagel has pointed out that because of "the heightened reality people have for us if they lead lives like ours and are engaged in similar enterprises" in small towns, it is "easier to put ourselves in their place, and their good and harm become vivid to us."[20] But if direct contact of the sort afforded by small-town life facilitates perspective taking,* the anonymity associated with population density promotes objectification. It is difficult to break that habit even when an individual steps out of the crowd and asks for help.

---

*This direct contact also has a darker side: the absence of privacy in small-town life seems suffocating to some people, and one also wonders whether helping and caring are not to some degree contingent on how closely the person being helped conforms to strict social norms. In general, the town versus city distinction may not be as clear cut as it first appears. The existing research on the question does not control for socioeconomic status or ethnic diversity, which may be confounded with size of community. Moreover, the measures of prosocial behavior are selective, excluding other expressions of caring such as organized philanthropy. (I am grateful to Marian Radke-Yarrow [personal communication, March 1989] for raising these objections.)

Another explanation, not incompatible with this one, is offered by the researchers who conducted the child-request study: "City people adjust to the constant demands of urban life by reducing their involvement with others."[21] These demands, we might add, are of several types. The frenzy of a downtown amounts to a sensory assault that desensitizes even—or especially—those people who are unaware of it and who count themselves as lovers of the city's bustle. Second, the danger of a literal assault in large cities is not conducive to a posture of openness to others' predicaments—openness even to recognizing their distress, let alone to taking steps to help. One is too busy attending to one's own safety. Third, the sheer scale of misery surrounding a city dweller, particularly with the mushrooming problem of homelessness over the last decade, overwhelms the impulse to reach out. "There are practical limitations to the Samaritan impulse in a major city," Stanley Milgram wrote twenty years ago in an article whose analysis seems even more germane today. "If a citizen attended to every needy person, if he were sensitive to and acted on every altruistic impulse that was evoked in the city, he could scarcely keep his own affairs in order."[22] When it was unusual to find a man sprawled out on the sidewalk, one was moved to stop, to ask if he was all right, to get him food or medical assistance. When, by contrast, one's daily commute to work involves passing by (or even stepping over) destitute and desperate people as a matter of course, one comes to regard them as so many annoyances, if one regards them at all. That one can continue to live—and, more to the point, live well—in a system that reduces so many to so much misery is a fact one would rather not digest. Turning aside is one way of not digesting it. As columnist Charles Krauthammer put it:

The city, with its army of grate-dwellers, is a school for callousness. One's natural instincts to help are suppressed every day. Moreover, they have to be suppressed if one is to function: there are simply too many homeless. . . . [To help] is not a simple act of mercy of which most people are quite capable. It is a major act of social work that only the professional and the saintly can be expected to undertake. To expect saintliness of the ordinary citizen is bad social policy. Further, to expose him hourly to a wretchedness far beyond his power to remedy is to make moral insensitivity a requirement of daily living.[23]

Finally, just as the probability of helping seems, roughly speaking, to vary inversely with the number of bystanders present and the size of the community, so can it be inhibited by social norms. It is important not only to be aware of the extent to which altruism is regarded with suspicion (or at least with mixed feelings) in our society, but to recall this in the context of environmental factors relevant to prosocial activity. Beliefs and values, while indirect in their influence and difficult to quantify, nonetheless make for a compelling set of influences on behavior. If our cultural training includes the message that only a sucker lets herself get drawn into other people's problems, this constitutes an environmental variable as surely as does the number of bystanders present at an event.

Interactive Elements of the Situation

Some of the situational factors that have attracted the attention of researchers deal with the relationship between the helper and the person being helped. These clearly represent aspects of the situation rather than of the helper's character, but they are interactive and thus conceptually distinct from the features discussed so far. There is not very much to be said about these findings, however, because they tend to echo our intuition. The less ambiguous someone's misery, the more likely we will be to help. Direct exposure to that misery is more likely to call forth a prosocial response than hearing about it indirectly, largely because the need is more difficult to deny.[24] Being contacted personally by someone who is soliciting help in behalf of a third party is more likely to result in a contribution than is a written request for money—which explains the recent growth of telemarketing by nonprofit groups.

Much has also been made of the fact that the probability of helping someone increases if one likes, or is similar to, that person. These findings are well established and unsurprising.[25] (The fact that residents of a small town are relatively likely to be homogeneous—that is, similar to one another—may partly explain the higher levels of helping in such communities.) The functional significance of these factors is reduced considerably, however, in the case of an emergency: normally someone might be more inclined to give you a hand if the two of you are united by a similar political outlook, but that person will yank you out of the path of an oncoming car regardless of what she has in common with you or how much she cares to spend time with you.

Similarity is often taken for an objective reflection of people's relationships to each other. It therefore bears mentioning that our proximity to others is both subjective and inconstant. That graduate students may be 27.3 percent more likely to assist other graduate students with a task than to assist chimney sweeps is not a finding that lends itself to generalization. Researchers may have to control for all but one or two variables, but real life is under no such constraints. Thus, do you regard as similar someone with whom you consider yourself an ideological soulmate but who speaks a different language? How about someone with whom you are in agreement about the arms race but not economic policy? Does skin color count for more than occupation in a judgment of similarity?

Even if we can answer these questions to our satisfaction, we are still obliged to ask whether *any* of these factors must be as salient a consideration for one person as for another—or whether the relevance of similarity is instead simply an outgrowth of a larger world view which, in turn, can be modified. In the words of the psychologist Harvey Hornstein,

The size and meaningfulness of the gap that we imagine to exist between similar and dissimilar others is not fixed by the traits they possess which are being compared. . . . Rather, the gap that we perceive when comparing these traits depends upon the social conditions that surround us when we look at similar and dissimilar people. *There is nothing inherent in any distinction between human beings that compels us to see others as they.* [26]

Moreover, if similarity along one axis does matter for a given individual, must it affect his willingness to perform a prosocial act? And what sort of prosocial act?

None of these questions is trivial. They do more than highlight the difficulty of operationalizing the idea of similarity; they call into question the meaningfulness, usually assumed rather than demonstrated, of typical findings in social psychology. More precisely, they challenge the usefulness, to say nothing of the determinative status, of situational factors said to control our willingness to reach out to other people.

Individual State

The likelihood that helping will take place is affected not only by certain features of the environment but also by certain characteristics of the would-be helper. For the moment, let us consider those characteristics that describe someone's state at a particular moment of time. Most research of "state" (as opposed to "trait") features that are relevant to prosocial behavior has concerned mood. The most straightforward and well-established finding here, by Leonard Berkowitz, David Rosenhan,

Alice Isen, and their respective colleagues, is that contented people are more likely to extend themselves to others: the rule is "feel good, do good." Children encouraged to review pleasant memories are more likely to donate pennies than those asked to recall unhappy events that befell them. To be absolutely accurate, though, most of the research has confirmed the rule: "Have nice things happen to you, do good." Experimenters arrange for people to unexpectedly receive free stationery, some cookies, too much money for a task just performed, or a coin in a phone booth. These people, whose mood presumably has improved, turn out to be unusually willing to make a telephone call on behalf of a stranded traveler, volunteer time to help another researcher, donate money, mail a lost letter, help a confederate who has dropped some papers, and so on. (Naturally, the subjects are not told of any connection between the two segments of the study, the gift and the opportunity to help.) Likewise, those who are informed they did well on a test have also been shown to be especially generous. In all of these cases, we should note, it is not that the subject has simply helped her benefactor as a way of reciprocating; rather, the event presumed to have enhanced her mood seems to dispose her to help anyone who comes along.[27]

While good mood clearly enhances one's prosocial inclinations, the effects of bad mood are more complicated. On the one hand, seeing a sad movie may depress contributions to charity,[28] and someone apparently put into a negative emotional state as a result of an unpleasant environment (such as one containing distracting background noises[29] or cigarette smoke[30]) is less likely to engage in prosocial behavior. On the other hand, failure at a task sometimes—perhaps I should say with some individuals—*promotes* helping. At the least, failure often produces the same likelihood of prosocial activity as no intervention at all, while success increases it. More strikingly, people who feel sympathetic sadness or guilt are often among the most likely to help.*

What accounts for these mixed results? First, positive mood is associated with an increased chance of helping in everyone, but negative

*There may be widespread agreement that the sadness brought on by another's distress is associated with taking steps to help that person, but there is a pronounced split among theorists when it comes time to explain the nature of this connection. Some argue that we help to make ourselves feel better, and anything else that works to cheer us up is essentially interchangeable with a prosocial response. Others challenge this egoistic view, maintaining that genuine sympathy or empathy (depending on how these terms are used) is fundamentally an other-regarding, rather than a self-regarding, motive; that your distress puts me in a bad mood suggests the existence of genuine altruism. We will return to this dispute.

mood is likely to have a similar effect only on adults. When children feel rotten, they are apt to be less generous. Second, all negative moods are not alike: sadness and anger, for example, appear to have different consequences. The former may well contribute to prosocial behavior, while the latter probably will not.[31]

Another mediator of the effects of negative mood is self-awareness, and this turns out to be an interesting factor even apart from how it interacts with mood. It has been proposed that if people feel bad but do good, it is because they are thinking about the misfortunes of the person to be helped, whereas if feeling bad reduces prosocial behavior, it is because they are preoccupied with their own state of mind. There is some truth to this formulation, but there is also more to the story. Self-awareness creates complications of its own.

It is surely plausible to argue, on the one hand, that if someone focuses on himself, he is distracted from your needs. Indeed, in a study where people were asked to imagine that a close friend was dying of cancer, those who were encouraged to think about their own reactions to the death were less likely to help out a graduate student than were those who adopted the dying friend's point of view.[32] In a second study, elementary school children who were asked to talk about something sad that had happened to another child were more generous in donating prize chips than were those who recalled something sad that had happened to themselves.[33] Still another experiment, offering a different perspective on self-awareness, found that those subjects who were asked to think about the *reasons* they had earlier agreed to help someone else subsequently rated themselves as more selfish than those who had not engaged in this exercise of critical self-reflection.[34]

But there is another hand. Some investigations have shown that inducing awareness of the self can actually enhance helping behavior.* Examining the circumstances in which that happens can help us to reconcile this finding with the studies on self-awareness that produce the opposite effect. First, self-reflection can promote prosocial action to the extent that it reminds one of moral obligations or internalized expectations— the gap between what one is doing and what one ought to be doing. Thus, we would not expect the effect to occur for someone who has no such set of expectations of herself. Second, mood and self-awareness might be

---

*Complicating the picture even further is the finding that a version of self-awareness in which one pictures the other's predicament happening to oneself can enhance perspective taking and empathy. This adds yet another layer of ambiguity to the discussion, since empathy, in turn, can affect prosocial behavior.

called reciprocal mediators: just as self-awareness helps to determine the consequences of being in a bad mood, so may being in a good mood help to determine the consequences of being self-aware.[35] Or perhaps it is more accurate to say that self-awareness is turned into prosocial behavior because one thinks charitably of oneself. It may, in other words, be the content, the affective charge, of self-reflection that determines its effect on helping others.

Two researchers explored the nuances of these issues in an article published in 1982. In a pair of preliminary studies, they found that simply heightening self-awareness (placing people in front of a mirror or playing their own voices back to them on tape) had a detrimental impact on helping. Then they ran another experiment, this time telling subjects that they had done either well or poorly on an analogy test. Those who had not been informed that they had failed (and thus presumably were not bogged down by self-concern) reacted *more* quickly to assist someone else if they had been facing their own reflection. Self-awareness, the authors concluded, can promote prosocial action as long as "the person's mind is freed of personal anxieties or other individual concerns (including a bad mood) that may rob one of perspective-taking potential." If external cues and internalized norms of helping can be made salient—and, specifically, are not washed out by preoccupation with one's own problems—then heightened awareness of oneself need not preclude acting in the interest of others.[36]

In addition to mood and self-awareness, there are two other characteristics of a person's state that are related to the willingness to engage in prosocial activity. The first is a sense of being proficient at the activity in question. "Unless they feel competent in performing them, students are unlikely to actually undertake helping acts or feel internal satisfaction from doing them," writes Pearl Oliner,[37] and this fact is obviously not restricted to students. While donating money or expressing sympathy does not require any special skill, changing a tire or pulling someone out of a river does. People who feel confident in their ability to perform a given task are more likely to do it.

Finally, a number of studies have demonstrated that if a person feels guilty over something else he did recently, then he will be more likely to come to someone's aid—even if it is not someone to whom he feels indebted.[38] Make a subject feel responsible for having broken some equipment or given an electric shock to another subject, and he will offer to be of help more readily than others—regardless of whether the transgression was intentional, whether he believes that other people know about it, and (in some cases) whether the help was explicitly requested. Sometimes, simply being present while someone else harms a third party is enough to predispose the observer to be of help when given the opportunity. (For children, however, one study suggests that causing someone pain calls up a different pattern of responses—including more distress but less emotional concern—than merely observing someone in pain.)[39]

Individual Traits

By definition, a snapshot of a person at a particular instant—how good she is feeling and how capable she believes she will be at performing a task, whether she is preoccupied with herself or troubled by guilt—does not provide us with much information about the likelihood of her being a reliably prosocial person over time. Of course, any of these state characteristics may be a reflection of enduring traits: perpetual crankiness, a tendency toward self-absorption, an immunity to feeling guilty, or a persistent feeling of incompetence. Such an individual is relatively unlikely, all else being equal, to help. But we cannot infer trait from state—some personality theorists doubt whether we can infer trait from *anything*[40]— and it is therefore important to treat the former as a separate category.

Self-Esteem A zero-sum view of the world might suggest that how favorably we think of ourselves is inversely related to how inclined we are to benefit others. However, as we shall see when we examine the issue from a developmental perspective, it turns out that the same approach to child rearing that is likely to produce a person with healthy levels of self-esteem* is also likely to produce someone who is caring and helpful. Moreover, there appears to be a *direct* relation between self-esteem and prosocial inclination. One psychologist has written: "Children who are encouraged to feel good about themselves may be more inclined to empathize with others than children who are preoccupied with personal inadequacies and other concerns about the self";[41] empathy, in turn, often predisposes one to reach out to others. (Notice that empathy, which will be explored in greater detail in the following chapter, is an affective

---

*I am not referring here to a grandiose view of the self that permits no acknowledgment of deficiencies. I mean rather a core of respect for and faith in oneself, an acceptance of one's own worth that is not contingent (at least, not for an adult) on acceptance from others or on a certain level of accomplishment.

response that may be connected to, but is not an example of, prosocial behavior.) Conversely, as Ervin Staub puts it, "A poor self-concept makes it more difficult to extend the boundaries of the self in benevolent ways."[42]

Once again, however, there are qualifications to slow us down. First, it may be, as Staub goes on to suggest, that children with an extremely high opinion of themselves are less connected to others and therefore less likely to help. Perhaps a "positive but more moderate self-concept" is more reliable in this respect.[43] Second, not all studies have found the predicted relations—at least not with both sexes. In one experiment, prosocial behavior in boys (but not girls) was actually associated with a *negative* self-image.[44] In another, children who viewed themselves negatively were more accepting of a fictitious peer said to have various social problems.[45] (Of course, this may have reflected identification with a troubled individual rather than an empathic disposition as such, and it tells us little about actual prosocial behavior.)

Less doubtful is the association between helping and an internal locus of control—that is, the belief that one can influence events and affect things that happen to oneself. Several studies have confirmed this relation,[46] which makes sense given that a related concept, a generalized sense of competence, also predicts prosocial behavior. While a feeling of being able to direct one's own life often goes hand in hand with high levels of self-esteem, the two concepts are nevertheless distinct.[47]

It may be that high self-esteem serves to facilitate responsiveness to others' needs by freeing us from the self-absorption that a precarious view of our worth can generate. But self-esteem apparently does not *guarantee* generosity; it is more a prerequisite for it, with other ingredients required as well. Moreover, as Nancy Eisenberg, one of the leading investigators of children's prosocial behavior, suggests, lower levels of self-esteem may independently contribute to helping behavior, but for qualitatively different reasons, such as seeking approval of others—at least in environments where helping is highly regarded.[48]

Assertiveness and Interpersonal Skills   People with relatively high levels of self-esteem may also be more likely to help because they have the psychological wherewithal to act, particularly in social situations. This should, however, be regarded as a factor in its own right rather than as just a function of self-esteem. Assertiveness also needs to be distinguished from aggressiveness, something that researchers and laypeople alike sometimes fail to do. Not only are the two concepts—standing up

for oneself and hurting others—separable in theory, but, for boys anyway, they tend to diverge with age: by the third grade, an assertive boy
is not especially likely to be aggressive.[49] (Some clinicians, in fact, suggest
that aggressive youngsters would profit from assertiveness training.
Their reliance on bullying others may stem in part from an inability to
express or satisfy their desires by other means.)

There is in some quarters a naive assumption that caring for other
people must be mutually exclusive with taking care of one's own needs.
Taken to its illogical extreme, this position points toward the conclusion
that only wimps are prosocial. The evidence, which is strongest for children, suggests otherwise. Not only are the two inclinations compatible,
but they appear to be complementary in many instances. Those who are
helpful are also likely to be assertive, and vice versa. "Characteristics that
promote positive behavior seem optimal also from the standpoint of how
effectively a person pursues his or her *own* interests."[50] The evidence for
this proposition includes a study showing that, particularly among children who have good inferential skills, assertiveness is associated with
prosocial behavior: if they can understand what is going on with other
people, then being assertive allows them to act on this understanding by
being helpful. Even assertiveness by itself is more useful in predicting
spontaneous prosocial activity than awareness of others' situations by
itself.[51]

Staub and others have shown, finally, that popularity with peers and
helpfulness are likely to go together—although it is not clear whether this
association is a function of interpersonal skills or assertiveness. One
study, for example, found a strong correlation between ratings of preschoolers' sociability and their willingness to help an adult.[52] Another
found that sixth graders with close and lasting friendships were more
generous and caring on both a self-report and a behavioral measure.[53]
By contrast, a preliminary survey taken during the 1960s of people who
rescued Jews during World War II found that social marginality, the
feeling of being an outsider, was frequently found among the twenty-
seven interview subjects.[54] This attracted some attention among people
in the field of prosocial behavior, but a recent study of more than four
hundred rescuers (along with a number of nonrescuers for purposes of
comparison) has cast doubt on the finding. The latter study found no
significant difference between the two groups with respect to a sense of
belonging to their community.[55] Sociability (or something like it)
seemed, if not a definite predictor of this sort of prosocial behavior, at
least not a handicap.

Politics and Religion   It would be foolish to assert that helpfulness is a consequence of political affiliation, particularly inasmuch as prosocial patterns are often established at a point in life when the most relevant *"L* word" is *lullaby*. Yet the same comprehensive study of people who risked their lives to save Jews from concentration camps found that "rescuers were more likely than others to endorse egalitarian political views."[56] To the extent that the political left attempts to balance an emphasis on individual liberty with a commitment to the values of community and equity, the existence of a statistical association between politics on the port side and a tendency to help others should not be astonishing. ("Socialism," as the political theorist Michael Walzer has written, "has as much to do with compassion and solidarity as with justice.")[57] Interestingly, tests of moral reasoning have shown that people who score at relatively high levels are more likely to be liberal than conservative.[58] And the belief that the world is fundamentally just, that people who suffer must have done something to deserve their fate, is empirically related to political conservatism.[59]

This last finding shades into religious issues. In a society that teaches us to associate morality with religion, one naturally assumes that a strong relation exists between piety and pity, between God and good. After all, the sacred texts of Judaism and Christianity, like those of most supernatural belief systems, contain reminders to be compassionate and charitable.

These familiar injunctions, however, have not been sufficient to prevent the commission of a range of horrors under the banner of one religion or another, from the Hebrews, who "utterly destroy[ed] the men, women, and children of every city" as they invaded Canaan[60] to the barbaric Christian Crusaders to contemporary fanatics killing in Allah's name.[61] Less dramatically, there also exists a "long parade of findings demonstrating that churchgoers are more intolerant of ethnic minorities than nonattenders."[62] This is not the place to weigh whether these and other disturbing phenomena result from the faithful's failure to actualize the teachings of their religions or from aspects of the belief systems themselves. (If the latter, one might note that adherents are often encouraged to think of themselves as chosen people or as possessing absolute Truth, or that suffering is sometimes seen as illusory or else deserved, and humans as sinful and in need of salvation or enlightenment.)

The question at hand instead is what we can surmise about the likelihood of an individual's being caring and generous just from knowing that he or she is a believer. The answer is that religious faith appears to be neither necessary for one to act prosocially nor sufficient to ensure such behavior; in fact, there is virtually no connection one way or the other between religious affiliation or belief and prosocial activities.

This conclusion has emerged with remarkable uniformity from many different types of research over many years. A careful study of about two thousand Episcopalians in the 1950s turned up "no discernible relationship between involvement [in the Church] and charitable acts."[63] In a questionnaire-based study of altruism involving several hundred male college students in 1960, there was only a slight correlation between altruism and belief in God, and none at all between altruism and attendance at religious services.[64] In interviews with randomly selected adults in 1965, "the 'irreligious' . . . [were] nearly as frequently rated as being a good Samaritan, having love and compassion for their fellow man, and being humble as the most devout and religious of our group studied."[65] Two experiments with undergraduates during the 1970s found essentially the same thing: In one, students who believed in the Bible's accuracy were no more likely than others to come to the aid of someone in the next room who seemed to have fallen off a ladder.[66] In the other study, students were classified as being "Jesus people" (born-again Christians), conventionally religious, nonreligious, or atheists. There was no statistically significant difference among these groups in willingness to volunteer time with retarded children or in resisting temptation to cheat on a test. (There was only one group in which a majority did not cheat, however: the atheists.)[67] In a different sort of investigation, a researcher who surveyed more than seven hundred people from different neighborhoods in a medium-sized city expected to find that religious people were especially sociable, helpful to their neighbors, and likely to participate in neighborhood organizations. Instead, she reported in 1984, religious involvement was virtually unrelated to these activities.[68] Finally, as the Oliners' study of rescuers during the war found: "Overall, rescuers did not differ significantly from bystanders or all nonrescuers with respect to their religious identification, religious education, and their own religiosity or that of their parents."[69]

On the delicate topics of politics and religion, then, it would seem that beliefs or activism of the sort sometimes called progressive are generally (though, of course, not exclusively) associated with prosocial behavior. The presence or absence of religious belief, meanwhile, tells us absolutely nothing about the likelihood of someone's engaging in prosocial activity.[70]

Gender Roles By now, any reader hoping to learn of a personality trait whose relation to the prosocial realm is both reliable and uncomplicated has become accustomed to disappointment. This pattern continues as we survey the research on gender. The matter of women's and men's capacity for empathy will be treated in the next chapter; here our concern is with caring, sharing, and helping behavior. Our concern is also with *gender* differences, a term intended to reflect not only biological determination of sex but also the attendant social roles. This distinction is useful any time one asks whether men and women behave differently, but it is critical in the case of action so thoroughly shaped—indeed, defined—by one's milieu as is prosocial activity.

Those who believe that males (or at least people with high scores on measures of personality traits and attitudes said to define stereotypical masculinity) are more inclined to exhibit prosocial behavior can offer a plausible rationale as well as data to support their conviction. To the extent that helping others is facilitated by traits like assertiveness and a conviction of personal competence, masculinity seems to fit the bill. In one study, more men than women (and more sex-typed males than androgynous males) left their experimental cubicle to investigate when they thought another subject was choking—although the disparity was not very impressive.[71] Differences favoring men become remarkable only when helping is operationalized in terms of a task with which men in our culture are more familiar, such as fixing a flat tire,[72] or when research excludes the sort of helping that takes place in the context of intimate or other long-term relationships.[73]

Those who believe that females, or at least people with high scores on measures of stereotypical femininity, are more inclined to exhibit prosocial behavior can offer a plausible rationale as well as data to support *their* conviction.* In our culture, women report themselves to be more empathic (chapter 4) and more prone to guilt[75] than men, and these characteristics may well be tied to helping and caring behavior.[76] In a choking-victim study published less than two years after (and in the same journal as) the one cited above, high scores on a measure of masculinity were associated with a *reduced* tendency to help, leading the researchers

---

*In one study—albeit one conducted with only a few dozen undergraduates—women were less likely than men to assume the worst about human nature after having heard a radio broadcast featuring bad news.[74] If this finding is replicated with larger and more representative samples of the population, it may be viewed not only as a kind of projective test result but also as a causal factor relevant to prosocial behavior.

to describe masculinity as a "response inhibitor in emergency situations" because such men feel a need to appear poised and are reluctant to risk making fools of themselves by helping unnecessarily.[77] The fact that men are socialized to be chary of helping others has been pointedly described by some feminist scholars.[78]

Those who believe that gender differences are the exception in most sorts of helping behavior, and that the differences that do turn up are generally slight, seem to have most of the evidence on their side. As noted in chapter 1, scores of studies contain passing mention of the fact that no gender differences were found, and these reports are decisive when taken together. Consider a few of the research reports already described here in other contexts. When Eisenberg-Berg and Hand discovered that helping/comforting, sharing, and moral reasoning are three distinct phenomena, they also found no sex differences in any of them.[79] While it was discovered that subjects who thought others were present responded more slowly to an apparent epileptic fit in the next room, it also turned out that "male subjects responded to the emergency with almost exactly the same speed as did females."[80] Children with a newfound competence in some activity were more likely than others to use that skill to assist others; boys and girls were equally likely to do so.[81] Finally, Yarrow and her colleagues, after reviewing a number of studies of children's prosocial inclinations, found that while girls have a *reputation* for being more altruistic, and while (according to one study) they express more verbal sympathy than boys, there seem to be no significant gender differences in actual prosocial interventions.[82] This, indeed, is the gist of many studies conducted with both children and adults. Where gender differences do emerge, they are typically weak, partial, and buried in qualifications.[83]

The Individual versus the Situation

We have considered the relation between prosocial behavior and specific factors, both individual and situational. But there remains the larger question of which sort of factor plays the more important role. Consider the following two statements:

Individual difference variables account for remarkably little variance in helping behavior. . . . Anybody can be led to help or not to help in a specific situation. Characteristics of the immediate situation may have a more important influence on what the bystander does than his personality or life history.[84]

Although rescuers and nonrescuers knew similar facts [about the plight of vic-
tims], at some point rescuers began to perceive them in a personal way. . . .
Objective risk conditions were no less threatening for rescuers than nonrescuers.
. . . What distinguished rescuers from others was their readiness to act despite
perceived risks. . . . Rescuers did not simply happen on opportunities for rescue;
they actively created, sought, or recognized them where others did not. Their
participation was not determined by circumstances but [by] their own personal
qualities. . . . [It was] a choice prefigured by an established character and way of
life.[85]

These conclusions sit like bookends on either side of a continuum
of thought on the issue. In light of all the available research, neither
extreme verdict is easy to justify. The situationalists quoted here are
Latane and Darley; their efforts to find personality traits that function as
predictors of prosocial behavior could be described charitably as less
than exhaustive. The other side is represented by the Oliners, whose
conclusion is based on the study of only one target behavior, and an
extraordinary one at that: rescuing Jews from the Nazis. (Moreover, their
dismissal of at least one of the environmental variables—being asked for
help—seems premature even with respect to their own data. Two-thirds
of rescuers got involved only when someone requested their assistance,
whereas three-quarters of nonrescuers were never asked.[86] It may well
be, as the Oliners contend, that rescuers were asked because their altruistic reputations were already known, but the authors seem too ready to
dismiss the possible relevance of an environmental factor.)

To ask whether the individual or the environment counts for more
is simply to invite more questions in reply. Are we talking about trait or
state characteristics of the person, about general features of the environment or those peculiar to the relationship between the subject and object
of helping? Are we trying to formulate a general law of prosocial action
or looking for causal factors in a given instance of helping?

If most researchers, at least until recently, have been concerned with
environmental variables, it has been for a reason. The particulars of
circumstances are always important in defining the need to help and
turning a personal prosocial proclivity into action. But this very lopsided
research agenda affects, rather than just reflects, an assessment of the
truth. Spend your time examining only situational influences, and you
will likely conclude that they are important—that is, you will conclude
that all your work has not been a waste of time.

Lately, more people in the field have turned their attention to personality determinants of helping behavior.[87] This, too, makes sense, and recent work has lent more credibility to the idea of an "altruistic personality."*

It does seem to be the case that very young children show pronounced differences in emotional arousal and responsiveness to their environment, and these could form the bases of enduring individual differences in prosocial behavior.[90] How enduring these differences really are, however, is unclear. We already know that various behaviors classified as prosocial do not always correlate with each other. Even more damaging to the trait theorists is the discovery that correlations are also low (or even nonexistent) in some studies that followed a given individual across different situations and recorded instances of just one sort of behavior.[91]

All of this leaves us facing the fact that two people in the same situation may have different motives for helping, and one person may have different motives for helping in each of two situations. Even if an altruistic personality or prosocial orientation exists, this hardly means that someone so characterized will rush to aid other people without taking environmental factors into account. If nothing else, such basic situational variables as whether helping is likely to bring rewards (or reciprocity) will mediate the effects of dispositional helpfulness. (The promise of a reward makes some people more likely to help and others less likely; one needs to know something about the person *and* the situation, then, to make a prediction.)[92] It has long been part of the conventional wisdom in personality theory that the salience of the cues provided by the environment largely determines which of these two will be more useful in predicting behavior: where the situational factors seem less clear cut, dispositional factors will become more relevant.[93]

One interesting perspective on this debate was provided by Joseph Adelson, a critic of the situationalists. He reasoned that this position appeals to some people by virtue of its implicit refutation of human evil: if our unwillingness to help is attributable to environmental contingencies (number of bystanders present, size of community, and so on), then

---

*Even if a prosocial orientation proves to be a useful construct, the question of whether one exists that can properly be called an *altruistic* personality is a matter of some controversy. Batson and his collaborators showed that at least some personality scales used to define such an orientation did not, in fact, predict to nonegoistic helping—that is, to a genuinely altruistic motivation.[88] Eisenberg, however, contends that she has described just such a disposition on the basis of evoking sympathetic reactions from her subjects.[89] (A fuller discussion of altruistic and egoistic motivations for prosocial behavior can be found in chapters 7 and 8.)

we cannot be accused of being deficient human beings. The danger of this strategy, Adelson implies, is that its casualties include not only intrinsic evil but intrinsic good.[94]

The issue can be approached from a different direction, though. We may wish to regard skeptically any talk of an inborn nature—good *or* evil—irrespective of our position on the importance of situational factors. The Oliners, for example, flatly reject these factors, but they do not do so in the name of innate goodness. Rather, they talk of stable character traits that can be traced to certain patterns of child rearing. Keeping in mind that the personality/environment dispute does not simply collapse into the question of whether human nature is basically good, let us turn now to the contribution of various child-rearing styles to prosocial behavior.

RAISING CHILDREN WHO CARE

From a distance, the matter of how to bring up children who care about others might seem reassuringly uncomplicated: explain to a child why helping is better than hurting, be forceful about it, demonstrate prosocial behavior and give the child a chance to experience it for herself, and be a warm and empathic parent; the child will grow up caring and sharing and helping.

Recipes, however, work more dependably in the kitchen than in the nursery. Even the most robust findings require qualification. No sooner does a researcher discover what appears to be a reliable way to promote prosocial behavior than someone else comes along and changes the type of target behavior, making the effects vanish. Scrutinized closely, findings are sometimes unclear and even contradictory. Is it the measure that is unsatisfactory? Was the sample too small? Do the variables interact in some way not yet understood? Part of the problem for researchers in trying to tease apart factors and isolate variables is the difficulty of finding certain combinations occurring naturally—say, parents who are low on prosocial values but high on empathy, or who assert their power with children but do not use physical punishment. Even though it seems relatively easy to enumerate a set of destructive parenting principles— How Not to Raise a Child—this, too, fails to provide us with airtight guarantees: "The lives and backgrounds of many individuals have been marked and sometimes marred by suffering, conflict, and strife, yet these persons emerge as compassionate and adaptively aggressive."[95] Once

again we are reminded that human beings refuse to accommodate social
scientists by acting as predictably as objects in the natural world.

But do parents make a difference? Unquestionably. Their convictions and actions not only shape children's traits, but also indirectly affect
their mood or self-awareness at a given moment and even help to determine the relevance of situational factors associated with prosocial behavior. In one study that speaks not only to the overall significance of early
life experiences but also, by extension, to the controversy regarding
individual versus environmental factors, volunteers at a telephone crisis
hotline who continued helping for at least six months were generally
distinguished by "childhood experiences of nurturant parents who mod-
eled altruism." Those without such childhood experiences sometimes
reached this same level of helping, but only if they were trained for the
work in a highly cohesive group. External inducements could promote
prosocial behavior, in other words, but people whose parents had in-
stilled an intrinsic commitment to it did not require such inducements.[96]

The Absence of Aggression

Before we explore in more detail the approach to child rearing that tends
to promote helping and caring, let us briefly consider what sort tends to
discourage aggression.[97] To begin with, a parent must have and communicate a deeply felt disapproval of hurting other people. It is not enough
merely to *say* that aggression is wrong; there must be an emotional charge
to the prohibition. It will be counterproductive if a child senses that,
despite a verbal prohibition, the parent is actually undisturbed—or,
worse, even amused—by his kicking a playmate. (Notice how the tacit
assumption that aggression is an inevitable part of human nature, and
therefore that acting to restrain a child would be pointless, is a particularly potent self-fulfilling prophecy here.)

Second, explaining to children just why it is that hurting people is
undesirable proves to be far more effective than responding punitively,
particularly if the latter involves severe physical punishment. There is an
immense collection of research on this point. The psychologist Diana
Baumrind has shown that authoritative parenting (warm and responsive
but also firm and directive) succeeds better at discouraging aggressiveness than either an authoritarian approach (controlling and coercive) on
the one hand or a permissive approach (nurturant but lax) on the other.
(The worst of both worlds is offered by the parent who manages to be

both permissive *and* punitive, perhaps letting children do as they please most of the time but occasionally and unexpectedly exploding with anger and applying harsh sanctions.) Disciplinary techniques that rely on pure assertion of power or withdrawal of love, as the influential developmental theorist Martin Hoffman and others have demonstrated, can elicit conformity in the short run but will discourage genuine internalization of norms. For such a child, being "good" consists of adhering to an externally imposed demand. Just as citizens in totalitarian countries may continue to think subversive thoughts but will not express them out loud, the child of totalitarian parents is not truly committed to the idea that hurting people is wrong. He is concerned mostly with not getting caught. If a parent not only fails to reason with a child about the consequences of aggression but *uses* aggression to enforce her point, the child learns that might really does make right. The use of some power by the parent can serve to drive home the importance of the lesson; there should be enough so the child pays attention but not so much that power *becomes* the lesson.

Listing methods of discouraging aggression is not tantamount to describing how to promote prosocial behavior. It is easy to imagine a child who neither hurts nor helps much, and, conversely, researchers have found that some children tend to do both. Today, few serious students of developmental psychology believe that aggression and prosocial behavior are simply opposite ends of a single continuum.[98] In fact, some writers have emphasized that a disciplinary technique restricted to prohibition (of aggression or anything else) can lead a child to become preoccupied with her own behavior, and this is not particularly conducive to a posture of responsiveness to others' needs.[99] We proceed therefore to the separate question of how to promote prosocial activity.

The Presence of Caring

Secure Attachment and Nurturance More basic than the techniques for encouraging particular behaviors is the practice of nesting all discipline and instruction in a warm, nurturant, and empathic relationship with a child. The theory here is that meeting a child's needs frees him from being preoccupied with them and allows him to be open to others' needs. He feels safer, less defensive, and bolder about reaching out to people around him—even those who are different from himself.

Indeed, the research suggests that an infant judged to be securely attached to her primary parent grows up to be more assertive and inde-

pendent—and also more sympathetic in responding to other people—
than those insecurely attached.[100] Nurturant caretaking makes a difference after infancy, too, although here some of the findings have been
mixed, depending in part on the gender of both parent and child.[101] One
cannot confidently predict subsequent prosocial inclinations just by
knowing how much nurturance a child received; it is one element of
successful parenting but not the only one. (The same may be said about
all of the approaches described in this section. One can imagine virtually
any strategy being mis- or overapplied, particularly if it is singled out and
implemented in the absence of the others.) If caring for a child slides into
permissiveness, for example, the consequences may not be favorable. But
children whose parents are interested in and supportive of them usually
distinguish themselves as socially competent and healthier on a range of
other measures. Such parental support, according to other research, is
particularly important during periods of crisis.

Warm, caring, empathic parents do several things at once. They help
the child to assume that the world is a benevolent, safe place in which to
act. Rousseau saw this clearly: "A child is therefore naturally inclined to
benevolence because he sees that everything approaching him is inclined
to assist him; and from this observation he gets the habit of a sentiment
favorable to his species."[102] (Someone whose experience with others
leaves her feeling threatened rather than safe is likely to be busy looking
out for herself at the expense of helping others.) Caring parents also
provide the child with necessary confidence. In effect, they consistently
model helping and caring behavior, and they become the sorts of figures
who can easily be objects of identification as well as effective instructors
of values.

Guiding and Explaining   It may seem too obvious to bother noting,
but parents who themselves value helping, sharing, and caring are more
likely to bring up children with these values than are parents who are
perpetually worried that someone is about to take advantage of them,
who are defensive and self-centered, who view life as a zero-sum game
in which the measure of success is how many people one has defeated
rather than how willing one is to help.

Similarly, the extent to which prosocial values are implemented by
a child turns on the sense of inclusiveness with which the parent views
(and encourages the child to view) others: Is life a contest between Us and
Them, with most people seen as Them? Or are parents more likely to
encounter another person with an emphasis on the humanity they share,

seeing each as someone to whom they, themselves, are connected, who is more like them (with respect to the things that matter) than alien? If parents do erect boundaries between people similar and dissimilar to themselves, where are those boundaries placed? (How many people are left out of the inner circle?) Are they rigidly fixed? (Can a member of an excluded group be reclassified, upon closer inspection, as someone similar to themselves?) How relevant are these boundaries to their actual behavior? (Will a parent feel entitled to ignore the misery of someone defined as one of Them—or even to bring about that misery?) These attitudes about whether we meet others with our hands extended or clenched in fists, and how we are inclined to perceive those others relative to ourselves, are evident to our children. It makes a difference whether a child hears his parent refer to other people as subjects or objects, as unique human beings just like us or as instances of roles or functions or ethnic classifications.

It also matters whether prosocial activity is promoted (or pursued by parents themselves) on the basis of self-interest: "Michael, if you don't share your toys with Linda, she won't let you play with her dinosaur" has an undeniable appeal for a parent, but it is a strategy more likely to inculcate self-regarding shrewdness than genuine concern for others.

Parents not only need to have humanistic values and a commitment to prosocial behaviors, per se; they also need to communicate them quite directly to children. Ervin Staub points out that preaching about the desirability of a given behavior is probably less effective than being explicit about what is expected. The idea of "controlling" one's children is regarded by some as repugnant, but direct guidance need not entail coercion or trickery. Children are going to be influenced by parents regardless of whether they have deliberately set about shaping their children's values (or whether the parents are even conscious of the process), and irrespective of what those values are. Not saying anything when a child acts selfishly sends a message just as clearly as saying something, and the message received by the child has more to do with the acceptability of selfishness than it does with the virtues of nonintrusive parenting.

Obviously parents must decide when silence is the best response, just as they must struggle to communicate disapproval of selfish or aggressive behavior without permitting the child to infer that their love is in doubt—a balance far trickier to strike in practice than in print. It does seem that setting out rules and expectations becomes far more effective when accompanied by explanations fitted to the child's age and ability to understand. Just as children should be made to understand why hitting is bad, so they must hear why—not only be told that—helping is good. ("When you share your tricycle with Marcia, she gets to have fun, too, and that makes her happy.")

Hoffman calls this inductive discipline and says that, as applied to prosocial behavior, it can take advantage of and build on a child's predisposition to empathize with others. The point is not just to tell but to explain, not just to praise but to specify which behavior is appreciated and why. (Staub emphasizes the importance of the latter, which he calls "embedded induction"—matching the explanation to a child's own prosocial actions.) Children should be encouraged to wrestle with moral questions and to think for themselves about such matters but also to compare their inclinations and actions to others'.* The more the child is led to take an active role, made a partner in the development of her own prosocial sensibilities, the less danger there is of provoking defiant opposition as a reaction to inductive guidance, a risk that appears to be greater with boys.[104]

Of the many investigations of this style of child rearing, two stand out. One is the Oliners' study, which found that the parents of children who later chose to rescue European Jews during World War II had been more likely to emphasize reasoning (rather than physical punishment or simple obedience) in bringing them up than had the parents of nonrescuers. The inductive style, according to the Oliners, "communicates a message of respect for and trust in children that allows them to feel a sense of personal efficacy and warmth toward others. . . . In contrast, punishment implies the need to curb some intrinsic wildness or evil intent."[105]

The second piece of research retrospectively examined the childhoods of more than a thousand undergraduates during the 1960s. It turned out that those students who were involved both in social service activities (community volunteer work) and political activism (protesting in behalf of a cause) were more likely to have been raised in homes characterized by a rational rather than punitive approach to discipline. Their parents, compared with those of other students, had expected

---

*At least one anecdotal account suggests that the style of parental instruction may be at least as important as the content. Unless the child is encouraged to question and use her reasoning skills, prosocial instruction may not produce a prosocial orientation. Consider one man who recalled being "taught that my highest duty was to help those in need" but learned this lesson in the context of the importance of "obey[ing] promptly the wishes and commands of my parents, teachers, and priests, and indeed of all adults. . . . Whatever they said was always right." The man speaking here is Rudolf Hoess, the infamous commandant of Auschwitz. The example is extreme, but it may serve as a powerful reminder of what can result from a parental emphasis on mindless obedience.[103]

responsible and mature behavior of them, had not permitted aggressiveness, and had generally seemed respectful of the children.[106]

Modeling Two other, smaller studies of, respectively, rescuing Jews
and political activism pointed to another feature of the subjects' families
of origin: parents had provided living examples of prosocial behavior.
Almost all of the rescuers interviewed by Perry London and his colleagues said they identified strongly with at least one of their parents who
served as a "model of moral conduct."[107] In a report appearing in the
same anthology that contains London's research, David Rosenhan described his interviews with people active in the early days of the civil
rights movement. Here, too, "one or both of the parents of the Fully
Committed"—those who spent at least a year working in the South for
racial justice—"were themselves fully committed to an altruistic cause
during some extended period of the respondents' formative years."[108]

The power of modeling is, of course, not restricted to prosocial
behavior—or even, for that matter, to children. Watching how a powerful
or admired figure acts is likely to produce imitation, particularly (though
not necessarily) if that figure seems to be rewarded for doing so. This is
how violence, too, is taught. But enough research has been done on the
effects of modeling helping behaviors in particular to make it clear that
the technique works quite well.[109] A child who had watched, even briefly,
as someone donated to charity is himself likely to donate more than most
other children even if months have elapsed since the exposure to the
model.

Several studies have established that showing works better than telling: children are more likely to donate when models exhort them not to
give but simultaneously set an example of generosity than when models
urge children to give but do not do so themselves. It is important to
recognize, however, that modeling in these studies is being contrasted
with simple exhortation rather than with explanation of the value of
generosity.[110] In fact, modeling shares this same failing: by itself, it does
not provoke children to think about the importance of prosocial behavior. It does, however, provide information—or offer a reminder—about
norms concerning how other people should be treated.

It is also useful to remember that this sort of research makes use of
contrived scenarios for testing the effects of modeling. Far more powerful
are examples that occur in situations like those a child is actually liable
to encounter, as well as examples set by people whom the child regards
as nurturing and warm. Studies with parents are somewhat more persua-

sive than one-time laboratory modeling sessions, then. They show that parents who value altruism are indeed likely to raise children with similar values, and this probably illustrates the power of modeling more than the approach to discipline used in the home (although these factors are easy to confound). Even while they are still unsteady on their feet, toddlers are watching and being influenced by the extent to which their parents react to other people's distress. Older children's behavior is affected by a parent's decision to talk about moral dilemmas and personal reactions to them. A parent who regularly considers the perspective of other people ("Boy, I guess that cashier must have had a pretty hard day to get mad at me like that, huh?"), and acts in accordance with that perspective, is modeling these behaviors constantly for a child.

Promoting a Prosocial Self-Image   Staub has been a leading proponent of providing situations in which children can experience helping first-hand: caring for pets, looking out for younger siblings, tutoring other children, and so on.[111] Furthermore, if a child hurts someone else, he can be encouraged to suggest ways of making reparation and then carry them out. That one learns more from personal involvement with prosocial action than from either hearing about it or watching someone else is a matter of common sense.

Less obvious but no less important is the fact that opportunities to try out prosocial values not only promote learning by doing but also encourage children to think of themselves as helpful, caring people. This notion dovetails with the idea of embedded induction (explaining these concepts in the context of the child's own actions) and with my caution about offering egoistic incentives for prosocial behavior. A child should get the idea that she gave half of her dessert to a playmate because she is altruistic: this sets into motion a self-fulfilling prophecy of a sort far more benign than most.* Two researchers, Joan Grusec and Theodore Dix, have noted that

children who come to believe that their prosocial behavior reflects values or dispositions in themselves have internal structures that can generate behavior across settings and without external pressures. By contrast, children who view

---

*This does not mean that parents should attribute altruistic motives to a child who obviously has acted so as to gain a reward. Apart from the dishonesty involved—which may itself become the lesson for the child—this blatant repudiation of reality may encourage her to deny the existence of her egoistic impulses. The idea ought to be to nurture altruism, not to put the child in the position of having to disavow or repress other motives.

their prosocial conduct as compliance with external authority will act prosocially only when they believe external pressures are present.[112]

It also stands to reason, although child development specialists generally do not address the issue, that children who view their prosocial conduct as self-interested will act prosocially only when they believe they will profit from it.

Practice Cooperating In a large study published in India and largely unknown in the United States, boys raised in institutions were found to be more generous (as measured by donations of marbles to an unknown poor peer) than were boys living with their families. Moreover, the longer a subject's stay in the institution, the greater his generosity. Group living, the researcher speculated, may serve "as an in-built mechanism for promoting concern for others," offering opportunities to practice and observe helping.[113] This would seem to be consistent with findings by other investigators that children raised in extended families are more likely to be generous in experimental games than those raised in nuclear families.[114]

But the opportunity to learn and play cooperatively appears to be beneficial even for those raised in Western-style households. The relative benefits of cooperative rather than competitive activity for children include higher-quality learning and achievement as well as enhancement of self-esteem.[115] Furthermore, even if cooperation, by virtue of being an activity in which two or more people work together for mutual benefit, is not considered an example of prosocial behavior, it nevertheless promotes such behavior. In one study, fifth graders who studied grammar in cooperative learning groups were more likely to give away prize tokens to a stranger than were those who studied on their own.[116] In another, kindergartners who played cooperative games for seven months donated far more lollipops to their friends and siblings than those whose recreation consisted of the usual competitive games.[117] Considerable research has established that cooperation also enhances children's ability to take the points of view of other people.[118]

Cooperation is an essentially humanizing experience that predisposes participants to a benevolent view of others. It allows them to transcend egocentric and objectifying postures, encourages trust, sensitivity, open communication, and, ultimately, prosocial activity. (It is not only one's fellow group members who are on the receiving end of this

generosity, incidentally; the effects typically generalize.) But raising children in a competitive environment not only deprives them of these advantages, it is also positively destructive. In fact, one group of researchers
has concluded that "competition may serve to suppress generosity to
others to a greater extent than cooperation serves to enhance it."[119]
While there are literally hundreds of studies documenting the harms of
competition, only a few have addressed its effects on prosocial behavior.
These, however, all point in the same direction. Children who were told
they should try to beat someone else at a bowling game donated fewer
prize tokens afterward than those who could simply play without competing.[120] A later experiment replicated these results even though the opportunity to donate this time was presented before the actual competition. The implication is that the mere expectation of a contest was enough
to undermine generosity.[121] The same goes for adults: subjects told they
would be competing against someone in a game responded "counterem-
pathically"—showing distress in response to the other's pleasure. The
expectation of a cooperative interaction, by contrast, promoted empathic
responses on several physiological measures.[122]

Other research has varied the children rather than the environment
in order to determine whether personal competitiveness is associated
with less willingness to help. In a word, the answer is yes. Conversely,
"high generosity seems to be part of a pattern which involves less intense
interpersonal competition," as one pair of researchers concluded on the
basis of a study with nursery school boys.[123] It has also been shown that
boys who were rated as particularly competitive—and, in yet another
study, boys whose *fathers* emphasized competition—turned out to be less
empathic than their peers.[124]

The zero-sum mindset mentioned earlier as representing the sort of
value that is inimical to helping and caring is, in reality, a predictable
product of a competitive culture. Competition can be defined as mutually
exclusive goal attainment, which means that others stand to profit at
one's own expense. It stands to reason, then, that experience in competitive environments teaches that others are obstacles to one's own success,
that their gains represent a problem for oneself. Under such an arrangement, prosocial behavior is simply irrational, and there is reason to think
that this lesson, too, generalizes to other environments. Whereas competition constitutes a sort of artificial scarcity in which each person naturally
comes to doubt the beneficence of others—after all, they regard him as
a rival, too, and are after what he has—cooperation encourages a sense

of security from which position one can, psychologically speaking, afford to wish others well and try to help them.

Taking Children Seriously

Implicit in many of these findings about the child-rearing approaches most conducive to prosocial behavior is a fundamental attitude toward a child. I am speaking, in sum, of taking the child seriously, treating her as a person whose feelings and preferences and questions matter. I have in mind the example set by parents who take the time to ask their two-year-old whether she wants to drink from her yellow or her blue cup at lunch today, or who recognize that her unhappiness is very real to her even if they can attribute it to the fact that she is teething or tired, who do not confuse their own preferences and sensibilities with hers, and who are concerned with how a roomful of grown-ups appears from *her* vantage point and not merely with whether they will find her appropriately well behaved. A child's preferences cannot always be accommodated, but they can always be considered and they need never be dismissed. The child is someone with a distinctive point of view, a unique set of needs, and her own way of reasoning (which is not merely "cute"). The parent who has taken all this to heart is not only warm and empathic but is also more likely to be the parent who cares enough to guide the child away from aggressive behavior, who prefers explaining to punishing, who communicates and models prosocial values, who gives the child a chance to experience herself as a caring person as well.

One may be forgiven for suspecting that this parent is an exception in our culture. There is some empirical evidence that few parents bother to attribute helpfulness to children (in order to promote a prosocial self-image) or systematically encourage children's responses of empathic distress.[125] Casual observation suggests an even grimmer picture, with parental affection too frequently made contingent on the child's behaving acceptably—and on the parent's moods. Children are often treated as objects of and for the parent, and are exposed to decidedly aggressive and selfish models.

While it is easy to condemn parents who do not provide children with the sort of home best suited to the flowering of a prosocial sensibility, we should also be quick to understand the possible reasons for this state of affairs. The parent may, for example, be distracted by his or her own needs—either psychological or financial. Those whose sense of self-worth is precarious are at a disadvantage not only for reaching out to others, but also for raising children to do so. Those who have to worry about whether a meager monthly check can be stretched to pay for both food and heat may themselves feel stretched to the breaking point; child-centered, inductive discipline may seem a laughable luxury. (One study found that simple obedience on the part of children was particularly valued by fathers whose work was closely supervised, and there is other evidence that the popularity of power-based discipline tends to increase as one slides down the socioeconomic ladder.)[126]

Then, of course, there are the parents who deliberately refrain from employing the style of raising children described here. Some are undoubtedly well meaning, like the mother who tries to protect her child from empathic reactions on the grounds that the child should not have to be " 'burdened by the agonies of others. . . . There's plenty of time later on for that' "[127]—as if adult empathy were unrelated to one's childhood experiences. More common are people who have simply absorbed the values and norms of American culture, which have more to do with competitive success than with helping and caring. "In structured interpersonal competitions, such as an athletic contest or a classroom exam, excessive awareness of and concern about the feelings of others may prove counterproductive," writes Mark Barnett[128]—and instead of taking this as evidence of the destructiveness of competition, we accept on faith the need for contests and try to discourage children from caring "excessively."*

Raising children with care—and to care—is an enormously difficult undertaking under the best of circumstances. And our society, with its emphasis on competitive individualism, creates circumstances that are unusually trying. If there *is* an urge to help, it is largely internally generated, and it exists more in spite of social pressures than in consequence of them. "People have little use for altruism in this society," Radke-Yarrow has commented, "except when it's institutionalized, as through charities and volunteer societies."[130] What the middle-class child (particularly the boy) learns—if not from explicit instruction, then simply from observation—is that other people's misery is none of his concern, that

---

*Similarly, when conservative economists point out that "altruism is not a trait with positive survival value in a competitive market,"[129] we are encouraged to view this fact as indicative of a problem with altruism as opposed to a devastating indictment of the economic system in question.

there is no reason to get upset just because someone else is in pain, that he has to look out for himself.

The point, then, is that identifiable reasons—psychological, economic, and ideological—rather than sheer perversity account for the widespread failure to set about raising prosocial children. In turn, the failure to carry out the sort of practices described by researchers—and, in many cases, suggested by one's own intuitions—goes a long way toward explaining the distance we remain from the altruism of which we are capable. There are gaps and inconsistencies in the research, but there is sufficient consensus on most of the points reviewed here to allow us to reverse patterns of self-absorption and cruelty if we are so inclined.

4

===

The Self
and the Other

I used to "jack" people—you know, with a gun or your hand,
just catch 'em and go into their pockets—because I thought it was
fun. But, you know, you get to the point where you wouldn't like
nobody doing you like that when you get old, and you wouldn't
like nobody just coming around you mother and just snatching her
purse and lapping her, you know, so I start thinking, I can't be
doing this no more, because somebody who do my mother like that
make me ready to kill anybody. *I started to be, like, sorry for*
things that I had done.

                                               —Gang member (Bing, 1988)

Although empathy may sound mysterious, remember that there is
much that sounds mysterious in the universe, only you have got
used to it; and perhaps you will get used to empathy.

                                             —H. S. Sullivan (1953)

THE OTHER AS SUBJECT

"Human behavior" is a misleading description of what psychologists study because we humans are interesting by virtue of our thoughts, feelings, and motives—not merely our actions. This is particularly evident in the present context: we do not exhaust an exploration of the human capacity to respond to others by considering only prosocial behaviors. The attitudes we take toward, and in the company of, our fellows are also of obvious relevance. The ways we understand and feel connected to others, the respects in which our view of ourselves is changed by having to do with others—these are not "behaviors" in the usual sense of the word but neither can they be ignored.

This chapter considers the capacity to imagine the way the world looks from a vantage point other than one's own, hereafter referred to as perspective taking, and also the capacity to share in the affective life of another, known as empathy. My intent is to undertake a close inspection of both of these processes, reviewing the way they work, their relation to each other, and the concrete manifestations of failing to engage in them.

As such, it is necessary to synthesize, and perhaps to try to advance, the work of a number of different scholars. Following the frameworks set out by Piaget and Kohlberg, cognitive developmentalists such as John Flavell and Robert Selman have considered the vicissitudes of perspective taking in some detail. Empathy, meanwhile, has been the central concern of Martin Hoffman and several other social and developmental psychologists, as well as of pioneering psychotherapists such as Heinz Kohut and Carl Rogers. The idea of human relationship has been addressed by a range of philosophers, of whom Martin Buber is probably the most prominent, while any number of social scientists have described the dynamics of dehumanization, a topic that may be understood in part as the failure to take others' perspectives or to respond empathically. Many researchers have undertaken empirical investigations of these and related topics, but there has been—as is so often the case—very little in the way of integration of the various strands of thought. A study of children's empathic responses to their playmates is useful, and so is a philosophical discourse on the nature of the "interhuman"; each, however, is of potentially greater significance when juxtaposed with the other, and when both are understood in a broader context.

The final—which is to say, most advanced—stages described in developmental models of perspective taking and empathy (such as Selman's and Hoffman's, respectively) can help us to conceptualize the most sophisticated ways we come to share in another's experience. Likewise, Buber's description of an I-Thou relationship, and the accounts of interdependence offered by Carol Gilligan and other students of the psychology of relatedness, help point the way to an understanding of the fullest response to others of which humans are capable.

The strategy that I have found useful for organizing all of these ideas turns on a twofold attitude toward the other. On the one hand, we appreciate, as it were, the other's otherness; on the other hand, we appreciate the humanness that we have in common. In itself, this dual emphasis on difference and similarity is hardly novel, but too few theorists of relationship or empathy have emphasized the importance of both and the tension between them. To dwell exclusively on the first is to risk sentencing each of us to life behind a barrier that is unique but opaque; to see only the second is to deny the particulars that define each person's place in the world and explain why, for example, an encounter with another person offers something that can never be equaled by solitary reflection.

One who appreciates both the dimensions of otherness and common humanness is able to apprehend a given individual's subjectivity—not merely avoiding objectification but affirmatively invoking, reclaiming, addressing the other's status as a subject. A subject is an actor, a knower, a center of experience, and while any two individuals share these features, each is also a *different* subject. Existentialist thinkers rebel against the intellectual systems and real-world practices that conspire to crush or deny the individual's subjectivity by reducing him to a part of a crowd, a scientific datum, a pale approximation of some transcendent reality. The point here is to extend this exploration and defense of subjectivity in order to take account also of the *other's* status as subject. You are not just an object in my world but the center of a distinct and distinctive world of your own. The fact of understanding this, finally, affects my view of myself—not only in the concrete sense that I am transformed by coming to know you, but in that the way we conceive the *Eigenwelt,* the realm of self-relatedness, is affected by the very idea of relationship.

These ideas will be explained, embellished, and, with any luck, clarified in the discussion that follows. I am chiefly concerned with the attitude toward the other, and the exploration of this topic is divided into two parts: a consideration of appreciating otherness and appreciating shared humanness, respectively. The first of these involves a look at perspective taking and empathy, including some thoughts on the implications of pursuing each of these without the other. The next chapter proceeds to inspect the complementary idea: shared humanness. This includes some reflection on the phenomenon of objectification, with special reference to a world view that distinguishes sharply between an in-group and an out-group, us and them. That chapter concludes with a look at one's attitude toward oneself, arguing that the self is best understood as a subject that can be temporarily objectified, and also as an entity distinct from, but connected to, the other.

PERSPECTIVES ON PERSPECTIVES

Perspective taking, sometimes called role taking,* has been described by Robert Selman as "a form of social cognition intermediate between logical and moral thought."[1] Indeed, the process of imagining the way another individual thinks about, feels in response to, or literally sees the world is a remarkable phenomenon, related to the domains of both intelligence and ethics, but wholly owned by neither. As George Herbert Mead saw it more than half a century ago, "This putting of one's self in the places of others, this taking by one's self of their roles or attitudes, is not merely one of the various aspects or expressions of intelligence or of intelligent behavior, but is the very essence of its character."[2] A certain level of cognitive development is a prerequisite for being able to imaginatively take in the world from someone else's perspective, and this skill, in turn, has been shown to promote learning.[3]

Still, more is involved than cognitive flexibility. Creative problem solving frequently requires one to question assumptions, reason counterfactually, and consider issues from a fresh point of view. But perspective taking adds the further requirement that one imagine a point of view other than one's own. This brings one outside of one's self rather than just outside of one's usual way of thinking. Under some circumstances, doing so seems to require not only intelligence but a certain degree of mental health: one must feel sufficiently unthreatened and free, psychologically speaking, to relax a vigilant watch over (and attachment to) the self and to risk adopting someone else's perspective.

To do so may also require a certain generosity of spirit, at least under certain circumstances, just as it may contribute to moral reasoning and behavior. In fact, as I will argue later, the concept of perspective taking has intrinsic moral resonances. Piaget seemed to suggest that the moral point of view is bound up with the process of peering into the intentions behind people's actions, and that perspective taking is an important source of information about those intentions, permitting one to compare one's own motives with those of others. Likewise, if it is good to consider others' needs, then imagining how others think and feel constitutes a very efficient way of understanding those needs. Kohlberg argued that " 'role-taking tendencies' and the 'sense of justice' are interlocked" and are part of the

*When George Herbert Mead talked about role taking, he had in mind the crucial developmental process of trying on social roles. Since then, role taking and perspective taking have been used more or less interchangeably, particularly by developmental psychologists.

same brew that includes sympathy and the resolution of conflict.[4] There is also evidence that the inclination to cooperate with others both promotes and is promoted by the ability to take the perspectives of others.[5]

Most writers on the topic have talked about three varieties of perspective taking: spatial or perceptual, cognitive, and affective. Just as with different kinds of behavior collected under the "prosocial" heading, the ability to engage in one of these versions of perspective taking does not necessarily imply that one can engage in the others; they are conceptually but not always empirically related.[6]

Piaget spent considerable time describing a child's acquisition of the ability to imagine how a visual space looks from someone else's point of view. It may be that this most literal sort of perspective taking is a prerequisite for the development of the capacity to imagine how someone else thinks and feels.[7] In this chapter, however, my interest is primarily with what it means to capture the way another person might approach an idea and how he might respond emotionally.

Imagining another's affect is not the same thing as actually *feeling* another's affect. When I refer to empathy, I have the latter in mind (although it may include some of the former as well). Some use the term in a much broader sense, which I believe has the effect of blurring this distinction. One would do better to follow John Flavell's example when he refers to "nonempathic inference" and observes that "the child who understands from strong facial-expression cues that the stranger in the picture is 'happy' is seldom overcome with joy herself in consequence. Why on earth should she be?"[8] Indeed, these two different processes are not always correlated for children or for adults: someone who can correctly identify another's joy is not necessarily able to feel it.[9] Using a very different language, Buber indicated his sensitivity to a similar distinction:

[By] "imagining" the real I mean the capacity to hold before one's soul a reality arising at this moment but not able to be directly experienced. . . . I imagine to myself what another man is at this very moment wishing, feeling, perceiving, thinking, and not as a detached content but in his very reality, that is, as a living process in this man. The full "making present" surpasses this in one decisive way: something of the character of what is imagined is joined to the act of imagining.[10]

The relation between "imagining the real" and "making present," which is to say between perspective taking (including the affective variety) and empathy, will be addressed below. For the time being, I will focus on how perspective taking develops and what its absence implies.

Without attempting to devise an age-linked Piagetian model, Flavell and his colleagues identified five components of perspective taking. One must be able to do these things: first, recognize that points of view other than one's own can exist; second, realize that it can be useful for one reason or another to make inferences about someone else's point of view; third, actually make those inferences; fourth, continue summoning the other's point of view to challenge one's own; and finally, apply it to one's own behavior. This model is relevant both to a child's development and to what someone goes through during any given encounter with an-other.[11]

Selman, meanwhile, has developed a more explicit stage theory. Not counting the initial, egocentric posture in which one remains locked into one's own point of view, he proposes four distinct levels. (1) Sometime between the ages of five and nine, a child realizes that the other has a subjective perspective that may be unlike her own, but she still assumes that only one point of view is the right one. (2) At age seven to twelve, she has a more relativistic perspective and realizes that not only is she viewing the other, but the other is viewing her. (3) At age ten to fifteen, she can step back to grasp a "third-person" perspective on this reciprocal viewing in order to coordinate the two points of view. And (4) from adolescence on, she can step back even further to grasp a societal (or, in Mead's term, a "generalized other") perspective that incorporates all possible third-person perspectives.[12]

Piaget believed that even purely spatial perspective taking is something that no child, however bright, can manage until about age seven. Considerable evidence has accumulated since then, however, that children several years younger can correctly identify the thoughts and feelings of others, and, if the task used for measurement is not too complex, spatial perspective taking can be discovered in children as young as two or three.[13]

Let me back up a moment here and reflect further on the provocative idea of egocentricity, which predates the capacity for perspective taking. This word has been variously defined as "the confusion of the self with the not-self,"[14] "embeddedness in one's own point of view,"[15] and "attributing to others [one's] own knowledge, viewpoint, feelings, and so on."[16] The egocentric child usually understands that he and the other are distinct entities but cannot grasp that each has a separate point of view.*

Except for discussions about sociopaths that describe them as people

*Being able to recognize that another person has a different point of view does not guarantee being able to imagine what that individual's point of view *is*, however. Con-

unable to manage perspective taking, virtually all talk of egocentricity not only takes place in the context of developmental psychology, but refers to very young children. Yet in common parlance we call adults egocentric or self-centered or "all wrapped up in themselves," and I believe we do so with reason. Where this characteristic comes from is unclear: such individuals may have some sort of endogenous incapacity (though I have seen no data to support this), or they may have had too little practice in perspective taking, or they may even have been positively socialized to be egocentric.[18]

I find it helpful to imagine three versions of egocentricity that often overlap in practice: it can derive from cognitive inability, from emotional need, or from simple neglect. In the first, and rarest, type—rare among adults, that is—one simply cannot imagine that others have points of view unlike one's own, or at least one cannot make use of various cues to figure out what those points of view are. In the second type, one encounters a person who cannot *afford* to leave the self behind even temporarily: here is someone whose gaze may be trained on the outside world but only in order to consider how each new development will affect him. Superficially, that is, he may attend to others, but the point of reference is always himself. The dominant affect is anxiety. That others may look at the world differently is, like so many other phenomena, perceived principally as a potential threat. Such an individual clings for protection to a fixed perspective; there may be cognitive flexibility, but there is insufficient emotional flexibility to allow one to take an imaginative leap into another's world. Karen Horney effectively distinguished these two versions of egocentricity, noting that it is usually the small child who is egocentric

because it has not yet developed a feeling of relatedness to others. It simply does not know that others have their needs, and limitations, too—such as the mother's needing sleep or not having the money to buy a toy. The neurotic's egocentricity is built on an entirely different and much more complicated base. He is consumed with himself because he is driven by his psychic needs, torn by his conflicts, and compelled to adhere to his peculiar solutions.[19]

Finally, one may be egocentric—or at least fail to consider others' perspectives—out of simple neglect. We may be tempted to put this down to cognitive insufficiency or emotional needs, but in many cases neither

---

versely, as Shantz points out, someone who is unskilled at perspective taking should not automatically be assumed to be egocentric.[17]

account seems well founded. Situational demands may, for example, distract one from considering how others are likely to regard one's actions or words.

Something very like egocentricity is widely seen as figuring into serious psychosocial dysfunction. Psychotics may have "delusions of reference," which is to say they may believe that unrelated events, such as remarks heard on television, are actually addressed to them. Some people are not speaking figuratively if they suggest that the moon follows them when they walk at night. And, as already mentioned, the failure to take others' perspectives has been identified as a prime indication of, or even cause of, sociopathic behavior.[20]

What particularly interests me is the relation between the egocentricity that seems to define people who can assault others and that which is present in far more common, and less horrifying, behaviors. The central joke of Arlo Guthrie's "Alice's Restaurant" was that the Army had reservations about drafting him to kill Vietnamese villagers on the grounds that he once had been arrested for littering. Yet the people who drop candy wrappers wherever they happen to be, or who block traffic by double parking, rip pages out of library books, and so on, seem to be locked into themselves, unable or unwilling to consider those who will have to look at their garbage, maneuver their cars around them, or discover a chapter missing. It seems intriguing to play with the possibility that what leads someone to toss garbage on the sidewalk might be conceptually related to what allows one to fire a weapon at a stranger.

This, of course, is not to argue that an empty potato chip bag will lead us to a killer. Casual carelessness and the willingness to take a life on command are separated by a gulf one can barely see across, to say nothing of the fact that violence has multiple causes. But to reflect on the practice of, say, leaning on one's car horn at midnight to summon a friend from his house is to recall Kafka's pithy account of war as a "monstrous failure of imagination." Reduce the scale, delete the "monstrous," and you have the late-night honker. While I do not pretend to regard this fellow from a disinterested distance (least of all when he is right outside my window), neither do I wish to write him off with reproving labels like "thoughtless" and "careless." These words may fit, but they open a discussion rather than ending one. They invite further inquiry into the nature of the thought and care—in short, the imagination—that he is missing.

In another age, and perhaps in contemporary small towns, this absence may have been rarer or, on another account, may simply have gone unnoticed. If an individual knows and is known to everyone with whom she comes into contact, she is accountable to them and there will be a price to pay for antisocial behaviors. Someone unable to engage in perspective taking might therefore refrain from such behaviors for fear of social sanctions, so that this inability would not be detected. But as I indicated in the last chapter's discussion of urban anonymity and its effects on prosocial activity, I do not believe that such sanctions adequately explain the big city versus small town difference. Where others are personally known to one, there is also a greater likelihood of caring about them and anticipating their reactions to one's own behavior. In a modern, urban society, however, neither of these is present: one is deterred not by anticipation of unfavorable consequences *or* by personal concern for those who are affected. Thus one must be skilled at taking others' perspectives and inclined to do so; more is required for one to decide to act responsibly.

EVERYONE, SOMEONE, AND YOU: THREE SEPARATE POINTS OF VIEW

It is customary to parse the idea of perspective taking on the basis of the nature of the other's experience (perceptual, cognitive, affective). But it is equally important to consider what we mean by *other*. Theorists and researchers sometimes blur what are actually fundamentally different directions that a person can take in moving outside of his own perspective. I suggest that one can take the point of view of everyone (the collective other), someone (the hypothetical other), or you (the concrete, specific other). These three, and the relationship among them, are represented in figure 1.

The Collective Other

To view an event or experience from a vantage point other than one's own is not necessarily to see it as another individual does. Possibly inspired by Adam Smith's impartial spectator, one ethical theorist has proposed that we imagine an "ideal observer" of our behavior when formulating moral principles and pay heed to that observer's perspective, which is, by definition, omniscient, disinterested, and dispassionate.[21] Theists frequently talk about God's point of view, and few people have

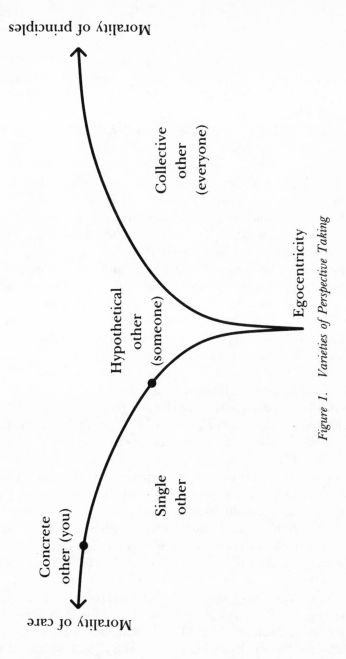

Figure 1. Varieties of Perspective Taking

not had the experience—sometimes liberating, sometimes desolating—of staring up at a night sky and thinking about human life (and specifically, one's own life) from a cosmic perspective.

Of the several possible abstract reference points that can be imagined, I want to focus specifically on that of one's society. This is what Mead called "the generalized other." The development of a complete, which is to say socialized, self includes a consideration of the interests and norms of the social group to which one belongs, he said. Perspective taking, then, can consist in internalizing the collective.[22] Notice that Selman, following Mead, has constructed his developmental model with this as the consummate form of perspective taking.

If there are social consequences of seeing with the eyes of the hypothesized collective other, they are mediated by the change in the way one sees oneself. Mead was mostly concerned with the process of socialization, but others, philosopher Thomas Nagel among them, have emphasized that to "regard oneself as merely one individual among many"[23] is the kernel of most ethical theories. It matters only that "one" has certain duties or rights or would benefit from a certain state of affairs; that the one happens to be you cannot be allowed to matter. An ethical prescription is fair if it has been universalized, and taking the view of an ideal observer or social collective is a means toward that end. (Another means is pretending that one does not know one's own place in society or other circumstantial particulars while one chooses moral and political principles—John Rawls's famous "original position.")[24] Thus, this version of perspective taking—but only this version—points the way to a morality based on abstract principles.

More prosaically, this process also explains how we leave behind the solipsism and inappropriate sense of specialness that is often part of egocentric experience. Children—and sometimes adults, too—may imagine that they, and the details of their lives, define a standard, the way life is supposed to be. Look, for example, at your hand. This is what a hand *ought* to look like; it captures the Platonic category of Handness. All other hands are too dark or too light, too fleshy or too bony, too hairy or too smooth. Or consider your hometown. This is, you may have vaguely assumed at some point, the right place to have come from (irrespective of your rational evaluation of it). There is something slightly suspicious about having grown up elsewhere, with the suspiciousness increasing in proportion to the dissimilarity between that place and your place. Or think about how neat you like to keep your house or apartment. Anyone who prefers a home even neater is compulsive; anyone who is satisfied with less tidiness is a slob. Goldilocks, we might say, supplies the language for elaborating on this variant of egocentricity.

Clearly, regarding one's own life as the standard has prescriptive consequences. Such an individual may feel a sense of entitlement or peculiar deservingness. But there is a descriptive component, too. Take as one illustration the fact that many men tend to use the male experience or male characters as a point of reference in telling stories, devising models of development, and so forth. When this is pointed out to them, such men react with genuine surprise: a male writer might protest that he intended no sexist slight just because he wrote, say, "How can anyone help feeling self-conscious in the presence of a beautiful woman?" The point, though, is that he has assumed that "anyone"—or, more precisely, the reader—must surely be male just as he is male.

This is the most insidious version of sexism (or racism, classism, ageism, as the case may be)—the result not of deliberately adopted attitudes but of a kind of thoughtless egocentricity. It is true that thinking of oneself, or the group of which one is a member, as defining the norm may be challenged by putting oneself in the place of another individual— in this case, a particular woman reader. But the larger point is that there are *many* potential women readers, that one's own circumstance may not be shared, that one's idea of tidiness is just one of many possible ways of keeping house. These and other examples of self-embeddedness, it may be argued, are best corrected by imagining how a collective or objective other views the issue—and views oneself. An abstract point of reference can help, so to speak, to "put things in perspective."

The Hypothetical Other

Notice, in figure 1, how, after an initial ascent from egocentricity, the idea of perspective taking can take two separate courses. These involve imagining the point of view of the collective other and of a single individual, respectively. In the first variant of the latter (represented by the lower section on the left arc) the identity of that single individual is beside the point. This is the hypothetical other, and it is what most people probably have in mind when they talk about perspective taking.[25]

Sometimes one makes a deliberate attempt to understand how "someone else" might regard a situation, while at other times a sudden shift of perspective seems to arrive uninvited. Even in the latter case, however, it is possible to prepare the ground for such an event by making

an effort to take others' perspectives whenever possible and by "exercising" one's cognitive and emotional flexibility. Certain professions seem
to demand a measure of perspective taking—at least if they are to be done
well. Any supervisor ought to be able to imagine how the prospect of
completing an assignment might look to a subordinate. A good dentist
pictures what it must be like to be on the other side of the drill (or to lead
a life in which flossing does not play a major role). A teacher cannot be
successful unless he or she can imagine how someone unfamiliar with a
given idea would respond to it for the first time. Piaget saw this, too:

Every beginning instructor discovers sooner or later that his first lectures were
incomprehensible because he was talking to himself, so to say, mindful of only
his own point of view. He realizes only gradually and with difficulty that it is not
easy to place oneself in the shoes of students who do not yet know what he knows
about the subject matter of the course.[26]

This pertains to cognitive perspective taking, of course, but there is a
spatial correlative: after some years of teaching, one may notice that when
he refers to something's being on the left he instinctively gestures to his
right, the students' left.

The perspective of the hypothetical other is taken when someone
becomes aware of how a given situation or idea—or how she, herself—
looks to another person. For example, imagine that you are sitting in a
theater, craning your head to see around the head of the person in front
of you, and growing increasingly irritated at this inconvenience. Suddenly, it dawns on you that the person in the row behind you regards you
in exactly the same way: you are not only blocked but blocking. Or
suppose that a subway is waiting at the platform as you arrive. You rush
toward it only to have the doors close in your face and the train pull away.
Your anger—"Would it have killed the conductor to have waited ten
more seconds until I got in?"—evaporates after you realize that from the
conductor's perspective, you are part of a steady stream of would-be
riders. He has to close the door sometime, and *someone* will just miss
getting on.

A deliberate and purely cognitive perspective taking can be useful in
understanding how others think about a particular issue, and how they
might have arrived at a position that seems to you indefensible. If one has
difficulty understanding how any human being could justify working for
the Tobacco Institute and spending his days denying the existence of a
causal link between smoking and lung cancer, it might help to reason by

analogy in order to get a better feel for this world view. Perhaps such an individual regards the effort to publicize the danger of cigarettes in exactly the way others regard the campaign to dissuade people from using marijuana. One's skepticism about the relevant research and one's defense of individual rights against governmental restrictions would then seem to follow logically. One may still strongly disagree with the conclusion or the premise, but at least the internal coherence of the viewpoint has become more accessible.[27]

Ideally, perspective taking not only requires flexibility but should itself be flexible. To take just one other point of view, or one other *kind* of point of view, may offer none of the advantages of perspective taking and may even exacerbate the ideological or psychological perils of embeddedness. During a visit to an ethics class at a prestigious business school, for example, I once heard an instructor describe a strict ethical code for doing business and invite his students to consider it from the point of view of a stockholder in, or the sales manager of, an affected company. The difference between these two roles, however—or, more to the point, between either one and the students' own perspective to begin with—may not have been great enough to challenge them to consider the problem in a new way. The perspective of a blue-collar worker, a consumer of the corporation's products, a resident of the town where the company is based, or simply of an ethical agent per se, seemed conspicuously absent from the exercise. A given role, or a set of roles within a narrow range, can become fixed, defeating the purpose of perspective taking.* One ought instead to try to live in "a space with many light bulbs, each of which illuminates a somewhat different side of every object and each of which provides a possible perspective from which to see a pattern of events."[29]

The Concrete Other

Carol Gilligan and a colleague have found fault with the idea of perspective taking on the grounds that this process, including "assum[ing] Rawls' original position or play[ing] Kohlberg's game of moral musical chairs"

---

*This is particularly true if perspective taking is "based on *existing* relations in an unjust society" and all the imagining is class-based and unidirectional. Nicholas Rescher makes this point well: "Internalization may work against social justice when the underdogs are moved to take pride in the successes of their more fortunate compeers, while the privileged neglect a reciprocal internalization (or internalize only the fate of their fellows in privilege)."[28]

lets one proceed "without specifically knowing anything about the other but simply by following the laws of perspective and putting oneself in his or her position."[30] This is quite true of the versions of perspective taking discussed to this point. If one is summoning up a collective other, there is, by definition, no single person involved. In the case of the hypothetical other, one need imagine only that there is *someone* sitting in the next row back in the auditorium, or someone working for the Tobacco Institute; who the individual is, and the unique details of her life experience, are irrelevant.

But I believe there exists a third variety of perspective taking, even though few theorists have attended to it or distinguished it from the hypothetical type. (In figure 1 it is located farther along on the same line that contains the hypothetical other.) Sometimes the identity of the individual whose point of view I seek to understand does matter; in fact, it is crucial to the enterprise. This is nicely contained in the description of "imagining the real." When I try to capture the thinking or feeling of another man, it is "not as a detached content but in his very reality . . . as a living process in this man," Buber told us. This distinction between a relationship with an interchangeable someone and with you in particular is a central theme in Buber's writings. To imagine the real, to engage in perspective taking in what he would regard as its fullest sense, is not merely to understand the implications of the role (for example, subway conductor) that someone else plays. Rather, it involves "a bold swinging . . . into the life of the other."[31]

What often passes for perspective taking—or empathy, as the word is sometimes used—is no more than the act of asking oneself: How would I like it if somebody did that to me? For a person who has hitherto failed to pose that question to himself, for a child or a sociopath, this is an exceedingly useful exercise. It is precisely what seems to have shaken the gang member (quoted in this chapter's epigraph) out of his dangerous egocentricity,[32] and it is, in the view of Thomas Nagel, Kurt Baier, and other ethical theorists, a solid basis for morality.[33]

But there is a world of difference—the difference between your world and my world, to be exact—between imagining yourself in someone else's situation and imagining *her* in her situation. It is the difference between asking what it is like to be in someone else's shoes and what it is like to have that person's feet. Sometimes, wrote Adam Smith, "I not only change circumstances with you, but I change persons and characters."[34]

If we are rarely alive to this distinction, it may be because in many situations it suffices for one to ask how he, himself, would like being in

it; the chances are good that neither he nor anyone else particularly wants
to be hit over the head with a tire iron. But in other circumstances, we
have different experiences and desires, and concrete perspective taking
proceeds from—and, at the same time, reinforces—the recognition of
people's unique realities.

The philosopher Max Scheler was quite clear about this. The question, "How would it be if this had happened to *me?*" he declared,

certainly has nothing to do with genuine fellow-feeling. If only because the
answer would very often be, "Had it happened to *me,* with *my* character and
temperament, it would not have been so bad; but being the sort of person he is,
it is a serious matter for him." True fellow-feeling betrays itself in the very fact
that it includes the existence and character of the other person as an individual.
. . . [To imagine oneself in the other's situation] would indeed appear,
phenomenologically speaking, to be directed merely upon our own sorrow or joy,
and would therefore be an *egoistic* [act].[35]

George Bernard Shaw put this more succinctly. "Do not do unto others
as you would have them do unto you," he said. "They may have different
tastes."[36]

The distinction between imagining oneself in the other's situation
and imagining the other in the other's situation has, as I shall argue
shortly, definite consequences for maximizing empathic reactions and for
the probability of acting prosocially. In fact, taking the point of view of
a certain other person permits us to understand perspective taking as an
end in itself rather than simply as a means for gathering information
about others. First, while affective perspective taking of a concrete other
is not the same thing as empathy, it does move us closer in the direction
of feeling as well as understanding how that person feels. Second, the
focus on a particular individual raises the possibility of imagining not just
a single affect or cognition or event but something more global. One can
come to understand the other's world, to imagine how he is likely to
experience things that have not yet occurred, to get a sense for what it
is to *be* him. In caring for others, one author suggests, "I must consider
their natures, ways of life, needs, and desires. And, although I can never
accomplish it entirely, I try to apprehend the reality of the other. . . .
Caring involves stepping out of one's own personal frame of reference
into the other's."[37]

If we are talking about perspective taking that is both cognitive and
affective, in which there is a concrete rather than a hypothetical other, and

in which that other's world (rather than just an isolated response) is grasped by us, then we are raising the possibility of an ongoing relationship with another.[38] This is the realm that Buber so well described, a realm of "dialogue" and figuratively "turning toward the other," in which a bridge is thrown "from self-being to self-being across the abyss of dread of the universe."[39] In such an encounter, "the other happens as the particular other . . . and is thus related to him in such a way that he does not regard and use him as his object, but as his partner in a living event."[40] Perspective taking is an ingredient in any such relationship, and the relationship itself makes such perspective taking more likely to take place.* From this scenario, as chapter 9 will argue, we can begin to construct a morality of a different sort than that suggested by the dictates of the collective other, and we can also glimpse something of a new perspective on altruism.

FEELING INTO

Whether empathy promotes prosocial behavior, the nature of its relation to perspective taking, whether gender differences exist with respect to it, and the role it plays in psychotherapy are all matters that turn on how the word is defined. Writers have used *empathy* to embrace affective perspective taking (or all perspective taking) or to refer to a feeling of sorrow in response to another person's predicament. In some cases the term has referred to a feeling that matches someone else's feeling, or an expression of understanding and support, or some combination of these things. None of these uses is objectionable in itself; a definition, after all, cannot be proved right or wrong but can only be shown to be more or less useful. The problem derives rather from the confusing situation in which different people are using the word differently.

Empathy was coined in the early part of the century by the U.S. psychologist Edward Titchener. The German word from which it was translated, *Einfühlung* (literally, "feeling into") was made popular by Theodor Lipps a few decades earlier to describe a mode of aesthetic perception: one could feel one's way into a painting, for example. In

*Perspective taking, however, is not a substitute for a genuine relationship with another. Even the most splendid act of the individual imagination pales beside the kind of dialogue Buber had in mind. In the context of direct knowledge about, and shared experience with, someone else, there may even be less need for deliberate acts of perspective taking.

those early years, *empathy* referred only to a sort of mimicry, with other forms of affect matching still called *sympathy.* [41]

Freud made few references to empathy,[42] but later writers on psychotherapy drew on the concept repeatedly. The two most influential in this regard have been Heinz Kohut and Carl Rogers. Kohut saw empathy as a critical component of the relationship between parent and infant, although he has been criticized for stretching the word to the point that it seemed to signify virtually any aspect of a positive affective bond.[43] He also used *empathy* to refer to what most researchers call perspective taking, a useful tool by which the therapist "gathers psychological data about other people and . . . imagines their inner experience even though it is not open to direct observation."[44] For Rogers, empathy—by which he, too, seemed to have meant something closer to affective perspective taking[45]—is one of the necessary and sufficient conditions for successful therapy: it is not only useful for understanding the client's state of mind but also has a curative effect. In the context of therapy, theorists frequently emphasize the need to balance this supportive demeanor with objectivity.

The various uses of empathy in different schools of psychotherapy could itself fill a chapter or even a book, but I want to discuss the concept from the perspective of social and developmental psychology. In so doing, I use *empathy* to denote something close to the original German notion of "feeling into" another person. In its ideal incarnation, this process builds on and draws from the capacity to take someone else's perspective and therefore is more complicated than simply "feeling with" someone.[46] In saying this I join Norma Feshbach, who sees emotional responsiveness as the third component of a process that also includes identifying another person's affective cues and understanding a situation from that person's perspective.[47] I also find Martin Hoffman's fine-tuned definition to be useful: empathy is feeling what is appropriate to someone else's situation—that is, what she *would* feel if she knew her own situation. (This distinction comes into play in instances of dramatic irony; for example, a truly empathic person would likely feel sad upon meeting a joyful individual who did not yet know that a loved one had just died.)[48]

More important is the distinction between *empathy* (feeling into) and *sympathy* (feeling for). The latter is a particular response to another's plight characterized by pity or concern, while empathy consists in sharing the other's affect, whatever it happens to be. Not surprisingly, the two concepts have been differentiated empirically as well as conceptually.[49] Yet there has been considerable confusion over which word should represent which concept. Ironically, while *sympathy* was once used to mean empathy, as, for instance, by Adam Smith, today there are some who use *empathy* to mean what I and others call sympathy.[50] Even more ironic is the fact that some writers have described sympathy as a fundamentally self-oriented[51] or distanced[52] response, while others embrace the concept (whatever name they give it) precisely on the grounds that it is other-oriented and suggestive of connection.[53] One way or the other, it is important to note that a response to someone else's situation which involves sympathy, empathy, or both can be distinguished from a response of personal distress in which the primary goal is to improve one's own mood. It is no easy task to sort out the internal dynamics—perhaps empathy calls forth a non-self-interested sympathy—but, as I will argue in chapter 8, people can be moved to come to another person's aid for reasons that have more to do with concern for that person's well-being than with a desire to make themselves feel better.

If perspective taking illuminates a space by turning on light bulbs, with empathy the metaphor shifts to the aural and the tactile. It is, in the words of the existential psychoanalyst Ludwig Binswanger, a *"sound* phenomenon, as when the poet Hoelderlin writes to his mother that there could not be a sound alive in her soul with which his soul would not chime in; or a phenomenon of *touch,* as when we say, 'your sorrow, your joy touches me.' "[54] Notice that these descriptions are predominantly receptive. As one writer asserts, when empathizing, "I do not project; I receive the other into myself."[55] Empathy in this view is primarily a response to the other's experience. But some theorists characterize it instead as reaching out to another, penetrating, feeling in. One writer justifies such a model on the grounds that receptivity is more a function of sympathy than of empathy.[56]

Neither of these exclusive positions is justified. Sympathy and empathy can continue to be distinguished even if both have an element of the receptive; being moved by someone's plight is not the same as chiming in with (or resonating to) that plight. Conversely, it seems unnecessary—indeed, virtually impossible—to rule out the active element of feeling into another's experience, particularly in the situation described earlier in which one feels the affective reaction appropriate to someone else's situation even if that individual does not (yet) feel it herself. This idea seems to have taken on unsavory connotations in some people's minds because of what the word *penetration* conjures up, or because of a hasty equation of active knowing with the excesses of Western rationalism in which all mystery and creative participation are lost.[57] In fact, *receptive* and *active* are not mutually exclusive in the way *passive* and *active* may be. To be fully receptive—to be a good listener, for instance—necessitates an active stance. Properly understood, empathy is kin to both elements.

It is the active dimension of empathy that allows us to make sense of the common phenomenon of feeling into the situation of someone who is not physically present. For many of the people who rescued Jews during World War II, "merely knowing that others were suffering was sufficient to arouse them."[58] Or, as one of Elie Wiesel's characters says: "There are only two possibilities for me: either I suffer your pain with you, or I'll suffer it without you; in a common absence, I mean. In any case, I'll suffer it."[59]

Before we delve into the empirical research, let us hear from Buber once again. He speaks of what is now usually called empathy not only as "making present" but as "experiencing the other side." For example, "The striker suddenly receives in his soul the blow which he strikes . . . [or] a man caresses a woman, who lets herself be caressed. Then let us assume that he feels the contact from two sides—with the palm of his hand still, and also with the woman's skin." Such an experience, says Buber, "makes the other person present to him for all time. A transfusion has taken place after which a mere elaboration of subjectivity is never again possible or tolerable to him."[60] In other words, one not only imagines but actually *feels* the sensual event, and the implications extend well beyond the sensual in creating a bond between the two individuals, a relationship that cannot be reduced to the sum total of their separate realities.

THEORY AND RESEARCH ON EMPATHY

The Development of Empathy

How one views the origin of empathy may depend, not surprisingly, on the school of personality theory to which one belongs. A behaviorist might assume, along with Justin Aronfreed and others, that classical conditioning can explain its development: if a child's pain or joy is paired with a signal of someone else's pain or joy, then the latter will become a conditioned stimulus, capable of eliciting emotional responses on its own.[61] Some psychoanalysts, meanwhile, argue that the unique relationship between parent and child provides a prototype for all subsequent sharing of affect. Harry Stack Sullivan concentrated on that which is unpleasant, pointing to "a certain direct contagion of disagreeable experience from significant adults to very young children"[62] and, elsewhere, to the way "the tension of anxiety when present in the mothering one induces anxiety in the infant."[63] Others have emphasized that a parent who responds empathically—or, better, perceptively and supportively—to the child permits the child to develop empathic skills of her own.

Martin Hoffman has offered the most influential and carefully elaborated model of the development of empathy, drawing from both learning theory and psychoanalytic conceptions.[64] He proceeds from the conviction that some rudimentary form of empathy, a predisposition to share in and respond to the affect of others, is present from birth. This conclusion is partly based on studies showing that newborns seem particularly disturbed by the sound of another infant's cry (chapter 3). After only a few months, an infant can discriminate among facial expressions; shortly thereafter, he or she can meaningfully interpret these expressions as reflections of emotions. As one writer summarizes the theory, "once the child imbues emotional expressions (facial, vocal, etc.) with emotional meaning, a capacity to respond vicariously to the emotions of others seems to follow soon afterward."[65]

Hoffman argues that there are four levels of empathic distress, as follows: (1) Global empathy: a distress reaction is possible even before infants have a clear sense that they and other people are distinct entities, with the result that they may "at times react as though what happened to the other happened to themselves."[66] (2) "Egocentric" empathy: children by this stage have a clear sense of personal identity, but they still cannot appreciate the existence of distinctive inner states—as evidenced by their assumption that what they find comforting at a time of distress will also be so regarded by others. (3) Empathy for another's feelings: children gradually become more responsive to cues about what others are feeling and better able to understand and share complex and even ambivalent emotions. (4) Empathy for another's life condition: a more sophisticated grasp of someone else's experience permits a fuller capacity to respond to that person's general condition (rather than only to his immediate situation), and also to respond to the plight of an entire class of people.

Other researchers have found that children do, indeed, progress "from early 'involuntary' empathic distress to differentiated discriminations and expressions" as Hoffman proposes.[67] This progression—particularly from the second to the third stage—is largely a function of the growing ability to take the perspective of others. In one study, children of different ages heard a sad story after having been instructed to "try to become as sad as possible because of what you hear." Fourth graders typically tried to imagine themselves in the place of the story characters, while younger children just concentrated on distressing events that were unrelated.[68] Given the early ability to share in others' affects, it is cognitive sophistication, and perspective taking in particular, that seems to be the key developmental variable in understanding the course of empathy as a child matures.

Paradoxically, the most sophisticated version of affective connection, including the ability to imagine how someone *would* be feeling if she understood her predicament, presupposes the ability to distance oneself from the other. One can thus respond "at least partly in terms of one's representation of the other's general condition and type of affective experience beyond the situation," according to Hoffman.[69] Yet this capacity must be monitored—although Hoffman does not mention this—lest one float off beyond the relationship with a concrete other and make present, as Buber says, only a "detached content" rather than a living subject. There is a real danger that one's cognitive and imaginative capacities will become so sophisticated that one has ceased sharing the experiences of real people.

Individual Differences in Empathy

If behaviors such as helping, sharing with, and caring for others are more pervasive than many of us assume—and no less "natural" than antisocial actions—the same may be said of empathy. Kohut believed the capacity to empathize is part of "the innate equipment of the human psyche."[70] While empathy permits us to experience vicariously the unique affect of a particular person, the broader capacity to do so is, said Kohut, "the resonance of essential human alikeness"[71]—a description that appears to echo Sullivan's famous comment that "everyone is much more simply human than otherwise."[72]

Hoffman, too, has described empathy as universal, overdetermined, and self-reinforcing,[73] while another writer speculates that "there are no emotions of other human beings that are not in principle matchable by every human being, and therefore none that are not in principle accessible."[74] But this idea is hardly new; nearly two and a half centuries ago David Hume offered this observation:

Wherever we go, whatever we reflect on or converse about, every thing still presents us with the view of human happiness or misery, and excites in our breast a sympathetic movement of pleasure or uneasiness. . . . One may venture to affirm, that there is no human creature, to whom the appearance of happiness (where envy or revenge has no place), does not give pleasure; that of misery, uneasiness. This seems inseparable from our make and constitution.[75]

The "natural benevolence" that Hume attributed to our species is a function of precisely this capacity for what is today generally called empathy.

This does not mean that every person is equally empathic or that empathy is unavoidable. It is possible for such tendencies to be squelched early in life, and for most people to choose at any given instant to override an inclination to feel someone else's pain. Most of us have a degree of voluntary control over the extent to which we feel into or with others. We are not inevitably empathic any more than we are inevitably hostile. But because the presence of hostile, violent, and selfish inclinations has received more attention than the fact that empathy, too, is in our repertoire, I linger here on the latter fact.

The topic of individual differences in empathy raises the question of how the phenomenon is to be measured, and this has surely proved to be a vexing challenge for students of the subject. Attempts to operationalize and quantify the extent—or, indeed, even to confirm the presence—of empathy in a given subject has led to the sort of frustration with which many researchers can empathize. Studies have used facial, verbal, questionnaire, and physiological measures—depending on the age of the subjects and the inclination of the researcher. Certain measures seem to minimize the danger of confounding empathy with the desire to meet social expectations or internalized norms: if one seeks to present oneself as empathic, it is easier to check off a certain answer on a piece of paper than it is to control one's facial expression, and easier to control one's face than one's heart rate. But the putatively "truer" measures are also the least sensitive to qualitative differences in, and cognitive mediation of, empathic response. The most developmentally sophisticated version of empathy—relying on perspective taking and amounting to something more than mere affect matching—is multidimensional, posing problems for anyone who wants access to it. Given that each way of measuring has distinctive disadvantages,[76] one is tempted to say simply that none can be relied on exclusively. But it is not at all clear that "putting several poor measures together in one study is better than using one poor measure alone."[77] The difficulties surrounding measurement and definition should be kept in mind while reading any discussion, including this one, that draws on research findings about empathy.

Whatever measure we use, it is clear that people respond with degrees of empathy that vary, as prosocial behavior does, according to the situation, an individual's state of mind, and enduring traits.[78] Like adults, children show marked differences in their empathic responses.[79] Some people seem to feel others' distress more intensely than their own, a fact more clearly understood by novelists than by psychologists. For example, Milan Kundera wrote: "Not even one's own pain weighs so heavy as the pain one feels with someone, for someone, a pain intensified by the imagination and prolonged by a hundred echoes."[80] (Camus, too, remarked that often "we cannot bear to see offenses done to others which we ourselves have accepted without rebelling.")[81] On the other hand, people with a history of antisocial behavior sometimes become *more* aggressive when they have evidence that their actions are causing others pain.[82]

One provocative framework for understanding these differences in dispositional empathy was proposed in an altogether different context by Ernest Hartmann, a psychiatrist. Our selves are bounded, he said, but the thickness of the boundaries varies significantly from one person to the next. At the "thick" end of the continuum we find people who are well defended and even obsessive, who have little spontaneous tendency toward fellow feeling; such individuals may also tend to objectivize and dismiss others. At the "thin" end are people characterized by gullibility, suggestibility, and sensitivity (in both senses of the word: fragility and responsiveness). They evince a greater vulnerability to psychological disturbance, and, if there is any talent present, more artistic creativity. This extremely useful theoretical framework, which I have embellished a bit, was developed as a result of Hartmann's work with nightmare sufferers.[83] I am proposing that it may help to sort out individual differences with respect to empathy—thin-boundaried people being, of course, more "naturally" empathic.* (Thicker sorts may have to work harder to achieve

---

*They may also, as Ervin Staub points out, feel more threatened and therefore more egocentric.

the same level of fellow feeling.) This suggests a series of testable hypotheses about the various personality and behavior patterns that might well be correlated with dispositional empathy.

Clearly, any number of situational factors and transitory moods can also promote or discourage empathic response. Let us return to that crowded theater where people are inadvertently blocking each other. As someone sits and waits for the film to start, she notices that a couple walking down the aisle are desperately scanning the rows, hoping to find two seats together before the lights go down. What is it that determines how the comfortably seated observer reacts—whether she vicariously shares their distress, feels smug about having arrived early enough to have her pick of seats, or remains indifferent to their plight? Many of the same variables discussed in the preceding chapter, including mood and focus of attention, are relevant here. It also might be useful to know whether she herself has recently been in their situation. Empathy is at least as dependent on the relationship between the two individuals as is prosocial behavior. Someone may be more inclined to empathize with a person who is perceived as similar to herself,[84] or who does not, for one reason or another, "touch either upon her unconscious conflicts or on areas of developmental deprivation and disappointment."[85] The implication here is that there would be no reason to expect an individual to exhibit a consistent level of empathy with everyone she meets.[86]

Several potential obstacles to feeling into someone else's condition are worth mentioning. Someone who is uncomfortable with her own emotionality probably will not be particularly responsive to another's. Someone who is anxiously monitoring her own internal state or behavior will be similarly handicapped—"I cannot listen to my child with empathy if I am inwardly preoccupied with being a good mother"[87]—and so will the person who is more interested in analyzing the other than in imagining and resonating to that person's feelings. This recalls my earlier distinction between seeing and seeing through; Buber, too, decried the "analytical, reductive, and deriving look between man and man."[88]

The person whose own needs seem more pressing than those of the other is also relatively unlikely to attend fully to that other person.[89] And demands placed on oneself by others can seem to drain one of the energy that empathy requires. A mother once described this to me quite pointedly: After a long day of "emotional focus" on her toddler, she felt unable to take anyone else's point of view. "It's something beyond fatigue," she said. "Some evenings I don't even have ears."

Gender Differences

At least in our culture, the features making up the "thin boundary" pattern are more commonly associated with women than men, and women also are perceived as being more concerned with the dynamics of personal relationships. Thus arises the question of whether hard evidence exists to support the idea of gender differences in empathy.

Nancy Chodorow's influential analysis of gender suggests that when the mother is the primary caretaker, girls should emerge from early childhood

with a basis for "empathy" built into their primary definition of self in a way that boys do not . . . [that is,] with a stronger basis for experiencing another's needs or feelings as one's own (or of thinking that one is so experiencing another's needs and feelings). . . . Girls come to experience themselves as less differentiated than boys, as more continuous with and related to the external object-world.[90]

Two points here are noteworthy. First, the description contained in the last sentence, which bears a certain similarity to the idea of thin boundaries, raises the possibility that the kind of empathy allegedly more natural for girls is distinguished by less differentiation between self and others than Hoffman and others contend is desirable. (If this is so, then we would seem to have the ingredients for a recapitulation of Carol Gilligan's critique of traditional stage theories of moral development.)[91] Second, the parenthetical qualification—that girls may simply *think* that they are more receptive to others' experiences—should be kept in mind as one reviews the experimental data.

On certain issues related to empathy, evidence for a gender difference—presumably a socialized one—seems fairly solid. Although sex differences usually do not appear in studies of children's perspective-taking ability,[92] a review of seventy-five studies showed that females do appear better able than males to judge the meanings of nonverbal cues of emotion; the difference is reliable, though not terribly large (about .40 of a standard deviation).[93] Also, "Boys are more motivated than girls to deny and mask negative emotions"[94]—a fact with possible implications for males' general discomfort with affective response as well as for the difficulty of responding empathically *to* males. (The latter is rarely considered in the literature, incidentally.)

Several studies with children have suggested that empathy may have different meanings and consequences for males and females. In boys, empathy has been shown to correlate with cognitive skills; in girls, with positive self-concept and prosocial behavior,[95] and, in another study, with general intensity of response.[96] As to whether girls and women display more empathy overall, several studies suggest that the answer is yes, although the difference is not always remarkable.[97] In 1977, Hoffman reviewed nine studies with sixteen samples and found that girls were more empathic in all of them—although the difference was not statistically significant in ten of the samples.[98]

Six years later, with Nancy Eisenberg and Randy Lennon's publication of a far more detailed review of more than 120 empathy studies conducted with children and adults, a different picture took shape. The existence or nonexistence of gender differences, they concluded, depends on how the concept is measured. If empathy is tested by asking people to rate themselves, then females are more empathic. But if physiological change or facial expression is taken as an indication of empathic response, the gender differences virtually melt away. Given that

emotionality and nurturance are both part of the stereotypic feminine role . . . it is highly likely that females would be more willing to present themselves as being empathic and/or sympathetic, even if there were no real sex difference in responsiveness. . . . The limited empirical research, at this time, provides little basis for the conclusion that the sex difference in empathy found for self-report measures is due to an innate mechanism or predisposition.[99]

(In the case of one type of measure used with young children, in fact, it seems that gender differences favoring girls appear only when the *experimenter* is female.)[100] When they returned to the topic several years later, having reviewed more recent studies, the authors found much the same thing: "gender differences in empathy may be an artifact of the method of measurement."[101]

From Feeling to Helping

While there may be disagreement over its development, measurement, and other particulars, there is a general consensus that empathy itself is a good thing—both intrinsically and in terms of its empirical relation to other desired states of being, such as mental health.[102] The absence (or at least malfunction) of empathy is also widely seen as a factor in sociopathy and delinquency,[103] although not all commentators have carefully distinguished between empathy and what I am here calling perspective taking. A widely cited study in the late 1960s found that empathy and aggression were inversely related in six- and seven-year-old boys,[104] while a 1988 meta-analysis based on several dozen studies found "modest but not entirely consistent support for the notion that empathic responsiveness may be an inhibitor of aggression."[105]

That a tendency to feel others' joy or pain may be associated with lower aggression does not mean that this tendency necessarily will translate into helping behavior. Casual observers have sometimes blurred the distinction between prosocial actions and empathy, even going so far as to use a single word like *altruism* to stand for cognitive, affective, and behavioral responses, as well as both state and trait characteristics, and both self- and other-oriented motivations. While it may seem intuitively plausible that empathizing and helping would go hand in hand—and indeed it has been argued that empathy evolved precisely to assure the preservation of helping behavior[106]—the relation has actually proved as complex as any other reviewed here. There are a number of complicating factors.

Type of Measure   Eisenberg and a colleague undertook a comprehensive review of studies on the subject and found, as they did with the question of gender differences, that correlations depended on how empathy was measured. To oversimplify a bit, empathy as reflected in picture/story tests was not related to prosocial behavior, while empathy as measured in other ways (such as by questionnaire) did turn out to be related.[107]

Age   "It appears that the association between empathy and prosocial behavior is somewhat weaker for children than for adults."[108]

Kind of Affect   Empathy with negative feelings, such as sadness, is more likely to predict to prosocial behavior than is empathy with joy.[109]

Extent of Arousal   Extreme empathic distress can be so unpleasant that "it may at times direct the attention of observers to themselves and thus actually decrease the likelihood of an altruistic act."[110]

Self- versus Other-Orientation   I noted above that a sympathetic/empathic response can be distinguished empirically from mere personal distress. The former, which is oriented to the other's condition, does tend to promote helping behaviors that are genuinely altruistic.[111] Moreover, recall from chapter 3 that children who were asked to describe unpleasant experiences suffered by someone else were subsequently more generous in sharing tokens than those asked to talk about something that had happened to themselves.

Cause of Plight   Hoffman has observed, reasonably enough, that one's actions and attitudes are dependent in part on what one takes to be the source of the other's suffering. If one concludes that no one is to blame, the response may be empathy, sympathy, and help. If one feels personally responsible, the result may be feelings of guilt and then attempts to make reparation. If one holds the victim himself accountable, empathy may be replaced by indifference or even hostility.* Finally, if someone else is believed to have caused the distress, the response may be moral anger directed at that third person. Rather than being experienced as the flip side of empathy, this last response may, as Piaget suggests, take the form of " 'vindictive joy' at seeing any sort of pain inflicted upon the author of other people's sufferings"—a self-sustaining hostility in which the original concern for the victim is forgotten.[113]

Feeling of Responsibility   There is some preliminary evidence that empathic response is more likely to lead to prosocial behavior when the responder also has a sense of personal responsibility for helping. Children in one study were given a projective test in which they were asked to describe how a story character was feeling about someone else's distress. The subjects who attributed something resembling empathy, prosocial behavior, or guilt to the character later proved more likely to come to someone else's aid themselves. The strongest predictor of helping, interestingly, was the attribution of guilt, which is to say, feeling a sense of responsibility for the person in need. The researchers concluded from this that "it may not be merely a tendency to feel the same affects as the other person (in the sense of 'trait empathy') that motivates helping, but a disposition to feel a responsibility toward the other person's well-being"[114]—a finding that corroborates what the Oliners found in their study of rescuers.[115]

While there is a cognitive dimension to the sense of responsibility, it is not the same as—though it may be empirically related to—perspective taking, another nonaffective response. To believe that one *ought* to

---

*Some people are inclined, as Melvin Lerner and Zick Rubin have shown, to believe that innocent victims (whom they personally cannot help) must have done something to deserve their fate. To the extent that this assumption is encouraged in a given society, as it may be in ours,[112] we would expect prosocial behavior to decline.

help is different from taking someone else's point of view. It should also be distinguished from a moral imperative based solely on abstract principles since the latter does not include an affective dimension such as guilt and since the sense of responsibility may be limited to a given individual with whom there is a personal connection.

Despite all of these qualifications about the empathy-prosocial nexus, people who empathize spontaneously as well as those who are specifically encouraged to focus on another's distress[116] are reasonably likely, all else being equal, to act on their feelings and do something in behalf of a victim. (If one responds empathically to a victim's or group's long-term plight rather than just to an immediate situation, then one may well be inclined to engage in sustained action to improve that plight— what Hoffman calls prosocial activism.)[117] We cannot know for sure that just because someone feels empathy while engaged in prosocial behavior, he must have helped *because* of the empathic reaction,[118] but it would seem reasonable to infer a relation unless there is some reason to believe otherwise.

The sometimes modest correlations between empathy and helping behavior actually may be misleading. This is true for various methodological reasons,[119] but also because a good deal of prosocial behavior occurs without the actor's having felt any empathic connection to the victim. Some people help because of internalized moral values and principles, much like Samuel Johnson, who was said to have remarked: "I have not so much feeling for the distress of others as some people have or pretend to have; but I know this, that I would do all in my power to relieve them."[120] Empathy may lead to helping, then, but helping does not imply empathy.* Whether perspective taking in itself inclines one to help is the topic of the next section.

IMAGINING WITHOUT FEELING

To ask whether understanding the other's point of view might nudge one into prosocial action is, more broadly, to explore what it means to imag-

---

*Another possibility is that prosocial behavior can cause empathy. Experience with helping others (for nonempathic reasons) might help to create an empathic connection that could, in turn, encourage further prosocial behavior. (The only empirical support for this possibility that I know of is a small study of female undergraduates in which it was found that those women who tutored inner-city children for ten weeks increased their empathy scores on a personality test.)[121]

ine the other's reality without also feeling it, to inquire whether the former offers us anything of value without the latter. (In the next section, the question is put the other way around.)

I have already mentioned that sociopathy has been described by some as betokening a failure to take others' points of view. The possibility that perspective taking may be conducive to helping, caring, and sharing also has been explored by several writers. The "capacity to put oneself in another person's shoes is behind most altruistic behavior," the philosopher Thomas Nagel asserts.[122] Several studies with children have indeed indicated that children with high scores on measures of perspective taking, as well as those who are specially trained in perspective taking for experimental purposes, tend to engage in prosocial behavior more frequently than their peers.[123] In fact, some investigators have argued that perspective taking is even more reliable than empathy as a predictor of helping behavior.[124] By way of explanation, the psychologist Dennis Krebs proposes that imagining the point of view of someone who needs help either can "produce a state of cognitive disequilibrium, which may be resolved by helping" or can "stimulate a sense of moral responsibility."[125]

Not all of the research has been quite so unequivocal,[126] but then not all of the research is concerned with the same sort of perspective taking (spatial, cognitive, affective) or the same measures of prosocial behavior (emergency rescuing, casual helping, sharing, and so on). Some researchers have found that children who are skilled at perspective taking are rated by their teachers as *less* altruistic or more disruptive than their peers,[127] but this may say as much about the teachers as about the children—and specifically about the fact that children who are popular with their peers and inclined to collaborate with them, as perspective takers tend to be, engage in behavior that has been ruled illegitimate in most American classrooms. (Typically, children are made to work alone or to compete against each other or both.)

On the other hand, if perspective taking is construed as just a means of gathering information about others, then it behooves us to ask why understanding would be expected to predispose one to care or help. It may be that perspective taking produces an empathic response that, in turn, leads to prosocial behavior. If the only connection is by way of empathy, then there is no reason perspective taking alone should have the same effect. Any number of writers have made the point that while the presence of perspective taking often facilitates moral, altruistic, or prosocial behaviors, it is not an element of all such behaviors, and neither does it guarantee that one will act ethically or prosocially. Perspective taking, in other words, is neither necessary nor sufficient for morality.[128] It is possible to understand the other's plight but remain literally unaffected.

One of the most persuasive (and depressing) pieces of evidence in support of this phenomenon is the fact that when the leading researchers, such as Flavell and Selman, set out to gauge a child's skill at perspective taking, they often do so in the context of a competitive task. These provide measures of recursive thinking employed in the service of deviousness and hinge on implicit questions such as: If you are trying to outsmart an opponent at a game, can you figure out that he is expecting you to make a certain move (and that he expects you to expect him to make it), and devise a strategy in light of this?[129] Clearly this is a far cry from the prosocial realm.

In fact, the jump from competition to altruism is a lot longer than that from competition to cruelty or outright sociopathy. If one can adopt the other's point of view for purposes of triumphing over him in a contest, one can surely do so for purposes of cold-blooded manipulation or sadism. Again, this has been noted repeatedly in the literature. "To victimize requires as much role taking skill as to empathize," said one psychologist.[130] Similarly, the philosopher Bernard Williams has observed that "the insightful understanding of others' feelings possessed by the sympathetic person is possessed in much the same form by the sadistic or cruel person; that is one way in which the cruel are distinguished from the brutal or indifferent."[131]

It seems undeniable that competitors, con artists, and barbarians can place perspective taking in the service of less than inspiring goals. But the writers who have stressed this point generally have not attempted to demonstrate the irrelevance (or diabolical possibilities) of imagining how someone else thinks or feels *at the time that person is in need.* Even though this skill can be exported to other realms, it may inherently be an impetus to praiseworthy action in a situation that seems to call for such action. Sociopaths excepted, and keeping all else constant, I would argue that a victim is more likely to be helped or comforted by someone who imagines what he is going through, how the world looks from his point of view, than by someone who does not. At the very least, one is less likely to be hurt by a perspective taker, as Feshbach points out:

The ability to identify emotion in other people, and especially the ability to see situations from the perspective of another person[,] can be expected to lead to greater social understanding. A child with such ability who wants to play with an attractive toy is less likely to react aggressively to the attempts of the peer to play with the desired toy than a child who lacks this understanding.[132]

The greater likelihood of helping (or not hurting), I would further contend, is a consequence of the perspective taking itself rather than of some other characteristic that is merely correlated with it. It may be that the people we would describe as prosocially oriented are also more likely to engage in perspective taking for other reasons, and that over the course of their lives they are more likely than others to use this skill in prosocial ways, but the act of perspective taking is not neutral. To consider the effect of one's action on someone else is already to be more inclined to help than to hurt.

The probability that helping actually will take place is further increased, however, when an affective dimension is added to the act of imagining. One strains to make sense of the proposition that someone could both understand and feel how the other feels yet remain indifferent or hostile to her. This borders on the inconceivable, the nonsensical. If my mind captures your world and my heart vibrates with its emotional impact, then I am on your side. If I can respond to your reality both cognitively and affectively, very little has been left to chance. In a word, empathy helps.

FEELING WITHOUT IMAGINING

The mirror image of Flavell's "nonempathic inference" is what he calls "noninferential empathy": feeling someone else's feelings without any mental representation of them.[133] The point here is that there are different routes to empathy, only one of which is marked "perspective taking." Hoffman notes that empathic arousal also can be due to an innate releasing mechanism (such as seems to be found in crying newborns), simple mimicry, or any of several patterns of conditioning and learned association.[134] In order to match someone else's affect it is not always necessary to use the imagination; one can simply use the eyes and ears to pick up on obvious cues or the memory to recall information about the other's past behavior. Few students of the field today would agree with Mead's flat declaration that empathy (which he called "sympathy") "always implies . . . taking in some degree the attitude of the person whom one is assisting."[135]

Nevertheless, perspective taking can add force to the empathic response[136] and permit that response to be more flexible and sophisticated. The very use of the conditional case—thinking in terms of what the other *would be* feeling (under specified circumstances)—presupposes that some imagining is taking place. Without perspective taking there can be "feeling with" but no authentic "feeling into." My point is not that there is something illegitimate about what Daniel Stern calls "affect attunement," but only that, because it occurs "largely out of awareness and almost automatically," it must be distinguished from a fuller version of empathy, which "involves the mediation of cognitive processes."[137] As Robert Selman has pointed out, a puppy will come up and lick someone who is crying, but this does not empathy make.[138] Likewise for "motor mimicry," in which we wince or recoil while watching someone else be subjected to sudden pain.[139] These involuntary or preverbal responses may represent the raw material of empathy—or primitive precursors to it, developmentally speaking—but no more than this.

Now when *empathic* is used in a much broader sense to include supportiveness, we have no trouble identifying people whose responses ring false. There are those who listen attentively, but mostly because they are on the lookout for something that could be threatening (or useful) to themselves. There are those who force a crude and unwelcome consolation on a victim (say, someone suffering from the death of a loved one) rather than being responsive to the other's needs. There are those who assure the sufferer that they "know just how you feel" when in reality they could not have the foggiest idea. And there are those who adopt a plastic therapeutic demeanor, self-consciously using techniques such as reflective listening rather than inviting genuine connection.[140]

But even if we are concerned with empathy proper, and with sincere efforts to engage in it, we must still be alive to the possibility of "pseudo-empathy," which inheres in every expression of vicarious emotion in which perspective taking plays no part. This is rather a stronger claim than the contention that perspective taking merely adds an element of cognitive sophistication to empathy. Without imagining the reality of the other, empathic feeling is ultimately self-oriented and thus unworthy of the name. The enterprise is reduced to an expression of affect whose reference point is one's own memories or emotional state. If, in place of imagining the real, an individual relies on the situation in which the other happens to be, then her emotional response will reflect little more than the way she herself would respond to being in that situation.[141] Alternatively, if she relies on obvious cues of the other's affect, then there is nothing else at work but an automatic matching of emotion. Either way, she is responding to herself.

This distinction is directly relevant to the practice of experimentally inducing empathic reactions. In a technique now used with some regularity, Ezra Stotland set up three conditions for his subjects. All of them watched someone else whose hand was strapped to a machine that they were told generated painful heat. Some were told just to watch the man carefully, some were told to imagine the way he was feeling, and some were told to imagine themselves in his place. There were two physiological measures of empathy: constriction of blood vessels and sweating of palms. The first showed a greater reaction on the part of those in the "imagine-him" condition; the second was higher for those in the "imagine-self" condition. Taken together with some other unexpected or only marginally significant differences among conditions, Stotland's results can be read only as showing that some kind of deliberate act of the imagination produces a response greater than just watching.[142] (The experimental design itself was enormously important by virtue of emphasizing that imagining the other is distinct from, and a realistic alternative to, imagining oneself in the other's shoes, as Scheler and Smith saw.)

Some writers have assumed that the imagine-self condition necessarily produces a more intense affective response than the imagine-him condition. I am not prepared to concede this,* but even if it were true, it should be kept in mind that intensity is not the only criterion for empathy. The issue is not just how weepy I become upon learning that your spouse has died; it is also whether I am merely recalling and reacting to a comparable loss in my own life or whether I am resonating to your unique set of circumstances—the suddenness of the death, the particular features of this person you loved that are especially vivid for you, your rocky marital history and the resultant prickles of guilt you are now feeling, the way your initial numbness is finally giving way to real pain, the respects in which your unconscious fears of being abandoned are about to be freshly revived by this event, the relationship that you and I have had up until now, and so on. Some of these particulars I simply remember, but most take on real meaning—and, more to the point, real relevance to your emotional life—only if I take your perspective, if I think as well as feel. Only then can one, as Buber said, not feel "a general

---

*I have already described two studies, one with adults and one with children, suggesting that prosocial behavior is enhanced by focusing on the other rather than on one's own pain or one's perspective on the other's pain (p. 74).

discomfort or state of suffering, but this particular pain as the pain of the other."[143]

Projection is one variant of pseudoempathy that deserves special attention. This is a classic defense mechanism, defined as the process of unconsciously attributing something about oneself to another person because it would be too painful to acknowledge ownership of that feeling; thus, someone who cannot bear to admit his own aggressive impulses may believe that it is everyone else who is hostile toward him. In empathy, one is responding to someone else's affect, while in projection the arrow is reversed and one "discovers" in the other what is really part of oneself. The processes are so different that one might reasonably say projection has nothing whatever to do with empathy,[144] yet in practice the two can easily be confused. People may purport to respond to another's distress when in fact the distress they are responding to is their own. The self-absorbed individual may appear for all the world to feel others' pain even though she really uses others as screens on which her own pain is projected. (The manifestation of this phenomenon in families, particularly in pathological identifications between mother and daughter, has been addressed by several writers.)[145]

Considering the different ways in which people can match another's feeling without really responding to that other—feeling with but not feeling for—calls to mind the classic definition of *knowledge* once used by epistemologists: justified true belief. The first modifier is the pertinent one here. One may for no good reason believe something to be true, and one may accidentally be correct, but one cannot thereby be said to "know" it. This is analogous to what is missing in empathy (or pseudoempathy) without perspective taking: one feels without any justification for the feeling, without any sense of what the feeling means for the other.

Imagining how one would feel—or actually has felt—in the other's situation is not without its uses, of course. It is one source of information about the other's likely reaction, providing that it is taken as no more than a provisional indication. Perhaps some sort of oscillation between imagine-self and imagine-him can be helpful. But what often seems to happen is that genuine, other-oriented empathy gives way after a moment to dwelling on one's own experiences. One starts by feeling *her* joy, but this calls up a memory of the last time something unexpected and delightful happened to oneself, and soon the other's reality has slid away. Hoffman calls this "egoistic drift,"[146] and the impact is that one's capacity for empathy is a function not only of whether one can respond to others but whether one can *continue* responding to others, persisting in the other-orientation.

One distinction that is rarely made in discussions on this topic is the extent to which the experience that provoked the other's affective response is universal. Let us assume that Stotland's subjects had responded much more strongly in the imagine-self condition than in the imagine-him condition. The fact is that, aside from quantitative differences in sensitivity, just about anyone would react in the same way to having his hand burned. Our experiences are interchangeable and I might as well put myself in your situation as imagine your reaction. Thus we need another criterion by which to judge the capacity for mature empathy: how well one can empathize with the other when his situation is outside of one's own experience.[147] Here the imagination is the sine qua non of empathy. As a man, I have to work hard even to approximate a genuinely empathic response to a woman who has just given birth. I may know what pain is, but I have never known this sort of pain (or exhaustion). Still, as Scheler emphasized, this does not mean that empathy must be confined to what we have personally experienced:

We can have a lively and immediate participation in joy or sorrow, can share with others their appreciation of value, and can even enter into another person's commiseration for a third party, without ever having sampled that particular quality of experience before.[148]

Imagine a continuum: on one side are universal experiences, where imagine-self will do (burning hand); on the other side are things one has not personally experienced, where imagine-him is obviously required (giving birth). The first thing to be said here is that the interesting cases are in the middle (death of spouse). One can get away with treating that example as a generic grief, but only at considerable cost to the integrity of the empathic response. Second, if one's capacity to empathize cannot be enhanced by developing perspective-taking skill, then at least one can try to broaden the range of one's experiences. The more frequently one can say, "I've been there," the higher the probability of managing something close to an empathic connection—at least of the imagine-self variety.

The vision of empathy offered here is one that might be said to flow from an existentialist rather than an essentialist understanding of human life, in the sense that Sartre had in mind when he said that existence precedes essence. When we talk about the feeling of joy, this is understood as something that the self feels, not as the instantiation of a larger, prior category of Joy. Philip's happiness is an attribute of Philip, and it cannot properly be understood outside of Philip's unique set of circumstances. Just as the phenomenologists told us that consciousness is always consciousness *of* something, so any affect must always be seen as *someone's* affect. Only if we begin to construe it more abstractly, presuming to speak platonically of Joy, does it appear possible to dispense with perspective taking. Naturally it is possible (and practically very useful) to abstract *from* Philip's concrete experience of joy and Nora's experience of joy and Craig's experience of joy to try to find the common denominator. But it is important to remember that "joy," per se, is an abstraction derived from these particular experiences and others like them. It is no more real than the number three, a concept that is based on our experience with three french fries, three flashlights, three ferrets, and so forth.

Feelings are particular to the person who feels them, and empathy, properly understood, is a way of taking account of that fact. But it is also a way for one person to acknowledge that the feeling of the other is saturated in his otherness. This has been implicit in the foregoing discussion: the topic here is not pain but *her* pain, and from my perspective the fact that it cannot be reduced to my pain is highly significant. There is no I-Thou relationship unless there is a Thou, said Buber, unless there is an "affirmation of the primally deep otherness of the other," unless I keep in mind that my partner in a dialogue is "different, essentially different from myself, in the definite, unique way which is peculiar to him, and I accept whom I thus see, so that in full earnestness I can direct what I say to him as the person he is."[149]

This has been the larger point of this chapter: perspective taking and empathy allow us to appreciate that you are not me and that we can be connected in spite of that. Cognitively and affectively, we can construct that bridge across the abyss and see how the unique other thinks and feels and makes a world. This is a source of wonder and inspiration, further evidence of what we humans are and what we can be.

5

The Self
with the Other

*The adolescent who insists upon a critical reexamination of
conventional wisdom is making himself into an adult. And the
adult whose concerns extend beyond family and beyond nation to
mankind has become fully human.*
—Leon Eisenberg (1972)

Part of what makes a lover exciting, a friend fulfilling, an author challenging, a dinner companion entertaining is the fact that their experiences are different from yours. There are as many ways of acting and reacting, construing and constructing, as there are people, and it is the irreducible otherness of these people's ways that we find intriguing—or, on other occasions, unnerving, perplexing, appalling. Perspective taking and empathy remind us of the general fact of multiplicity even while helping us to imagine what it must be like to be this particular other, the one sitting right over there, this person whom above all I am not.

But, then again, maybe not above all. Often unexpected similarities—shared idiosyncrasies and opinions—in the lives of two strangers stand out against a background of differences. And, just as important, figure and ground can be reversed: the differences can be appreciated in light of the fact that this person whom I am not is first of all *also a person*. It is this that allows us to bridge the gap, to feel into and imagine. Were we fundamentally dissimilar, we could scarcely apprehend the other's experience, let alone translate it into our own dialect. Buber reminded us that without distance there is no relationship, but it is also true that without shared humanness, there is no overcoming the distance.

That you and I belong to the same species is a reality to be savored. The word *humanization* sounds contrived, but the reality to which it refers is important to acknowledge lest we assume that the only alternative to dehumanizing is doing nothing at all. We would do well, once again, to imagine a continuum here. At the zero point is the absence of any thought or feeling regarding this issue. The line extending to the left represents increasing degrees of dehumanization; to the right, the growing appreciation for the other's humanity. Let us begin with a closer look at the negative—the various ways by which we sometimes regard our fellows as less than human.

THE HUMANITY OF HUMANS

Dehumanization

Before it flaked off into New Age supernaturalism, humanistic psychology offered a thoughtful critique of the discipline. It drew from existentialism and writings in the Eastern traditions, from the vigorous revisionism of the neo-Freudians and the growing discomfort of various heterodox personality theorists and researchers. Its mission was nothing less than the rescue of the human being from the rigid, positivistic science of behaviorism and from the dark, instinctivist determinism of psychoanalysis. Something of our potential is overlooked, the humanists argued, our three dimensions flattened into two, by these traditions and also by the uncritical and excessive reliance on natural science methods to study people. To experiment on subjects with the same essential methodology used to investigate microbes and quarks, to turn intangibles such as love or creativity or anguish over mortality into quantifiable variables, is to achieve precision at the cost of reducing us, fragmenting us, boiling us down. To see the person primarily as a mobile information processor or a clever rodent with vocal cords (man-as-computer, man-as-rat) is not only to create an inadequate theory but also to do violence to the reality of human life. With the best of intentions and credentials, theorists and researchers were said to have drained the humanness from the humans whose behavior and motivation they presumed to study.

To be sure, this precis collapses a varied set of critiques into a few phrases. The reason I include it here is that this line of criticism effectively charged Ph.D.'s with an insidious form of dehumanization. The implication is that our humanity is at risk not only because of the attitudes taken by individuals but also because of institutional forces. Of course, academic psychology represents only one of these forces, and hardly the most prominent of them. One thinks immediately of Marx's critique of the dehumanizing impact of capitalism, a critique that he did not confine to his early philosophic manuscripts. The methodical dry prose of *Capital*, too, suddenly erupts into a passionate indictment of a system in which those with power exploit those without it: "They mutilate the laborer into a fragment of a man, degrade him to the level of an appendage of a machine, . . . transform his life-time into working-time, and drag his wife and child beneath the wheels of the Juggernaut of capital."[1] Any number of social critics have called our attention to the effects of mind-numbing labor, chilly bureaucratic organization, the identification of each individual with a highly specialized task, and the society's relentless pursuit of technological efficiency. These interlocking phenomena have been decried by an assortment of critics for squeezing the juice out of human beings.

We do much the same thing on a smaller scale when we reduce someone to a label, an abstraction, or a single feature. When a man judges a woman solely on the basis of her appearance, he is engaging in an act that is not merely sexist but dehumanizing, one analogous to the identification of someone solely on the basis of, say, mathematical ability. These handles ("the math genius," "the one with the great body") are convenient and can even come to be accepted by the one so labeled: it is better for one's self to be identified with a single characteristic than not to have any identity at all. But this everyday reductionism leaves us with less than a whole and therefore less than a human—even if the descriptions themselves are intended to be flattering.

As the labels become less benign and the dehumanization more extreme, we begin to witness a cyclical relation between attitude and behavior. When we encounter people divested of dignity, destitute and desperate, we relate to them as subhuman and thus justify to ourselves turning away from, or even adding to, their misery. This is the secret of how the affluent of many cultures, cultivated and proud of their moral refinement, can accept (and profit from) the oppression of an entire class of people. Reduced by oppression to a ragged and pathetic state, deprived of opportunity to be otherwise, these people come to be seen as deserving their plight. Strip away their humanity and they seem unworthy of being treated as humans.[2]

Some people resist helping and then dehumanize the victim to justify this decision. Others—and I suspect there are more in this second group than we might imagine—are for one reason or another *unable* to help.

This creates a tension between desire and behavior that must be recon-
ciled. If a human being is suffering, I want to intervene; since I am not
intervening (or since my intervention is ineffective), I decide that this
must not be a suffering human being after all. To this extent, what we are
seeing is, paradoxically, a testament to our prosocial or empathic impulses as much as evidence of our ability to sever ties with others. It is
because our inclination to help has been frustrated that some of us
respond, in self-defense, by denying the reality before us.[3]

Philip Zimbardo saw something of this sort happening with caretak-
ers, people in the social services. "After repeated exposure [to someone in
distress], with improvement slow or not apparent, the individual feels
helpless to effect any change and views such people as emotional burdens,
to be serviced without personal involvement."[4] More dramatically, when
the Nazis began their program of genocide, many witnesses felt hopeless
and helpless to stop it. "These feelings, which encourage self-centeredness and emotional distancing from others, provide fertile soil for passiv-
ity," as the Oliners saw it.[5] In both examples, the absence of connection to
victims is simultaneously a cause and an effect of dehumanization.

This vicious cycle often rolls past mere inaction and toward acts of
outright violence. The farther one moves in the direction of stripping an
individual or group of humanity, the more license one feels to do harm;
the more violent one becomes, the more likely that one will dehumanize.
Several theorists have remarked on this self-reinforcing process,[6] and it
has been confirmed empirically by the well-known psychologist Albert
Bandura and his associates.[7]

So much is well established. But it may be that there is another
telltale sign of a dehumanizing social system, one which I offer now as
pure speculation. Perhaps when we cannot be of help, when we feel
overwhelmed by dehumanizing forces, we displace our responsiveness to
other species. Thus, the greater the diminution of a sense of shared
humanness (and, by extension, of respectful or compassionate treatment
of other people), the more fuss is made over animals. This is not to
suggest that an inverse relationship exists between a given individual's
concern for humans and for pets; the fact that Klaus Barbie was a devoted
cat owner proves nothing. But something of the sort may exist on a larger
scale. A society or historical period regularly characterized by dehumanization may be to that extent prone to a preoccupation with animals.

A television documentary was broadcast a few years ago about the
execution of a black man in Mississippi. The program permitted viewers
to come to know the man, to watch him—and the prison staff around

him—prepare for his death at the age of twenty-six. One short sequence
showed a rabbit being used to test the gas chamber in preparation for
killing the man. After the first airing of the documentary, the prison
warden said he received a great deal of critical mail—"more of it . . . angry
about the death of the bunny rabbit than of Edward."[8] This was also the
experience of Francis Ford Coppola, director of *The Godfather*. "Thirty
people were shot in the movie, but people only talked about 'cruelty to
animals,' " he told an interviewer.[9] Anyone who has watched another
Coppola film, *Apocalypse Now,* in a crowded theater may have noticed a
collective and heartfelt moan arise from the audience during a sequence
in which a dog is thrown into a river—this, of course, in the context of
wide-scale, savage human bloodletting that causes no one to miss a beat
of popcorn chomping.

Is it precisely the scale of violence in the films that inures us to it,
calls up a wall of defenses against it—a wall with a hole just big enough
for a puppy to wriggle through? This is very likely the case, and my point
is that something very similar may happen on a wider scale in real life.
Humans are treated as less than human, so animals are treated as more
than animals. That we concern ourselves about the fate of stray cats or
incarcerated calves is, all things being equal, a simple and commendable
expression of our noble impulse to help the helpless. But all things are
not equal: people go hungry while we lavish care on pets. Moreover, this
attention to the needs of animals is not merely one more luxury item to
be contrasted with widespread human misery. It is a deliberate, morally
informed attention, and as such the intriguing possibility is raised that it
is precisely a reaction *to* that human misery.*

Rehumanization

If we are talking about the dehumanization that results from political and
economic forces, then it would seem to follow that these forces will have

*I have heard several people explain their affection for animals on the basis of the
latter's "innocence." Since most of us tend to think of ourselves this way, too, it may be
that sympathizing with animals is an unconscious statement about the way we feel our own
innocence has been badly used, or how we should like to be treated. But if innocence
accounts for our compassion for the four-legged, this is revealing about our view of the
two-legged (excluding ourselves): Have we bought into the doctrine that our species is
fallen or corrupted? Do we regard a human as less worthy of sympathy because she "asked"
for what has befallen her, because she is culpable for her suffering? The corollaries of what
Marx might have called animal fetishism disclose attitudes about humans that some will find
disturbing on reflection.

to be addressed if we are to rehumanize ourselves. The principles to guide any such structural changes are also applicable to altering individual interactions. One way or another, all of them deal with ways of making another person's humanness as difficult as possible to avoid.

"Studies of aggression have yielded at least one clear generalization: an awareness of our own and of others' humanity lessens the likelihood that aggression will occur."[10] The confidence in this finding impels us to try to figure out how to reach and maintain such an awareness, how to bring us together. One approach to reducing figurative distance is to reduce physical distance. Virginia Woolf may have overstated things a bit when she wrote that it is "almost impossible to dislike any one if one look[s] at them,"[11] but her point is basically sound. Unless one is skilled at objectifying others or in the grips of some malevolent passion, merely coming face to face with the other can have the effect of making her humanness sharper and more salient. More often than not, one is inclined to root for someone who is here in the flesh. Rivalry and cruelty thrive on distance because distance allows us to turn people into abstractions.

Studies by Milgram and others have shown that subjects are less likely to give severe shocks to people whom they can see, hear, and touch (p. 285n.41). The less remote the other is, the less willing we are to hurt him—precisely because it is more difficult to dehumanize someone who is palpably, undeniably human. (It is in this spirit that one psychologist proposes that arms control negotiators be required to talk to each other in the nude.)[12] The story is told of a terrorist group that took control of a train in the Netherlands in 1975 and prepared to execute a passenger as an example.

Before doing so they allowed him to dictate a final letter to his family. In that letter [the passenger] reflected on his life, dwelling on both accomplishments and shortcomings. . . . After completing the letter, his captors decided not to execute him. Instead they shot another hapless hostage without allowing him to compose a parting letter.[13]

Researchers have found that making even superficial eye contact or conversation with a stranger increases the probability that one will subsequently help that person.[14] Giving people the opportunity to communicate with each other before playing a laboratory game, meanwhile, makes it more likely that they will play cooperatively rather than just trying to maximize personal gain.[15] Mediation programs that bring thieves and their victims face to face have had the effect of leading offenders to regret their actions and victims to abandon their desire for revenge.[16] Finally, even this direct exposure to others is unnecessary for people whose capacity for empathy is most fully developed: for them, "direct personal contact . . . is not essential for building bonds of *we.*"[17]

In chapter 4, I argued that if perspective taking is to help us capture the unique reality of the other, it must be conceived as a process of imagining him, not imagining oneself in his situation. Here I want to qualify this: if the objective is to retain or recapture a sense of the other's humanness—what we share rather than how we differ—then the imagine-self strategy may do nicely. The fact that one person regards another as similar to herself will tend to facilitate empathy, but empathy and perspective taking also can promote that sense of similarity. If I reflect on how I would react in another's situation, I come to recognize that I very well could be in her situation. To realize that I would likely be overcome with despair is to realize that this is likely how she is feeling—and perhaps it also means that I will share that feeling. In any case, this process facilitates the recognition of what we have in common. Small wonder that people who are asked to imagine themselves in the other's place are less likely to blame that person for his predicament and more likely to react with compassion.[18]

The antidote to dehumanization, then, is to appreciate not only the other's distinctive point of view but also to see that other as a human subject—and to recognize that we share this attribute. This "emotional realization of the unity of mankind as a species"[19] is not a contrivance to be employed on special occasions; it is a mode of being in the world, a way of living. It emerges from the acknowledgment that one's meaning—one's own humanness—depends on affirming the subjectivity of others. Such a humanizing affirmation has the concrete consequence of reducing aggression, making life safer and more pleasant. But it is also an end in itself.

There's No "They" There

I am looking at two photographs that are sitting on my desk. The first, which I clipped out of a newspaper, is of a teenage girl. She has a charming smile and shoulder-length hair, and she is wearing a T-shirt emblazoned with the message: "Thank God for AIDS." I look at the photo for a long time, searching for clues in her face to explain this. I wonder how bigoted a pair of parents would have to be to produce someone who would pull this shirt over her head in the morning. Presumably she has never known a homosexual, or, for that matter, someone dying of an incurable disease—but something other than a simple lack of experience is at work here and I am not entirely sure I know what it is.

My eyes drift to the second photo, which immediately transfixes me just as it did the first time I saw it reproduced in a scholarly article on dehumanization.[20] It is a photo of a southern lynch mob: a crowd of white men and women in the foreground and the bodies of two black men hanging from a tree above and behind them. Eight or nine of the white people are facing the camera, several of them smiling as if they were at a picnic; one man points with his index finger so the viewer should be sure not to miss the two dead men or his own satisfaction with what has been done to them. In the lower left—and this is the area I keep returning to—stands a young couple. They are both looking at me and grinning. They seem friendly, the sort of folks I might enjoy having dinner with. She is holding her right hand behind her back and he is grasping her thumb affectionately.

How can this be? I am asked to accept not only that A can kill B, not only that C, D, and E can watch while this happens, but that C can hold onto D's thumb. This pushes my imagination to its limits. How can these people be casual, relaxed, *pleased* when two corpses (which were people a short while before) are swinging from a linden tree not fifteen feet away? I continue to watch their faces intently as though it were sensible to hope that the gravity of what they have seen, what they have allowed to happen, will begin to sink in and their smiles will vanish before my eyes and their faces will turn ashen and he will drop her thumb and they will realize they are not on a date but present at a murder. At the same time the teenager in the other photo will look down at her chest and she will blink a few times in disbelief and, very softly, she will mumble, "Oh my God" and stand frozen with horror as tears well up in her eyes until suddenly she rouses herself and rips off the T-shirt, preferring the embarrassment of nakedness to the obscenity of applauding mass death.

But the subjects in the photographs continue to smile until at last I turn away from them. I cannot bear to see, nor manage to understand, these illustrations of what happens when a whole group of people—in this case, blacks or gays—is objectified. This is the logical conclusion of failing to appreciate the humanity one shares with the members of an out-group. In wartime, it happens predictably. It happens necessarily, in fact; otherwise, killing is not possible. Nazis did not shove human beings into gas chambers; they rid the Fatherland of *Untermenschen* as if they were skimming scum off the surface of soup. American soldiers in Vietnam did not pump bullets into people's bodies; they simply exterminated Communist "insects."[21] Israeli soldiers are not (as I write) shooting children to death who could be their own younger siblings, or crushing bones by slamming down their rifle butts on the hands of innocent shopkeepers; they are protecting themselves from "terrorists."

While the psychological dynamics in each of these examples is similar, the examples themselves obviously are not analogous, let alone interchangeable. Neither are they exhaustive; virtually any instance of war or violent subjugation of a population will lead us to the same conclusion. That conclusion was well summarized by Sam Keen:

> As a rule, human beings do not kill other human beings. Before we enter into warfare or genocide, we first dehumanize those we mean to 'eliminate.' . . . The hostile imagination systematically destroys our natural tendency to identify with others of our species. . . . A full-bodied imagination would lead us to the recognition that those we are fighting against are like ourselves. They hurt when struck, fear death, love their children, hate going to war, and are filled with feelings of doubt and impotence.[22]

To take a frightfully ironic example of how the other's humanity must be denied in order to do him harm, some of the most unspeakable violence against other cultures has been justified on the grounds that these people "do not value human life the way we do."

The reduction of individuals to mere parts of a group, meanwhile, is an invitation to dehumanization—or else it is simply a special instance of dehumanization, the kind that operates on the collective level. One researcher summed up the experimental findings on the topic as follows:

> When categorized as a group member, a person's behavior is judged to be less informative about her or him, is attributed less to dispositional and more to situational causes, is considered more homogeneous and similar to other group members, and is perceived to be less credible and less independent of the others in the group. . . . Certainly, when intergroup conflict is great, deindividuation of outgroup members dehumanizes them, increases their threatening nature, and facilitates aggressive responses toward them.[23]

Reversing this procedure is not as straightforward as rehumanizing an individual. It is impossible to subjectivize or humanize a group because a group is not a subject or a human in the first place. What can be done is to reduce the salience of group membership, to appreciate both the individual's unique point of view and the species membership that she shares with us. That is to say, we can see beyond group membership in two directions at once. She may be one of Them, but she is mostly (a) a person, just like me, and (b) an individual, distinct from the others in her group.

Maximizing personal knowledge, minimizing distance and anonymity, are useful not just for humanizing in general but specifically for overcoming the obstacle of deindividuation. Assumptions about a particular group are shattered as one comes into contact with its members, one by one. At first, the stereotypes persist and remain in uneasy coexistence with direct knowledge about an individual: He's one of the *good* X's. Eventually, as one comes to know too many counterexamples—and the chief reason prejudice endures is that this happens too rarely—the stereotypes tremble and collapse. Along with the sweeping assumptions about this particular group, the epistemological framework by which individuals are seen principally as members of one or another out-group is challenged. Concrete details nudge one upward toward seeing shared humanness, and downward toward seeing uniqueness. The combination makes it nearly impossible to objectify or to harm.

Real-life examples of this process point the way out, the way beyond those snapshots of hate on my desk. Here is a college instructor describing a discussion with his students:

The prevailing attitude in class threw me for a loop: People with AIDS deserve to die. Others would say, "I want nothing to do with them." There was hardly any show of compassion. And yet when I showed them a film on AIDS and the dying, they were disturbed. Some in the class cried openly.[24]

And here, on a different topic, is the writer Judith Viorst:

For a long time, it has been fairly easy for Israelis, for American Jews, for me, to . . . [focus] on Israel's survival and [treat] the issue of something called "Palestinian rights" as a troublesome invention of Israel's enemies. But the . . . uprising in the occupied territories has put flesh and blood on the Palestinian "problem." In newspaper pictures, on television and, for me, on a painful trip to Gaza, Palestinians have acquired a human face.[25]

Coming to see others as more simply human than one of Them represents so drastic a conceptual shift, so affecting an emotional conversion, that there may be no greater threat to those with an interest in preserving intergroup hostility. Heinrich Himmler, head of the Gestapo, paid homage to this phenomenon when he sarcastically complained in 1943 about how there are

eighty million upstanding Germans, and each one has his decent Jew. Of course the others are swine, but this one is a first-class Jew. Of all those who talk like this, not one has watched [the actual extermination], not one has had the stomach for it.[26]

Start by admitting there is one good Jew and pretty soon the larger project of dehumanization has broken down. With it goes the suspicion, the hatred, and the willingness to murder. Eventually the fact of someone's being a Jew—or a *goy* or a gay or a black—is not nearly so important a fact as his being a person. We come to see, to paraphrase Gertrude Stein, that there's no *they* there.

To take this view seriously, to see it as more than a banal affirmation that we are all brothers and sisters under the skin, is to call into question not only the value of patriotism but the consequences of defining oneself primarily with respect to membership in any subset of the human race. It will be, to this extent, a very controversial position among those on both the left and the right. Difference and diversity are to be celebrated in some respects, but any time people draw bold lines around their group—even a group that is in the minority—there is exclusion, and where there is exclusion, there can be a We-versus-They polarity and an objectification of the They. The problem is not so much with taking pride in elements of one's own culture as with the fact that this pride can become defiant, exclusive, irrational, and ultimately deadly.

Historically, most of this sort of ugliness has been a result of powerful interests doing the defining, the branding of and discriminating against people said to be importantly different: members of minority groups. (This is why denunciations of affirmative action programs are resolutely ahistorical, either naively or disingenuously so: entrenched patterns of discrimination will not vanish even if majority groups suddenly stopped taking notice of race or other ethnic criteria.) It is easy to see how those in an oppressed minority would be inclined to pull together and take pleasure in the very group identity that has been disparaged by others. Nevertheless, calls among people of a certain group to maintain a public show of unity, to avoid letting outsiders see any evidence of intragroup criticism, should be deeply troubling to anyone whose ultimate allegiance is to humans as humans. Similarly, to respond to a particular event—say, a war between two nations—by asking first how it is likely to affect one's own nation is a morally bankrupt stance.[27]

It may be unrealistic to expect any person to express equal concern for all human beings, but there would seem to be an obligation to resist, or at least to attempt to moderate, a fundamentally partisan world view.* In the absence of such an effort, one may become indifferent to the news that people who are not in one's own clan are suffering—or even pleased by this news if the in-group might somehow benefit. One may come to help one's own not only to the exclusion of, but even at the expense of, others. Apart from the fact that lives can be lost as a result of this world view, it is intrinsically objectionable to narrow one's vision in the way that leads one immediately to ask of some development, "Is it good for the X's?"

It is surely a discouraging fact that many people do just this. Yet a closer look at the psychology of group membership offers some reassurance. First, invoking an out-group, creating a common enemy, is not a necessary consequence of working with others. Cooperation does not require hostility toward or competition with another group. Of course it is technically true that the formation of any group entails at least a formal distinction between those who are and are not members. If a bus driver gives a genial wave to the other bus drivers he passes on the highway, he may feel a vague sense of connection to those in this fraternity; he does not wave to the drivers of other vehicles. But his camaraderie is not conditioned on enmity toward cars and trucks. There is no clearly defined and emotionally charged identification of an out-group.

Many of us have come to associate cooperation with intergroup competition; our experience with competitive athletics, corporate capitalism, and international rivalry has taught us that if a group of people is working together it must be for the purpose of defeating another group. Happily, this need not be true: it is a function of socially constructed decisions rather than of the nature of groups. Classroom research demonstrating the benefits of cooperative learning—in terms of both enhanced achievement and greater esteem for fellow team members—

---

*It is sometimes suggested that if each individual identifies with several groups simultaneously, any two people will likely share membership in one group even if they are on opposite sides of another divide. As Morton Deutsch has written, "Cross-cutting memberships and loyalties tend to function as a moderating influence in resolving any particular intergroup conflict within a society."[28] This, however, is a high-risk strategy that may ultimately multiply the perils of We/They thinking rather than cancel them out.

has shown clearly that these advantages are not dependent on intergroup competition and may even be diminished by the addition of this element.[29] Similarly, a series of studies by the Dutch psychologist Jacob Rabbie found "no evidence for a greater ingroup solidarity in the [competitive] condition. If anything there is a slight but nonsignificant tendency in the opposite direction."[30] This, he pointed out later, debunks the "very popular notion . . . that intergroup competition leads to ingroup cohesiveness."[31] Even in the Army, another study found, the men in each squad did not come to look upon each other more favorably, or to know each other better, when they were in competition with other squads.[32]

Many studies of adult cooperation do not specifically test for the effects of intergroup competition, but here, too, the absence of an outgroup does not seem to interfere with the formation of group identity— an identity that, in turn, leads people to put aside narrow considerations of self-interest.[33] In short, as psychologist Harvey Hornstein put it, feelings of intragroup amity simply do not require intergroup enmity; the former "can spring forth independently, as a natural response to one's fellows."[34]

A second line of research, mentioned in chapter 3, is also encouraging. It emphasizes that similarity is not a function of objective proximity or characteristics held in common, but reflects a subjective experience of the significance of what is shared. What matters is the meaning of the differences between two individuals or groups—or the absence of meaning. Recall Hornstein's observation that "there is nothing inherent in any distinction between human beings that compels us to see others as *they.*" The impact of such distinctions is not fixed but dependent on socialization patterns and individual character traits. One study found that racial differences between the observer and the observed affected the empathic responses of black children less than it did those of white children.[35] Another study asked undergraduates to pass judgment on (and choose a punishment for) a fictitious student who may have cheated on a test. They were told, among other things, how this student felt about various social issues. Both the likelihood of finding the student guilty and the severity of the punishment depended on whether the student's attitudes on these questions were similar to the subject's own views—but only for those subjects who scored high on a test of authoritarian personality features. Attitude similarity was not as salient for—or at least did not affect the judgment of—the others.[36]

Here, then, we have two heartening discoveries: to work with a group is not necessarily to work against another group, and to acknowledge the

existence of differences among groups is not necessarily to be preoccupied with those differences. Nevertheless, the more permanent one's
membership in a given group is—skin color being, after all, a different
matter than cooperation with a group of strangers in a laboratory—and
the more one's self-definition depends on that membership, the greater
the dangers are of excluding and dehumanizing those in an out-group.
Hatred of homosexuals is not an inevitable consequence of the existence
of different sexual orientations; the pleasure one takes from some feature
of one's homeland need not occasion a rivalry with people who have
other homelands. But our experience with the frequency and devastating
consequences of We versus They views of the world suggests that where
shared humanness and individual uniqueness can be emphasized over
group membership, this would be much to the good.

The idea of shared humanness has been expressed by some writers
in terms of expanding the We until it embraces everyone. This characterization is often offered descriptively as well as prescriptively. "The central
fact of history, from a psychological point of view, may be said to be the
gradual enlargement of social consciousness and rational cooperation,"
wrote the sociologist Charles Horton Cooley in the early part of this
century.[37] More recently, Peter Singer, invoking something akin to what
I have called taking the collective other's point of view, argued that moral
thinking has, since ancient times, been moving steadily to a "fully universal" perspective:

Altruistic impulses once limited to one's kin and one's own group might be
extended to a wider circle by reasoning creatures who can see that they and their
kin are one group among others, and from an impartial point of view no more
important than others.[38]

What is particularly useful about this conception is the fact that such
expansion is not conceived as a duality—either there is the universal We
or there is widespread discord—but rather as existing on a continuum.
We may never get to the point where someone's having a different skin
color or preferences regarding religion is no more likely to promote
dehumanization or discourage caring relationships than that person's
having a different hair color or preferences regarding sleeping position.
We probably do not *want* to trivialize attitudes on social and political
questions, but we can gradually approximate a state of affairs in which
membership in such a group remains less salient than one's humanness
and thus is not apt to lead to the dehumanization of those who do not

share such membership. In place of flags, statues of war heroes, and
bumper stickers saying "Kiss Me, I'm X," we could do no better than to
display Leon Eisenberg's words: One whose "concerns extend beyond
family and beyond nation to mankind has become fully human."[39]

The Other as Subject

Unless the perception is systematically blotted out, it is probably not so
difficult to keep in mind that the other is a human being. Although they
are answered in very different ways, the same existential questions apply
to all of us: what to make of mortality and finitude, identity, autonomy
and relationship, how to make meaning and confront meaninglessness.
Likewise, it may be practical to speak of the great majority of humans as
being able to appreciate the uniqueness, the otherness of others. Perspective taking and empathy, as the last chapter detailed, give us a
glimpse into the life of that person and that person alone. We can understand what we share with the other and we can understand how we differ.
The trick is to entertain both simultaneously. Then, and only then, do we
truly experience the other as a subject.

I say "experience" rather than "understand" because something
more than an intellectual apprehension is required. It is the same as with
mortality. Everyone knows that death is inevitable, but there are not many
(some would say there are not *any*) who really know that one day they will
cease to be and there will be no self to experience this or anything else.
Here, too, we can *say* the other is a person just like us and yet a person
like no other, but the connection I am describing must be felt viscerally
as surely as one's own humanness and uniqueness are felt.

Yet even this last formulation gives us pause. It is easy to use one's
own features as a point of comparison and wish that we could appreciate
the other's subjectivity as we do our own. But it is not clear that everyone
does experience his or her own subjectivity. Having explored both sides
of the process of appreciating the other, I turn now to a somewhat briefer
look at the implications for one's relationship to oneself.

FROM OUTSIDE THE SELF

To bring the concept of "subjectivity" down to earth is to bring it down
to ourselves. Each of us is the reference point for his understanding of

what it means to be a subject—one who acts—as opposed to something that is merely acted upon. But there is more to the story than this. In order to make the *other* into a subject by taking her perspective, one must (in a very particular sense) make the self into an object. We speak of this in everyday language when we urge that someone maintain a "sense of perspective" about her problems or when we admire someone who does not take herself too seriously or can laugh at herself. Nagel built into his notion of collective perspective taking the recognition that each of us is merely one individual among many. The point is not only to change the way we regard others—namely, as being just as important to themselves as we are to ourselves—but also to change our self-perception. Each of us has, under the moral system that follows from this, no special entitlements. We come to see this because we come to see ourselves from the outside, the way others see us. In Mead's words, "The self has the characteristic that it is an object to itself. . . . He becomes a self in so far as he can take the attitude of another and act toward himself as others act."[40]

This is not always easy to do. Someone who becomes aware of being the object of another's perceptions and judgments, watched and weighed by that subject, is inclined to resist this by struggling to rescue her own subjectivity. The rescue is effected by objectifying the other: if you act on, look at, or think about me, I will do the same to you. I will try to deny you your power to objectify me by objectifying you as only a subject can do. (This was the essence of Sartre's early caricature of human relationship.)[41] But someone confident in her subjectivity, unafraid of being object to another, can afford to resist this temptation and can join with the other in seeing herself from the other's point of view. This is the healthy self-objectification I have in mind.

Still, there is no question but that this process is tentative, temporary, and deliberate; it is in the interest of self-knowledge or morality or connection to others. The *total* absence of subjectivity is more likely to signal schizophrenia—as the late R. D. Laing's brilliant phenomenological portraits made clear—than skillful perspective taking. And if the self is objectified, this does not bode well for one's relationships with others. "To the extent that [one] is dehumanized, he loses the capacity to act as a moral being," writes Herbert Kelman, so dehumanization of the self and the other end up reinforcing each other.[42] The loss of the sense of self as human, as subject, as agent, is ominous indeed. Having shown experimentally that subjects who remain anonymous are more likely to deliver shocks than those treated as individuals and addressed by name,[43] Zimbardo also notes that "prosocial behaviors are encouraged by environmental and interpersonal conditions which enhance one's sense of recognition and self-identity."[44]

The need for the self as subject is also manifested in the fact that one cannot effectively empathize unless one can empathize with oneself. Alice Miller remarked that a "lack of empathy for the suffering of one's own childhood can result in an astonishing lack of sensitivity to other children's suffering."[45] Childhood aside, one who cannot tolerate his own range of feelings, or who is essentially a stranger to himself, is unlikely to forge an affective connection to someone else. A degree of self-knowledge and comfort with one's own affective life facilitates both knowing and being known to others.[46]

How Can You Be in Two Places at Once When You're Not Anywhere at All?[47]

The idea of taking another person's perspective presupposes that that perspective is different from one's own. There would be no possibility of carrying out this act of imagination, and no *need* to do so, if the identities of the two individuals were not distinct. With empathy, however (the sort that does not include perspective taking), people may think that the process of feeling the other's affect hints at a mystical union with the other. Of course, an extended experience of anything like complete fusion is extremely rare,[48] but some people contend that it is a state devoutly to be wished, and that empathy so conceived represents a higher state of affective sharing.

Such a state of being has implications not only for the idea of empathy but also for the status of the empathizer, affecting the self as well as the relationship. It is with an eye to both that I want to challenge this position, and I want to make it clear that in doing so I stand with the great majority of those who have thought seriously about the issue, from philosophers to social psychologists. Perhaps the most impressive name on this roster, because of his credentials in opposing individualism, is Buber. As the premier theorist of relationship, the most articulate exponent of the idea that the fulfillment of human life is what happens between one person and another, Buber consistently opposed anything resembling fusion, characterizing it as a distortion of genuine encounter with the other. "One cannot stand in a relation to something that is not perceived as contrasted and existing for itself," he said.[49] This position, which is stated somewhat differently in the title of this section, led him to distance himself from the implications of mysticism despite his passionate interest in a Jewish mystical sect:

The flight from the common cosmos into a special sphere that is understood as the true being is, in all its stages, from the elemental sayings of the ancient Eastern teachings to the arbitrariness of the modern counsel to intoxication, a flight from the existential claim on the person who must verify himself in We. It is flight from the authentic spokenness of speech in whose realm a response is demanded, and response is responsibility. . . . The fugitive flight out of the claim of the situation into situationlessness is no legitimate affair of man.[50]

In fact, Buber felt so strongly about this that he rejected the word *empathy* because he was concerned that it connoted the loss of the self in the process of experiencing the other. He used different language to emphasize the fact that one participates in the other's life "without forfeiting anything of the felt reality of his [own] activity. . . . A *great* relation exists only between real persons. . . . One must be truly able to say *I* in order to know the mystery of the *Thou* in its whole truth."[51]

Contemporary students of empathy have come to much the same conclusion. Says Martin Hoffman: "Although empathy may be a major, perhaps *the* major, social bond, it does not allow one to become the other."[52] And elsewhere: "The empathic reaction must depend heavily on the actor's cognitive sense of the other as distinct from himself."[53] Norma Feshbach similarly emphasizes that "empathy, to have constructive consequences, demands separation between self and object. The vicarious experience of affect should not reflect the merging of observer and object, but should derive from the observer's ability to assume the perspective and share the feeling of the object."[54] Essentially the same point has been made by the psychoanalyst Rudolf Ekstein,[55] the psychotherapist David Shapiro,[56] the psychologist Ervin Staub,[57] and the philosopher Milton Mayeroff.[58] For Carol Gilligan, whose vision of human development and morality turns on relationship, "Love does not imply fusion or transcendence . . . [and co-feeling] does not imply an absence of difference or an identity of feelings or a failure to distinguish between self and other."[59]

If the question, then, is: What happens to the self when it feels into the other? the answer is: All is not lost. There are different ways of describing the ideal form of empathy, but none of them requires that the self become submerged in the other any more than that its subjectivity be demolished. I may feel his feelings and I may feel in response to his feelings, but there is never any doubt that the subject of this sentence continues to be *I*. If empathy were a business transaction (which, thankfully, it is not), it would be a cooperative venture, a partnership, rather than a merger or an acquisition.

But we cannot leave matters at that. The larger focus here is on appreciation of otherness, and to say simply that empathy is not fusion is rather like defining a benefactor as someone who does not give away *all* her assets to charity. If they are worthy of their names, empathy and perspective taking (at least taking the perspective of the concrete other), not only leave the self intact but also leave the self transformed. In chapter 9, I will talk more about a world view grounded in relationship rather than in the conduct of discrete individuals. The point here is that selves who meet to feel and imagine each other are discrete and yet they are also connected.

This paradox, which presupposes the value of preserving the self, has been noticed by feminist theorists and clinicians. It is true, writes Judith Jordan, that "in order to empathize, one must have a well-differentiated sense of self . . . [because] without an adequately articulated and relatively constant set of self-representations or self-images, any temporary identification might become a threat to the constancy of the self." But at the same time, the boundaries between self and other must be flexible to "allow for a sense of 'we-ness' or affective joining with another" so that one can "experience a sense of feeling connected and . . . at the same time [separate]."[60]

Separateness in the sense that the integrity of the self is retained does not imply separateness in the sense that one relates to the other from afar. The latter neither describes the reality of empathic connection nor offers a picture of mental health. Gilligan remarks wryly that a clinical observer may be correct in identifying someone who is in danger of having no self, but this observer may himself be in danger of having no other.[61] As with empathy, we reflect that two clasped hands are still two hands—but they are also two hands touching, the warmth and pulse of one accessible to the other.

PERSPECTIVE TAKING IN THE REAL WORLD

Denouncing Evil

This chapter and the previous one have considered ways of appreciating the other as other and the other as simply human. Empathy and perspective taking are the focus of the former, and ways of overcoming dehumanization and deindividuation are addressed in the latter. I would now like to turn to some ethical implications of perspective taking and empathy as well as some concrete problems of application in the world that is home for us as individuals and citizens of nation-states.

Objectifying others is a useful measure for carrying out certain tasks—not only killing but healing, for instance. The surgeon manages to slice into someone's belly only by banishing the awareness of the human subject he is invading; it is just an abdomen. Even with "selective and transient dehumanization," though, there is always the danger that "the constructive self-protection it achieves will cross the ever-shifting boundaries of adaptiveness and become destructive, to others as well as to the self."[62] As a general rule, one ought to struggle in all situations and with all people to maintain an appreciation for the other's subjectivity and humanity.

But what about those who commit unspeakable, unforgivable acts? Are we to affirm our common humanity with the directors of death squads, the molesters of children? In a word, yes. Someone who has been directly touched by evil will not manage this without effort, but the dismissal of fiends as less than human is too easy and too dangerous. It is an attempt to circumvent the agonizing problem of human evil by denying that the evildoers are as human as we. And it is inadvertently to accept *their* premise that some people can be exiled from the human community. "Despite yourselves," Camus wrote in his essay addressed to an imaginary German during World War II, "I shall still apply to you the name of man."[63]

Does this carry with it a call to take the perspective of such individuals, to see what the world looks like to a rapist or a murderer? To begin with, we are restrained by the limits of our capacity to imagine. It is not always easy to put ourselves in the position of those who cannot do the same.[64] But while it may be difficult to accomplish this leap of imagination, it is not morally problematic to do so. The view that one ought not to try to capture the point of view of villains seems to be based on the premise either that their villainy is contagious or that *tout comprendre c'est tout pardonner*. The latter is exactly what led Bruno Bettelheim to criticize Robert Jay Lifton for trying to figure out how German doctors could lend their expertise to the Nazi cause.

I shied away from trying to understand the psychology of the SS—because of the ever-present danger that understanding fully may come close to forgiving. I believe there are acts so vile that our task is to reject and prevent them, not to try to understand them empathetically as Dr. Lifton did.[65]

The fact that I happen to think this position is dreadfully misconceived does not prevent me from seeking to puzzle out how Bettelheim arrived at it (perhaps from his own experience in a concentration camp); conversely, the fact that I can understand his point of view is not a barrier to my objecting to it. I do not mean to suggest that my reaction to Bettelheim's view is comparable to his (or my) reaction to the SS, but rather that perspective taking is not mutually exclusive with judging. It is true that perspective takers and empathizers will tend, all else being equal, to be more tolerant than others.[66] (This helps to explain why some religious followers may be reluctant to imagine how their doctrine appears to those of other faiths; the mere act of doing so threatens to undermine the conviction that absolute truth resides in their own beliefs.) But judging remains compatible with understanding because neither understanding nor empathy demands agreement.

"No matter how mean or hideous a man's life is, the first thing is to understand him," said Charles Horton Cooley, "to make out just how it is that our common human nature has come to work out in this way. . . . This sort of morality does not, however, dispense with praise and blame."[67] Cooley, of course, wrote before the SS existed, but others have not only said the same thing in the post-Nazi era, they have struggled to understand this very evil by means of perspective taking. Alice Miller, for example, describes how she overcame her initial reluctance to imagine how the world looked to Hitler himself, to regard him as a human being and to learn about his childhood. "If we turn our backs on something because it is difficult to understand and indignantly refer to it as 'inhuman,' we will never be able to learn anything about its nature."[68]

Sometimes we will need to take action against evil, not merely to understand it. Sometimes that action must be harsh, not at all the way we would prefer to treat another human being. Does the process of understanding preclude such action? When it does—when we find ourselves, for example, unable to cage someone like an animal after having come to recognize his humanness—then the action is illegitimate. We should not have to objectify, to silence our empathic response, in order to incarcerate. The need to act must be so compelling—as indeed it sometimes is—that we find ourselves reluctantly prepared to do what has to be done in spite of our full awareness of the evildoer's humanity.

Taking the other's perspective and otherwise trying to understand him not only can coexist with judgment—including negative judgment*—of his actions; in some cases judgment supplies the *motive* for that act of understanding. It is precisely to prevent evil that we need to figure out how it comes to happen; we need to grasp its appeal from the inside. In an interesting article on empathy and the law, one scholar has observed that "understanding how and why Nazism was so attractive to the German people, or how and why lynchings were and are so attractive to members of the KKK, is important to preventing those evils from recurring."[69]

The assumption that empathy excludes the possibility of judging is based on a false dichotomy: either we look down from a distance and pass judgment, thus objectifying this individual, or else we become one with her and accept her attitudes, her vision, her world. That value judgment does not entail objectification is the subject of another book, yet to be written. That empathy does not entail trying to *become* the other person is a central argument in the preceding section. Ultimately, most expressions of reluctance to empathize with bad people can be traced back to an unstated assumption that empathy requires a sort of merging of self and other. If this is false, then we can begin to understand how one individual can understand and feel into another, yet still be able to make a decision about the other and his actions. Our task can be to reject and prevent the vile acts of which Bettelheim speaks—and also to understand them empathetically. In fact, the latter may help us to prevent their recurrence.

So far I have been speaking of how we *ought* to approach the other, taking for granted that we can decide whether or not to judge. I am not convinced that this is so—any more than we can talk seriously about value-free social science or education or journalism. We can avoid being "judgmental," in the way that word is usually understood, but it may not

---

*Not all judgments are critical judgments. Very often those who exhort us not to make judgments about other people's behavior (or about other cultures) really mean that we should not make *negative* judgments. They fail to see that approval is just as much a value judgment as disapproval. (They also fail to see that their attempts to discourage disapproval are themselves value judgments.)

be possible to set aside our values in order to understand another person or idea. Our response to her is shot through with judgment because we are, for better or worse (I think for better), judging creatures. Perspective taking can color and shape the judgment, and, if one is open-minded enough, may even prompt a radical reconsideration of one's position. But it does not erase the judgment or deny its existence. In a way, this is to say nothing more than that perspective takers do not entirely give up their own points of view when they try on others'. A point of view, assuming that we are not being literal and spatial here, is, among other things, a set of values.

Deterring War

The idea that understanding the appeal of evil can help us to know how to prevent it raises the broader question of what can be accomplished from the act of perspective taking. The answer begins with the observation that it offers a profoundly important way to promote social change. Martha Minow, a legal theorist, sees it this way, too:

The most powerful device to expose and challenge . . . unstated assumptions [is] looking at an issue from another point of view. . . . The effort to do so may help [you] recognize that [your] perspective is partial and that the status quo is not inevitable or ideal. . . . You may find that you had so much ignored the point of view of others that you did not realize that you were mistaking your point of view for reality. Perhaps you will find that the way things are is not the only way things could be.[70]

To be frozen into a single, conventional perspective is generally to cling to an existing set of behaviors or laws. To ask how someone else might view or be affected by the usual way of doing business, of assigning blame, of distributing resources, or of resolving conflicts is to call established norms into question and, at the least, to raise the possibility of change.

So far from requiring a suspension of judgment, perspective taking suspends the suspension of judgment and suggests that things may be neither as settled nor as satisfactory as they appear from the customary vantage point. This makes perfect sense in light of what we already know: to transcend egocentrism by imagining another person's point of view frequently leads to modifications in behavior, to prosocial activity and the avoidance of aggression. It changes individual lives. There is every reason to expect that becoming similarly unembedded with respect to the impact of social practices or structures can also stir things up.

Perspective taking is also the very essence of collective, consensus-based decision making. There is no need to understand the needs and views of others in that version of coercion known as adversarial majoritarianism. At its best, this model decrees that the candidate most people support will assume office, the policy most officials support will be implemented, and those who object will just have to live with it. But real democracy is characterized by dialogue and listening, as the political philosopher Benjamin Barber saw:

"I will listen" means to the strong democrat not that I will scan my adversary's position for weaknesses and potential trade-offs, nor even (as a minimalist might think) that I will tolerantly permit him to say whatever he chooses. It means, rather, "I will put myself in his place, I will try to understand, I will strain to hear what makes us alike, I will listen for a common rhetoric evocative of a common purpose or a common good."

Such perspective taking, Barber concluded, "has a politically miraculous power to enlarge perspectives and expand consciousness in a fashion that not so much accommodates as transcends private interests and the antagonisms they breed."[71] With each of us able to see how things look to others, the desire to triumph and impose our will on those others gives way to a desire to reach consensus. Mead was absolutely right to connect role taking to democracy: the communication that is at the root of self-governance is "a process of putting one's self in the place of the other person's attitude."[72]

Perspective taking offers a deep way of taking account of others when making decisions with them or for them. But it also offers a way of detoxifying the poisonous We/They structure of nationalism. It is, to be blunt, what must be done if the superpowers are not to exterminate each other and the planet. Each side must consider how the other views any given situation. I do not know whether this is done by leaders of the Soviet Union, but it seems evident that there is altogether too little effort in the United States to see things from the Soviet point of view. This, Ralph White argued in his book *Fearful Warriors*, is the prerequisite for moving the clock's hands back from midnight. We need to ask: "How would I feel if I were faced with the situation the Soviet Union now faces? . . . How would I interpret recent American behavior?"[73] Notice that

these questions require no compassion, no suspension of value judgment, not even a motive other than self-interest. Moreover, they represent a rather rudimentary version of perspective taking, the sort where
one only imagines oneself in the other's situation rather than imagining
the other in the other's situation.

All that is asked is that American policy makers consider how they
would feel if they lived in a country that had a history of being invaded
(which ours does not), a country that had lost fifty people for every one
we lost in World War II, a country surrounded by a concatenation of
hostile powers and missiles. To imagine this situation is to loosen defensive postures and soften hostility, yet evidently it is rarely done in Washington. Robert Scheer, a journalist who probed the thinking of numerous
people in the Reagan administration, including George Bush and Reagan
himself, during interviews in the early 1980s, said this:

They think, to a man and woman in the higher positions of this Administration,
that the Russians wear black hats and we wear white hats. . . . [People outside the
government] say, "Put yourself in the Russians' shoes." I don't think there's
anyone in this Administration who would ever say that.[74]

Whether or not there has been movement since then in the direction
of appreciating otherness, there has surely been improvement on the part
of U.S. citizens in coming to appreciate common humanness. The impetus was, as it almost always is, personal contact. Mikhail Gorbachev may
be substantively different from his predecessors, but overshadowing his
policy preferences was the fact that he came to New York and to Washington and revealed himself to be a human being. Media coverage of the
Soviet Union during these visits began to capture the ordinary humanity
of Soviet citizens. "It's very hard to dehumanize people when the images
are that vivid and crisp," said social psychologist Scott Plous. "To see
them as human beings, as opposed to abstract, conceptual dots called
'Russians' or 'communists' gives us a dimension that we really need," said
the psychiatrist Robert Jay Lifton.[75]

To subjectify them is also (in the salutary sense) to objectify us, to
realize with an unpleasant start how our actions may appear to others. In
the first chapter, I recounted how a U.S. warship killed 290 innocent
people in 1988 when it shot down a commercial airliner. This event was
covered in the foreign press exactly as the U.S. media would have reported the event if any other country had been responsible. But taking
the collective other's point of view (let alone that of the aggrieved party)

does not come easily to our reporters or scholars, our politicians or citizens. In the last decade alone, the United States has sponsored a war against Nicaragua, bombed Libya, invaded Grenada and Panama, shelled Lebanon, and armed dictators against their own people. If Americans are insulted or bemused or angered by the intensity of resentment their flag inspires around the globe, it may be in part because cross-national perspective taking occurs so rarely. We are not accustomed to asking how such violence might appear to an outsider, someone not trained from childhood to "know" that any such actions are always—indeed, by definition—undertaken in the interests of Freedom and Democracy, and in response to someone else's provocation.

I do not choose these local and inflammatory examples because I think the United States is uniquely evil.* Self-righteousness runs deep here, but not only here; perspective taking does not appear to be a national pastime in France or Japan or Argentina either. But it is too easy to fault someone else's parochialism or to inveigh against it in the abstract. We will not be inclined to see ourselves from another point of view unless we are first made uncomfortable with evidence that *we* normally fail to do so.

Regardless of where one's passport was issued, it would be a useful exercise when reading in the newspaper about the activities of one's country (and the pronouncements of its leaders) to imagine that one was reading about something being done or said by another country, particularly the designated enemy. Would they still seem justified, defensive rather than offensive? To raise this question will offend no one as long as it is couched in generic language. But point out that our freedom fighters would be described as terrorists if they weren't ours, and the issue becomes charged.

The same exercise is appropriate with respect to any number of practices to which we have become accustomed. Are Americans who refuse to eat dogs any less irrational than Hindus who refuse to eat cows? How would we react upon learning that all children in another country (say, a Communist country) had to begin every school day by reciting a loyalty oath to their nation? Would it make any difference if that oath

---

*As Noam Chomsky likes to point out, criticism of U.S. foreign policy is defined as radical if it argues that the United States is *not* exceptional. To argue that this country operates precisely as other nations throughout history have operated—only, perhaps, more forcefully because it has the force available—is to defy the conventional wisdom that the United States is an historical anomaly, motivated by noble desires and handicapped only by its good intentions.

were called a pledge of allegiance? Of course one can spin out examples
of this sort indefinitely. And that is exactly what I am recommending that
we do. One of the most remarkable advancements in human knowledge—
and one of the most underappreciated features of modernity—is our
ability to transcend the culture-bound perspective that had hitherto limited human beings. Cross-cultural comparisons are both infinitely liberating and enormously humbling since they help us realize that the way we
do things is not the way things have to be done. Perspective taking is one
mechanism by which we put this knowledge into practice, using it to melt
suspicion and to enrich our own lives.

Turning on the Receivers

Compassion and connection are most efficiently promoted by giving
people a chance to experience the life circumstances of others. To spend
time talking with street people—to learn how they fear falling asleep in
the wrong places lest someone steal what little they have, how they drink
to blot out the hopelessness, how fiercely loyal friendships blossom in the
alleys and parks—this is to turn an abstract problem (homelessness) into
real human beings. Of course no one should congratulate himself on
having "experienced" homelessness by dint of having visited its victims
on the way home. But anyone who has directly known distress cannot
look at a similar event again in quite the same way and cannot easily pass
by someone else in similar trouble. The person who has spent a few hours
stranded on the highway is thereafter more likely to offer assistance to
another such motorist. One businessman reports that he no longer walks
past unconscious strangers on the streets—now that he has known what
it is to be injured and ignored. "I lay there, retching, somewhere between
life and death without a helping hand. This incident has surely cured me
of this social disease," he writes.[76]

Broadening people's range of experiences is a remedy for indifference. But even better—although the two approaches are, of course, not
mutually exclusive—is to hone perspective-taking skills and enhance empathic responsiveness so that one can imagine, feel, and help someone
even without having personally been in his or her predicament. Can this
be done? Our optimism will depend partly on whether we conceive of this
process as creating something or as recovering it. If cruelty exists because
people's empathy and perspective taking are in eclipse, so to speak, then
unblocking them would seem a simpler task than trying to develop such

an orientation from scratch. Whether or not empathy is seen as natural—
or more natural than its absence—a case can be made that it is a human
capacity that will flourish unless some force interferes with its development and actualization. Notice, for example, how gender differences in
empathy seem to reflect social norms and concerns about self-presenta-
tion more than a disparity in innate potential. What Buber said to account
for the infrequency of authentic dialogue may be pertinent to empathy
as well: "Most of the time we have turned off our receivers."[77] There is
reason for hope if our charge is not to construct receivers but merely to
turn them on again.

In experiments conducted by Stotland, Aderman, Batson, and others—some already described, some to be discussed in later chapters—
people asked to imagine themselves in someone else's situation, or to
imagine how the other is experiencing her situation, are more likely to
respond physiologically to that person's distress, more likely to be sympathetic instead of derogatory, and more likely to help for purely altruistic
reasons than subjects not invited to partake in the other's inner experience.

Longer-term programs of "empathy training" for children, meanwhile, have achieved a measure of success, although typically the focus
of these programs, too, is perspective taking rather than empathy per
se.[78] Teaching perspective taking to younger children has positive effects
on prosocial behaviors, although it is not clear how long these effects
last.[79] One experiment with older children was also promising. For half
a day each week over ten weeks, fifteen delinquent boys received "reme-
dial training in deficient role-taking skills" and were helped "to see themselves from the perspectives of others." Not only did these boys exhibit
better perspective-taking skills afterward, but they had committed fewer
"delinquencies" than a control group after one and a half years. (Certain
qualifications about the method and the effect size raise questions about
the significance of these results, however, even if they do remain promising enough to justify more attempts at replication than have actually been
performed.)[80]

If our concern is with children—a sensible concern if we wish to help
our society to move beyond selfishness—then we ought to look not only
at what can be done at home (as was discussed in chapter 3) or in the
laboratory, but also in schools. The following chapter describes several
experiments, with special emphasis on a long-term study under way in
California, to help children become better at perspective taking, more
caring, and more responsive.

6

The ABCs of Caring:
A Case Study

Schools do affect character, whether you like it or not. There are only two ways they can go about it: unaware and badly, or consciously and well.

—Amitai Etzioni

READING, WRITING, ROLE TAKING

If we had to pick a logical setting in which to guide children toward caring about, empathizing with, and helping others, it would be a place where they regularly come into contact with their peers and where some sort of learning is already taking place. The school is such an obvious choice that one wonders how it could be that the active encouragement of prosocial values and behavior—apart from occasional exhortations to be polite—plays no part in the vast majority of American classrooms. This would seem to be due either to a lack of interest in the idea or to some objection to using the schools in particular for this purpose.

Both factors probably play a role, but I will concentrate here on the latter and consider three specific reservations that parents, teachers, policy makers, and others may have about classroom-based programs to help children develop a prosocial orientation. The first is that this agenda, by virtue of being concerned with social and moral issues, amounts to teaching values—a dangerous business for a public institution. The second—and this one dovetails with the broader absence of interest in the prosocial realm—is the fear that children taught to care about others will be unable to look out for themselves and succeed when they are released into a heartless society. The third is that taking time out to teach these matters must be at the expense of attention to academics. Such a shift of priorities is apt to be particularly unpopular at a time when we entertain ourselves by describing how much students do not know.

To begin with the first, there is no escaping the fact that a prosocial agenda is value laden, but neither can an honest observer deny that the very same is true of the status quo. The teacher's presence and behavior, her choice of text, the order in which she presents ideas, and her tone of voice are all as much a part of the lesson as the curriculum itself. Values are also present in the way children are led to regard each other. There are two principal models for learning in most U.S. schools: children work either competitively (against one another) or individually (apart from one another). Collaborative effort is generally seen as inappropriate; for that matter, social interaction of any sort is reserved for free time and discouraged in the classroom. A student who helps another to learn is guilty of cheating. Finally, the assumptions that guide a teacher's method for enforcing discipline and keeping control of the classroom—and the very fact that these issues are viewed in terms of discipline and control in the first place—are also steeped in values. In short, to arrange our schools so that caring, sharing, helping, perspective taking, and empathizing are actively encouraged is not to *introduce* values into a neutral environment. It is to examine the values already in place and trade them in for a new set.

It is sometimes said that moral concerns and social skills ought to be taught at home. I know of no one in the field of education or child development who disagrees with this. The problem is that such instruction—along with nurturance and warmth, someone to model altruism, opportunities to practice caring for others, and so forth—is not to be found in all homes. The school may need to provide what some children will not otherwise get. In any case, there is no conceivable danger to providing these values in both environments. Encouragement from more than one source to develop empathic relationships is a highly desirable form of redundancy.

In practice, if the case study to be discussed below is any indication, prosocial education will not be nearly as controversial as anxious principals and school board members may fear. If the assumptions and operative principles of such school programs are explained clearly, with objections anticipated and adequately addressed, parents and other community members from across the political spectrum will likely find the values fundamentally unobjectionable, if not long overdue. They may simply translate these goals into a language with which they are more familiar, expressing satisfaction that their children are being provided with the skills of win-win negotiation or the values of positive citizenry or the capacity to balance concern for self with concern for others. One educator, noting that "American schools are generally reluctant to endorse explicit values," recommends that a prosocial program be framed as "citizenship education rather than moral or values education."[1] The idea here is not to misrepresent the nature of such a program but to allay fears that one's child is being brainwashed. There is nothing subversive—except in the literal sense of subverting selfishness—about a plan to raise children to be nicer and more caring people.

The idea that a product of such a program will be gullible and spineless, destined to be victimized by mean-spirited individuals, can be traced back to the prejudice that selfishness and competitiveness are efficacious social strategies. While it may seem paradoxical, however, those whose mantra is "Look out for Number One" are at more of a disadvantage in any sort of society than those who are skilled at working with others and inclined to do so. A well-designed program of prosocial instruction will include training in cooperative conflict resolution and methods of achieving one's goals that do not require the use of force or manipulation. Competition and the single-minded pursuit of narrowly conceived self-interest typically turn out to be counterproductive.

There is thus considerable benefit to the individual in learning to share and cooperate rather than in avoiding others or trying to defeat them, and any effort to teach prosocial values can include such skills. But even without such a component to a school program, the enterprise of encouraging children to become responsive to others, to empathize and help, does not constitute a handicap. These values may not specifically benefit the actor—and, indeed, even if they sometimes do benefit him, they should never be presented on this basis—but they do not, under most circumstances, work *against* his interest either. It is true that such a child may grow up to care more about his friends than his funds, and may occasionally miss a business appointment in order to tend to someone in distress. In this respect, it would not be incorrect to speak of a trade-off, of choosing what sort of person one ultimately wants to be (or wants one's child to be). For the most part, though, there is nothing about caring for others that implies not caring for, or looking after, oneself. Assertiveness, healthy self-esteem, and popularity are all compatible with, and even correlates of, a prosocial orientation (chapter 3).

The concern that social or moral instruction and academic instruction are inversely related is clearly mistaken. So far as I am aware, there is absolutely no evidence to suggest that prosocial children, or the sort of learning experiences that help to create them, are mutually exclusive with academic achievement. Quite to the contrary. As noted in chapter 4, perspective-taking skills tend to promote cognitive problem solving more generally. And in one study, girls' level of empathy at age eight or nine was a powerful predictor of performance on reading and spelling tests taken two years later—an even better predictor, in fact, than their original test scores.[2]

Not only are the ingredients of a prosocial orientation conducive to academic excellence, but the educational process itself does not require a choice between teaching children to think and teaching them to care. It is possible, as I will shortly explain, to integrate prosocial lessons into the regular curriculum; as long as a child is learning to read and spell and think critically, she may as well learn with texts that encourage perspective taking. Cooperative learning, meanwhile, which has an important place in a prosocial classroom, has been shown in literally hundreds of studies to enhance achievement regardless of subject matter or age level.[3] So consistent and remarkable have these results been that schools and individual teachers often adopt cooperative learning models primarily in order to strengthen academic performance, with the promotion of prosocial values realized as an unintended bonus.

Dimensions of Prosocial Learning

Any educator has an effect on how children come to regard and interact with others in four ways: by regulating *what* is being learned, *how* it is being learned, *with whom* it is being learned, and *in what context* the learning occurs. The various strategies for encouraging prosocial interaction—and, for that matter, the relevant aspects of any educational experience—can usefully be evaluated within this framework.

The first category refers to the content of the lesson, which embraces a wide range of activities, from explicit training in perspective taking or moral reasoning to discussions about values that can, in turn, include either "clarification" of the beliefs that students already hold or old-fashioned lectures on character and morality. Most of the debate on the subject occurs between proponents of just such programs, each accusing the other of being relativistic or of seeking to indoctrinate. Far less consideration is given to the possibility of integrating such issues into the regular curriculum.* As an alternative to special units devoted to one of these approaches, children can use texts in conventional subject areas that have the additional benefit of encouraging perspective taking.

For the moment, let us linger on the idea of specific training in perspective taking. One such program, tested by Norma Feshbach in the 1970s, is worth considering. She worked with ninety-eight third- and fourth-grade students in the Los Angeles public schools who represented a variety of ethnic backgrounds and included a fair number of aggressive children. They were divided into three groups: one received "empathy" training, the second worked on cognitive problem-solving skills, and the third served as a control group. For ten weeks, the children in the first two groups met with a trainer for three 45-minute sessions each week. Before and after the intervention, measures were taken of self-concept, aggressiveness, and prosocial behavior.[5]

Children in the "empathy" training condition (which actually focused more on understanding others' points of view and emotions than on feeling them) participated in several dozen exercises developed by Feshbach and her associates, which have been published separately.[6] Some of the activities are designed to facilitate the recognition of others' emotions: children try to identify feelings depicted in photographs, play a silent version of "telephone" in which they must pass along a facial expression from one to the other, and discriminate among different affective intensities as they correspond to real-life situations. Other activities promote perspective-taking skills: the task might be to imagine how story characters feel, to act out situations from the points of view of different participants, to guess what classmates might want to receive as a gift, to mirror someone else's emotion, and so forth.

The results of this study, "while not spectacular, reflected systematic and statistically significant positive changes in children who participated in the empathy training activities. . . . [They] reflected a more positive self-concept and displayed greater social sensitivity to feelings than children in the two control conditions." Aggression declined for children in both the empathy and the problem-solving training sessions, leading Feshbach to conclude that any positive experience in a small group,

*A distinction, though not a sharp one, can be made between teaching morality (or about morality) per se and helping children to be positively connected to others. The latter is my focus here, and some writers have argued that, particularly for younger children, it ought to be the primary focus in the schools, too. "Unless the young child has acquired a positive propensity towards other persons," says one educator, "subsequent moral education will become virtually impotent."[4]

regardless of content, may have such an effect. But prosocial behavior increased only for those whose training sessions focused on perspective taking, as opposed to merely cognitive skills. Such an intervention, Feshbach decided, can be "useful for the average child as well as for the very aggressive child."[7]

This experiment is one illustration of how a change in the curriculum—in the content of what children learn—can affect prosocial attitudes and behavior. But attending to the other variables I mentioned is at least as important. Consider the matter of *how* the instruction takes place. Having children learn from each other, rather than merely from the instructor or the texts, creates powerful bonds among them, sending a very different message than does having each child work on her own—or, worse, leading each child to assume that people must work at cross purposes, the success of each being inversely related to the other's. Cooperative learning does not presuppose the existence of prosocial motives. It amounts to an enforced structural interdependence in which students must rely on each other while they work on a task. This is done by specifying, for example, that no one can be considered to have successfully completed that task until everyone in the group has mastered it. Each has a built-in incentive to help. Prosocial attitudes and behaviors tend to sprout from this arrangement, as does a subjective sense of group identity and a greater acceptance of others, including those who are different from oneself with respect to ethnicity, ability level, or other criteria.[8]

There are many models of cooperative learning: some depend more heavily than others on grade manipulation to create incentives for working together, some involve cooperation among as well as within groups, some provide for a strict division of labor in completing assignments (such that each group member has access to only some information while everyone is responsible for learning all of it). Various measures are used to balance interdependence with individual accountability. In any case, cooperation does not imply unanimity or the absence of conflict. There is evidence that encouraging students to discuss controversial issues and to disagree with each other (but within a context of cooperation)—thus rejecting the false dichotomy of competitive debate on the one hand and the absence of conflict on the other—is particularly effective at developing perspective-taking skills.[9] But any of these approaches to cooperative learning will, as a general rule, lead children to understand and care about each other far more than the learning that takes place individually or competitively.

The third issue in educating for prosocial values is the question: With whom will students learn? Most researchers recommend that children be assigned to groups that maximize heterogeneity. But not since the days of the one-room schoolhouse has children's learning involved interaction with those who are of different ages. This possibility is worth pondering. For an older child to guide someone younger is to experience firsthand what it is to be a helper and to be responsible for someone dependent on him.[10] For the younger child, this cross-age interaction presents an opportunity to see a prosocial model who is not an adult. Anecdotal accounts suggest that this works well in practice,[11] and an Israeli study indicates that age variation is significant even within a single grade. Kindergartners whose classmates ranged from barely four years old to nearly six were more generous and expressed more caring attitudes than those from classes where everyone was about the same age.[12]

Finally, there is the question of the context in which learning takes place. As with the last factor, this can refer either to the way a classroom is organized or to the structure of the entire school. The latter has been the subject of some provocative projects by the late Lawrence Kohlberg and his associates. Their "just community" high schools give students practice at making moral decisions together in the course of exercising real responsibility for governing their schools.[13]

Within the individual classroom, a key issue is how and by whom decisions are made about children's conduct. It is normally accepted that the teacher explicitly or implicitly generates rules and norms by which order is maintained and behavior controlled. Typically the teacher's style of "discipline" is identified on a continuum stretching from extreme rigidity to a completely laissez-faire style, depending in part on how much noise and self-generated activity the teacher chooses to accept. The method for restraining students—and the teacher's role is indeed commonly conceived of in terms of restraint—may be harshly punitive (the old style) or it may involve manipulating rewards to assure compliance (the new style). In either case, the decision is the teacher's alone and the technique consists largely of artificial inducements.

Some educators are beginning to challenge this way of framing the issue by arguing that children of all ages can and should play a role in making decisions about how their classroom is to be run. Discipline would thus be reconfigured as mutual problem solving. Such an approach will be preferred by anyone who favors the idea of autonomy and democratic decision making, but it may also be argued that purely practical considerations recommend it since children are more likely to follow rules that they have helped to devise than rules dictated to them.* In urging that children be given a voice, I do not mean to say that teachers should not intervene in a crisis situation, but only that externally imposed guidelines for behavior will be effective only so long as rewards and punishments (sometimes called "consequences") continue to be meted out. If the goal is to encourage children to internalize these guidelines, then common sense suggests that promoting a sense of ownership in them is likely to be singularly effective.

To have children help decide how their classroom is to be set up—by which I include not only rules about talking and hitting but also how to celebrate birthdays and decorate the walls—is to invite them to take part in a process of discussion, an opportunity for cooperation and consensus. To this extent, it is a chance to practice perspective-taking skills, to share and listen and help. It is, in short, a way of providing a framework for prosocial interactions that supports other such opportunities; it turns housekeeping matters into another opportunity to learn about and practice caring (and, incidentally, thinking as well).[15]

This is by no means an exhaustive survey of the possibilities that might be fit into this framework. These few pages should be sufficient, however, to make plain that an educator need not be confined to curricular adjustments in order to help students become more responsible and responsive to one another. Children do not learn to care about each other just because their teacher tells them to do so or even shows them how to do so, although these may be significant contributors. While the available research on innovative ways to use the classroom toward this end is distressingly incomplete, one program that began in the early 1980s not only has offered some useful and relevant data on the general issue, but also has made use of each of the factors I have described here, thus providing a model for a comprehensive plan of prosocial education.

---

*This, of course, assumes that following rules is in itself a desirable goal. More broadly, educators need to ask themselves and each other about the ultimate objective of discipline. Even if one of the conventional programs of behavior control, such as "Assertive Discipline," did succeed in keeping children quiet,[14] do quiet children learn more effectively or merely make fewer demands on the teacher? (One proponent of cooperative education likes to say that a principal walking through the school corridors should be concerned if she hears no sound coming from a classroom: this means that real learning probably is not taking place.)

THE CHILD DEVELOPMENT PROJECT

Dyke Brown, a lawyer by training, helped to start the Ford Foundation after World War II and later opened California's first integrated, coeducational boarding school. In the late 1970s, he turned his attention to the pervasive individualism and self-preoccupation he believed were undermining the American social structure. After a year of interviewing almost seventy-five child-development specialists, educators, and social psychologists, Brown persuaded the Hewlett Foundation, the largest philanthropic organization on the West Coast, to support a program that would test a strategy for promoting prosocial values and behavior in the schools. The Child Development Project (CDP), and its parent organization, the Developmental Studies Center, grew out of that proposal. CDP is the first long-term, comprehensive, school-based project of its kind, employing not only educators to implement its program but also researchers to assess its effectiveness.[16] In the spring of 1988, I had the opportunity to observe the schools in which the CDP operates and to talk not only with its staff[17] but also with dozens of children, teachers, parents, and other members of the surrounding communities.

After being invited to work in the San Ramon Valley Unified School District, about thirty miles east of San Francisco, the CDP carefully matched two sets of three elementary schools in the district for size and socioeconomic status. A coin flip then determined which of these sets was to receive the program and which would be the comparison schools. The first teachers were trained in preparation for the 1982–83 school year. Staff researchers focused on a group of children, then in kindergarten, and are now in the process of following them into junior high school to assess whether their attitudes, behavior, and achievement differ from those of their counterparts in the comparison schools. In the fall of 1988, the program was introduced into two elementary schools in nearby Hayward, a district more ethnically diverse than the white, affluent suburbs in San Ramon Valley.

Apart from the large number of children, teachers, and staff members involved, what makes the idea of the CDP so compelling is that its method amounts to a kind of immersion for the students, saturating all aspects of their school experience and some of their time at home as well. Its program attends to each of the four educational variables discussed in the last section, one objective being to ascertain the relative importance of each in shaping children's prosocial orientation. I will take them in order.

With respect to curricular content, the CDP does not add special exercises of the sort favored by Feshbach. Rather, the texts used for some of the regular lessons are selected to encourage perspective taking and to model prosocial behavior.[18] First-graders might practice their reading skills on a story about a child who is ridiculed by his peers for being stupid; the subsequent class discussion asks them to reflect not only on the meaning of the story but also on the nature of friendship and feelings. Sixth-graders may read about a white boy who meets a black person for the first time, after which the students proceed to consider whether it is reasonable for the boy to worry that his new acquaintance will be insulted if asked whether his forebears were slaves.

The CDP places at least as much emphasis on the method of teaching as on the content. For at least part of the day, children are encouraged to learn from each other, either in pairs or in slightly larger groups.

At the start of a lesson, the teacher describes the task and helps children to see intrinsic reasons for engaging in it, talks about the prosocial values that will be most relevant to performing it, assigns interdependent roles to the group members, and explains the specific skills that will be necessary for achieving the relevant academic and social goals. The children are then left to work on the task in their groups.[19]

In an attempt to discourage students from seeing cooperation as only a means to some other end, teachers do not use extrinsic motivators such as grades or intergroup competition to encourage or reward group work. (Cooperative games are also used on the playground.)

The idea of cross-age interaction is another feature of the project. On a regular basis, two different classes—say, of fifth-graders and second-graders—come together so that students can work with their "buddies." Older students are also invited to devote some of their free time to tutoring younger children.

Finally, there is the issue of the context for learning. Just the sort of approach to classroom management described above, in which children decide together with the teacher how they want their class to be run, is used here. Styled "developmental discipline" by the CDP, the emphasis again is on developing intrinsic motives to participate productively and prosocially. Teachers are encouraged to develop warm relationships with the children, both to model caring behavior and to reduce the number of discipline problems. The idea is to create an environment in which children *want* to learn and help each other, and in which they play a part in creating that environment. Periodic class meetings are held to discuss various issues, and children sometimes help to make decisions about the timing and content of their academic work. Teachers are asked to reconsider some of their usual practices: "Is it necessary that the children walk in line to the lunch room? ask permission to use the bathroom? complete a learning activity exactly as prescribed?"[20] When a problem develops, the question for the children is: What can we as a class do about it?, as opposed to: What will the teacher do for us—or to us?

In talking with teachers involved in the program, one repeatedly hears how skepticism has been transformed into amazed enthusiasm: to give children—even very young children—some collective responsibility for making decisions, to assume that they are basically well intentioned (if sometimes lacking in understanding or self-control),[21] and to work at creating an atmosphere of warmth and excitement about learning appear to set the tone for the other components of the program. It would not be surprising to learn, once all the research has been completed, that this aspect is the most powerful contributor to children's prosocial values and behavior.

The CDP also has students undertake community service projects such as the adoption of a needy family in the area (whose names are withheld but whose circumstances are described to the children in detail) rather than just collecting toys for something called "charity." Other activities include periodic homework assignments that are specifically designed to be done with parents: a second-grader may, for example, bring home a poem about a child who is teased by a sibling. Parents are invited to share their own childhood memories, to help their son or daughter compose a poem on the same subject, and then to describe the whole experience in writing. Certain science projects are also intended to be done by the whole family in order to foster collaboration at home, and children may be assigned to interview their own parents about the family's history. Special schoolwide activities include family film night, an afternoon of outdoor noncompetitive games for parents and children, and a day in which students bring their grandparents to school for a cross-generational perspective on education and social norms.

In their writings, those on the CDP staff have distinguished their approach to teaching values from those of better-known models. Unlike certain variants of character education, the CDP approach makes no attempt to bribe or threaten children into adopting a set of moral guidelines. The emphasis, as should already be clear, is on helping them to understand the reason for a given value rather than simply insisting that they accept it or behave in a certain way because they were told to do so. Unlike purely child-centered approaches, however, the CDP is committed to the importance of adult socialization: the teacher's job is to teach, to guide, to enforce, to facilitate cooperation, to model—in short, to be much more than a passive bystander. Prosocial values come from a synthesis of adult inculcation and peer interaction, and these values—in contrast to the programs developed by some moral reasoning theorists— emphasize caring for others as well as applying principles of fairness.

Prior to the project's implementation, students randomly selected from the three program and three comparison schools proved to be similar not only demographically but also on a range of social attitudes, values, and skills. Then, over the next five years, thirty-seven program classrooms and thirty comparison classrooms were visited by observers blind to the condition (and, after the first year, unaware that there was any intervention at all). These reports, together with open-ended interviews of children, showed that teachers were indeed implementing the various components of the program. Program children perceived their classrooms as more supportive, reported a greater emphasis on prosocial values, and were more likely to say that they had participated in developing class rules than were children in comparison schools.

On the other hand, not all teachers were equally successful at learning or understanding the CDP training, and while most grasped it adequately, few mastered it entirely. Staff members readily concede some deficiencies in those training procedures—notably in expecting teachers to put the program into practice while they were first learning its concepts, and in training teachers one grade level at a time, with the result that the whole faculty was not involved in the project from the beginning. To the extent that the preliminary results could have been more impressive, the variation in teachers' skill at implementing the various components of the program may be partly responsible.* (There are plans to perform a statistical analysis to determine whether teachers' implementation skill does indeed correlate with children's prosocial attitudes and behaviors.)

After five years of interviews and observation of the children from

*Another possible confound is the fact that cooperative learning, now becoming increasingly popular in California, has independently been adopted by at least two and possibly all three comparison schools. While they have not used the particular approach to cooperative learning developed by the CDP staff—or, of course, implemented the various other components of the program—common sense suggests that the results may not be as striking as if the teachers in the comparison schools had relied exclusively on individualistic or competitive models of instruction.

the original cohort each spring,[22] significant differences between program and comparison school students have emerged. The former engaged in more spontaneous prosocial behaviors in class, seemed better
able to understand hypothetical conflict situations, and were more likely
to take everyone's needs into account in dealing with those situations. In
some instances, they played together more harmoniously and collabora-
tively. On other measures, however, such as observed behavior outside
of class and style of participation in structured group tasks, differences
between conditions did not consistently reach statistical significance.[23]

With little or no prompting, parents of these children recount how
their sons and daughters now take the initiative to resolve disputes (and
do so successfully) while playing games with friends. In some cases parents also talk of having decided, on the basis of the changes they have
witnessed, to involve their children in family decisions. Moreover, a casual observer of classes in the program schools is struck by how children
help each other off the floor without being asked, actually listen to each
other during unsupervised discussions, and turn naturally to each other
for assistance on difficult assignments.

It may be useful to review the CDP's experience with respect to the
three general challenges to the idea of prosocial education considered
above. Even a visitor deliberately looking for San Ramon Valley residents
who are opposed to the program's commitment to teaching values has
difficulty discovering any resistance. Conservative school board members, liberal administrators, and protective parents all generally seem to
be puzzled at the suggestion that the CDP's mission might be regarded
as controversial. Qualities such as helpfulness, consideration, and responsibility are uniformly seen as commendable, and the project is cred-
ited with having helped to promote them in children.

Likewise, there is neither evidence of concern nor objective reason
to support any fear that caring children will be unable to stand up for
themselves. On a questionnaire, program students were more likely than
their counterparts in the other schools to believe that one has an obligation to defend one's position even if it seems unlikely to prevail. Teachers
and parents corroborate this finding by telling stories of children who
have become more assertive even while becoming more prosocial. A
genuine balance seems to have been reached between concern for self
and concern for others.

Finally, on the question of achievement, students and teachers in
program schools seem to recognize that, as one ten-year-old boy put it,
cooperative learning is "like you have four brains." Given such anecdotal

reports as well as the existing research on cooperative education, one would expect program children to enjoy an advantage in the acquisition of learning skills. However, while CDP's emphasis has not required any sacrifice of conventional achievement as measured by standardized test scores, neither has it provided its students with any significant advantage over those in comparison schools. This may well be due to a ceiling effect: students in the district already score in the top 10 percent for California, so there is less room for improvement.

Part of the purpose of the CDP is to determine which methods are most effective in a school-based program devoted to raising prosocial children. Because such studies, particularly of this magnitude and with this combination of techniques, had never before been conducted, the commitment of resources has of necessity been enormous: the Hewlett Foundation has spent something on the order of one million dollars a year for eleven years, its largest grant ever. It is not yet clear what level of expenditure, what commitment of time for training and supporting teachers, and what kind of effort to assure community backing will be required of other school systems that decide to adopt all or part of the CDP's program. But even as the project wears on and the data continue to be analyzed, even as researchers assess how far prosocial values can be promoted without making fundamental changes in our society's institutions, the CDP already has made the point that children can be raised to work with, care for, and help each other, and that schools can play a major role in that process.

III

FROM ME TO YOU
TO US

7

Altruism Lost

Man depends, to a very great extent, on the idea he has of himself, and . . . this idea cannot be degraded without at the same time degrading man.

—Gabriel Marcel (1951)

SONGS OF SELFISHNESS

There is overwhelming evidence that we often act to help people in need, that we can see the world through others' eyes and feel their pain, that certain ways of raising and educating children can promote these prosocial dimensions of human life so that they become at least as basic as the capacity to do harm. But what, asks the skeptic, does all this amount to? Wouldn't an unbiased inquiry into why we take someone else's perspective or come to her aid—or why, for that matter, we do *anything* for or with others—lead us eventually to the motive of self-interest?

This is the challenge of egoism, or, as moral philosophers know it, psychological egoism. The term is generally defined as the view that individuals always try to further what they believe to be their own interests, and it is distinguished from ethical egoism, which holds that individuals *ought* to do so.[1] (It is also distinguished from egotism, which is not a coherent theory of human motivation but a synonym for conceit or self-absorption.)

The first thing to be said about egoism is that it is predicated on the existence of a split between what is good for me and what is simply good. There are plenty of cultures in which the idea of such a discrepancy is unfamiliar and, if described by an outsider, would seem contrived if not incomprehensible. In fact, the distinction as we understand it today is fairly new even in Western culture, having come into being—with the egoism/altruism dispute in its wake—only about three centuries ago.[2]

After Hobbes, philosophers beat the drum for egoism rather loudly and frequently. Even those whose reputations rested on having corrected his bleak view of human nature were careful to make obeisance before the ultimate reality of self-interest. Bishop Butler, whose sermons in the early eighteenth century are regarded as the classic critique of Hobbes's framework, paused (in a passage now rarely cited) to assert that "every particular affection, benevolence among the rest, is subservient to self-love."[3] John Stuart Mill wrote, "Of the social virtues it is almost superfluous to speak; so completely is it the verdict of all experience that selfishness is natural." The people we regard as moral are simply selfish in a different way, he continued. Theirs is a "sympathetic selfishness; *l'égoisme à deux, à trois,* or *à quatre.*"[4]

Today it would no longer be appropriate to refer to the "challenge" of egoism because this position has become the dominant, not the dissident, one in our culture. The belief that humans are naturally aggressive may be widespread, but at least this is still recognizable as a belief that must be defended and can be disputed. By contrast, the belief that humans always act in the final analysis so as to benefit themselves has become, to borrow from computer parlance, the default assumption. Rarely does anyone bother to offer a defense of egoism; it is the premise for other claims rather than itself the subject of disagreement. Everyone knows people are really out for themselves even when they appear to be doing good. Books arguing for the universality of selfishness—which is to say, for the nonexistence of genuine altruism—are not written. They do not have to be written. Rather, books proceed from this assumption by debating the *desirability* of universal selfishness or the wisdom of basing public policy on it.

My concern in this chapter is to offer a quick sketch of how egoism colors contemporary biology, economics (along with other social sciences), and psychology—or at least influential schools of thought within these disciplines. The following section will examine the reasons for our reliance on this assumption, just as the first two chapters proposed explanations for the appeal of biological determinism and the belief in innate aggression. Then, in the next chapter, I will reconsider whether there is actually good reason to believe that real altruism is just an illusion.

Philosophers, as I shall show, have largely jettisoned the notion of *Homo avarus.* But this has not caused most of the rest of us to miss a beat in our songs of selfishness. Barry Schwartz wrote not long ago that evolutionary biology, economics, and behavior theory share a common vision of what it means to be a person. . . . [In this vision] human beings . . . are out to pursue self-interest, to satisfy wants, to maximize utility, or preference, or profit, or reinforcement, or reproductive fitness. They are greedy, insatiable in the pursuit of want satisfaction.[5]

Let us look a little more closely at each of these disciplines in turn.

Biology

Edward O. Wilson has referred to altruism as the "central theoretical problem of sociobiology,"[6] and it has even been suggested that the field of sociobiology, which attempts to apply biology to social behavior, was *invented* to explain the existence of altruism.[7] Indeed, altruism does seem to pose a problem: If survival is the engine of natural selection, how can we account for those individuals across many different species who go to great lengths to benefit others—sometimes even at the cost of their own lives? The sociobiological response has not been, as some casual readers assume, to offer a biological grounding for what we generally call altruism. Quite the reverse. It has attempted to define real altruism out of existence, reducing it in each case to a variant of selfishness. Pop-sociobiologists have unhesitatingly used this same technique to explain away the significance of *human* prosocial behavior. Thus, Richard Dawkins tells us that anyone who still talks about altruism simply has not faced facts: "A human society based simply on the gene's law of universal ruthless selfishness would be a very nasty society in which to live. But unfortunately, however much we may deplore something, it does not stop it being true."[8]

Two theories dominate the contemporary sociobiological account of altruism. The first, devised by W. D. Hamilton and popularized by Dawkins, is known as inclusive fitness. It flourished after an attempt to show that natural selection worked on groups rather than individuals (thus purporting to explain how acts of self-sacrifice were consistent with Darwinian theory) was not well received. Hamilton argued that selection operates not on individuals *or* on groups but on genes. Thus individuals will sacrifice themselves if there is a high probability that this act would assure the survival of their genes in close relatives. The closer the relative (that is, the more genes held in common), the greater the likelihood of sacrifice—and the fewer such relatives who would have to survive to make the sacrifice a sound decision from the cost-benefit perspective that is assumed to govern evolution.

The second major theory is Robert Trivers's idea of reciprocal altruism—quid pro quo transformed into a law of nature. One individual saves another because this increases the probability that the favor will someday be returned. Hamilton observes of this arrangement that "the term altruism may be a misnomer: there is an expectation of benefit of the initiating individual."[9] Appropriately enough, Trivers reciprocates, noting that Hamilton's model and others "that attempt to explain altruistic behavior in terms of natural selection are models designed to take the altruism out of altruism."[10]

There are, then, two major biological theories of the phenomenon, and the author of each says the other has wiped out any altruism worthy of the name. Both, of course, are correct. Those who have come along afterward—writers enamored of such explanations and persuaded of their relevance to our own species—have viewed them as exhaustive. Thus, says Wilson, there are only two kinds of human altruism. The first is "hard-core" and essentially amounts to what Hamilton called inclusive fitness; the second, "soft-core" altruism, refers to prosocial behavior calculated to bring some reward to the actor. (The former sort of egoism, Wilson warns, is more dangerous since, by virtue of benefiting one's kin group, it makes global harmony impossible. But he pronounces himself "optimistic" since "human beings appear to be sufficiently selfish and calculating" to favor the latter version, and—in a passage that should have settled once and for all the arguments about Wilson's political convictions—"true selfishness, if obedient to the other constraints of mammalian biology, is the key to a more nearly perfect social contract.")[11]

Other biologists have added their voices. "Evolutionary biology is quite clear that 'What's in it for me?' is an ancient refrain for all life, and there is no reason to exclude *Homo sapiens,*" writes David Barash.[12] And from Michael Ghiselin, this oft-quoted bit of Scroogean sentiment: "Given a full chance to act in his own interest, nothing but expediency will restrain him from brutalizing, from maiming, from murdering—his brother, his mate, his parent, or his child. Scratch an 'altruist,' and watch a 'hypocrite' bleed."[13]

Richard Alexander has expanded this view into a book. Generosity and altruism are for him nothing more than "complex forms of reproductive selfishness," moral systems are self-serving arrangements of indirect reciprocity, and conscience is "the still small voice that tells us how far we can go without incurring intolerable risks. It tells us not to avoid cheating but how we can cheat socially without being caught."[14] Alexander's central point is that there *is* no brighter side of human nature and nothing beyond selfishness.

The point here is not that every practicing biologist accepts these conclusions, which Philip Kitcher rightly calls "gratuitous Hobbesian speculations that have no basis in biology or any other science."[15] It is rather that the branch of this science that presumes to address human behavior has seen fit to deny the reality of genuine altruism, making the claim of universal selfishness appear to be absolute by arguing that it can even, with enough embellishment and conceptual fiddling, explain away all instances of prosocial behavior. This enterprise both reflects and contributes to the egoism that underlies other disciplines and the culture as a whole.

Economics and Other Social Sciences

Egoism is not *an* assumption but *the* assumption underlying neoclassical economics, which is, in turn, the dominant approach to the discipline in this country. "The first principle of Economics is that every agent is actuated only by self-interest," wrote Francis Edgeworth in the 1880s.[16] "The only assumption essential to a descriptive and predictive science of human behavior is egoism," said economist Dennis Mueller in the 1980s.[17]

The model is based on the premise that every individual is merely trying to maximize his own utility, weighing choices in order to arrive at the option that yields the most advantageous outcome for himself. This is true whether he is acting as investor or laborer, producer or consumer, and also regardless of whether or not he *appears* to be egoistically motivated. Everyone is always engaged in the business of trying to make rational choices—rationality having been defined here as nearly coextensive with egoism—whether selecting a deodorant, hiring a secretary, or deciding about moving to a new city. The good news, Adam Smith reassured us, is that no one need ever try to transcend his egoism since everyone profits when each works to benefit himself.[18] This is the theory; the rest is commentary.

Such unyielding reliance on the a priori assumption of self-interest can seem reasonable enough when the activity under consideration is, say, a bidding war for a property between two investors, which is just the sort of thing with which many economists are chiefly concerned. When they continue to cling to the same model to explain charitable or self-sacrificing behavior, however, as some do, they tend to call attention to themselves in the process. The question of how to account for "the passerby who jumps into the lake to save a drowning swimmer . . . from the standpoint of economics is a challenging one"—but not too challenging for an economist and a legal scholar, conservatives William Landes and Richard Posner. Those who risk their lives to save someone else, they propose, "get their names in the newspapers and this may be the 'real' reason why they rescue complete strangers." And why does someone who sees a flowerpot about to fall on another person's head call out to warn her? Certainly not out of concern:

A, though he presumably does not know what B's wealth was before the flowerpot toppled over, does know that B's expected wealth is now very small and that his own wealth, however slight, is almost certainly much greater than B's. Moreover, if the cost to A of effecting the rescue is very small (the cost of a shout), A can transfer wealth to B at a very low cost to himself. Thus, even though, because they are strangers, A presumably values a dollar to himself much more highly than he values a dollar to B, the rescue may still be a "profitable" transaction for A.[19]

These remarks, which appeared not in the *Harvard Lampoon* but in the *American Economic Review,* are unusual only for giving concrete reality to assumptions widely shared in the field. Another economist has argued that there are only three reasons people give money to charity: direct benefits to the donor, indirect benefits to the donor, or a "Kantian motive" in which "a donor benefits neither directly nor indirectly from the consumption of the charitable good, but merely from the act of giving."[20] The inclusion of the third possibility appears at first to represent a departure from orthodox self-interest theory, but a close reading of that sentence makes clear that the third motive is still unrelievedly egoistic; the source of the benefit to the donor merely shifts from product to process. Kant, to say the least, would not want his name lent to such a motive.*

Another economist, in a book entitled *Selfishness, Altruism, and Rationality,* argues that there is

*And neither should we be satisfied with it. It seems commendable to help someone without receiving any *tangible* benefits for doing so—which describes how many people often act. The more interesting question, which will be addressed in the next chapter, is whether we are sometimes motivated to meet others' needs without looking for *any* sort of personal benefits, including self-satisfaction or the avoidance of guilt or distress.

no more need to distinguish between the bread Smith buys to give to the poor and that which he buys for his own consumption, than to distinguish his neighbor's demand for sugar to make cookies from his demand for sugar to make gin in the cellar. . . . It is ordinarily both convenient and reasonable for economics to . . . treat the individual as satisfying his preferences without dealing explicitly with the possibility that his preferences include a taste for helping other people.[21]

In fact, such economists *cannot* distinguish between acting to benefit oneself and to benefit someone else lest cracks appear in the rigid assumption of universal egoism and the whole structure come crashing down. This is why they are apt to say things like, "A person is reliable if and only if it is more advantageous to him than being unreliable."[22] With their blind loyalty to the idea of self-interest, these economists appear very nearly as ludicrous as the banker in the Monty Python sketch who literally cannot grasp the concept of charity. Asked to contribute to the orphans' fund, the banker becomes increasingly puzzled when told this would be neither a loan nor a tax dodge. After hearing that he is simply being asked to donate a pound that will be given to the orphans, the man frowns and shakes his head. "I don't follow this at all," he says. "I mean, I don't want to seem stupid but it looks to me as though I'm a pound down on the whole deal."

Just as neoclassical assumptions play a prestigious role in contemporary economics, so are there influential models in the other social sciences that rely exclusively on the belief that everyone acts only to benefit herself. In fact, these theories do not merely *rely* on this belief; they seem to be nothing more than so many elaborations of it. Exchange theory in sociology, associated with Peter Blau and the late George Homans, proceeds from the premise that beneath the evidence of "seeming selflessness an underlying 'egoism' can be discovered." With the exception of a few "saints," those who help others expect that doing so "will bring social rewards." The only interesting question with regard to wealthy people's contributions to charity is whether they are more concerned with earning "the social approval of their peers" or "the gratitude of the individuals who benefit from their charity."[23] Friendship, too, on this account, can best be understood as "a social-exchange system in which altruistic action is one of the goods exchanged."[24]

Alvin Gouldner has systematically set out the mechanisms of reciprocity in society, a phenomenon that presumably begins as direct exchange but soon takes on the properties of an autonomous norm. The idea that we give in order to get, which is "no less universal and important an element of culture than the incest taboo," may strike one as egoistic, Gouldner concedes. So be it. Reciprocity is simply a way of "mobiliz[ing] egoistic motivations and channel[ing] them into the maintenance of the social system. . . . 'Private vices make public benefits.' "[25]

But egoism is not just the property of specific schools of thought, such as exchange theory in sociology and public choice theory in political science (to say nothing of the popularity of game theory models across the social sciences). It also informs the mainstream in these disciplines, since the average scholar (like the rest of us) simply takes for granted that members of a polity always act out of perceived self-interest—including when they decided to become members of the polity in the first place. From Locke onward, the dominant political philosophy of Liberalism—not to be confused with present-day liberalism—has grown from the rocky soil of individualism and egoism. As the political theorist Benjamin Barber has observed, "Relationships founded on motives other than self-interest narrowly defined have clearly fallen outside the pale of liberal political theory."[26]

The latter half of this chapter discusses some of the reasons why egoism persists in the culture at large. For social scientists, the assumption is particularly appealing because of its conceptual elegance, which is to say, its simplicity. One who believes everyone is motivated exclusively by self-interest can spin out models and hypotheses and predictions, and can quantify the results. Robert Frank points out that the assumption is also adopted defensively:

The flint-eyed researcher fears no greater humiliation than to have called some action altruistic, only to have a more sophisticated colleague later demonstrate that it was self-serving. This fear surely helps account for the extraordinary volume of ink behavioral scientists have spent trying to unearth selfish motives for seemingly self-sacrificing acts.[27]

If, for whatever reason, the idea of altruism is regarded as inconsistent with the assumptions of social scientists, their response for the most part is simply to ignore it. And if some example of prosocial behavior or empathic response cannot be ignored, then it will be shrunk to fit the egoistic theory—anything to avoid having to confess that the theory itself is incapable of capturing all the multifaceted richness of human beings.

Psychology

The same tendency to ignore or distort unsettling evidence appears again in the field devoted to understanding the behavior and motivation of the individual. There is, in fact, a certain measure of unintentional irony in the occasional declaration by sociobiologists that psychology needs what they have to offer: a more "realistic" understanding of human nature. To the extent that this account of realism rests on a foundation of egoism, psychologists seem to be managing quite well on their own. They may not talk about inclusive fitness or differential reproductive success, but their sketch of a wholly self-regarding organism looks remarkably similar to that framed by biologists.

I am generalizing, of course. Psychologists often do not even speak the same language among themselves, let alone converse in the same tongue as biologists. Yet psychoanalysts and behaviorists, experimentalists and therapists, specialists in prosocial activity and those attending to other problems—all really do appear to have egoism as their common denominator. This point has been made with special force by Michael and Lise Wallach in their book, *Psychology's Sanction for Selfishness.* "Psychological theories of motivation are, almost without exception, fundamentally egoistic, in a nontrivial manner," they have written.[28] The number of drives attributed to the human may have grown over the years, but the nature of these drives never seems to change: it is always the satisfaction of one's own needs that is supposed to motivate the individual. This is taken on faith.

It is surely true of psychoanalytic theory, which has leached into popular culture and thus been influential far out of proportion to the number of its practitioners. "Very few examples can be found in psychoanalytic literature that deal directly with positive forms of behavior and do not focus primarily on the aspects of unresolved conflict," says the analyst Rudolf Ekstein.[29] The tendency of Freudians to see pathology in every behavior is well known. (Recall the old joke about the underlying meaning of the patient's time of arrival for her analysis: if she comes early, she is anxious; if late, hostile; if on time, compulsive.) But this facility for taking anything innocuous (or vaguely wholesome) and interpreting it to death is in particularly fine form with regard to people who help or care for others.

Show the analyst an illustration of altruism and he will see a means for resolving intrapsychic conflict, a sign that guilt or anxiety is not yet under control. Before a child is grown, what we call "altruistic impulses and morality will awaken in the little egoist," Freud informed us, but this is just an overlay on his primary character, which has already been established. Through the windows into the unconscious processes we espy the true, self-serving functions of this ostensible concern for the welfare of others. Just look at the dreams, Freud urged. But stop looking at them if they should contradict the theory: if "a dream seems to have been provoked by an altruistic interest, we are only being deceived by appearances."[30]

In general, an apparent desire to help constitutes a reaction formation, an unconscious reversal, against one's *real* desire, which is usually to hurt. If those suffering from fatal diseases try not to infect anybody else, said Freud, we can be sure they are merely defending against their "unconscious wish to spread their infection on to other people."[31] The more altruistic the act appears, the more profound the actor's secret greed or envy or sadism. And if this set of hypotheses fails to persuade, the psychoanalysts have others in reserve. Moral motives could be construed as nothing more than responses to our "original helplessness," Freud wrote in an early letter.[32] His daughter Anna continues in the same vein in her best-known work, *The Ego and the Mechanisms of Defense,* which devotes a full chapter to debunking altruism. People's "surrender" to this impulse suggests their need to overcome the fear of death or their underlying masochism or some other defensive process, she says.[33]

Given this theoretical groundwork, the reaction to altruism on the part of analytically inclined—even if not orthodox Freudian—psychotherapists is fairly predictable. After all, Freud himself warned that "all who wish to be more noble-minded than their constitution allows fall victims to neurosis."[34] The therapist's job is to interpret, and to interpret properly one must be able to spot the egoistically driven defense mechanisms that (almost by definition) give rise to what an untrained observer might call "being a nice person." Since women are more likely to profess prosocial inclinations in our culture, women will more often be on the receiving end of these interpretations. So reasons Jean Baker Miller: "Clinicians . . . may think they see through to the fact that the woman is serving herself through serving others. They may stress attempts to discover what she is *really* after and to show that she is just as self-serving as everyone else."[35]

Thus the descriptive premise that selfishness motivates our every action becomes a prescriptive framework for the therapeutic enterprise:

"Look out for your own needs" seems less objectionable if it is packaged as self-discovery rather than pure exhortation. It is significant that progressive and conservative social critics have, in effect, joined forces recently to censure the institution of therapy for precisely this reason. Robert Bellah and his colleagues note that "the question 'Is this right or wrong?' becomes 'Is this going to work for me now?' . . . The very language of therapeutic relationship seems to undercut the possibility of other than self-interested relationships."[36] Allan Bloom is more succinct: "Psychology has distinctions only between good and bad forms of selfishness."[37]

From depth psychology we move to the other major approach to personality theory: behaviorism, or learning theory. One of the most striking points of agreement between these rival schools of thought concerns egoism. Not only the vulgar versions of classical and operant conditioning but also the newer forms of behaviorism take self-interest as their point of departure. Even when blended with elements of cognitive theory or packaged as social learning theory, the actor is—again, virtually by definition—motivated to benefit himself. Freud's pleasure principle and the behaviorist's idea of reinforcement are (in this respect, at least) not very far apart at all.

The inflexibility of the self-interest doctrine is most noticeable when psychologists, notably those enamored of "equity theory," insist on using it even to explain love. "The amount of romantic love a person feels for someone is supposed to be a direct function of the benefits he or she derives from the relationship," David McClelland has observed. Those who take a different view of their passion have made "attribution 'errors.' "[38] Such analyses are sometimes condemned, and understandably so, for representing the worst sort of coldblooded reductionism. But this should not distract us from recognizing that the principal feature of this model is egoism. One of the most influential and widely cited books in the field, we should notice, does not begin by championing scientific (as opposed to poetic) approaches to human relationship. Rather, the reader is welcomed with these words: "Politicians contend that 'Every man has his price.' Equity theory, too, rests on the simple, but eminently safe, assumption that man is selfish."[39]

Consider, finally, those psychologists who have specifically investigated prosocial behavior and empathy. Why do we reach out to other people? Most social behavior theorists, who dominate the discussion of the issue, point to one of three reasons: (1) we are seeking some sort of reward—if not explicit payment or public recognition or praise, then self-approval; (2) we are seeking to avoid some sort of punishment—either condemnation by others for violating a social norm or guilt for violating an internalized standard; or (3) we find someone else's pain distressing, and relieving that pain is often the most efficient way of improving our own emotional state.

Almost all of the research reviewed in chapter 3 on the relation between helping and mood or self-awareness has been guided by some variation of these egoistic assumptions. In a single recent issue of a leading journal, one psychologist talks about how positive mood leads people to help more readily because they "regard themselves more favorably than they otherwise are inclined to,"[40] while another group of authors proposes that even empathic individuals, who feel sad when "viewing a suffering victim . . . help for egoistic reasons: to relieve the sadness in themselves."[41] Likewise, if prosocial activity occurs when we are attuned to our own affective state, it is because we are attempting to benefit ourselves. If prosocial activity occurs when we are attuned to others, it is because doing something about their situation will be rewarding to us. Positive mood, negative mood, self-aware, not self-aware—the precise empirical findings hardly seem to matter since they are invariably perceived through an egoistic filter.

Even before grappling with the substance of this theory, I should make it clear that none of these accounts of prosocial behavior can be dismissed out of hand. There is a prima facie plausibility to each, just as there is to each of the interpretations of the time at which the psychoanalyst's patient arrives for her appointment. That something is problematic here may not occur to us until we see the whole picture and recognize the pattern. It is undoubtedly true that some people help others for self-serving reasons, and the reasons generally proposed (public recognition, escaping guilt, and so on) are as credible as any. But the possibility of genuine altruism has been ruled inadmissible by most investigators, all of their ingenuity having been devoted exclusively to explicating the mechanisms of egoistic motives. Nor is this tendency peculiar to neobehaviorists, as C. Daniel Batson explains:

By around 1920 . . . theories of motivation based on behaviorism or psychoanalysis were sufficiently sophisticated to provide an egoistic account of any behavior that might appear to be altruistically motivated. Continued dominance of psychology by modern descendants of these early egoistic theories of motivation may explain why the recent upsurge of interest in and research on helping behavior . . . has not led to a parallel upsurge of interest in the classic question of whether at least some helping might be altruistically motivated. When asked why we act prosocially, all major psychological theories of motivation—Freudian, behavioral, and even humanistic or "third force" theories—are quite clear in their answer: everything we do, including all prosocial behavior, is ultimately done for our own benefit.[42]

As a general rule, investigators across various theoretical schools assume that if they cannot identify the self-interested motive behind helping behavior or empathy, it is because they are not looking hard enough or in the right places.[43]

Once one starts to realize the extent of this bias, its presence becomes hard to ignore. Data that are compatible with either an egoistic or an altruistic interpretation are automatically viewed in terms of the former. Read Darley and Latane as they imagine the conflict that bystanders must suffer in deciding whether to help: these people do not want to make fools of themselves by overreacting but they are also "worried about the guilt and shame they would feel if they did not help"[44]—this self-interested worry being the only conceivable motive for coming to the aid of someone in distress. Or read David Rosenhan and his colleagues as they discuss the relevance to prosocial behavior of focus of attention. "Subjects who focused on the victim's feelings presumably experienced greater empathy *and, with it, the hedonic sense that helping could be particularly rewarding.* "[45] It is assumed as a matter of course here that empathy is fueled by a quest for personal reward—even though Rosenhan himself had complained a decade earlier about theorists who explored helping or rescuing and *"decreed* on the basis of little concrete evidence that there must be 'something in it' for the actor, even when nothing is apparent."[46]

Ervin Staub, one of the leading, and most sophisticated, theorists of the development of prosocial behavior, is not immune to the dominant assumptions of the discipline. He distinguishes clearly between altruistic and egoistic motives, suggesting that they may both be present, but then seems to cast doubt on the existence of the former:

If behavior that demands various sacrifices is not reinforced in any way, it would extinguish over time. As people develop concern for others' welfare, they are likely to learn to gain satisfaction from promoting others' goals and reducing others' needs. . . . When a person behaves prosocially out of altruistic intentions, purely to benefit another, he is still likely to have some anticipation of, and certainly the experience of, such reinforcement.[47]

The idea here is that even people who do not pause to consider how they will benefit from being a good samaritan, even those who help spontaneously, can best be explained by what in the final analysis is Skinnerian behaviorism. What *really* accounts for helpfulness, should one be inclined to dig deep enough, is self-reward.

Finally, this belief also informs the work of some theorists who are more interested in the way we think about morality than in the way we behave. Dennis Krebs approvingly describes the position in stark terms: "Subjects tailor their moral decisions to the alternatives that advance their self-interest, and adjust their moral reasoning in support of their decisions."[48] Regardless of the way one approaches ethical issues, in other words, and one's apparent commitment to the needs and rights of others, this is in every case just a charade designed to rationalize one's selfish desires.

These instances of ideological commitment to egoism are among the general organizing principles of sociobiology, mainstream economics (as well as other social sciences), and psychology. That these disciplines all share the belief that humans are actually out for themselves even when they go out of their way for others is helpful for understanding why the reality of altruism is typically doubted in the society at large. But there are other features of the society that sustain this doubt and make egoism appear to be a matter of common sense. These explanations, taken together, offer a telling look at our social milieu.

BEHIND THE APPEAL OF EGOISM

In principle, of course, it is entirely possible that egoism is so popular because it is true. But as with other prevalent assumptions in our culture, we do not need to accept that people are by nature interested only in themselves in order to arrive at a convincing account of why so many of us assume that we are. As I have already noted, this belief in particular is so ingrained in our scholarship and popular culture that explicit indoctrination is practically superfluous.

We have been persuaded that altruism is only a chimera partly by the promulgation of explicit self-interest ideologies. We are told not only that each member of our species is destined to be preoccupied with his own well-being, but that such preoccupation is the path to individual and social fulfillment. Morality is married, or at least friendly, to the idea of doing for oneself. This is the view known as ethical egoism, and it has been decried by philosophers for centuries. Kant, in the *Critique of Practical Reason,* showed us how self-love and morality pull in opposite directions; two centuries later John Rawls came to essentially the same conclusion.[49] The notion that each of us should pursue her own rational self-interest irrespective of its effect on others, says the philosopher Kai Nielsen,

is an ancient and recurring one in the history of ethical thinking. It is a belief that many people who reflect about ethics naturally come to have. This is particularly true of people living in cultures such as our own. However, the vast majority of moral philosophers in the past three hundred years have rejected it as thoroughly confused.[50]

Nevertheless, versions of ethical egoism continue to soothe economists with an invisible hand, to reassure needy seekers of themselves who live by the tenets of the human potential movement,[51] to excite new generations of adolescents captivated by the meretricious screeds of Ayn Rand. We elect presidents who ask us to consider whether each of us is better off than he was four years ago—with the emphasis on financial well-being—as if one's personal bank account were the most appropriate basis on which to gauge the success of our leaders.

Sometimes ethical egoism stares out at us from the covers of vulgar self-help books, and sometimes it takes a subtler guise. Imagine a middle-class woman who says she is weary of taking responsibility for the well-being of others. She wrestles with the question of whether she should stop making herself available to counsel someone who has long been depressed, or perhaps with whether to challenge a business colleague for a promotion the latter wants badly. Over lunch she describes her dilemma to a friend, and instantly the friend provides her with support for this proposed shift in values: You've got to start putting yourself first, she is told. You're not obligated to solve other people's problems.

Whether or not they are articulated in therapeutic jargon ("Give yourself permission to take responsibility for processing your issues"), such reassurances are widely seen as the preferred response and are offered without apology. They are, to be sure, generally well meaning and understandable. Mary Belenky and her colleagues have described something similar as a stage through which many women pass after having viewed themselves as less important than the people they take care of: "The claims of others, for years so salient for them, are often suddenly disregarded when the women begin to assert their own authority and autonomy."⁵² We are talking, in other words, about an exaggerated, reactive self-concern to compensate for an earlier debilitating loss of self.

We are also talking, to put this in context, about women whose retreat from a commitment to caring and relatedness is simply more conspicuous than the egoism (and egotism) of many men who have been chronically alienated from those values.⁵³ But however sympathetic we may be to the concerns of the individuals involved, pep talks about putting oneself first represent a key component of contemporary society's veneration of self-interest, and, by extension, a climate in which altruism is made to seem an idealistic fantasy of the sort one is expected to outgrow.

Closely related to advice about looking out for Number One is the reflexive counsel to "stop feeling guilty"—an exhortation offered cease-lessly in books,⁵⁴ articles, seminars, and informal conversation that ig-nores the question of whether a given person may have done something about which he or she *ought* to feel guilty. Guilt is perceived as analogous to dandruff; the only question is how to get rid of it most efficiently. After all, guilt is an unpleasant feeling, and a relativistic society whose watch-word is "Who are you to judge another person's life?" is left with plea-sure as the only criterion by which to evaluate action and affect. Our imaginary lunch companion tells her friend that she has no reason to feel guilty—a phrase prepared well before hearing the account of what the speaker actually has done. Such a stance reinforces the egoistic vision, which, in turn, contributes to the dismissal of all guilt feelings.

Ethical egoism, in short, begets psychological egoism—that is, a common belief that we *should* restrict ourselves to self-interest, however that belief manifests itself, will ultimately incline us to see this exclusive devotion to the self as a fact of life. In turn, the way we see ourselves, as Marcel pointed out (see this chapter's epigraph), affects the way we really do behave. Thus such ideas set a vicious circle into motion: we act in accordance with these images and thereby provide support for them.

The mechanism by which this process operates is not particularly mysterious. The invention of "rational economic man," says Barry Schwartz, "led to the formation of social practices and institutions that were consistent with it but that undermined previous forms of social organization." The same is true of the egoistic assumptions of behavior theory, which seem to us valid "not because work is a natural exemplifi-cation of behavior theory but because behavior theory principles, in the form of scientific management, had a significant hand in transforming work into an exemplification of behavior theory principles."[55] On the individual level, too, we act selfish because we believe we are, and we believe we are because we see ourselves acting that way.

Our acceptance of the inevitability of this devotion to self is a function not only of our attitudes about egoism, but of the way we construe altruism. So many writers, whose picture of the human being is truncated, all genuine and irreducible concern for others having been lopped off, try to bolster their case by defining the only alternative to egoism as something hopelessly utopian. Unless we are prepared to accept the "altruistic perfection" of "a race of saints" (Wilson)[56] or a "theory which regards man as a sacrificial animal . . . who has no right to exist for his own sake" (Rand),[57] we are compelled to cast our lot with the apologists of self-interest.

Whether this false dichotomy represents a debater's trick or an honest limit of the imagination, it is widely shared by the lay culture. Even if we concede that altruism exists, we are convinced that it is fantastically rare. We associate it with the odd self-sacrificing individual of our acquaintance and with the list of twenty or so rescuers honored at the end of each year by the Carnegie Hero Fund Commission—people who risk their lives to carry children out of burning buildings and so forth. Such extraordinary tales of selfless, saintly behavior paint an image of something quite different from ourselves. In fact, the image is often defined precisely in terms of its remoteness from us.

Of this practice we can say several things. First, it does each of us an injustice by seeming to put part of human nature beyond our reach. In *The Plague,* Camus has his narrator deliberately refrain from praising the honorable efforts of residents of the disease-infested town. His rationale is that

by attributing overimportance to praiseworthy actions one may, by implication, be paying indirect but potent homage to the worse side of human nature. For this attitude implies that such actions shine out as rare exceptions, while callousness and apathy are the general rule. The narrator does not share that view.[58]

Second, to linger on saintliness communicates the reassuring message that a few larger-than-life characters have become specialists in helping others. In taking on a life of this sort, they relieve us of the responsibility of having to go and do likewise. We call them exemplary but they are not literally examples to us. (This is rather like the function that moral philosophers play in the academic community. Experts in various fields can slough off the ethical implications of their work, secure in the knowledge that others are being employed to worry about such things.) In fact, one experiment showed that subjects who read about people who did an exceptional amount of volunteer work subsequently rated themselves as slightly less altruistic than those who read about individuals who were less helpful.[59]

Third, and most germane to an account of egoism's popularity, this approach has the effect of turning altruism into an all-or-nothing proposition. If our private definition of the word ends with: "See 'Mother Teresa,' " and if we are sure we could never be like her, then we may stretch out comfortably in a life devoted to self-aggrandizement. (This is why either/or thinking is always so popular: it makes choosing easy.) Again we witness a self-fulfilling prophecy: if I know altruism is not within my reach, why bother trying to act that way—or seeking to cultivate it in my children?

It is bad enough to narrow the field in this manner, but our culture, while reserving its adulation for the heroically selfless, also seems frequently to disdain the very idea of helping. This is a curious ambivalence. We praise rescuers, and yet "accepting help may be seen as weakness, and offering help, as intrusion."[60] Many of us, as I pointed out in chapter 3, raise our children to compete rather than to share. And rescuing people in peril—even at minimal cost to oneself—is almost never required by law. One legal scholar has written, "It is not a great overstatement to suggest that the supreme command of this mighty repository of Anglo-American thought and experience is: 'Mind your own business!' "[61]

With the help of such traditions as psychoanalysis, prosocial behavior is viewed suspiciously and altruism is reduced to self-interest. Notice the contempt with which we refer to "do-gooders,"[62] how ready we are to point out and ridicule pseudo-helpers (those who obviously have ulterior motives) as well as pseudo-victims. Our folklore is filled with welfare queens driving Cadillacs, healthy beggars who use crutches as props, and the like—these examples being far more salient to us than their actual prevalence would justify. We cherish examples of such deception, nodding our heads knowingly and twisting our lips into a satisfied smirk of vindication. "It takes only a few obvious frauds . . . to snap the compassion of skeptical marks and cut off their charity completely."[63] We are predisposed to look for such examples and to regard them as more decisive than the obvious misery that surrounds us; this allows us to reassure and justify ourselves for not helping. As Jerome Kagan puts it:

The idea that humans always act in the service of self-interest has created serious mischief. So many citizens have come to accept the truth of that assumption about human nature that the average person now treats it as a natural law. And because they believe they should not violate a natural law, they try to obey it. . . . What worries me is that the presumptive validity of the law of self-interest is becoming a self-fulfilling prophecy.[64]

On the occasions when we overcome our suspicion of the whole affair and commend prosocial behavior to our children and to each other, notice how we do so. It is not just that enlightened self-interest is said to encompass helping others, but that helping others is almost always justified in terms of what the helper may get out of it. The only alternatives we have laid out for ourselves are enlightened self-interest and unenlightened self-interest. Glaucon's brother, Adeimantus, challenged Socrates by making this observation about ethical behavior more generally: "All you who profess to sing the praises of right conduct, from the ancient heroes whose legends have survived down to the men of the present day, have never denounced injustice or praised justice apart from the reputation, honours, and rewards they bring."[65]

Notwithstanding the philosophical repudiation of ethical egoism, there seems little doubt that when we as a society are not busy justifying or rewarding selfish behavior, we are promising that prosocial action will redound to the benefit of the actor. Fairy tales are replete with magical creatures or royalty who pose as unfortunates and reward charitable acts. The same moral is found in a magazine advertisement for charity that carries the headline: "How Helping a Poor Child Will Make You Feel Rich," and also on a billboard that stands not far from my home: "Lend a hand! A friendly act is rarely forgotten." Many religious traditions emphasize egoistic inducements, promising that those who act rightly will be rewarded with a pleasant afterlife or a state of enlightenment, sometimes by earning the equivalent of cosmic merit badges.* In a newer version of this egoistic appeal—one not restricted to children or the religious—we are promised that volunteering our time for good causes will bring us a healthier immune system, lower cholesterol levels, and longer life. Two leading proponents of this view put it as follows: "In these tough times, we need to develop plenty of virtuous strength—even if it takes a little enlightened selfishness to drive us."[66]

---

*As the New Testament puts it, "When thou doest alms . . . thy Father which seeth in secret himself shall reward thee openly" (Matthew 6:3–4) and "When thou makest a feast, call the poor, the maimed, the lame, the blind: And thou shalt be . . . recompensed at the resurrection of the just (Luke 14:13–14)."

What happens when this same frame of mind drives public policy? Here are excerpts from three newspaper articles, representative of hundreds of others, that happened to appear within the span of a single month:

A Federal commission today called for a comprehensive policy to combat infant mortality, saying that it costs far less to support health care for pregnant women and newborns than to pay later for critical and long-term care for infants.[67]

"Family violence costs employers millions of dollars annually in lower productivity, turnover, absenteeism and excessive use of medical benefits," said Deborah Anderson, executive vice president of Responses [to End Abuse of Children, Inc.][68]

Those [illiterate people] who cannot find work end up costing the Government billions of dollars in welfare and unemployment compensation. Some end up turning to crime.[69]

The message here is that we ought to try to reduce infant mortality, family violence, and illiteracy because it is in our own best financial interest to do so. If we do not act now to help suffering people, it will only cost us more down the road.[70]*

Our economic system is based on just such calculations, and on reducing noneconomic issues, including such "externalities" as human suffering, to dollars and cents. A corporation exists for only one reason, and that is to provide a favorable return on investment to those who own it. From the corporate sector one therefore fully expects to encounter a world view in which wife beating is disapproved because it leads to the excessive use of medical benefits. But since the business of America is business, this perspective seeps out of downtown skyscrapers and suburban industrial parks and becomes the lifeblood of public policy, too. Thus our treasury is tapped to reduce infant mortality if and only if this can be shown to be a wise investment. (We do not ask: If preventing babies from dying is not a sufficient reason to tap the public treasury, then what is the point in having one?)[71] Soon we are all reasoning this way in our personal

*The point of such declarations, of course, is to create or mobilize a constituency to support a given program. I do not mean to deny the need for such support in light of scarce resources and other contenders for funding. The point, rather, is to emphasize that the criteria for disbursement invariably relate to financial self-interest. If we are to choose between a campaign to end homelessness and some other budget item, we have already accepted that the first (and perhaps last) question to ask is: Which will benefit us taxpayers more?

lives, justifying each decision about how to treat others in terms of what we will get out of it, or following Tom Lehrer's wry musical advice to the Boy Scouts: "Be careful not to do/Your good deeds when there's no one watching you."

Policy analyst Lisbeth Schorr has declared (in a reporter's paraphrase) that "the political will and economic resources to expand" programs to reduce teenage pregnancy and child abuse "will come not from altruism but from concerns about productivity and the high cost of crime and unemployment."[72] This assumption obviously informs those quoted in the above news stories. But if so, let us reflect on just how profound an indictment we have thereby leveled against the society in which we live.

Let us also pause to ask whether this assumption is even *true*. The issue is generally framed so that those who would make an appeal to something like altruism—who would say we should stop domestic violence or provide care to newborns just because it is the right thing to do—are perceived as naive. Those who appeal to the self-interest of the donor, on the other hand, are seen as shrewd pragmatists, willing to trade lofty moral appeals for references to the bottom line in order to get the job done.

The problem is that, from a long-range perspective, this may be a self-defeating strategy. To understand how this is true, we need to take a step back and recall the research that has found extrinsic (external) incentives can undermine the very performance they are used to promote.[73] Unless applied with care and discretion, rewards such as money, victory in a contest, grades, and even praise can be counterproductive, particularly if the activity in question requires creativity. This is true for several reasons, most of them having to do with the effects of rewards on intrinsic motivation—that is, on one's liking for the activity in question. No artificial inducement can compensate for an absence of interest in a task; people do their best work when they find it fun, not when they are in it for the money. But the data take us even further: they show that rewards actually *erode* intrinsic interest. What once may have been done for pleasure comes to be thought of as a chore, a prerequisite for obtaining the extrinsic incentive. Remove the reward and there is no longer any desire to continue performing the task. Moreover, people who see themselves as motivated by rewards also tend to feel controlled by them. The result, once again, is often poorer performance.

These findings challenge the behaviorist view that it is always expedient to dangle a reward before an organism (including an organism with two legs) in order to encourage a desired activity or attitude. This suggests that there is a need to rethink the way bonuses are used in the workplace and grades in the classroom. But the implications extend beyond productivity: the research also points up the folly of trying to encourage prosocial behavior by the use of extrinsic incentives or other appeals to self-interest. This strategy tends to make one dependent on what is, in effect, a bribe for helping. It offers no reason to help in the absence of rewards, and it effectively drowns out the intrinsic value of meeting other people's needs. And not only does it wind up snuffing out altruism, but it also promotes a cynical tendency to assume that no one would help without getting something out of it.

Consider some of the experimental evidence:

- Second- and third-graders who received rewards for donating to another child—or fines for not helping—were less likely to explain their own behavior in words suggesting an intrinsic motivation to help than were children who received no rewards or punishments.[74]
- Among children who gave away some of their game winnings after watching a model do so, those who were told they had made the donations "because you're the kind of person who likes to help other people"—or who were simply told they had "shared quite a bit" (without any attribution)—were subsequently more generous than those told they had donated because they were expected to do so.[75]
- The likelihood of children's donating increased in one study both when they were praised and when they were led to think of themselves as helpful people. But in a follow-up experiment, it was the latter who turned out to be more generous than those who had received verbal reinforcement. In other words, praise promoted generosity in a given setting but ceased to be effective outside of that setting, whereas children with an intrinsic impulse to be generous continued to act on that motivation in other circumstances.[76]
- Elementary school students whose mothers believed in using rewards to motivate them were less cooperative and generous than other children.[77]
- Adults who were offered money for agreeing to help a researcher rated themselves as less altruistic than those who either received no payment or were told *after* they said they would help that they would be paid. "Extrinsic incentives can, by undermining self-perceived altruism, decrease intrinsic motivation to help others," these researchers concluded. "A person's kindness, it seems, cannot be bought."[78]
- Women offered money for answering a questionnaire over the telephone were less likely to agree to a similar request two or three days

later in which no money was involved than were women who had not been paid for their participation in the first survey.[79]

• Repeated blood donors who were reminded of altruistic reasons for giving blood indicated that they were more willing to do so again than those who were reminded of the personal benefits of what they were about to do. Focusing attention on personal benefits actually reduced the motivation to go through with the donation.[80]

• Adult subjects who were told that a personality test showed they were kind and thoughtful people were more likely to help a confederate who "accidentally" dropped a pile of cards than were those told they were unusually intelligent or those given no feedback at all. This is important because it suggests that being led to think of oneself as generous does not affect behavior merely because it is a kind of reinforcement, a mood enhancer; this label apparently promotes prosocial action because it helps to build a view of the self as altruistic.[81]

The lessons of these studies, when taken together, are straightforward. When we are rewarded for prosocial behavior, we tend to assume the reward, and not altruism, accounts for our having acted as we did. If we do not see ourselves as altruistic, we are less likely to act prosocially once the extrinsic reward for acting that way is withdrawn. In this respect, verbal reinforcement for helping is worse than nothing, and material reinforcement is worse yet. Conversely, encouragement to think of oneself as a generous person—an appeal not to self-interest but to genuine altruism—seems to be the most reliable way to promote helping and caring over the long haul and in different situations. The research reviewed here dovetails with a classic study that warned against giving in to the temptation of paying blood donors.[82] And it means that we cannot dismiss as impractical an educator's assertion that

self-interest alone may be insufficient in promoting productive activity. Self-transcendence and the idea that one can be of service to others may be far more effective in persuading some to develop their skills and abilities. . . . Rather than appealing to self-gain, teachers might be better advised to urge students to act on behalf of others without regard to their own immediate gratification.[83]

There is a lesson here, too, for those who propose to clean up the scandals and rein in the naked greed of the business world by proclaiming that "ethics pays." At the very least, all the research findings aside, it should be obvious that such a strategy serves principally to legitimate personal gain as the only relevant standard for one's behavior. If a situation arises in which immoral conduct *is* more lucrative, we have offered no basis for rejecting it.

More broadly, this discussion has pointed to the existence of two distinct self-fulfilling prophecies. First, we tend to "live down to" the assumption that we are basically selfish, or up to the assumption that we are given to act prosocially. Both of these orientations feed on themselves. Helping is like lying: one finds it difficult to stop with just one generous act. Second, we also live down to the view that when we *do* help others it is only for egoistic reasons, and we live up to the view that we are basically altruistic. What we believe to be true about ourselves and others affects how we behave, which, in turn, affects our assumptions about human nature.

Consider a likely scenario. A young child, yet insensible of motivational considerations, attributes altruism to others on the simple basis of how many helpful acts they perform. As he grows, he begins to think about *why* people act to benefit others. Where he sees such behavior rewarded in one way or another, he assumes that the reward accounts for the inclination to help. Since he himself is offered extrinsic incentives, he figures that he, too, is generous only because of what he gets out of it. In fact, he generalizes, whenever people seem to act altruistically, there must be good (that is, egoistic) reasons for it.

Outside of emergency situations, the child is also less likely to help people if he does not admire them, and he is less likely to admire those people he suspects of having selfish motives when *they* help. Since he will come to suspect most, if not all, people of having such motives, he will be increasingly disinclined to help. This, in turn, may make others less likely to reach out to him, so he will be even less likely to respond positively to them or to believe in the existence of altruism. Thus does another vicious circle close in.

Selfishness, like the belief in its ubiquity, is fully understandable without any invocation of "human nature." The use of extrinsic incentives to promote generosity combines with the collapse of altruism into saintliness, with a commitment to the value of putting oneself first, and with several distinct academic traditions premised on psychological egoism to create a powerful, self-reproducing framework in which talk of altruism is instantly discounted as wishful thinking. If we can break the spell of these ideological forces, we can examine without prejudice the philosophical arguments and empirical evidence on the question of whether it is reasonable to assume that real altruism exists.

8

Altruism Regained

*The voice of nature and experience seems plainly to oppose the
selfish theory.*

—David Hume (1751)

*Selfishness is in human nature in the same way that the David
was in the marble before Michelangelo touched it.*

—Barry Schwartz (1986)

THE ILLOGIC OF EGOISM

It is common in our culture to hear cynical sentiments of the sort voiced
by George Santayana: "Generous impulses are . . . self-deceptive hypocri-
cies. . . . Dig a little beneath the surface, and you will find a ferocious,
persistent, profoundly selfish man."[1] Those who do not remember the
full range of our species' possibilities, however, are condemned to repeat
such slanders. While there is reason to doubt whether the existence of
genuine altruism can ever be empirically demonstrated—at least to the
satisfaction of skeptics—I will try to show in this chapter that someone
who argues for the reality of altruism stands on ground at least as firm
as that beneath the egoist.

What I hope emerged from the preceding chapter was a sense that
egoism is not only widely accepted but generally taken for granted even
among scholars. One can hardly avoid noticing how rarely anyone both-
ers to justify the assumption that each of us is always acting to benefit
himself even when appearing to help someone else. As the moral philosopher Joel Feinberg has written, "Empirical evidence of the required sort
is seldom presented in support of psychological egoism. . . . It is usually
the 'armchair scientist' who holds the theory of universal selfishness."[2]

Let us endeavor to be clearer than those who wander casually onto this turf about what altruism and selfishness mean and do not mean. To begin with, we should emphasize again the distinction between prosocial behavior and altruism. It is a simple matter to demonstrate the falsity of the proposition that people are universally selfish in the sense that they never help or share with others; such activity obviously goes on all the time. The question at hand is *why* people are prosocial, whether some expected benefit to the self must motivate this behavior.

To argue that altruism exists is not to deny the existence or value of what is sometimes called self-love. Put the other way around, self-love is not at all the same thing as selfishness. This distinction was emphatically made by Rousseau. On the one hand, he wrote, there is *amour de soi*, the sort of natural and necessary inclination to care about oneself that lies behind the impulse of self-preservation and is "contented when our true needs are satisfied." It is perfectly compatible with—indeed, a prerequisite for—"the gentle and affectionate passions." On the other hand, there is *amour-propre*, which puts one's own needs ahead of others' and demands that everyone else take note of one's claims; it is the source of competitiveness, envy, vanity, and other "hateful and irascible passions."[3]

The idea that loving oneself not only does not exclude but actually facilitates loving others has been featured in the work of many writers. Erich Fromm, for example, noted that "the love for my own self is inseparably connected with the love for any other self"—and, conversely, that "selfishness and self-love, far from being identical, are actually opposites. The selfish person does not love himself too much but too little; in fact he hates himself."[4] What we moderns call self-esteem is relevant here. Recall that the approach to raising a child that promotes a sturdy faith in the self overlaps markedly with the approach that increases the likelihood of the child's caring about and helping others.

Just as selfishness bears no resemblance to healthy self-love, so must it be distinguished from the tendency to simply look out for one's own interests.[5] There is surely nothing objectionable about waiting until no cars are in sight before crossing the street or arranging the furniture in one's living room in the way that seems most pleasing. Consideration of self-interest may well be universal, and it may under some circumstances even allow one to help others more effectively. Think, for example, of the recommendation that airplane passengers first secure their own oxygen masks so that they can tend to their children's needs.

Interest, however, can be compounded to the point that one loses sight of principle. The fact that taking care of oneself is morally neutral or even praiseworthy can easily become a rationalization for excessive concern with one's own desires and for overlooking or even actively trampling the claims of others. (Fromm has argued that this confusion is often a deliberate strategy to rationalize greed.)[6] The latter is closer to *amour-propre* or selfishness, which can lead to a life devoid of the prosocial or even distinguished by the antisocial. Or it can make room only for those helpful behaviors that are designed to benefit oneself.

This distortion of self-interest is not benign, and it is also, to return to our primary concern here, not inevitable. "Self-love may be prominent in our natures without necessarily being sovereign," as the psychologist Gordon Allport wrote.[7] Likewise, selfishness may be prominent in our society without necessarily defining human nature. We may agree that each person is alert to her own interest without concluding that this is her *only* consideration, and we may agree that some people are thoroughly selfish without concluding that this is true of *everyone*. To assume otherwise is to mistake a description of pathology for an account of the human condition—a criticism that has been made of Freud's work.

The distinction between self-interest (or self-love) and selfishness illuminates our approach to the idea of altruism. To be altruistic is not necessarily to be self-abnegating. (In the last chapter I tried to show how turning altruism into something narrow and nearly unattainable makes it easier to dismiss the whole idea as farfetched.) The philosopher Ronald Milo took a step in the right direction when he wrote, "The altruist is to be characterized not as one who puts the interests of others ahead of his own, but as one who puts the interests of others on an equal footing with his own."[8] This definition, however, with its stress on an economic balance of interests, does not adequately capture the reality of nonegoistic helping, which often seems to proceed without any regard to whether the helper will benefit. Notice that "without any regard to" does not mean "at the expense of." The helper's concern may simply be to improve the welfare of another—period.[9] As Mary Midgley, another philosopher, put it:

People define altruistic behavior negatively, as activity which while helping others does nothing for the agent, which he himself does not at all want, or which is necessarily to his disadvantage. This negative conception seems to destroy the possibility of motivation towards it. The word however means something positive. The act is done *for* the benefit of the other.[10]

Here we have a notion of altruism that is neither suspiciously restrictive nor so broad as to define away the challenge of egoism.

Before looking at empirical data on the question, it will be useful to consider just how specious the egoist's arguments really are, keeping in mind that we are dealing with a strong version of egoism here, one holding that the ultimate goal of every human action must somehow be to benefit the actor. It might surprise social scientists and laypeople, who take psychological egoism for granted, to learn that this is very nearly a dead issue in philosophy—not because everyone in the field accepts its truth but because almost no one does. The people who make it their business to examine the logical foundations of such beliefs have, with startling unanimity, found this one wanting. In 1960, one writer apologized for raising the problem in a journal article, acknowledging that "nowadays there appear to be few philosophers who hold" the view.[11] Two decades later, another philosopher who tried to resurrect the issue began his paper as follows:

Psychological egoism is, I suppose, regarded by most philosophers as one of the more simple-minded fallacies in the history of philosophy, and dangerous and seductive too, contriving as it does to combine cynicism about human ideals and a vague sense of scientific method, both of which make the ordinary reader feel sophisticated, with conceptual confusion, which he cannot resist. For all of these reasons it springs eternal, in one form or another, in the breasts of first-year students, and offers excellent material for their philosophy instructors, who like nothing better than an edifice of sturdy appearance but with rotten foundations on which to display their skill as demolition experts.[12]

Such attempts at resurrection are becoming even rarer. Articles in the journals are hard to find, and the best anthology on the subject— featuring an introductory essay that carefully distinguishes the various versions of egoism[13]—was published in the early 1970s but soon went out of print, apparently assigned by few philosophy instructors. The following are some of the reasons that few in the field even take the idea of psychological egoism seriously.

Words Are Stretched Out of Shape.	If all actions are said to be selfish, then the term no longer has much meaning. Chesterton observed that it is an extraordinary extension of the word *self-indulgent* that would allow us to so describe someone who wants to be burned at the stake.[14] In practice, egoists often stretch words like *selfishness* or *self-interest* to the point that the argument becomes unfalsifiable. What would it take, one wonders, to convince the egoist that a given action really was altruistic?

If every conceivable piece of evidence can be explained away as being in the actor's own interest, then the game is rigged.

Even Altruists Can Want *to Help.*   Egoists sometimes point out that even when I want to extend myself to others, this is still an expression of what *I* want, so altruism must finally be illusory. But this, as many philosophers have pointed out, is a logical error. What matters for determining the truth or falsity of egoism is not the subject of the desire but the object. Obviously anything that I want is something that I want; to claim that this point is decisive is to base the whole argument not on a psychological truth but on a tautology. The question is whether *what* I want is motivated by self-interest.

Finding Gratification Is Different from Seeking It.   It may be true that helping others brings one pleasure,[15] but this is not the same as showing that one helped *in order to* please himself. In many cases, as the philosopher Nicholas Rescher points out,

the case is reversed—his own augmentation of happiness is a strictly incidental reactive product of that of the other. In normal circumstances, at any rate, one welcomes another's benefits just *because* they are his benefits, and not because they somehow benefit oneself through the mechanism of internalization as an oblique way of furthering one's own good. . . . Accordingly, an unselfish act does not become less unselfish because one gets satisfaction from its performance.[16]

The distinction may not always be easy to make in practice, but it is critical nevertheless. The egoist must do more than point to the smile on the face of the rescuer if she means to show that the rescuer had that pleasant afterglow in mind before administering CPR to the victim. (Likewise, the fact that prosocial behavior apparently contributes to healthy self-esteem or self-confidence[17] does not bolster the egoist's case.)

It is a Zenlike paradox that one ends up deriving more pleasure from helping if that pleasure is the farthest thing from one's mind upon deciding to help.* This point has been made by a number of thinkers, including John Stuart Mill[19] and, perhaps more surprisingly, Herbert Spencer:

---

*More broadly, failing to deliberately pursue our own interests often works in the service of those very interests, whereas fixing our minds on the most rational means for benefiting ourselves can turn out to be a counterproductive strategy. This is the central argument of Robert Frank's recent book, *Passions within Reason.* Unfortunately, Frank's governing (and unproved) assumption is that this must be *why* we often do not pursue our own interests. Altruism is allegedly undertaken only in order to benefit ourselves in the long run—even though this hypothesis requires that we somehow remain in the dark about why we are "really" helping others.[18]

Egoistic enjoyments are aided by altruistic actions. This increase of personal
benefit achieved by benefiting others . . . is fully achieved only where the act is
really unselfish. . . . In the truly sympathetic [individual], attention is so absorbed
with the proximate end, others' happiness, that there is none given to the pro-
spective self-happiness which may ultimately result.[20]

Indeed, casual reflection does seem to suggest that the people we
know who might be classified as unselfish are rather more likely to be
content than those who are selfish. The contentment may not in every
case be a consequence of being unselfish, but it does seem that selfish
people are at least as prone to unhappiness as any other subset of the
population.[21]

My larger point here is that when pleasure does result from generosity, it need not have been—indeed, probably was not—the point of the
act. But egoists are unable to show that pleasure always *does* result; they
cannot make sense of prosocial actions that bring no apparent satisfaction
to the actor—unless, of course, they fall back on the question-begging
assertion that some sort of satisfaction *must* have been present or the
action would not have taken place.

It could always be argued that although we *think* our intentions are
altruistic, we are motivated unconsciously by self-interest. Here we run
into the longstanding controversy about the extent to which psychoanalytic theory lends itself to empirical validation. That there is good reason
to think repressed wishes or memories exist and affect our behavior we
may readily concede. That all of us are exclusively bound by egoistic
motives of which we are unaware is considerably more problematic.

Freudians and neo-Freudians have drawn our attention to an array
of putatively generous people who give in order to control others, including "self-sacrificing" parents and lovers who not only do more harm than
good but act so as to reassure themselves of their worth as caring individuals. These insights from depth psychology are invaluable for distinguishing altruistic from pseudo-altruistic behaviors. But it is another
matter to assert that unconscious conflicts and cathexes constitute the
real reason all of us care about others. One of the consequences of this
proposition, which seems to be based on faith alone, would seem to be
that any altruist who underwent a successful analysis (in which unconscious material was made conscious) would be transformed into a self-
conscious egoist.

Such arguments, in any case, make it difficult to do philosophy, as
several representatives of that field have argued.[22] Moral philosophers

are obliged to concern themselves with the decisions of conscious, free agents. To wave away the apparent reasons that we act one way or the other—by invoking psychoanalysis or any other version of determinism—is to collapse the whole business into an epistemological riddle.

Malice, Too, Lies beyond Self-Interest. Egoism, to be technical about it, is unsatisfactory because it denies the existence not only of altruism but of a variety of other motives whose existence would seem to be very real indeed. Consider the fact that cruelty is every bit as unselfish as benevolence. Robert Paul Wolff writes: "Once a sceptic has admitted that it is logically possible for one man to want another to suffer, he cannot very well deny that it is equally possible . . . for one man to want another to be happy."[23] Indeed, speaking historically, self-interest was first defined in opposition to malevolence rather than to benevolence.[24] The presence of either inclination belies the claim that one can want only what is in one's own interest.

Advance Planning Refutes Egoism. To take the last argument a step further, egoism, strictly construed, is concerned exclusively with attempts to benefit the *present* self, the me that I now experience. Thus egoism cannot explain why we engage in behaviors that are advantageous to us only in the long run. Henry Sidgwick raised this objection in the late nineteenth century:

If the Utilitarian has to answer the question, "Why should I sacrifice my own happiness for the greater happiness of another?" it must surely be admissible to ask the Egoist, "Why should I sacrifice a present pleasure for one in the future? Why should I concern myself about my own future feelings any more than about the feelings of other persons?"[25]

Of course, simple prudence demands that I take into consideration how today's action will affect me next month. But given the narrow perspective of egoism, my future self is as remote from me as is someone else's present self—perhaps more so. To attend to the presumed interests of next-month's-me (without regard to what I favor right now) may be experienced as essentially an altruistic act.[26] And, of course, it is done anyway.

Self-Interest Has No Patent on Rationality. Egoism has acquired much of its force by hitchhiking on the idea of rationality, particularly in economics and the other social sciences. To talk about our natural and irrepressible desire to maximize our self-interest is to appeal to the idea of making rational decisions. Thus it is not at all unusual to read about " 'hard-core' altruistic acts, in which there is no prospect of personal reward . . . [and] other sorts of seemingly irrational behavior."[27] Thus it is, too, that games like prisoners' dilemma[28] seem fascinating and unsettling because what seems rational from each individual player's perspective turns out to be irrational from the perspective of the dyad. The shock of such results, observed Rescher,

> inheres solely in [the] ill-advised approach to rationality in terms of a prudential pursuit of selfish advantage. . . . To disregard the interests of others is not rational but inhuman. And there is nothing irrational about construing our self-interest in a larger sense that also takes the interests of others into account.[29]

Even if one were convinced that the quest for rationality were universal, in other words, nothing about the validity of egoism would thereby be established. Rational decisions may be made in the interest of benefiting someone else as surely as to benefit oneself. Or, put the other way around, "Altruists are neither more nor less rational than nonaltruists. They are simply pursuing different goals."[30] Thus is egoism deprived of one of its choice bits of ammunition.

The Psychological Egoist Cannot Be an Ethical Egoist. I argued in the last chapter that someone who believes we *should* always put our own interests ahead of others' may well convince himself that this is in the nature of the organism; ethical egoism, that is to say, elicits psychological egoism. But this does not mean that one view logically entails the other, nor that the relation works the other way around. Quite to the contrary, in fact. It is not surprising that psychological egoism is incompatible with ethical altruism: if everyone in fact cares only about himself, then there is little point in telling people they ought to do otherwise. But Kai Nielsen has made the intriguing observation that, strictly speaking, the psychological egoist cannot subscribe to ethical egoism either. If we cannot help putting ourselves first, it is useless to prescribe *any* sort of conduct with respect to whose interests we should consider. We might as well tell the psychological egoist not to grow blue hair as tell him not to be an altruist.[31]

On one level, this is just an amusingly ironic consequence of psychological egoism. But it also reminds us of what follows from any assertion about the existence of a fixed human nature. If selfishness is assumed to be a given rather than something chosen, then questions of value and moral culpability are so many exercises in self-deception. Happily, egoism seems not merely false but, unless offered in a much weaker form, incoherent as a concept. It is for this reason that one of the few modern philosophers to take the idea seriously nevertheless concedes:

Rarely has Psychological Egoism been independently propounded as an intrinsically significant moral doctrine. It seems to have been most commonly used to support the advocacy of some specific moral outlook or social policy . . . [such as] to persuade people to treat others always as if they were incorrigibly and systematically self-centered.[32]

It is worth pondering what motivation one might have for wanting people to do so. And it is also worth looking again at the various disciplines that have assumed egoism to be true in order to see how they have actually justified and used the assumption.

WHY FITNESS DOESN'T FIT

In the last chapter, I tried to show that the attention sociobiology lavishes on altruism suggests the diligence of an undertaker, not of a suitor. If its theories have the consequence not of explaining, but of explaining away, human altruism, then we are now obliged to ask whether there is any point in listening to what sociobiology has to say on the subject. I think the answer is no, above all because biologists are not interested in motives. A writer like Richard Dawkins is impatient with critics who think he is attributing to genes the desire to be selfish. It's just a figure of speech, Dawkins replies; the only issue is what organisms actually do and what we can infer about natural selection from their behavior.[33] In fact, he says, on a strictly behavioral understanding of the term, one could offer as an illustration of altruism a genetic predisposition to have bad teeth: useless molars mean reduced food consumption, which in turn means more food for everyone else.[34]

Now sociobiologists have a penchant for sliding back and forth between the two meanings of certain words—the version that merely describes the behavior of many species and the one that captures a uniquely human phenomenon—so a reader can be forgiven for concluding they think animals (or genes) really are selfish or altruistic. When sociobiologists summon up evidence to prove something about altruism, what they have in mind bears only a superficial resemblance to the concept we normally discuss in the context of human affairs. For obvious reasons, there is little to be said about an insect's "choice" to sacrifice its life so that another can live. By contrast, there is a great deal to be said about why a human being does so. Motives matter. We clearly are more impressed with someone who tries to rescue another but fails than with the person whose self-serving action has the unintended consequence of saving a life. But we cannot expect to hear much of interest on the subject of human altruism from a field that (of necessity) disregards the question of motive and cannot distinguish between bad teeth and good morals.[35]

Notice that the absence of motivational consideration cuts two ways. We cannot conclude that humans are truly altruistic just because members of other species help one another (or just because humans themselves help one another, for that matter). But we also cannot conclude that humans really are selfish just because an argument like inclusive fitness turns on the "self-interest" of the gene. In fact, we cannot conclude very much at all about why you and I are helpful on the basis of such data.

Consider the specific sociobiological formulas for altruism. Is our behavior really bound by the imperatives of inclusive fitness? If so, how do we explain the fact that we frequently help those who are unrelated to us, including those who will never bear or help to raise our offspring? For that matter, what evolutionary sense can we make of the fact that a disproportionate share of acts of human violence are committed against close relatives? To the extent that we do favor our kin with special generosity, Marshall Sahlins has shown that "no system of human kinship relations is organized in accord with the genetic coefficients of relationship as known to sociobiologists."[36] In other words, our socially constructed decisions about whom we will regard as near or distant often bear faint relation to the bloodlines that form the basis of biological calculations.

Much of what we call altruism, of course, does not involve the actual sacrifice of the rescuer's life. But even when it does, we find plenty of examples that inclusive fitness theory cannot easily explain, such as people who become martyrs to promote political causes.[37] In short, given the significance of human choice, inclusive fitness seems of dubious value for explaining human altruism. As Philip Kitcher saw,

there is no evidence to lead us away from the natural idea that, given the traits with which evolution has equipped us, we are able to set ourselves personal goals and to perform actions that detract from our inclusive fitness. It is possible to take the evolution of *Homo sapiens* seriously and yet to deny that natural selection has fashioned dispositions to behavior that lead us always (or almost always) to maximize our inclusive fitness.[38]

Reciprocal altruism, the other major biological contribution to the topic, turns out to be no more promising as an explanation of our prosocial behavior. Robert Trivers's determination to find an egoistic account of such behavior is embarrassingly obvious: "Were this an isolated case, it is clear that the rescuer should not bother to save the drowning man," he says.[39] There *must* be some self-maximizing advantage to rescuing or no one would do it; this is the premise, not the conclusion, of his discussion.

Back in the real world, it is common to help strangers even though there is virtually no chance—particularly in urban settings—that they will someday return the favor. (In fact, as Sahlins points out, we even help people who may well be construed as genetic competitors.)[40] All Trivers can offer in response is the speculation that "selection may favor a multi-party altruistic system in which altruistic acts are dispensed freely among more than two individuals."[41] In other words, the existence of precisely what would appear to refute a theory limited to self-maximizing, reciprocal-helping behavior is made to seem like a confirmation of it.

If Trivers's formulations strike us as being unfalsifiable, Richard Alexander's peremptory pronouncements endow that word with new meaning. As with Trivers, egoism is not the deduction but the premise, and he goes to extraordinary lengths to explain why individuals "so often *seem* to be altruistic" (his emphasis) and to try to account "for the altruism of moral behavior in genetically selfish terms."[42] Like other sociobiologists, Alexander approaches the topic having already apparently ruled out the possibility of genuine altruism. The presupposition may be stated in the form of a syllogism: (1) all human behavior can be understood in terms of genetic predisposition (phenotype is entirely reducible to genotype); (2) genes are "selfish," concerned exclusively with preserving copies of themselves; therefore (3) all human behavior is really selfish, appearances to the contrary notwithstanding. What remains for the sociobiologist is merely to figure out how to explain away all those pesky examples to the contrary.

This is Alexander's assignment in *The Biology of Moral Systems,* and he is nothing if not inventive in carrying it out. *Nepotism rules,* he begins. *If people help each other, it is just to preserve their own genes.*

Oh? (we respond). And what about the fact that we routinely help strangers?

Simple (replies Alexander). *Reciprocity.*

But don't we commonly help people who obviously will never return the favor?

Well, yes. But this can be explained as—and all of morality can be collapsed into—something called "indirect reciprocity." A helps B so that C will help A.

But what about all the occasions in which no C in a position to reciprocate witnesses the act, or in which prosocial behavior takes place anonymously?

Don't be naive. The apparent anonymity is shrewdly calculated to make the helper seem that much more praiseworthy so he can collect even more rewards in the long run. He who does good simply benefits from convincing others that "he does not really believe in individuals opportunistically acting according to their own interests in individual situations."[43]

And how do you explain people who clearly don't calculate at all, who simply respond to another person's need without any thought of getting something out of it?

Isn't it obvious? They're not just fooling others but themselves as well. "It will be in the egoist's best interest not to know (consciously) or to admit to himself that he is an egoist. . . . By convincing themselves that they are selfless, private donors may become better able to convey an appearance of selflessness to others."[44]

And so it goes. Under the guise of "eliminating the aura of mystery that has surrounded the concept," Alexander reveals that morality is just a matter of trying to "outguess, outmaneuver, outdo those others," to sneakily manipulate them into acting contrary to their own interests so that one gets back more than one gives up. "When we speak favorably to our children about Good Samaritanism, we are telling them about a behavior that has a strong likelihood of being reproductively profitable."[45]

Does all this fly in the face of what we see around us—even in one of the world's most competitive and ungenerous societies? Does it seem to say more about the author than about the species he professes to describe? Do we find no evidence to support this sour cynicism that is passed off as science? Alexander is unfazed. "Maybe we resist finding out about the genes and their mission . . . [because] accepting the arguments of evolutionary biologists is like admitting that one is, after all, an egoist."[46] The more you deny his theory, the more you prove him correct.

Far more reasonable a conclusion, based on what people actually say and do rather than on an a priori commitment to biological determinism, is the following: most of what is human and prosocial does not seem to fit into either inclusive fitness or reciprocity theory, and it cannot be made to fit even if we sit on the suitcase and tie it up with rope. This does not mean that we are beyond the call of biology; it means there are other variables that prove, in cases such as this, more decisive. It does not mean that inclusive fitness theory is inadequate to account for the self-sacrificing behavior in other species; it means that human culture and values have evolved to the point of becoming influences in their own right.[47] We have, and regularly exercise, the power to make decisions that are not adaptive—which includes those that are maladaptive as well as the much larger set of choices that are neutral with respect to evolutionary considerations.

If sociobiology were theoretically powerful and practically relevant to human behavior, its impact would be to undermine genuine altruism because its theories are ultimately egoistic. Since it is neither powerful nor relevant, we ought to look elsewhere to decide whether altruism is real. But there is a tendency among many social scientists to believe that until some biological grounding has been found for one's view of human behavior, that view is as good as useless. This tendency reflects a widely held, often unarticulated, sense that something linked directly to genes or neurotransmitters is more "real" than something without such a connection. Some of the reasons we are inclined to think this way were discussed in chapter 1: traces of biological determinism and materialism, the habit of equating the natural sciences with knowledge itself, and so forth. Even if we were not social creatures at birth—even if our original equipment, so to speak, disposed us to care only about ourselves—there would still be no need to assume that all subsequent motivations can be collapsed into egoism. Gordon Allport described how we acquire motives as we grow that become "functionally autonomous" of what gave rise to them. A desire to help others can become as potent and enduring a motive as any other regardless of whether, or when, it was learned.[48] To grope desperately for biological bases is, wittingly or unwittingly, to deny the reality of what Allport described. Yet many writers who are highly critical of egoism have scrambled to demonstrate that altruism is biologically rooted. How successful have they been?

The first sort of claim we come across is that cooperation is usually adaptive. Using the prisoners' dilemma game as his model, the philosopher Peter Singer argues that when two early humans were chased by a tiger, they both stood a better chance of surviving if they worked together to fight the animal off than if each just worried about himself and made a run for it.

This makes intuitive sense and is fine as far as it goes. But the fact of an evolutionary advantage to mutual aid does not tell us much that we want to know about our own prosocial behavior. How will such behaviors be manifested? How can we promote them? Why do some people choose them more often than others? Why does someone become more or less generous as she ages? What biology can do for us is explain how a range of human possibilities came to evolve—not predict which one each of us will choose to actualize or determine that any of them is binding on contemporary human attitudes and behaviors. Even if helping is favored by evolution, it is not a biological given. Does biology support the idea of a brighter side of human nature? Yes, providing we understand just how little is contained in the word *support*.

Philosophers and social scientists ought to keep in mind that it is a risky business to dismiss biological arguments when their conclusions seem distasteful but embrace them when they seem to paint a portrait of a kinder, gentler species. If we can choose to repudiate violence and selfishness, we can also decide to abandon the empathic and helpful tendencies that are part of our nature. We have the genetic capacity for both. Just as arguments about fitness and the like fail to disprove the existence of genuine human altruism, so ostensible biological bases of helping do little more than explain what else we *can* do.

There is another problem, too. Singer—and he is not alone in making this sort of leap—deduces from the wisdom of cooperation the existence of "an evolutionary advantage in being genuinely altruistic instead of making reciprocal exchanges on the basis of calculated self-interest."[49] Unless he is using "genuinely altruistic" in a peculiarly weak sense, this seems unfounded. All that is shown in the example of two men and a tiger is that it is advantageous to work together, not that working together is done for altruistic reasons. (Of course, if cooperation is more adaptive than competition in a variety of settings, as appears to be the case, this is not a fact to be passed over lightly. I am not lingering on it here only because it does not show that *altruism* is adaptive.)

Is it possible to ground altruism in biology, even if Singer fails to do so? Most writers in this field are satisfied with an egoistic account of both prosocial behavior and ethics, a fact that should give pause to those looking for biological evidence of real altruism. Nevertheless, several people have undertaken just such a search. Martin Hoffman, for example, has reasoned that, from a biological perspective, purely egoistic explanations for helping are not persuasive since self-interest is not predictably tied to doing good. Helping, sharing, and cooperating are clearly adaptive, he argues, so we need a more reliable, biologically based mediator of these behaviors to explain how they developed and persisted.[50]

In a sense, Hoffman is following in Darwin's footsteps here, since the latter, at least by the time he wrote *The Descent of Man* in 1871, attributed to our species an "instinct of sympathy" that was an elaboration of the "social instincts" found throughout the animal kingdom. Morality itself, he said, was to this extent a product of evolution.[51] For his part, Hoffman nominates empathy to serve as the biological mechanism. Unfortunately, his version of empathy, as we have already seen, is at least partly egoistic. Moreover, while the link between empathy and prosocial behavior may be empirically based (albeit complex), the evolutionary basis of empathy is speculative, and there is, in the words of one psychobiologist, "no substantive neurobiological evidence about brain mediation of altruism."[52]

Two studies in the last decade have, however, attempted to show that empathy (and, in one case, altruism as well) are highly heritable. The first, published in 1981 by Karen Matthews, C. Daniel Batson, and their colleagues, found that identical twins were more similar in their responses to an empathy questionnaire than were fraternal twins (.41 versus .05).[53] The second, a 1986 study by J. Philippe Rushton and his colleagues, produced comparable findings on a measure of empathy (.54 versus .20) and also on a twenty-item self-report of prosocial behavior (.53 versus .25).[54]

Leaving aside for a moment the questions about Rushton's credibility given his outrageous claims about the genetic inferiority of blacks (see p. 276n.35), both of these studies tell us only how subjects describe themselves, not how they actually behave. Self-description would seem particularly susceptible to environmental influences, in which case the claim of a genetic factor is cast into doubt. (It also suggests the possibility that the pencil-and-paper measure of empathy was actually picking up social responsiveness, as Matthews et al. concede.) In any case, these are both studies of twins reared together, which are of questionable usefulness for isolating genetic factors. Rushton's study, to make matters worse, was of a self-selected sample: questionnaires were mailed to 1,400 twin pairs, and the 573 pairs who returned them became the subjects. No consideration was given to the possibility that those who decided to take part may have been unrepresentative of the other twins or of the population at large. Finally, even if none of these methodological problems existed, we should not forget that the studies concern only heritability—the extent of genetic contribution to individual differences with respect to the trait and not the extent to which the trait itself is determined by genetic factors (see chapter 1).

We seem to be left, then, with the idea that biologists have so far contributed to our understanding of altruism only a model that reduces it to egoism—rather like a laboratory technician who needs to clean a tissue sample before studying it but has available for that purpose only a strong acid that dissolves what he is trying to inspect. In this analogy, we would not conclude that there is really nothing there to be studied after all, but rather that we ought to send the work to a laboratory better equipped for such research. As a general rule, moral and psychological phenomena cannot be reduced to biology any more than biological topics can be reduced to the stuff of physics. The specific question of whether human prosocial behavior can be motivated by a sincere and irreducible desire to help is not, finally, a matter for biology. If biological accounts of altruism deny its existence, there are other alternatives available to us besides the judgment that all behavior is egoistic.

WHY UTILITY DOESN'T FUNCTION

Despite the domination of economics by a model that sees all behavior as exclusively self-interested, there has been a stirring of dissent in recent years. The idea of "economic man" has long been criticized as a misleading (as opposed to useful) fiction since the calculating, consistent, fully informed actors on which the model depends bear little resemblance to people in the real world. More recent, however, are sustained critiques of the egoism at the core of this conception. Acting rationally simply is not tantamount to acting in one's own self-interest, these writers have argued. And even in economic matters (which in practice do not constitute a realm unto themselves, divorced from, say, political or personal matters), people routinely attend to noneconomic, nonegoistic considerations. Social scientists need to acknowledge these other considerations, whether we refer to them collectively as morality (Michael McPherson), the moral dimension (Amitai Etzioni), commitment (Amartya Sen), civic values (Greg and Paul Davidson), or something else. These and other writers—from within economics and from neighboring fields—have lately challenged the discipline to break free of the hegemony of egoism.[55]

Still, the numbers and influence of these challengers should not be overstated. Neoclassical economists continue to dominate the discipline,[56] and they typically defend the model in two ways: first, they argue that egoism is not an empirical finding but simply an assumption from which useful hypotheses can be derived; and second, they say that the idea of self-interested economic actors can adequately account for altruism, if it exists: one's utility function (that is, set of preferences) can include anything, including a desire to help others.

With respect to the first point, the usefulness of the model is precisely what some are beginning to question—at least with respect to phenomena outside of the world of commerce. Such economists have handicapped themselves by using a tool that fails to distinguish between self-oriented and other-oriented preferences. Of course one can begin with *any* assumption irrespective of its truth value and proceed to spin out predictions; indeed, economists often seem to pride themselves on the volume and rigor of what can be generated from a sentence that begins with "Assume. . . ." But one's ability to say meaningful things about the real world is compromised if the supposition, though plausible and widely accepted, is ultimately false—if, for example, one posits universal egoism even though it does not account for how people actually think and feel and act. More generally, the question of how our preferences came to be what they are—a question that economists deliberately avoid by taking preferences as givens—is not only intellectually interesting but also practically important.

An economist who wants to say that the welfare of others is just one of many possible preferences that an actor can have, meanwhile, places himself in something of a dilemma. Either self-interest means something substantive or it does not. If it does, then altruism cannot be understood as an example thereof without doing violence to the concept. Altruism by definition is not a subset of egoism. If the economist takes this path, he had better be prepared to defend the idea that everyone really is self-serving. (Some have argued that in terms of applied economics the discipline need not and should not dispense with altruism: a society in which people try to meet each other's needs can have an efficient economic system as readily as one in which each is trying to meet her own.[57] Moreover, collapsing everything into self-interest promotes an infatuation with rewards and punishments that makes for bad management.)[58]

The only way to preserve the integrity of the idea of altruism, then, is to choose the other possibility and pump up the idea of self-interest until it takes in everything (including real altruism) and, as a result, signifies nothing. To say people are motivated by self-interest is, once

again, to say nothing more than that people want what they want. As a
consequence, one has a weaker science for failing to differentiate between
the desire to benefit oneself and the desire to benefit others.

Although it can be argued that an economist who neglects morality fails to be a
good *person* . . . [he or she also] fails to be a good *economist*. . . . [The attempts]
of many economists to explain *everything* in terms of self-interest . . . are balanced
awkwardly between tautology and falsehood.[59]

The economists who argue this way are generally more interested in
the nature of theories and models than in how helpful or selfish most
people really are. Because of this, and because these economists presumably witness the same examples of prosocial behavior as the rest of us,
it is hard to see how citing a few more instances of it will convince them
that they are missing something.

There are, however, a few bits of evidence from within economics
that are worth noting. If we are motivated by economic self-interest, for
example, our decisions about giving money to charity should be highly,
if not exclusively, reactive to tax incentives. (After all, why help the
unfortunate unless there is some financial benefit to the giver?) Yet there
are data to suggest that while tax deductions may play some role in
convincing one to increase the amount of a gift, the initial decision to
donate—particularly by those who are most generous—is made for other
reasons.[60] Experience with recent changes in the tax laws have offered
further reason to doubt the self-interest hypothesis:

In 1982, after the top individual rate was cut from 70% to 50%, there was an
actual *increase* in the rate of giving, perhaps because people then had more to give
away. And, when nonitemizers were first permitted to begin deducting charitable
gifts, there was no discernible increase in generosity. In both cases, tax deductions appear not to have been the primary concern. Preliminary reports indicate
the same is true for the 1986 [Tax Reform Act]. Insofar as it has affected contributions at all, it appears to have increased them. . . . There have always been, and
presumably always will be, people motivated only by natural kindliness or a sense
of social justice or religious conviction.[61]

Melvin Lerner, in his challenge to the economics-based "cost-accounting" approach to social behavior, has, with his co-workers, conducted several studies that indicate people do not seem to act primarily

as profit-maximizers, even if profit is reinterpreted more broadly as plea-sure. In one experiment, subjects who were asked to volunteer for an-other study, and to contribute a portion of the payment they would receive to a needy family, signed up for more sessions than did those who were not asked for a contribution—provided they were being paid fairly for their time.[62] Lerner argues that people seem preoccupied with self-interest only when they sense that someone is taking advantage of them. Give people what they deserve and they will do what they can to make sure others get what they deserve, too. In this sense, it is not self-interest but "the theme of justice [that] serves as the central organizing principle in most human endeavors."[63]

In the political arena, where economists and other egoists have long insisted that we make all our decisions on the basis of trying to maximize our individual gains, "the single most compelling and counterintuitive discovery of research on political attitudes and behavior over the last thirty years is how weak an influence self-interest actually exerts," accord-ing to Gary Orren.[64] What is far more likely to predict someone's position on an issue of public policy is a deeply held principle. Attitudes about issues ranging from desegregation to unemployment tend to reflect value commitments more than they do one's personal stake in a given policy.[65] Similarly, people who have had occasion to interact with police officers and judges are usually at least as concerned with the fairness of the procedures as with how well they personally fared.[66]

Take another example—the so-called free rider effect that is sup-posed to reflect egoism in all its glory. The idea here, as elaborated by Mancur Olson and others, is that people will always try to take advantage of others' efforts—even to the point of persuading them to make those efforts—without bearing any of the costs themselves. (Thus, each citizen benefits from the existence of an army to protect him, but would avoid serving in that army unless compelled to do so.) The problem is that this supposed law of nature often fails to work; people do pitch in when, according to the theory, they should just be trying to catch a free ride.[67] Here is sociologist Gerald Marwell:

In over 13 experiments we have found that subjects persist in investing substan-tial proportions of their resources in public goods despite conditions specifically designed to maximize the impact of free riding and thus minimize investment. The prevalence of such economically "illogical" behavior was replicated over and over. Nor do other experimenters find their subjects behaving much differently. . . . Whether we [choose to take a free ride] varies as a function of individual situation, individual character, the nature of the public good, and other unknown factors.[68]*

This is not an artifact of contrived experimental procedures. In the real world, too, people regularly do things like contribute to public television and radio stations even though self-interest theory predicts everyone should wait for others to contribute and then watch or listen for free. For that matter, it is difficult to explain on the basis of this theory why anyone ever goes to the polls. Since elections are almost never decided by a single vote, everyone should take a free ride by letting others do their civic duty.

The free rider problem, like prisoners' dilemma and the "tragedy of the commons,"[70] exemplifies a situation in which what is advantageous for each of us is bad news for all of us, and vice versa. Typically, social scientists have assumed that the only way out of this conundrum is to artificially arrange things so that each individual has a direct, personal interest in pursuing the common good—or a reason to avoid pursuing his private interests. A central authority may be empowered to punish selfish behavior, for example, or incentives may be set up to make cooperative behavior more attractive to each individual.

These solutions take for granted what we have already begun to see is a dubious model of narrow, self-interested motivation. Thus we should not be surprised to learn that a series of studies by Robyn Dawes and his associates has shown that none of these egoistic inducements is actually necessary for promoting behavior that is in everyone's best interests. People will usually cooperate with others in a group so long as they are given an opportunity to feel a sense of belongingness to that group. Allow someone to meet and talk with the others and he or she will subsequently tend to make decisions in the group's interest rather than trying to take advantage of the others.[71]

In the face of such arguments and data as have been summarized here, some economists and others have acknowledged that there is more to human nature than egoism—and then proceeded cheerfully to ignore

*It also seems to vary as a function of how well one has been trained to accept the self-interest model—say, by studying economics. In a series of twelve free rider experiments with various groups of subjects, the people most likely to look out exclusively for their own individual interests were economics graduate students. (Specifically, they were unlikely to invest tokens in a group exchange from which everyone benefited, preferring instead to be parasitic off others' investment.) In a follow-up questionnaire, the economics students tended to say that fairness was not a consideration in their decisions—or else they simply did not respond to this question.[69]

their own admission. The economist Thomas Downs, for instance, conceded: "In reality, men are not always selfish, even in politics. . . . In every field, no account of human behavior is complete without mention of . . . altruism." But by the very next page he was announcing: "We accept the self-interest axiom as a cornerstone of our analysis."[72] Another strategy, as we saw, is to acknowledge the existence of altruistic motivation but to file this with any number of other possible preferences in the drawer marked Self-Interest, thus appearing to rescue the axiom. Nevertheless, however they manage to do it, many economists continue to insist that our motivation for all activities is egoistic even though this assumption is wholly unjustified.

THE LIMITS OF RECIPROCITY

If the destination is getting what one wants, the usual vehicle for getting there is trade. There is no such thing as a free lunch, as speakers are fond of declaring to business groups at expensive luncheons. This, of course, alludes to the idea of reciprocity that we hear sociobiologists promoting and that we find in all the social sciences in one form or another. I give you this and you give me that. More precisely: I give you this *only because* I expect you will give me that (or because you already gave it to me).* Such, allegedly, is the way of the world.

The wisdom of this as a prescriptive foundation for an economic system is not what concerns me here. Rather, I want to ask whether this arrangement of give and take is what always and necessarily lies behind prosocial behavior. This is important because reciprocity is a far cry from altruism: there is a vast difference between treating others as you would *like* them to treat you—the Golden Rule—and treating others as they *have* treated you or as you expect them to treat you. In fact, the two are not only dissimilar in theory but, it would seem, inversely related in practice. A study of Israeli preschoolers found that the more likely children were to justify sharing in terms of their own future benefit, the less generous they were as compared with their peers.[73]

There is no question that our culture is studded with examples of reciprocity. But there is considerable question as to whether giving must always be understood as half of an exchange. A market-based economic

---

*I am leaving aside here the possibility of defining *reciprocity* more broadly to include acts of helping that, while following the experience of being helped, may be motivated by gratitude or something else besides pure self–interest.

system is typically seen to have emerged as a natural concomitant of "human nature," while the fact that our thinking about what is natural may be affected by our economic system is overlooked. Likewise, attention is rarely paid to the power of the self-fulfilling prophecy. If we have been socialized to expect a tat for every tit, to keep score silently in relationships so that things are nearly symmetrical (and to feel uncomfortable when they are not), to construe the act of helping as doing a favor that ought to be repaid, then these expectations can create a reality as real as any determined by natural egoism. Ideas about ourselves, once again, shape how we act and help determine who we are. "The idea that exchange is the basis of intimate relationships may actually have the effect of impairing such relationships," as two psychologists have emphasized.[74] But not everyone who suffers from this syndrome will have the presence of mind to realize that the relationship has unraveled because of culturally based assumptions about the need for reciprocity—rather than because the relationship failed to exemplify a transcendent law of quid pro quo.

In some cultures, after all, the emphasis is on gifts rather than exchanged commodities. These gifts move, as Lewis Hyde explained, "from one hand to another with no assurance of anything in return."[75] Even within a given culture, a reciprocity orientation varies with gender and class, reminding us just how contingent that orientation really is. In the Israeli study, middle-class boys shared more candies when they were told their identity was to be made known to the recipient—that is, when reciprocity was a possibility—than when the donation was to be anonymous. However, generosity was not affected by donor anonymity among middle-class girls or among lower-class children of either sex. And when the children were asked in general terms why it is appropriate to share, there was a direct relation between the occupational level of the father and the likelihood of an answer that invoked reciprocity norms.[76]

If we look to the way friendship is perceived, it should immediately be clear how restrictive, even immature, it is to think in terms of reciprocity. This is the way a six-year-old sees things: "She's my friend because she pushes me on the swing and then I push her." Within a few years, most children grow past this conception of friendship, and the "more developed concept of relationship is more than an advance in reciprocity. It is supraordinate to reciprocity."[77] Friendship is a commitment to someone else that no longer demands any sort of precise exchange.

What is true of friendship is also true of helping. In one study, grade school children were more favorably impressed by fictitious character A, who returned a favor, than by B, who did a good turn for someone who had earlier refused to help B. Adults, meanwhile, gave a more positive evaluation to B than to A, signaling a greater appreciation for something closer to altruism than to reciprocity.[78]

This does not mean that conspicuously failing to return a favor is not generally viewed as obnoxious. Children and adults alike strongly disapprove of people who refuse to help someone who did them a favor earlier. But it is important to be careful about the conclusions we draw from this. That reciprocating is perceived as preferable to not reciprocating does not mean that an ethic of reciprocity exhausts our understanding of how prosocial behavior operates or should operate. We sometimes help strangers just because they need helping, not because we expect to get anything out of it; we care about their well-being without regard to how we may benefit. This is more regularly true of some people than of others, but it is clear that reciprocity is characteristic of only a limited subset of prosocial behavior. Other such behavior is more properly called altruistic, and people who score as such on questionnaires are actually more likely to help others when they are *not* expecting to receive any compensation.[79]

Likewise, the fact that a lopsided relationship may eventually collapse does not suggest that all caring between two people can be understood exclusively—or even principally—as an exercise in mutual back scratching. The acts of generosity that take place between two friends or lovers can, as a rule, be explained in terms of that caring relationship. (The relationship cannot in turn be reduced to simple reciprocity or the sum of the participants' needs.) Even among children, as Ervin Staub and a colleague showed two decades ago, "prior sharing affected subsequent sharing by nonfriends, but its effect on sharing by friends was slight."[80]

Margaret Clark, a psychologist, has emphasized that caring, or, as she prefers, "communal," relationships operate differently than "exchange" relationships—a distinction that recalls Buber's discussion of meeting the other as a Thou or as an It. In one paper, Clark and her co-workers set out to show that people are pleased to have their favor returned if they have expected an exchange relationship, but are actually disappointed with the reciprocated aid if they had hoped to establish a communal relationship with the other.[81] In another paper, she proposed that if a communal relationship is expected, two people working together are less concerned about keeping track of who did what, even if a reward is offered for successful completion of the task.[82]

Unfortunately, Clark's preferred way of demonstrating this difference—in these studies and in a subsequent one[83]—has been to use young men as subjects and pair each one with an attractive woman. The communal condition is said to be in force when they are told she is single, while the exchange condition means only that she has been introduced as married. This would seem a most unconvincing way to operationalize both concepts, particularly the former. The men's efforts to impress the woman might well be seen by an economically (or sociobiologically) minded observer as nothing more than long-term investments in a type of exchange whose pay-off is expected after the experiment has ended. Whether or not this is true, the richness of an I-Thou, a communal, or even simply a non-exchange-based relationship is hardly captured by this study in flirtation.

Somewhat more meaningful was a study of married couples in which subjects were asked to respond to a measure of marital adjustment as well as a questionnaire tapping their attitude about an exchange orientation (how important it was for them that what they do for others is neither more nor less than what others do for them). It was found that those who were preoccupied with getting as much as they gave tended to have less satisfying marriages.[84]

Given these trends, it is all the more disappointing—and remarkable—that so little research has been done to demonstrate empirically the limitations of reciprocity theory. Fortunately, as we have seen, there is such confirmation of the limits of egoism more generally. And if we take a fresh look at the dogma of reciprocity, we may well agree with Lerner that it is really

a theoretical invention to explain, or explain away, the overwhelming evidence that contradicts the common assumption that people are motivated by self-serving ends. In fact, for the most part, people *do not act* in obviously self-serving ways. As citizens, parents, spouses, good employees, etc. we devote most of what we have and our efforts for the benefits of others; and we do it as naturally, if not more so, than what we might do for "ourselves."[85]

SUI GENEROUS

In proposing that the existence of genuine altruism can offer a plausible account of many, though not all, instances of prosocial behavior, this chapter has concentrated chiefly on showing the weaknesses of egoism. Philosophers have had good reason for rejecting the proposition that all people must act so as to benefit themselves, I have argued. For their part, sociobiological accounts of genetic "selfishness" are of extremely limited value in explaining actual human behavior, and a reduction of prosocial activity to mere fitness considerations is unwarranted because of the significance of both cultural influence and individual choice. The commitment of neoclassical economists to explaining everything, including all helping behavior, in terms of self-interest is hard to justify conceptually or empirically. Reciprocity does not account for how most adults conceive of what prosocial activity should be or must be. In short, we do not act the way egoism would predict—unless the idea of egoism is expanded to the point that it includes everything and thus can never be disproved.

From the perspective of most writers who have addressed the topic, the existence or nonexistence of altruism rides or falls on the status of egoism; the two concepts are defined so as to be reciprocally related. Logically, if we act prosocially, and if it cannot be demonstrated that we did so for self-serving reasons, one may conclude that we probably did so altruistically—at least if it is conceded that *altruism* need not be reserved for positively self-denying acts. As a lawyer might put it, the burden of proof rests equally on the proponents of egoism and altruism; the latter endures no greater responsibility to prove her case. If humans care and help frequently, and do so starting very early in life, then we have what might be called a prima facie reason to assume that such behavior means exactly what it seems to mean: the actor really cares about and seeks to help the other.

The simplest way to validate this is just to ask the person performing the prosocial activity. (Most social psychology research of the topic not only excludes so uncomplicated an approach but deceives subjects by telling them that something else altogether is being studied.) Naturally it is possible that an individual is ignorant of his true motives or is deliberately misrepresenting them. But there is surely some value in hearing what people have to say on the subject of why they decided to help.

Nancy Eisenberg and Cynthia Neal took this approach with a group of subjects who seemed unlikely to try to deceive them: four- and five-year-olds. A researcher followed the children around their preschool and watched for unprompted acts of sharing, helping, or comforting. When such an act was observed, the child was asked why he or she did it ("How come you gave that to John?") and the answers were sorted into general categories of explanation. Not one of the children made reference to the demands of authority figures or to a fear of being punished for failing to help. Very few said they expected to benefit in some way by helping or that they acted to receive social approval. The most frequent explanations referred either to pragmatic (nonmoral) reasons or to the simple fact that the child they helped had *needed* the help (for example, "He's hungry").[86] This, of course, is the core of altruism.

In his mammoth study of blood donors (p. 328–29n.82), Richard Titmuss, too, asked why people had acted the way they did. Most said something about having either a duty or a desire to help others, or talked about wanting to express gratitude for being in good health or for having received someone else's blood in the past. Only 1.8 percent of the donors said they were hoping to receive some benefit from donating. Titmuss emphasizes that almost all respondents "employed a moral vocabulary" and that for most "the universe was not limited and confined to the family, the kinship, or to a defined social, ethnic or occupational group or class; it was the universal stranger" they wished to help.[87]

Sometimes people do more than bring a cookie to a playmate or part with a pint of blood, and dramatic acts of helping or rescuing—often performed, it would seem, without any time for calculation—are frequently explained in the direct, undramatic language of pure altruism. Consider a few examples from World War II, which forced questions of goodness and evil to the extreme. Philip Hallie investigated the French village of Le Chambon, whose residents agreed to hide Jews despite the enormous risks this involved. Here is his central conclusion:

If we would understand the goodness that happened in Le Chambon, we must see how easy it was for them to refuse to give up their consciences, to refuse to participate in hatred, betrayal, and murder, and to help the desperate adults and the terrified children who knocked on their doors. . . . We fail to understand what happened in Le Chambon if we think that *for them* their actions were complex and difficult. . . . The Chambonnais think, when they think about it at all, that they are at the sea level of human decency. If you insist upon discussing the matter, they will tell you that they are not morally better than anyone else. . . . One way of judging the Chambonnais is their way—with a shrug of the shoulders and the question: "Well, where else could they go? I had to take them in."[88]

Where the stakes are highest, the explanation is simplest. The helpers do not see themselves as self-interested on the one hand, or as heroic on the other—and protestations about the latter rarely sound like false modesty. These people typically say that they simply did what had to be done, they answered a call, they made the obvious choice. Camus captured this tone in *The Plague,* which is widely read as an allegory about the Nazi occupation of France. His Dr. Rieux works tirelessly with the plague's victims, taking chances with his own health, but explains this matter-of-factly:

I have no idea what's awaiting me, or what will happen when all this ends. For the moment I know this: there are sick people and they need curing. . . . There's no question of heroism in all this. It's a matter of common decency . . . [which] consists in doing my job. . . . Heroism and sanctity don't really appeal to me, I imagine. What interests me is being a man.[89]

The Oliners, in studying individual rescuers of Jews, found exactly the same thing. From some of their informants they heard: "I did nothing unusual; anyone would have done the same thing in my place" and "I insist on saying that it was absolutely natural to have done this" and "I feel that I only did my duty. I am not a hero."[90] Furthermore, the Oliners' study contains other indications that much of the rescuing was genuinely altruistic. The costs were very high, for starters, and the rescue activity usually continued from two to five years. More than half of the rescuers felt that even the first act of helping was extremely risky to themselves and their family. (In some cases, the rescuers even sent their own children away so they would not share the risk.) Usually there had been no prior personal connection to the victim(s); more than 90 percent helped at least one complete stranger. Furthermore, as Jews, the victims were from an out-group, widely despised at the time, so the decision to help them cannot be dismissed as a case of looking after one's own. The victims were also, with few exceptions, in no position to compensate the rescuers or return the favor, so reciprocity presumably was not contemplated as a possibility.

Particularly impressive is the fact that some rescuers had the chance to avoid responsibility for the victims while keeping their consciences clear. Had their motivation been only to feel good about themselves or to escape guilt, they would not have interfered when the Jews who were living with them considered turning themselves in or running away for various reasons. Yet they did interfere, refusing to allow those in their custody to risk their lives even though this would have let the rescuers themselves off the hook.[91] Overall, even the most doctrinaire egoist would be hard put to deny the altruism at work here.

But is it more plausible to account for ordinary helping as a calculated bid for social approval or acceptance, as many egoists insist is the case? This is undoubtedly true of some people, including those whose sense of their own worth is especially dependent on others' judgment. But in their study of fourth-graders, Ervin Staub and a colleague found a significant *negative* relation between need for approval and simple sharing, suggesting that at least this prosocial behavior is not motivated by a need to impress others.[92] Consider also an early study of undergraduate males by Leonard Berkowitz and Louise R. Daniels in which each subject was asked to play the role of a worker and construct paper boxes under the guidance of an unseen supervisor. Those who were told their performance would affect how the supervisor was evaluated turned out more boxes—regardless of whether they had been led to think the supervisor was going to hear about how productive they had been. Even under conditions of anonymity, in other words, people worked harder simply in order to benefit someone whom they had never met.[93]

So it is for tiny acts of helping outside the laboratory. I am eating a sweet roll at a reception and someone comes up to me with a napkin. "If it's as sticky as mine was, you'll need this," he says simply. Now it is possible he acted so as to curry favor with me or impress me with his thoughtfulness. But in the absence of evidence in this direction, I see no reason not to regard his action as genuine helping. And it is grounded not on a rule that One Should Give Napkins to People with Sweet Rolls— or even that One Should Be Nice to People. It is grounded in perspective taking. It is other-oriented and straightforward and undramatic. It is the opposite of egocentrism. And it is the basis on which to build a human community.

The egoist may rejoin that the rewards and punishments motivating prosocial behavior have been internalized: people help just to feel pleased with themselves or to avoid guilt. And once again we concede that this account describes at least some part of the motivation of at least some people. But can it really explain all prosocial behavior in lieu of altruism?

There are some writers who believe we can never know for certain, that we can only hope to arrive at a point where altruism is shown to be no less plausible than egoism, after which each of us is on his own to attribute either motive (or some combination) to a given act of helping. After all, even the true altruist may feel pleased after having helped. Her pleasure was, by definition, not the *reason* for helping, but how can we ever distinguish between pleasure that follows from reaching a prosocial goal and pleasure that *is* the goal? Many people argue that we cannot and that the existence of genuine altruism can never be demonstrated empirically.

Dan Batson does not share this view. He has spent more than a decade in his University of Kansas laboratory creating artificial situations "in which one person is confronted with an opportunity to help another perceived to be in need" and introducing "changes in the situation— manipulations—that enable us systematically to disentangle the relationship between different potential ultimate goals of helping."[94] From these intricate experimental designs—which are, depending on one's perspective, either ingenious or contrived—Batson has attempted to rule out one egoistic hypothesis after another and see whether prosocial behavior may not, at least for some people, reflect a combination of sympathy and perspective taking. For subjects who respond in this way to another's distress—either spontaneously or as a result of experimental induction* —genuine altruism may provide the most economical explanation of why they helped. Any benefits, emotional or otherwise, that these people might realize are "not the goal of helping; they are simply consequences of helping . . . because the ultimate goal is to increase the other's welfare, not [their] own."[95]

To demonstrate the plausibility of this hypothesis, Batson first had to come to grips with the argument that prosocial behavior is motivated by nothing more inspiring than an attempt to reduce one's own vicarious distress. Because you are in pain, I am in pain; I want not to be in pain, so I help you. The story is told, for instance, of how Thomas Hobbes once gave money to a beggar and explained to a surprised observer that he was merely trying to relieve his own distress at seeing the beggar's distress.[96] One group of researchers, proposing that we come to the aid of victims in emergencies only to reduce our own emotional arousal, note explicitly that "the major motivation implied in the model is not a positive 'altruistic' one, but rather a selfish desire to rid oneself of an unpleasant emotional state."[97]

Now there is no question that distress—by definition an unpleasant sensation that one is inclined to try to escape—often does attend exposure to someone else's plight. What we want to ask is whether this is the *only* response one can have. Both Batson and Nancy Eisenberg have teased apart distress and sympathy (which Batson calls empathy), showing that there is a qualitative difference between feeling anxious or apprehensive, on the one hand, and sad or concerned, on the other. (Batson

---

*Batson contends that subjects in the high empathy condition of his experiments tend to help according to the same pattern regardless of whether they responded to a given situation empathically without any prompting (as measured by questionnaires) or were induced to be empathic by means of an instruction to try to imagine how the victim feels.

has done so through factor analysis and experimental manipulation;[98] Eisenberg through a combination of self-report data and analysis of facial expression and heart rate.)[99]

Given that self-oriented distress can be distinguished from other-oriented concern, Batson next had to show that the latter was more than just another impetus to escape something unpleasant. He did this by demonstrating that the people he calls empathic are just as likely to help even if the experimental design allows them to reduce their distress easily by escaping from the suffering victim. In one of his early studies, there was nothing to stop students from simply ignoring a written appeal to help a senior whose parents had been killed in a car accident. But it seemed that high-empathy students were not interested primarily in relieving their own distress; they wanted to help the young woman and they agreed to do so although they could have simply left the room.[100]

A second constellation of egoistic accounts proposes that people help in order to gain a reward or avoid a punishment, even if these are internally generated. Again, this seems plausible as far as it goes, but Batson has tried to show that it does not go far enough to explain all instances of helping behavior. He reasoned that a helper's needing to feel personally responsible for alleviating a victim's distress would prove she was motivated by a need for approval or internal reward. Therefore, if she feels just as pleased when someone else steps in to help, she may not have been interested in taking credit herself for being a rescuer but only in making sure that the victim's distress was relieved—an altruistic motive. In one study, Batson told his subjects that by performing well at a task involving numbers, they might be able to help someone else (whose voice they had just heard) avoid mild but unpleasant electric shocks. A little later, some subjects were informed that the other person would not be receiving shocks after all. Those who had scored high on a questionnaire-based measure of empathic response to the other's plight did report a more positive mood if the other's shocks were avoided, but those who were responsible for this reprieve were no happier than those who learned that the other subject had been spared unexpectedly through no action of their own.[101]

But what about the idea that we help simply in order to avoid guilt? In yet another study, Batson decided to make it easy for subjects to avoid helping by requiring them to pass a test in order to qualify as a helper. If they were told in advance that most people could not pass the test, the subjects who volunteered just to stave off guilt feelings presumably could justify failing it and thus not helping; it was not their fault. If, however, they made a serious effort to pass even when given an out, Batson figured they were truly interested in helping the victim. As predicted, "Providing justification for not helping . . . had a dramatic effect on the helping of low-empathy subjects; it had little effect on the helping of high-empathy subjects . . . [which is] precisely what we would expect if . . . feeling empathy for the person in need evoked altruistic motivation to have that person's need reduced."[102]

Although both of these experiments are consistent with the possibility of real altruism, neither offers an airtight proof. In the first one, it is possible that the subjects whose mood improved after the victim was helped by a third party were actually pleased, at least in part, because of their own *willingness* to help even though they never got the chance. The premise of the second study is also suspect: People motivated to help solely in order to avoid guilt might not let themselves off the hook so easily; they might well expect to feel bad for failing to try hard to pass the qualifying test. The idea that guilt-motivated subjects could bail out with a clear conscience suggests a failure to recognize the depth and range of self-punishment. (On the other hand, Batson did indeed find that low-empathy subjects made less of an effort than high-empathy subjects to qualify to help when told the test was difficult—that is, when given an easy out—than when told the test was simple.)

A very specific and sophisticated challenge to Batson's tentative rescue of altruism has been made by Robert Cialdini. His contention is that even empathic individuals help others only to relieve their own sadness, which is caused by the others' plight.* If different means are used to improve the mood of an empathic person, he or she will no longer be more helpful than anyone else—suggesting that personal gratification and not genuine altruism lies behind the prosocial behavior.[103]

Notice that Batson and Cialdini are in agreement that empathy leads to increased helping, that the empathic person feels sad upon encountering someone else in distress, and that this sadness probably will be reduced after helping that victim. The difference is that Batson insists that the goal of helping is altruistic for these empathic individuals. Beyond the specific methodological criticisms he has offered of Cialdini's latest study,[104] his method has been to show that, contrary to Cialdini's results,

---

*This is subtly different from the aversive arousal hypothesis mentioned above. Cialdini is not claiming here that helpers feel only distress that they seek to escape. He agrees that they may feel real sadness but says they help primarily as a way of enhancing their own mood. Affirmative mood enhancement is not identical to the act of freeing oneself from something unpleasant.

empathic individuals do not help less just because they expect to have their mood enhanced by other means (in this case, by watching an enjoyable video). But, again, this is true only of subjects who respond empathically to suffering. For others, helping does indeed appear to be motivated at least partly by a desire to improve their own mood.[105]

Several studies by two other groups of researchers, all published in 1988, seem to substantiate the view that at least some helpers are genuinely altruistic. The first of these, conducted by David Schroeder, John Dovidio, and their colleagues, is noteworthy because they did not expect to confirm Batson's empathy-altruism hypothesis. Subjects were given a pill that was described to some as a placebo and to others as having the effect of fixing in place whatever mood a person has upon taking it. (Presumably no correlation exists between empathy and gullibility.) The researchers assumed that empathic individuals would be less likely to help if they thought helping could not alleviate their sadness because of the drug. In fact, though, there were no significant differences between the placebo and mood-fixing conditions. These results supported the altruism hypothesis: subjects apparently were not agreeing to help just to cheer themselves up.[106]

The other series of studies, conducted by Nancy Eisenberg and her associates, is of interest because it is apparently the first to distinguish between altruistic (or at least sympathetic) and personal-distress motives in accounting for the prosocial behavior of children. Operationalizing a distinction between sympathetic and distress reactions in toddlers was no easy feat since questionnaire-based methods are obviously impractical. In two studies, Eisenberg's group had shown that heart rate accelerates in reaction to an anxiety-producing stimulus and decelerates in response to a stimulus reported to produce sadness or concern; these different patterns usually matched facial reactions, although it was not clear whether the latter response could be described as entirely other-oriented.[107]

Having laid this groundwork for the idea that sympathetic reactions do not collapse into mere distress—and therefore that it is possible that some children's prosocial actions, like some adults', may properly be described as altruistic—Eisenberg then tried to replicate Batson's findings with four- and five-year-olds. The children were shown videotapes of other children being injured on a playground. Adults judged whether the facial expressions and gestures of the young viewers were sad and concerned or anxious and apprehensive. (There was little problem distinguishing concern from distress; interrater reliabilities were .83 and .96, respectively.) Ten days later, each child was given a toy and left in a room with another child, with observers noting how willing he or she was to share the toy both spontaneously and upon request. It turned out that the children who had reacted with concern to the film were more likely to offer the toy voluntarily (comparable to Batson's easy-escape condition), while those who had reacted with distress were unlikely to share unless they were asked.[108]

Many of these investigations are quite different from one another in terms of how empathy is defined and measured (and whether it is seen as responsive to a particular situation or as reflecting an enduring trait), how prosocial behavior is construed, when egoism can be considered to be ruled out, and so on. The respective findings also vary depending on which statistical tests are performed on the data, and some correlations are higher than others. Another important matter is whether prosocial action means helping in an emergency or nonemergency situation. (Batson and his colleagues have argued, for example, that a genuinely altruistic motivation to help someone who is not in distress may depend on there being a preexisting emotional connection between the two individuals,[109] recalling Clark's distinction between communal and exchange relationships.) Readers interested in pursuing the methodological fine points and further qualifications of the research summarized here are urged to consult the studies themselves.

Even if empathic or sympathetic individuals are indeed likely to help for altruistic reasons, this does not mean that self-interest concerns vanish. Batson asserts that they may still "perform a relative-benefit analysis before acting" and that their empathy-based altruism can be "easily crushed by overriding egoistic concerns."[110] And, indeed, to say that we can attend to (and be motivated by) the need of another is not to say that we do not also attend to our own needs—or that we should not do so.

The problem with theories of motivation based on self-interest is not that they are false but that they are only partly true. They contain just enough that sounds plausible to persuade us that we have heard the whole story when we have not. When theorists are pressed to defend their egoism in the face of a world full of people who act to benefit others, they merely embellish the egoistic theory. In the Wallachs' apt metaphor, they are rather like pre-Copernican astronomers, wedded to the idea that the earth is the center of the universe, who

devised more and more convoluted "epicycles" to account for the new evidence without giving up the geocentric assumption. . . . A narrow sense of self is [said to be] at the center of all motivation and behavior . . . [and] whenever the physical or social environment seem[s] to pull the organism to do things, needs for the self [are] always posited as being served.[111]

What is true of psychologists is, of course, equally true of biologists and economists. David Collard, an economist, notes that we regularly give gifts, donate blood, help victims of natural disasters, pay our taxes, and sacrifice for future generations. All of these acts, he concedes,

could, with ingenuity, be explained in terms of self-interest. But the more these acts multiply, and the more intricate the explanations, the greater is the temptation to make a clean sweep and abandon self-interest as a universal assumption. Indeed, there is much to be said for making non-selfishness the general case. ... In other words it may now be appropriate to turn the usual argument on its head: it is not that selfish men sometimes appear to behave unselfishly, but that unselfish men sometimes appear to behave selfishly.[112]

If the latter formulation seems implausible or at least impossible to prove, no less can be said of its opposite, the canard that selfishness is the natural state of humankind. The swirling complexity of human history can be arranged so as to accommodate any number of theoretical constructs; cited selectively, almost any feature can leave the ground and become the figure. That we choose to see self-interest as the organizing principle of our species says as much about the interests of the viewer as about the nature of the viewed. Whether one accepts that the evidence and arguments reviewed in this chapter support Collard's contention that nonselfishness is the general case, they surely challenge the cynical supposition that all of our finer moments are only so many displays of cleverly repackaged selfishness. By any reasonable standard, altruism is real.

9

Beyond Altruism

Where men are friends there is no need of justice, but men may be just and still need friendship besides. In its highest form, indeed, justice would seem to contain an element of friendship.
— Aristotle (fourth century B.C.E.)

UP TO US

Having simplified the issue of prosocial motivation by setting up a polarity of egoism and altruism, I now want to complicate matters once again. If the point is to challenge the egoists by arguing for the existence of non-self-interested activity, it is sufficient to confine the discussion to these two alternatives. But if we want a finer resolution, a more detailed account of helping behavior, it becomes necessary to admit those cases that lie between and beyond the obvious possibilities. What are we to make, for example, of people who sacrifice for the benefit of their families or for some other group of which they feel a part? Neither egoism nor altruism seems adequate to account for this sort of thing. It is not egoism because, while group identification can have the effect of benefiting the self, loyalty to a collectivity often becomes a goal in its own right. On the other hand, it does not seem quite correct to reduce this group identification to altruism either—unless altruism is defined as anything other than egoism. (It is even less appropriate to blame the destructiveness of intergroup conflict on an excess of altruism as some writers have done.)[1]

Let us set aside group interaction and also nonprosocial activity in order to concentrate solely on a case in which one person helps another. If I help you, it is possible to identify four accounts of whom I was intending to benefit by this act. These possibilities may be denoted by the following shorthand: (1) me, (2) me because of you, (3) you, and (4) us. Strictly speaking, only the third constitutes pure altruism,[2] but a careful

treatment of the limits of psychological egoism requires that we understand altruism in the context of these closely related alternatives. The
introduction of *us* as a point of reference radically recasts the entire
discussion and will be the touchstone for the remainder of the chapter.

I should begin by emphasizing that even with this (or any) attempt
to sort out the various motives for prosocial behavior, there are bound
to be messy cases. Real people do not oblige us by sorting themselves into
the right box. A given individual may, depending on her state and situation, be motivated by any of these considerations or by some combination
of them, and she may become more responsive to one or another motive
over time.*

Me   There are any number of clear-cut instances of helping in which
the motive is obviously self-gain. In such cases, the prosocial act is not
regarded as intrinsically valuable but is seen as a means to some personal
reward, such as money, praise, prestige, or a greater likelihood of being
helped in return. While I have argued strenuously that this explanation
cannot adequately account for all prosocial behavior, it is important to
acknowledge that it does fit some.

Self-interest is even more clearly tied to the idea of cooperation with
more than one other person. In a society that venerates competition and
solitary effort, the suggestion that we ought to work together is regarded
as either refreshingly humanistic or suspiciously un-American. The fact
that writers who point out the advantages of cooperation to teachers,
managers, and policy makers are often seen as radicals or visionaries says
more about our devotion to narrow individualism than it does about
cooperation itself. The simple truth is that most proponents of teamwork
emphasize—and most participants realize—its benefits to each individual
who takes part. "Cooperative behaviors traditionally have been defined
more in terms of consequences for the self than the other, that is, as
coordinating one's behavior with that of another in order to achieve one's
goal."[4] Even Hobbes was essentially recommending a cooperative solution to the threat of anarchic violence: because we share an interest in
peace, we can and should agree to abide by the dictates of a central
authority. The proposition that people usually will profit from exchang-
ing their talents and resources seems on the face of it a nonideological
assertion, easily confirmed by empirical study and approximately as con-

*The schema is also incomplete in one respect, as Dan Batson has noted. If one helps
purely out of a conviction that one ought to do so—that is, in order to fulfill a principle—
then none of these possibilities really captures the operative motive.[3] (The relation between
principles and a personal connection to other people is discussed later in this chapter.)

troversial as the suggestion that task performance will be enhanced by getting a good night's sleep. Cooperation as such, like some prosocial behavior, leaves egoistic motivations undisturbed.

Me Because of You   The decision to relieve someone else's distress is sometimes motivated by a desire to relieve one's own vicarious distress. This, as I have noted several times, is not altruism. If an individual's prosocial behavior can be traced to a desire to reduce her own discomfort, to avoid guilt, or to feel pleased with herself, then the self is the ultimate beneficiary of the act; meeting the other's needs is, again, just a means to that end.

It may not be altruism, but intuitively we recognize a distinction between this motivation and straightforward egoism. Moreover, we are simply more impressed with a person who is truly saddened by someone else's sadness than by his counterpart who cheers people up in order to cultivate a reputation as a good fellow. The idea of taking pleasure from giving pleasure, which contributes to, among other things, a satisfying sexual relationship, does not seem to us particularly objectionable. It would not seem especially troubling even if we were unable to prove the existence of real altruism and were left with the fact that humans feel better for having made others feel better. Actually, this interdependence speaks rather well for our species and provides a reasonably firm foundation on which to construct positive norms and institutions.

It is rather striking, when one stops to think about it, that most of us do feel good about helping and bad about not helping. We ought not to take this for granted. Ponder for a moment the fact that we are likely to feel guilty when we choose not to come to someone's aid unless we take active steps to override or defuse this feeling. Thomas Nagel said that guilt "is precisely the pained recognition that one is acting or has acted contrary to a reason which the claims, rights, or interests of others provide—a reason which must therefore be antecedently acknowledged." Likewise, he argued, sympathy is not just feeling bad upon encountering other people's pain; built into the concept is "the pained awareness of their distress as *something to be relieved.*"[5]

Being unwilling or unable to help also prompts another reaction in many people, as I observed in chapter 5: a tendency to rationalize the failure to act by derogating the victim. We labor to convince ourselves that she brought her problems on herself, that she is evil or lazy and generally unworthy of our prosocial efforts. Herman Melville put this quite precisely in "Bartleby," his story of quiet rebellion:

So true it is, and so terrible, too, that up to a certain point the thought or sight of misery enlists our best affections; but, in certain special cases, beyond that point it does not. They err who would assert that invariably this is owing to the inherent selfishness of the human heart. It rather proceeds from a certain hopelessness of remedying excessive and organic ill. To a sensitive being, pity is not seldom pain. And when at last it is perceived that such pity cannot lead to effectual succor, common sense bids the soul be rid of it.[6]

What is here expressed poetically has also been described more clinically: "When we are unable to help an innocent victim, however, our desire to live in a just world is threatened. In such situations people may restore cognitive balance by deciding that the victim is in fact blameworthy."[7]

Whatever the role of the desire to live in a just world or to avoid cognitive dissonance, it seems consistent with the phenomenon of derogating the victim to suggest that we do so because a deep-seated inclination to relieve another person's pain has been frustrated. This impression is strengthened by other research findings. First, such derogation apparently can be prevented simply by asking people to imagine themselves in the victim's situation; they then respond with compassion rather than rejection.[8] Second, even if people have convinced themselves of the unworthiness of the victim, they will still respond prosocially in many instances if given the opportunity.[9] Finally, the failure to help, as Darley and Latane discovered (p. 68), sometimes leads people to evince physical signs of discomfort—as if there were a price to pay for choosing not to (or being unable to) follow through on the urge to alleviate another's suffering.

It may reflect well on us, then, that failing to help leaves us either feeling badly or trying to convince ourselves that there was no need to help after all. Likewise, attending to another's pain for reasons having to do with one's own well-being may have to be classified as a kind of egoism, but it is a kind quite different from what we usually call selfishness.

You   That I may help you just to help you is an idea defended at length in the preceding chapter. But it is often difficult to tell the difference between "you" and "me because of you"—that is, between genuine altruism and the vicarious motivation just discussed. As Steven Kelman, a political scientist, has observed,

Most people who display concern for others, and feel good because they do so, do not try to distinguish whether their "real" motivation is to help others or to feel better themselves, since they accomplish both goals at the same time. . . . The fact that this linkage exists does not mean that one type of behavior is "really" another.[10]

Philosophers point out, quite rightly, that the fact of feeling pleasure after helping does not allow us to infer that the expected pleasure *motivated* the helping. Notwithstanding the experimental work of Batson and others, though, many psychologists despair of being able to tease apart the reasons for prosocial behavior. The fact that they "do not necessarily fall neatly into egoistic and altruistic categories . . . create[s] serious difficulties in attempting to integrate research findings."[11]

Paul Schervish, a sociologist at work on an investigation of unusually generous millionaires, reports that he ran into a "dead end" trying to categorize the nature of their philanthropy; often, there was no "clean motive." Some donors felt bad because they had inherited money from greedy or unethical parents and wanted to give away this tainted fortune. Some were trying to "give something back" since they had been helped by others—a motive clearly different from helping in the expectation of subsequent gain. Some said they felt "diminished by others' suffering" or that they could not live with themselves if they did not help.[12]

This last response is commonly heard from people who perform extraordinary rescues. A man who leapt onto the subway tracks in New York City to save a child—very nearly losing his own life in the process—told a reporter that had he not acted, "I would have died inside. I would have been no good to myself from then on."[13] In another incident, a man who dove into the Potomac River to pull someone from a sinking car said, "I just couldn't watch the guy drown. I think I jumped into the water out of self-defense. I wouldn't have been able to live with myself if he had drowned and I had done nothing."[14]

A theorist or researcher is inclined to frown in consternation at the difficulty of ascertaining whether these people helped out of true altruism or a sophisticated version of egoism.* Others, notably those more concerned with results than with motive, are inclined to dismiss the question

---

*While self-reports cannot always be taken at face value, these particular descriptions are striking by virtue of the helper's apparent *need* to act—not only in the sense that it was objectively urgent that someone do something, but that they personally felt as if they had no choice in the matter. Many definitions of psychological health turn on the notion of flexibility or freedom; neurosis (although the label is no longer used by clinicians) is characterized by being at the mercy of intrapsychic forces, feeling compelled (or unable) to act in a certain way. This raises troubling questions. How do we view people who feel they "have to" help—either in a given circumstance or as a general rule? Is a sense of agency relevant to our determination of whether an act was altruistic?

as unimportant. But perhaps our response should be to *celebrate* the difficulty of answering the question since the source of this problem is not so much the inadequacy of our method as the inextricability of human desires to benefit the self and to benefit others.

Distinct from the challenge of separating egoistic and altruistic motives—and also from the indirect or vicarious benefit to the self—is the possibility that the two may coexist. I may want to help just because you require help *and also* because it will make me feel better to give you that help. The latter does not cancel out the former's claim to be altruism unless altruism is defined as a self-sacrificing act—one that must entail risk or disadvantage for the actor—or as an act that must not result in any advantage accruing to the actor. (I have taken pains to repudiate just such a definition.) Finally, the presence of both motives should not be confused with the process whereby I weigh your needs against mine before acting: here, my own needs incline me to help just as my recognition of your needs does.

Us   Some people regard altruism as unsavory and ripe for transcendence because it smacks of piety or self-congratulation or unhealthy self-sacrifice. These associations, though, seem to reflect the dominant view of altruism in a culture beholden to an ethic of self-interest more than something inherent in the idea of altruism. With only one exception, there is no reason that helping someone simply because he requires help should be suspicious or troubling to us.

The single exception is the framework of individualism on which altruism—or more precisely, the egoism/altruism dichotomy—rests. Here is a self with a bundle of interests and preferences. The egoist says it always attempts to maximize them. The nonegoist replies that it sometimes looks after the interests of another self. But both take for granted the existence of separate selves, each with its own set of (sometimes overlapping) interests. It is important to recognize, as Edward Sampson did, that egoism and altruism are "in opposition only in an individualistic setting; their opposition is not written in granite, genetics, or our fundamental human psychology."[15]

The implication of challenging individualism, per se, will be discussed in the following section. For the time being, let me just emphasize that such a challenge does not involve a blurring of identities or a reversion to the sort of mystical fusion discussed in chapter 4. Consider the case of prosocial behavior. To speak of an "us" in this context is not to lose sight of the you and the I who make up the us. It is, however, to recognize that there are some occasions in which one could not—even with perfect self-knowledge—reduce a prosocial act into an attempt to benefit either of the individuals involved. This is not just because one's own affect is reactive to the other's or because it stands side-by-side with the other's or because one has difficulty ascertaining whether she has helped the other egoistically or altruistically. It is rather because she defines herself as being related in an important way to the other and, as a result, finds herself acting without intending to benefit *just* the other *or* herself *or* the two separate selves added together. Pressed to explain, she will say not that she cannot tell what she has in mind, but rather that the question is misconceived because her reference point is something beyond either of the two partners: it is the connection between them.

I present these distinctions with some tentativeness. They are not blindingly obvious, and the "us" motive is easy to confuse with, on the one hand, the simple inability to distinguish between egoism and altruism, and, on the other hand, a merging of one person's identity with the other. Describing what I believe to be a unique and irreducible phenomenon is further complicated by the fact that many writers who have referred to transcending the egoism/altruism dichotomy seem to have had in mind exactly what I am trying to distinguish it from. One philosopher champions a kind of transcendence attendant not on concrete relationship but on a larger Good that is neither mine nor yours.[16] Those influenced by Eastern traditions mean something else altogether,[17] and others have made such references so fleetingly that it is difficult to tell exactly how they conceive of transcending the dichotomy.[18]

The four-component model offered here is not intended as a stage theory, but the idea of helping for the benefit of us rather than you is, in some respects, conceived as a step beyond altruism. If the question is asked, "But what do you get out of helping?" the self-aware egoist replies, "Peace of mind" or "A respite from guilt." The altruist replies, "Maybe nothing, but that's OK: personal gain was not the point of my helping." The person thinking about "us"—there is no obvious label for him—replies by challenging the premises of the question, since the idea of self- versus other-gain seems, above all, irrelevant. The relationship in which such helping occurs (and out of which it emerges) begets a motive that cannot be understood by a neoclassical economist or an equity theorist any more than a three-dimensional object could be apprehended by a two-dimensional creature.

For the philosopher Lawrence Blum, relationship—specifically, friendship—provides a context for understanding altruism that subverts

moral systems based on impartiality. But, more than this, it is also a
context that nudges us beyond the idea of altruism.

The terms "egoism" and "altruism" as usually understood serve us ill in describing acting from friendship. . . . Friendship involves persons being bound up with
one another. The different sorts of emotions and feelings which the friends have
towards one another get their meaning and significance from the entire relationship of which they are a part. . . . This is why the caring and the acts of beneficence
in friendship are not separate from my own interests, from what is personally a
good to me; it is not, in that sense, "disinterested." [It is also, he notes later, not
just motivated by a *combination* of egoism and altruism.] In fact friendship is a
context in which the division between self-interest and other-interest is often not
applicable. The friendship itself defines what is of importance to me, and in that
sense what is in my interest. In that sense I do not generally sacrifice my own
interest in acting for the good of my friend. I act with a sense of the friendship's
importance to me, even though it is the friend whose benefit I directly aim at (i.e.,
which is my motive for acting), and not my own.[19]

　　Two years later, Carol Gilligan proposed a strikingly similar formulation that grew from her study of the moral development of women and
girls. Beyond caring for the self and caring for others, she wrote, there
exists a "perspective [that] focuses on the dynamics of relationships and
dissipates the tension between selfishness and responsibility through a
new understanding of the interconnection between other and self."[20]
　　This phenomenon does not transport the individuals involved to a
plane far above the issues of empathy and distress, self and other. Someone may well find that his mood is affected by the other's—in an intimate
relationship it could hardly be otherwise—but this does not mean that
talk of "us" can be collapsed into Cialdini's negative state relief model
in which the real point of helping is to improve one's own emotional state
(chapter 8). Vital to Cialdini's idea is the hypothesis that any other mood
enhancer will do just as well as, and is interchangeable with, helping.
What I am describing is a state of interdependence in which my vicarious
sadness or pain can be relieved *only* if your distress is relieved.
　　In the case of us, then, empathy must be thought of as neither
egoistic nor altruistic. It is a function of the relationship itself. Heidegger took note of this in his classic work, *Being and Time:* " 'Empathy'
does not first constitute Being-with; only on the basis of Being-with
does 'empathy' become possible."[21] It is because we are related that I
feel into and respond to you. Of course, this works reciprocally: my
empathizing also helps to "sustain and contribute to the social bond or

attachment to that other person."[22] Empathy, based on what I earlier referred to as global perspective taking—the inclination to imagine life *as* the other, rather than discrete experiences *of* the other—can come to define the relationship.

Since a sense of us develops over time, it is reasonable to speak of some combination of egoism and altruism giving way to a relationship. Such a transformation has important implications for prosocial behavior. When we first meet, conventional motives explain my helpfulness; as we become friends, I begin to think and act in terms of us. Initially, empathy may be a matter of vicarious distress or other-oriented sympathy and concern, but eventually it is a reflection of our relationship.

Something of the sort describes the change that often occurs in group interaction. Harry Stack Sullivan suggested that cooperation means that "*I* play according to the rules of the game to preserve *my* prestige and feeling of superiority and merit. When we collaborate, it is a matter of *we*. The achievement is no longer a personal success; it is a group performance."[23] This has been the experience of many teachers who structure their classrooms to facilitate cooperative learning: at first, children help each other to learn because they have to, because their grade depends partly on the others' achievement. But typically a sense of group identity, an us, develops and the egoistic incentives become less salient (although they do not always disappear altogether). Now, instead of tutoring you because I will benefit from your improvement, I am genuinely interested in the performance we manage as a group. This group identity, described by Robyn Dawes and his colleagues, among others, does not appear to be a matter of members' weighing the benefits to self and group before selecting the latter. That there may be a trade-off is an assessment made by an outside observer—one steeped in an individualistic frame of reference. The issue for the group-identified participant, as for the person who feels connected to a friend or lover, is no longer simply "What can I do for her—and will it be at my expense?" but "What can I do for us?"

BEHIND THE APPEAL OF INDIVIDUALISM

To move from me to you to us in the context of one's motivation for prosocial behavior is, by extension, to call into question the ideology of individualism itself. Most of this book has attempted to challenge the notion that humans are necessarily selfish, but the affirmation of altruism

encourages an inquiry into the overlapping issue of how we are related
to each other—as opposed to just how we act toward, or what we want
for, each other.

"Human life as radical reality is only the life of each person, is only
my life. . . . It is essentially *solitude, radical solitude,*" said the Spanish
philosopher Ortega y Gasset,[24] echoing a number of other Continental
thinkers. Such a declaration may be too extravagant for our tastes, but
the English political theorists whose voices are more familiar to us proceeded from a similar world view. Hobbes may have been the first individualist; in the seventeenth century, as MacPherson put it,

the individual was seen neither as a moral whole nor as part of a larger social
whole, but as an owner of himself. . . . The human essence is freedom from
dependence on the wills of others, and freedom is a function of possession.
. . . Society consists of relations of exchange between proprietors.[25]

While there obviously are important differences among them, all the
architects of democratic liberal theory and capitalism—Locke, Hume,
Smith, Bentham, and Mill—spoke a similar language. If we are part of a
society, they said, it is only because each of us decided as an individual
that it was in his interest to give up something in order to come together.
If we exchange goods or ideas with each other, it is because we are
persuaded that venturing out of our shells will pay off. If we are exhorted
to consider the interests of others, it is by summing up the benefits and
costs to each person; there is no social good, per se, but only your
preferences plus mine plus hers plus his. (The utilitarians may have
rejected ethical egoism, but they still offered a ringing affirmation of
individualism.) If we endorse the idea of freedom or political rights, Marx
reminded us, these are only the rights

of man separated from other men and from the community. . . . Liberty is,
therefore, the right to do everything which does not harm others . . . [a liberty]
not founded upon the relations between man and man, but rather upon the
separation of man from man. It is the right of such separation. The right of the
circumscribed individual, withdrawn into himself . . . wholly preoccupied with his
private interest and acting in accordance with his private caprice.[26]

It was the implicit psychology of liberal theorists—their view of
human nature—that informed this political vision. Now that psychology

has emerged as a discipline in its own right, we find that almost every branch, school, specialty, and theory within it is premised on individualism. For Freudians, humans are antisocial by instinct and driven principally by intrapsychic forces. For behaviorists, the laws of learning pertain to the individual organism as it responds to the contingencies of its environment. For humanists, the *summum bonum* is *self*-actualization, with the human potential movement undertaking "the deification of the isolated self . . . . an unembarrassed denial of human reciprocity and community."[27] Developmental psychologists generally equate maturity and health with autonomy and individuation; theories of achievement and motivation focus almost exclusively on the individual. The entire discipline, according to Edward Sampson, "plays an important role in reinforcing an individualistic, self-contained perspective; it helps play down the importance of interdependent values."[28]

Beyond politics and psychology, individualism is the central theme of our everyday lives, and its measure has been taken by French observers from Tocqueville to the anthropologist Louis Dumont, the latter summarizing our predicament in one blunt, damning phrase: "The whole has become a heap."[29] Writing in the late 1960s, Philip Slater remarked that our success at freeing ourselves from various constraints has left us "disconnected, bored, lonely, unprotected, unnecessary, and unsafe."[30] Fifteen years later, Robert Bellah and his colleagues pointed out that we tend to think of our social life and commitments primarily in terms of personal fulfillment and individual well-being.[31] Indeed, we need only watch the celebration of personal heroism in movies and on television, or notice the mythology of individual greatness that sustains our economic system even in a corporate age. We betray ourselves in our advertising campaigns ("I believe in me") and our poster slogans ("God bless my personal space").

The symptoms of our ideology, in short, are ubiquitous, and they range from these prosaic particulars to the underlying metaphysical commitment—very rarely called into question or even into awareness—that divorces being from what Heidegger called being-with or being-in-the-world. In our view, the isolated self comes upon the scene and then decides whether to be part of a community. Our political debates often resolve into a tension between liberty (of individuals) and equality (among individuals). Our moral bedrock is the principle of noninterference: if you do no harm, you may act however you individually choose. Our discussions about the meaning of life distinguish between the nobility of self-realization and the vulgarity of simple self-satisfaction. The unspoken common denominator is always the self, the discrete individual.

In light of this, we are extraordinarily suspicious of any suggestion that our world view might not be reality itself but only a socially constructed version of reality. The idea that individualism is descriptively incomplete—that it is one way, but only one way, of making sense of the world—will seem incomprehensible to many. The separate self as the fundamental level of analysis seems to us simply to reflect the way life is.

The suggestion that individualism is prescriptively inferior, meanwhile, will be received as a challenge to all that is holy and good. We are on guard against anything that sounds remotely like collectivism, since this raises the specter of weakness or of the submersion of one's identity in a faceless group.[32] Perhaps it is for good, or at least historically understandable, reasons that we champion the privileged status of the self, but now we can see only in dichotomies: on one side is institutional tyranny, on the other is the besieged individual. Too rarely do we ask, What is missing from this picture?

What is missing, of course, is human relationship, a very different alternative to individualism. In making space for a self that has the right to choose, we have distanced ourselves not only from autocracy but from the idea of connection with other selves. Is this simply a function of stereotyped thinking, or do we resist such connection because it seems threatening somehow?

Let me answer by way of an analogy. When we come across someone who makes a point of announcing that she has shaken off all the values with which she was raised or that she never lets herself get depressed, our reaction is to suspect that she doth protest too much. That someone finds it necessary to speak with such emphasis may suggest that she is trying to ward off doubt; what is declared to be firmly grounded may in fact be precariously situated. So it is for the commitments of a society, and specifically for our society's cult of the self. The more the preservation of privacy, self-reliance, and freedom from all commitment are trumpeted as virtues, the more one suspects that the sense of self is actually in danger. The defensive defense of individualism may bespeak the fear that there is really nothing left to defend.

Any number of social critics have pointed to the frantic mobility in American society, the lack of community, the absence of commitment to shared values or to the value of what is shared. We are divided from each other, cast back upon ourselves to the point that it is profoundly unsettling to acknowledge our alienation. Instead, like a lonely soul who noisily boasts of being free from constricting attachments, we insist this is not a predicament but a choice, indicative not of crisis but of an advanced set of values.

The United States is only the reductio ad absurdum of this state of affairs, which is recognizable, more or less, in all Western cultures. Likewise, our current symptoms are only the latest indications of something that has been around for several centuries. And it is against this backdrop that we can begin to understand not only the emphasis on self-interest but also the belief that concern for self is more real than concern for others. The self is threatened and therefore made more salient; its preservation becomes a priority and comes to seem "natural."

But what is it that threatens the self, leading us, paradoxically, to assert the idea of selfhood all the more vehemently? It is the very style of our individualism. The circle is vicious: we turn for our redemption to the very idea that undoes us. Notice how often we express our individuality in a dreary, predictable way, like the old joke about wanting to be a nonconformist . . . just like everybody else. One sociologist recalls what Tocqueville noticed about the United States: "The individual . . . achieves freedom and power only under the condition that he become isomorphic, or similar in form, to all the other individuals in the society. . . . The individual is free . . . to expand as a standardized individual."[33] Our miserable individuality is screwed to the back of our cars in the form of personalized license plates.

Nor is this the only paradox we encounter in seeking to understand the roots and fruits of individualism. Consider the widespread appeal of belief systems that promise transcendence. It is our detachment from others that has turned us into hitchhikers, anxious to escape the self in the first vehicle that comes down the road—even one that propels us right past humanity. Chodorow has cogently criticized Norman O. Brown, who "alternates extreme individualism with total merging . . . interweav[ing] this extreme arelationship with a[n] equally extreme vision of oneness and union, where there is no differentiated person to become part of society or culture."[34] The point, of course, is that these putatively opposite modes are really not so different from each other because they share the feature of missing anything to do with being-with. In a similar vein, Peter Marin recounts a conversation with someone much taken with "spirituality" and mysticism.

"I know there is something outside of me," he said. "I can feel it. I know it is there. But what is it?"

"It may not be a mystery," I said. "Perhaps it is the world."

That startled him. He had meant something more magical than that, more exotic and grand, something "above" rather than all around him. It had never occurred to him that what might be calling to him from beyond the self were the worlds of community and value, the worlds of history and action—all of them waiting to be entered not as a saint or a mystic, but in a way more difficult still: as a moral man or woman among other persons, with a person's complex nature and needs. Those worlds had been closed to him, had receded from consciousness as he had ceased to inhabit them fully or responsibly or lovingly, and so he felt their ghostly presence as something distant and mysterious, as a dream in which he had no actual existence.[35]

* * *

Steven Lukes is undoubtedly right to warn that even those of us in the West who would criticize individualism are nonetheless a part of this world view and we should not pretend that we can view it from the outside.[36] Still, critics from several traditions have called attention to the implications and deficiencies of our self orientation. Various writers have emphasized one or another of these traditions, but it is particularly impressive to see them gathered together.

First, of course, there are the historians and anthropologists who remind us that the idea of the individual self as we conceive of it is, so far from being a simple reflection of reality, actually an anomalous concept among human beings. The very word *individualism* did not exist until the nineteenth century, and the world view it signifies is hardly taken for granted in Eastern and nonindustrialized societies. The anthropologist Clifford Geertz speaks for many other social scientists:

The Western conception of the person as a bounded, unique, more or less integrated motivational and cognitive universe, a dynamic center of awareness, emotion, judgment, and action organized into a distinctive whole and set contrastively against both other such wholes and against its social and natural background, is, however incorrigible it may seem to us, a rather peculiar idea within the context of the world's cultures.[37]

The existentialist tradition also emphasizes that the self is always a self-in-the-face-of-others (to adopt the indigenous habit of hyphenation). Kierkegaard, Nietzsche, and Sartre did not exactly devote their respective careers to addressing the issue of ideal human relationship,[38] but the movement as a whole does not deserve its reputation for exclusive con-

cern with the individual. "Being-with is an existential characteristic of
Dasein [human being] even when factically no Other is present-at-hand
or perceived," according to Heidegger. "Even Dasein's Being-alone is
Being-with in the world."[39] This theme is echoed by Karl Jaspers,[40]
Gabriel Marcel,[41] the later Camus,[42] and, of course, Buber.

Marx, as his critique of liberal political theory suggests, also helped
to give us some distance from individualism. "Not only is the material of
my activity given to me as a social product (as is even the language in
which the thinker is active)," he said; "my *own* existence *is* social activity,
and therefore that which I make of myself, I make of myself for society
and with the consciousness of myself as a social being."[43]

Feminist theory has added its voice, pointing out, as Mary Midgley
put it, that "the whole idea of a free independent, enquiring, choosing
individual, an idea central to European thought, has always been essentially the idea of a male."[44] And, as another writer notes, this idea is
"fundamentally undercut by an examination of female experience."[45] It
has been suggested that the defense of the separate self represents for
many men not an expression of autonomy and strength so much as a
retreat from connectedness and vulnerability, which can be, at least at an
unconscious level, deeply threatening. In any case, the feminist critique
over the last few decades has made it all the more difficult to accept
uncritically the ultimate reality of the separate self.

Even in psychology there have been pockets of resistance. Family
systems theory takes a step beyond the self; so does the branch of psychoanalysis known as object relations theory, which offers a model of human
intersubjectivity that balances relatedness with autonomy.[46] Freud's exclusive attention to the motivational forces within the individual has been
challenged by Fromm, Horney, and Sullivan, the neo-Freudians. In "The
Illusion of Personal Individuality," Sullivan declared:

The personality . . . can be observed and studied only in relations between
personalities or among personalities. . . . One of the greatest difficulties encoun-
tered in bringing about favorable change is this almost inescapable illusion that
there is a perduring, unique, simple existent self, called variously "me" or "I,"
and in some strange fashion, the patient's, or the subject person's, private property. . . . It makes no sense to think of ourselves as "individual," "separate,"
capable of anything like definitive description in isolation. . . . No great progress
in this field of study can be made until it is realized that the field of observation
is what people do with each other, what they can communicate to each other
about what they do with each other.[47]

While all of these challenges to individualism share a dissatisfaction with our view of the centrality, or logical priority, or naive celebration of the self, they do not offer identical metaphysical systems to replace that self. Heidegger was not a Buddhist and Sullivan was not a Marxist; feminists, like existentialists, disagree among themselves. What most of these critics share, though, is the idea not only that every person is nested in social relationships, but that the very notion of personhood is dependent on those relationships. We are social beings; each of us is already in a world, willy-nilly. One might even say that the idea of an individual self is abstracted from the given reality of interconnection— as opposed to the view that it is society that is a reification and only separate selves are real. Even to affirm the notion of individuality, as Bellah and his colleagues slyly pointed out, is to enter the social world of ideas.[48] Rationality itself is a product of social interaction, of shared knowledge and criteria.

It is also important to recognize what these critics are *not* doing. They are not just arguing that individual selves are inclined alternately to express their individuality and their ties to others. (One thinks, for example, of David Bakan's description of "agency" and "communion," or Andras Angyal's model of "autonomy" and "homonomy," both of which speak to our duality, our need to be separate but also to be part of something larger.) The point is rather to question the idea of a separate self that *has* urges of this sort or that. These critics also are not simply saying that each of us comes to know herself by interacting with others. It is true, as Ortega y Gasset and others acknowledged, that we must rely on our fellows even for self-knowledge.[49] But moving beyond an individualistic world view is not commended to us merely as a means for self-discovery. Our relationships are an end, and collectively they also describe the human condition at least as convincingly as a model based on separate selves.

Even when we recoil from deliberate cooperation, from intimacy or community, we are interdependent creatures, a point that has been explored by writers from many different disciplines. Biologically speaking, as Lewis Thomas remarked,

a good case can be made for our nonexistence as entities. We are not made up, as we had always supposed, of successively enriched packets of our own parts. We are shared, rented, occupied. . . . The whole dear notion of one's own Self— marvelous old free-willed, free-enterprising, autonomous, independent, isolated island of a Self—is a myth.[50]

Other biologists have also called our attention to the deliberate cooperation that occurs so regularly both within and among species as to make
it clear that both competition and self-sufficiency are the exception in
nature rather than the rule.

Psychologically speaking, the self is "a composite structure which has
been and is being formed and built up since the day of our birth out of
countless never-ending influences and exchanges between ourselves and
others. . . . We are members one of another."[51] This does not mean that
we are symbiotic, fused, or selfless; it means that we do not exist or
develop independent of others. The idea that a child's natural egocentricity must be overridden in order to make him social (or prosocial) is a
belief whose popularity "is attributable to an overemphasis on individualism" in developmental psychology; in fact, "to understand individuals
fully, one must first grasp the relationships from which the individual is
derived."[52]

Sociologically speaking, the very idea of society presupposes interdependence. Even in an individualistic society, we rely on each other,
work with each other, interact with each other in innumerable ways.
The pioneers whom we revere would not have survived without being
willing to cooperate. Increasingly we are forced to reckon with the fact
that even whole societies are themselves interdependent. Nuclear accidents and oil spills know nothing of national boundaries. If one country
revalues its currency or adjusts its interest rates, the reverberations are
felt around the world—and the U.S. stock market is as vulnerable to
such changes elsewhere as is any other component of the world economy.[53] We are all of us strapped together for the duration of the journey.

Failing to recognize this fact, persisting in the rituals that are prescribed by the cult of the self, is concretely harmful in many ways. It leaves
us naive, unable to deal with the complexities of the real world. The
evidence on links between isolation and pathology (both mental and
physical) has been rehearsed many times. Ironically, this very individualism adds insult to injury by denying its victims—and the rest of us—
needed services. As the writer Suzanne Gordon has observed:

America's traditional . . . devaluation of the meaning of human relationships, and
its emphasis on competitive individualism and self-reliance have created a situation in which care giving is an endangered activity and care givers are an endangered species.

She points to the "exodus from the helping professions"—notably the shortage of nurses, child care workers, and teachers. The combination of burn-out and abominably low wages that has produced this shortage may indirectly be the result of our individualist ethic.[54] Prosocial behavior in general, to say nothing of altruistic or "us"-motivated prosocial behavior, is discouraged and even made to seem alien to human nature. Our moral vision is blurred by a self-based metaphysics and by practices that serve to isolate us. In fact, a world view based on the individual self as opposed to the self-in-relationship has striking moral implications, as does the wider set of issues—altruism, empathy, and selfishness—discussed to this point.

SOURCES OF MORALITY

Reuniting Desire and Duty

For all its influence, Kant's ethical system is hardly the only one designed since the Enlightenment. Whereas he spoke of duties, others have talked of rights; whereas he was interested in the intrinsic value of actions, others have been more concerned with results. But Kant's prescriptions do exemplify two features that have reigned supreme in Western thought. First, morality is resident in the individual; it is the autonomy of the self rather than its relation to other selves that is integral to the idea of moral agency. Second, morality is manifested in principles that ought to be adopted just because our reason tells us that they are right.

For the present, let it suffice to say about the first of these that the individual focus is not a neutral, purely formal context for moral discussion. If we begin with the self, we *value* the self, and there are material consequences to this in terms of valuing independence over interdependence. Lucien Goldmann has observed that it is precisely Kant's emphasis on the autonomous self that leads him to imagine a tension between what one wants to do and what one should do. "So long as the *individual,* the *I,* is the subject of action, the search for happiness is not universal but egoistic, and as such, contrary to virtue."[55]

Whatever the role of individualism, though, one of the most striking features of Kant's thought is surely this incompatibility of duty and desire. The will should conform to the moral law and not to what one wants to do. In fact, he says, "It is even *dangerous* to allow other motives (for

instance, that of interest) even to cooperate *along with* the moral law."[56]
The more clearly we distinguish between oughts and preferences, the
better. There are

many persons so sympathetically constituted that without any motive of vanity or
selfishness they find an inner satisfaction in spreading joy and rejoice in the
contentment of others which they have made possible. But I say that however
dutiful and amiable it may be, that kind of action has no true moral worth.
. . . [If one acts] only from duty and without any inclination—then for the first
time his action has genuine moral worth.[57]

This holds true for empathy, too. We have the capacity to share in
others' feelings and we ought to cultivate this capacity as an important
tool for doing our moral duty. But there is value only in the empathy that
is deliberately willed, not in the kind that occurs spontaneously.[58] Moreover, even the preferred version of empathy is not seen as valuable in its
own right but only insofar as it helps us meet our rationally recognized
moral obligations.

Not all ethicists who have followed Kant chronologically have followed him in this repudiation of all that is not willed. But our lives
indisputably have been influenced by the view that morality must be
imposed, that ethical sense must be, as it were, hammered into children,
that the right thing to do is almost by definition the thing we would rather
not do. If moral behavior is an externally imposed duty, we should not
wonder that it comes to be viewed as a chore and is undertaken reluctantly. Together, Kant and Hobbes have left us a legacy of permanent
struggle between, on the one hand, the person's desire for pleasure at the
expense of others and, on the other hand, an obligation to transcend that
instinct. Given this way of framing reality, it was understandable for
Freud to have concluded that pleasure will usually prevail, that "instinctual passions are stronger than reasonable interests."[59]

Traditional morality also has held, following Kant, that the identity
of individuals must be irrelevant, that principles are to be formulated
dispassionately, impartially, universalizably. There is no room for feelings here because feelings offer an unreliable basis for any ethical system;
they are tantamount to bias, which is precisely what we seek to eliminate.
Almost all ethical systems regard this as axiomatic, even when the talk
turns to altruism. It is not a coincidence that the *altruism* entry in the index
to John Rawls's book *A Theory of Justice* directs the reader to "*see* Mutual
disinterestedness." And Thomas Nagel's influential book, *The Possibility*

of Altruism, begins with the declaration that morally significant altruism "is not a feeling." The word *rational* or *rationality* appears six times in Nagel's first seven sentences. Later, he summarizes his position as follows:

Altruism and related motives do not depend on taste, sentiment, or an arbitrary and ultimate choice. They depend instead on the fact that our reasons for action are subject to the formal condition of objectivity, which depends in turn on our ability to view ourselves from both the personal and impersonal standpoints, and to engage in reasoning to practical conclusions from both of those standpoints.[60]

Two recent books stand in opposition to this view of altruism—and of ethics more generally. Lawrence Blum's *Friendship, Altruism, and Morality,* as I have already mentioned, locates altruism in the context of relationship. More than this, Blum argues that an act, such as seeking to benefit a friend in need, may qualify as moral even if it is neither impartial nor universalizable. To act compassionately, with sympathy and care, is in itself to enter the moral realm. *Some* emotions may be changeable and capricious (and therefore incapable of supporting morality), but not all emotions, and not all altruistic emotions, can be so described.[61]*

Nel Noddings's *Caring* is not concerned with altruism as such, but, like Blum's essay, it rejects both the idea that morality must be universalizable and the assumption that personal connection is too capricious to sustain a system of ethics. Noddings is chiefly concerned to establish that meeting and caring for the other is more valuable than upholding principles or rules about right action. Thus, she "locate[s] the very wellspring of ethical behavior in human affective response," in concrete concern rather than abstract obligation.[64]

The idea that morality can be based on feelings rather than reason is generally traced back to David Hume. "Reason is, and ought only to be the slave of the passions," he argued—an opinion he conceded was "somewhat extraordinary." Fortunately, said Hume, these passions of ours are mostly benevolent: we generally respond empathically and sympathetically to others, making their concerns our own and endeavoring to bring about what is in their interest. All of what we call the virtues are

---

*Interestingly, Nagel and Blum offer remarkably similar definitions of *altruism.* Nagel speaks of "a willingness to act in consideration of the interests of other persons, without the need of ulterior motive,"[62] and Blum of "a regard for the good of another person for his own sake, or conduct motivated by such a regard."[63] It would seem that nothing in the concept of altruism per se demands that such an orientation be a matter of rational deduction and uniform application.

rooted in the fact that we applaud what benefits other people and oppose what harms them—just as we do with respect to ourselves. Justice contributes to the public good, and that good has meaning for us because of (and is defined in terms of) our empathic response to others. The result is that empathy, which he called sympathy, is "the chief source of moral distinctions."[65]

Speaking very roughly, my intention here is to contrast an individual morality with a relational one, a cognitive morality with an affective one, a principle- or rule-based morality with one grounded in care or empathy.[66] The conventional idea is that the former possibility in each pair is more reliable. Most philosophers have held that rational rules (such as "One should attempt to help those in danger if the cost to oneself is not prohibitive") are more durable than affective responses to another person and her predicament. However, this assumption is being questioned: in fact, not only have affects been defended as a solid basis for morality, but it has even been argued that rules are actually *less* trustworthy than feelings.

Imagine a person who is concerned to follow a general precept about the value of helping but who has no emotional connection to any victim, no felt desire to see anyone relieved of pain. Such an individual may fail to recognize another's distress correctly to begin with and may then help awkwardly or at the wrong times for lack of affective attunement with the victim. Moreover, Ervin Staub argues that "individuals characterized by a concern with rules and feelings of duty or obligation to them may be more likely to make the judgment that victims deserve their suffering and be less helpful under such conditions."[67] (I would qualify this by suggesting that it is not so much that rules predispose one to blame the victim as that empathy can curb such a tendency where it exists.)

The Oliners take this a step further: "Ideology, grand vision, or abstract principles may inure [one] to the suffering of real people."[68] To take a rather extreme example of this, one can almost hear the echoes of Kant in the speeches of Nazi mass murderer Rudolf Hoess. What is morally required, Hoess declared, has nothing to do with kindness, but with a "meticulous desire for justice and a fanatical sense of duty."[69]

Because of both the nature of the concept and the particular concrete meanings it can take on, duty may not be more reliable than care. What is more, if altruism is regarded as a moral good, then perhaps empathy and care approximate this good more closely than principled helping ever could. This, too, sounds surprising at first, since empathic helping is normally associated with some measure of gratification for the helper, while disinterested helping seems purely selfless.[70] However, a disinterested helper acts so as to discharge an obligation, to follow a rule, to live up to a principle. The response to the other is therefore mediated and indirect, the act of meeting the other's needs being only a means to achieving the ultimate goal of acting in accordance with the principle. Compassion, by contrast, will tend to facilitate the objective of helping just in order to help. It thus has a stronger claim to wear the mantle of altruism.[71] Now, it may well be that a person motivated by rules or principles will *develop* an affective commitment to helping or will come to care about the particular other being helped. (She may even come to think primarily about the relationship between herself and the other, in which case talk of altruism is beside the point.) But even here, principles contribute to altruism only indirectly—that is, only insofar as the act of helping elicits an other-oriented (rather than rule-oriented) motive.

Besides the fact that a Kantian approach to morality may seem chilly, unreliable, or removed from genuine altruism, its opposition between duty and desire virtually guarantees that moral behavior will be perceived as disagreeable, as something one would go out of one's way to avoid. It is common to complain about widespread immorality—cheating, dishonesty, exploitation, and so forth—but less common to inquire whether this just might be related to the way morality has been construed in the first place.

If Hume is right about the "naturalness" of benevolent passions, and if all of the evidence described earlier in this book has been persuasive, then we have cause to question the premise of traditional understandings of morality. Assuming a social and child-rearing context conducive to caring and helping, empathy and perspective taking, there is reason to think that what we *want* to do and what we *ought* to do are not so far apart after all. The apparent convergence of desire and duty should please everyone except he who makes a fetish of the will and of overcoming desire regardless of the nature of one's desires. This convergence, if taken at face value, hints at the possibility of an "organic morality"—one that is a natural outgrowth of who we are rather than a set of principles imported for the purpose of redirecting us.

A Place for Principles

The idea of a relational, affective, care-based, or organic morality makes for a refreshing alternative to traditional approaches to ethics. But before we abandon the latter altogether, let us consider its proposed replacement a little more carefully. To begin with, what exactly is the relevance to morality of the fact that humans are—or at least have the capacity to be—more empathic than is usually believed? It is one thing to observe that duty and desire may overlap but something else again to argue that this gives us information about the nature or role of duty. We may have been too quick to describe our species as selfish, but how does correcting this perception of what we are affect how we ought to be?

It may be permissible, as Blum and Noddings argue, to discard the requirements of universalizability and impartiality, but if the word *morality* means anything, it specifies something *ought*-related; it must prescribe rather than just describe. In the course of arguing that reason is not the source of moral distinctions, Hume paused to make what has become a very famous digression. He observed that philosophers frequently and unaccountably slide from talk about the nature of humans or of God into talk about how we *ought* to behave.[72] The tendency to assume that some moral significance resides in a description of, say, what humans need—or, more generally, to assume that one can ever derive a value from a fact— has come to be regarded as an instance of the naturalistic fallacy.

The issue is more complicated than I am making out here; in the early 1960s, the so-called is/ought problem was the subject of a number of disputatious monographs. But it seems clear to me that we must be very careful about assuming that any sort of morality can be constructed on the basis of an empirical finding about the capacity for empathy—or, for that matter, the capacity for reasoning, the need to be cared for, the historical prevalence of prosocial or antisocial acts, or anything of the kind.

Our beliefs about ourselves may, of course, affect our behavior. We may act more morally as a consequence of realizing that it is within our repertoire to do so. But the question at hand is not how often we engage in moral acts; it is how we come to call those acts moral. That is a matter of judgment and choice, not of discovery. Most people we know may accept the normative judgment that caring for others is a good thing to do, but that does not make it any less a normative judgment. Caring, like everything else, does not become good just because it is generally approved. Nor does it become good just because it may be "natural." Hurting is also natural; the operative question is which of our many natural capabilities we will decide to value. But even if caring *were* in some sense more natural than hurting, we would still not be able to conclude anything about its moral desirability from this fact.

The point of all this is that in contrasting two kinds of morality, we must resist the temptation to counterpose stiff rules ("One should help if . . .") with warm accounts of concrete caring. By virtue of being descriptions, the latter are not really moral statements at all. A morality of caring may tell us that it is desirable to help or care, to *want* to help or care, to nurture relationships in which helping can take place, or to attend to real human beings rather than to abstract rules. In place of "One should help if . . ." such a moral framework can say *"You* should help if . . ." or "You should help *your friend* if. . . ." It can even omit the *if.* But it cannot omit the *should.*

Noddings has made as good a case as can be made against principles, but ultimately she is unable to show that they can be banished from morality—not least because she ends up invoking some herself. The point, she says, is not to construct rules about stealing and killing—rules that will clash with each other and create their own exceptions—but to care deeply about others and let this suggest the proper actions. *"Each one* who comes under our gaze must be met as one-caring," she proposes.[73] But what is this if not a principle? It may be a principle concerned with the value of caring, and a very appealing principle, but it is unmistakably a principle.

At this point, let us set aside the issue of what constitutes a moral system or statement and simply ask whether the injunction to empathize offers us sufficient guidance so that we can get by without principles. Immediately we realize that it does not. In situations of conflict, the pressing question is: *With whom* should we empathize? The pregnant woman or the fetus? The victim of terrorism or the displaced and oppressed people in whose behalf the terrorist struggles? We need principles about fairness, justice, duty, or rights to help us decide. "But this is a false dichotomy!" comes the reply. "A humane choice can be made only by empathizing with *all* parties to the dispute." To which we answer: This is wise counsel indeed—and it is also a principle.

I want to recognize the importance and value of empathy but not assign to it a burden it cannot support. Empathy is not *necessary* for helping; some people are prosocial just because they think they should be. And empathy is not *sufficient* for ensuring moral behavior. The last statement, I hasten to add, does not hinge on empathy's being affective.* Perspective

---

*More broadly, Blum has argued that an altruistic response to someone is not a purely affective affair. "The crucial moral distinction is between concern for one's own good and concern for the good of others, rather than between emotional (or interested) considerations and rational considerations."[74]

taking is a cognitive phenomenon, yet it, too, is insufficient. "Whose perspective should we take?" is as sensible, and unsettling, a question as "With whom should we empathize?" or "For whom should we care?"[75]

To be sure, empathy and care are not interchangeable concepts. Empathy may increase the likelihood of helping, but it does not logically entail taking action. This is why the Oliners saw the need for a "conjoining of empathy for pain with personal responsibility."[76] The idea of care, by contrast, can be thought of as building in this responsibility so that to care for someone means not only to share her feelings but to act in her behalf.

Even the richer concept of care, though, requires a rule (or a meta-rule) for direction lest we exclude people to whom we are not personally connected. Such exclusion violates norms of fairness to which I think most of us want to be faithful. "The central facet of the vicarious affects is that when they come in the door, *impartiality* flies out the window," as Rescher put it.[77] Impartiality may be overrated, but even the most caring individual will often be troubled by its absence. John Stuart Mill warned us about people who "may be very amiable and delightful to those with whom they sympathize, and grossly unjust and unfeeling to the rest of the world."[78] Even Hume, for that matter, recognized the problem: "Sympathy with persons remote from us [is] much fainter than that with persons near and contiguous . . . . [so we know] to correct these inequalities by reflection, and retain a general standard of vice and virtue."[79]

It may be argued that the problem here is not that care is itself inadequate but just that we need to care for more people. In a sense this is true. Martin Hoffman proposes, in effect, that more and better caring, as well as making an effort to empathize with more people and to understand their common humanity, can help to reduce empathic bias.[80] Still, he acknowledges, the fact is that we will never care for everyone equally, and to that extent we will be inclined to favor those to whom we are most closely connected unless there is a principle that restrains us from doing so.

I would propose that such selectivity—let us avoid the loaded term *bias*—can be problematic on some occasions. Consider just one of many possible examples. More patients need organ transplants than can get them at present. Suppose that Fred is admitted to the hospital and gets such a transplant, only to have his body reject it. Should he be given priority for another operation or should he go back to the end of the line? The medical staff has by now come to know Fred and feel his plight concretely, whereas the other, equally needy, patients are just so many names on a computer printout to them. Should this be allowed to affect their decision, or should they employ rules to ensure fairness as a counterbalance to their personal involvement?[81]

What I am really talking about here, although the concept has acquired a pejorative reputation in some circles, is the need for abstraction. This is precisely what seems to be lacking in public officials who are genuinely moved by, and generous with, destitute individuals they encounter on the street but whose budget priorities create misery on a much wider scale. Likewise,

the news of an animal run over by a car, a child stuck in a well, or the preventable death of one individual evokes an outpouring of sympathetic response and upsets the emotional equanimity of many; yet reports of six million Jews killed in Nazi death camps or of a hundred thousand Japanese killed in Hiroshima and Nagasaki may cause but moderate uneasiness. Arthur Koestler has put it poignantly, "Statistics don't bleed; it is the detail which counts. We are unable to embrace the total process with our awareness; we can only focus on little lumps of reality."[82]

I think it is putting things too strongly to say that we are able to focus *only* on concrete, ready-to-hand reality—although obviously it is easier to do so. It would seem that there is often moral value in moving beyond what is in front of our faces or what "feels right" in our gut. Granted that human lives are sometimes sacrificed in the name of abstractions. Granted also that trying to keep people's concrete subjectivity before us is generally a more promising route by which to arrive at morality than is focusing on abstractions. Nevertheless, abstractions are often our only link to justice and a greater good. It is of little consequence whether we call this a higher-order morality of care[83] or decide that no morality of care is adequate by itself. What matters is the recognition that some moral claims are no less urgent for being intangible or physically distant or otherwise hard to feel. Camus wrestled with this issue in *The Plague,* describing his doctor protagonist's obligation to resist the heart-wrenching pleas of infected individuals who wanted to rejoin their loved ones outside of the quarantine area, or who resisted being torn away from their family and shipped to the hospital. "To fight abstraction you must have something of it in your own make-up," Camus wrote.[84]

Where Humanity Begins

All of these considerations suggest that what we need is a morality of thought *and* of feeling, of principle and of care. This may sound like a facile, even perfunctory, compromise, but apparently it is not obvious to everyone. Some champions of a care-based morality seem to be allergic to principles and rules, while a much larger contingent of Kant's intellectual heirs have dismissed affective connection as epiphenomenal or irrelevant or even inimical to ethics. What I have tried to do here, moreover, is not merely to say that a synthesis is required and let it go at that but to emphasize the reasons it is required, the deficiencies of each partial conception of morality.

With respect to the relative importance of thought and feeling, who can deny the poverty of one without the other? Which has been more deadly—bloodless rationality or fanatical passion devoid of reason? Both are inhuman because each is only part of the human. Impersonal principles were introduced in the first place because not all human passions are as benevolent as the ones that Hume (or, for that matter, this book) celebrates—a fact that we forget at our peril. Yet principles alone can justify mass purges and nuclear holocaust. As the philosopher William Barrett put it: "To be rational is not the same as to be reasonable. In my time I have heard the most hair-raising and crazy things from very rational men, advanced in a perfectly rational way; no insight or feelings had been used to check the reasoning at any point."[85]

But reason and care, principles and passion, are not really discrete ingredients that have to be artificially combined. They coax each other from their hiding places; each, by a miraculous alchemy, is transformed into the other. Someone may begin to help because she thinks she ought to do so. Soon she has before her a person, a subject, and she comes to care as well. The motive has evolved as the prosocial act has elicited a living connection. The Oliners quote one rescuer, initially motivated by a commitment to the idea of justice, who said, "I began to like the people I was helping and became very distressed at what was happening to them."[86]

Conversely, we might ask, where do moral principles come from? To some extent they can be learned in straightforward fashion. But here is another possibility: over time, one responds affectively to many people and this may prompt the conviction that one *ought* to help. One starts to think about guidelines for helping fairly and, more generally, about how to treat others. We resonate to others' feelings and these free-flowing responses eventually solidify: principles, in sum, might be understood as "congealed empathy." Approaching the same idea from a different direction, Hoffman proposed that

the empathic affect may be evoked independently, or empathic affect may be aroused first and then may prime the moral principles. Either way, the co-occurrence of a principle and empathic affect should produce a bond between them (or strengthen any existing bond). The result may be that the principle, even if learned initially in a "cool," didactic context . . . is encoded and stored as an affectively charged representation—as a "hot" cognition.[87]

Others, too, have suggested that care may be the main impetus for developing ethical ideas as well as supplying them with their content.[88] In any case, the two are more closely related than we might assume, and any program to promote prosocial attitudes and behavior ought to emphasize both justice and caring, principles and empathy—a view that even cognitive developmental psychologists like Piaget and Kohlberg gave some evidence of having embraced.[89] As one legal scholar put it, "Abandonment of the rules produces monsters; so does neglect of persons."[90] And whether our focus at the moment is on rules or persons, we ought to bear in mind that morality is a social product, a collective effort. As Carol Gilligan and Grant Wiggins have emphasized, "Strong feelings *and* clear principles are dependent on 'authentic' relationships" rather than being self-generated.[91]

The idea introduced in the first part of this chapter, that a relational perspective beckons from beyond altruism, has unmistakable moral ramifications. We are predisposed to help those with whom we feel a personal connection for reasons that are neither egoistic nor altruistic. It is the perfect transcendence of Kant's split between desire and duty. I have conceded that we need rules of fairness to guide our treatment of those with whom there is no feeling of us. But perhaps we need to try to act even with strangers *as if* there were or could be such a connection. Altruism—one self helping another without consideration of personal gain—is both realistic and commendable. But a model of relatedness that ripples out concentrically from our loved ones to those we know to everyone else has the potential of creating even sturdier bonds.

Our obligation, as Rescher reminds us, is not merely to treat individuals in a certain fashion but to work together to make structural changes that will facilitate caring. We should "act so as to realize a social order in which action for prudential advantage is—at least by and large— coincidental with action for the common good."[92] This means challenging the institutional and ideological supports for competition and individualism, replacing them wherever possible with a norm of cooperation. After all, we *are* interdependent, like it or not; we would do better to like it. We should try to enhance a prosocial orientation in our children and ourselves, attending to the development of perspective-taking and empathy skills. We should broaden our range of experiences to maximize understanding of, and identification with, others.

Relationship in the fullest sense is not a luxury for the few, dependent on specialized training or affluence. No one has spoken more passionately or poetically about the common nobility of connection than Martin Buber. His response to an imagined critic who asks whether dialogue is a realistic possibility in the modern world is worth savoring:

The life of dialogue is no privilege of intellectual activity like dialectic. It does not begin in the upper story of humanity. It begins no higher than where humanity begins. There are no gifted and ungifted here, only those who give themselves and those who withhold themselves. . . . I am not concerned with the pure; I am concerned with . . . the breaking through from the status of the dully-tempered disagreeableness, obstinacy, and contraryness in which the man, whom I pluck at random out of the tumult, is living and out of which he can and at times does break through.

Whither? Into nothing exalted, heroic or holy, into no Either and no Or, only into this tiny strictness and grace of every day, where I have to do with just the very same "reality" with whose duty and business I am taken up in such a way, glance to glance, look to look, word to word, that I experience it as reached to me and myself to it, it as spoken to me and myself to it. And now, in all the clanking of routine that I have called my reality, there appears to me, homely and glorious, the effective reality, creaturely and given to me in trust and responsibility. We do not find meaning lying in things nor do we put it into things, but between us and things it can happen.[93]

Buber's answer speaks also to those who equate altruism with unheard-of heroism, to those who assume that we are stuck in the quicksand of self-interest, to those who raise their children and plan public policy based on the premise that the prosocial is utopian. To reject these unjustified assumptions is not to take leave of the real world. It is, if I may recast a favorite saying of the cynics, to be not an optimist but a realist.

No imported solution will dissolve our problems of dehumanization and egocentricity, coldness and cruelty. No magical redemption from outside of human life will let us break through. The work that has to be done is our work, but we are better equipped for it than we have been led to believe. To move ourselves beyond selfishness, we already have what is required. We already *are* what is required. We are human and we have each other.

Appendix

The Seville Statement on Violence

Believing that it is our responsibility to address from our particular disciplines the most dangerous and destructive activities of our species, violence and war; recognizing that science is a human cultural product which cannot be definitive or all-encompassing; and gratefully acknowledging the support of the authorities of Seville and representatives of the Spanish UNESCO; we, the undersigned scholars from around the world and from relevant sciences, have met and arrived at the following Statement on Violence. In it, we challenge a number of alleged biological findings that have been used, even by some in our disciplines, to justify violence and war. Because the alleged findings have contributed to an atmosphere of pessimism in our time, we submit that the open, considered rejection of these mis-statements can contribute significantly to the International Year of Peace.

Misuse of scientific theories and data to justify violence and war is not new but has been made since the advent of modern science. For example, the theory of evolution has been used to justify not only war, but also genocide, colonialism, and suppression of the weak.

We state our position in the form of five propositions. We are aware that there are many other issues about violence and war that could be fruitfully addressed from the standpoint of our disciplines, but we restrict ourselves here to what we consider a most important first step.

IT IS SCIENTIFICALLY INCORRECT to say that we have inherited a tendency to make war from our animal ancestors. Although fighting occurs widely throughout animal species, only a few cases of destructive intra-species fighting between organized groups have ever been reported among naturally living species, and none of these involve the use of tools designed to be weapons. Normal predatory feeding upon other species cannot be equated with intra-species violence. Warfare is a peculiarly human phenomenon and does not occur in other animals.

The fact that warfare has changed so radically over time indicates that it is a product of culture. Its biological connection is primarily through language which makes possible the coordination of groups, the transmission of technology, and the use of tools. War is biologically possible, but it is not inevitable, as evidenced by its variation in occurrence and nature over time and space. There are cultures which have not engaged in war for centuries, and there are cultures which have engaged in war frequently at some times and not at others.

IT IS SCIENTIFICALLY INCORRECT to say that war or any other violent behavior is genetically programmed into our human nature. While genes are involved at all levels of nervous system function, they provide a developmental potential that can be actualized only in conjunction with the ecological and social environment. While individuals vary in their predispositions to be affected by their experience, it is the interaction between their genetic endowment and conditions of nurturance that determines their personalities. Except for rare pathologies, the genes do not produce individuals necessarily predisposed to violence. Neither do they determine the opposite. While genes are co-involved in establishing our behavioral capacities, they do not by themselves specify the outcome.

IT IS SCIENTIFICALLY INCORRECT to say that in the course of human evolution there has been a selection for aggressive behavior more than for other kinds of behavior. In all well-studied species, status within the group is achieved by the ability to cooperate and to fulfill social functions relevant to the structure of that group. "Dominance" involves social bondings and affiliations; it is not simply a matter of the possession and use of superior physical power, although it does involve aggressive behaviors. Where genetic selection for aggressive behavior has been artifically instituted in animals, it has rapidly succeeded in producing hyper-aggressive individuals; this indicates that aggression was not maximally selected under natural conditions. When such experimentally-created hyper-aggressive animals are present in a social group, they either disrupt its social structure or are driven out. Violence is neither in our evolutionary legacy nor in our genes.

IT IS SCIENTIFICALLY INCORRECT to say that humans have a "violent brain." While we do have the neural apparatus to act violently, it is not automatically activated by internal or external stimuli. Like higher primates and unlike other animals, our higher neural processes filter such stimuli before they can be acted upon. How we act is shaped by how we have been conditioned and socialized. There is nothing in our neurophysiology that compels us to react violently.

IT IS SCIENTIFICALLY INCORRECT to say that war is caused by "instinct" or any single motivation. The emergence of modern warfare has been a journey from the primacy of emotional and motivational factors, sometimes called "instincts," to the primacy of cognitive factors. Modern war involves institutional use of personal characteristics such as obedience, suggestibility, and idealism, social skills such as language, and rational considerations such as cost-calculation, planning, and information processing. The technology of modern war has exaggerated traits associated with violence both in the training of actual combatants and in the preparation of support for war in the general population. As a result of this exaggeration, such traits are often mistaken to be the causes rather than the consequences of the process.

We conclude that biology does not condemn humanity to war, and that humanity can be freed from the bondage of biological pessimism and empowered with confidence to undertake the transformative tasks needed in this International Year of Peace and in the years to come. Although these tasks are mainly institutional and collective, they also rest upon the consciousness of individual participants for whom pessimism and optimism are crucial factors. Just as "wars begin in the minds of men," peace also begins in our minds. The same species [that] invented war is capable of inventing peace. The responsibility lies with each of us.

Seville, May 16, 1986

David Adams, Psychology, Wesleyan University, Middletown, (CT) USA
S.A. Barnett, Ethology, The Australian National University, Canberra, Australia
N.P. Bechtereva, Neurophysiology, Institute for Experimental Medicine of Academy of Medical Sciences of USSR, Leningrad, USSR
Bonnie Frank Carter, Psychology, Albert Einstein Medical Center, Philadelphia (PA) USA
José M. Rodriguez Delgado, Neurophysiology, Centro de Estudios Neurobiológicos, Madrid, Spain
José Luis Díaz, Ethology, Instituto Mexicano de Psiquiatría, Mexico D.F., Mexico
Andrzej Eliasz, Individual Differences Psychology, Polish Academy of Sciences, Warsaw, Poland
Santiago Genovés, Biological Anthropology, Instituto de Estudios Antropológicos, Mexico D.F., Mexico
Benson E. Ginsburg, Behavior Genetics, University of Connecticut, Storrs (CT) USA
Jo Groebel, Social Psychology, Erzichungswissenschaftliche Hochschule, Landau, Federal Republic of Germany
Samir-Kumar Ghosh, Sociology, Indian Institute of Human Sciences, Calcutta, India
Robert Hinde, Animal Behavior, Cambridge University, UK
Richard E. Leakey, Physical Anthropology, National Museums of Kenya, Nairobi, Kenya
Taha M.Malasi, Psychiatry, Kuwait University, Kuwait

J. Martín Ramírez, Psychobiology, Universidad de Sevilla, Spain

Federico Mayor Zaragoza, Biochemistry, Universidad Autónoma, Madrid, Spain

Diana L. Mendoza, Ethology, Universidad de Sevilla, Spain

Ashis Nandy, Political Psychology, Center for the Study of Developing Societies, Delhi, India

John Paul Scott, Animal Behavior, Bowling Green State University, Bowling Green (OH) USA

Riitta Wahlström, Psychology, University of Jyväskylä, Finland

Notes

CHAPTER 1

1. D. E. Koshland, Jr., "Nature, Nurture, and Behavior."

2. B. Birns, "The Emergence and Socialization of Sex Differences in the Earliest Years," p. 229.

3. B. E. Ginsburg, "Developmental Genetics of Behavioral Capacities," pp. 188–89.

4. S. J. Gould, "Similarities between the Sexes." In *Not in Our Genes*, Richard Lewontin, Steven Rose, and Leon Kamin suggest that biological determinism assumes not only that individual behaviors "are the direct consequences of inborn physical characteristics," but also that social phenomena can be explained in terms of individual behaviors. The presence of this second form of reductionism, claiming that a society is no more than the sum of its constituents, is too often overlooked in discussions of the nature/nurture question, perhaps because we take this atomistic form of analysis for granted. Together, the two claims lead the determinist to draw "arrows of causality . . . from genes to humans and from humans to humanity" (p. 18).

5. "Behavioral genetics has little to say about universals of development (e.g., why the human species uses language) or about average differences between groups (e.g., why girls perform better than boys on verbal tests)" (R. Plomin, "Environment and Genes," p. 105). Plomin's choice of examples may itself be instructive since gender differences in verbal ability no longer exist. (See J. S. Hyde and M. C. Linn, "Gender Differences in Verbal Ability.")

6. R. Watson, "A Case of Human Error," p. 18.

7. E. F. Torrey, *Surviving Schizophrenia*, p. 2.

8. *New York Times* advertisement, September 27, 1988, p. C-21. Of course, to call something a disease is not tantamount to claiming that it is inherited; asbestosis is caused by exposure to an environmental hazard, namely asbestos. In fact, environmental factors ultimately may be of greater relevance than genetic

predisposition even with respect to cancer and coronary disease. (An editorial in the *New England Journal of Medicine* argues that "cultural transmission can be even stronger than genetic transmission" with respect to these diseases [R. R. Williams, "Nature, Nurture, and Family Predisposition].) But those who claim that schizophrenia is a brain disease typically use this language to emphasize that it is not caused by environmental factors, which in this case have more to do with familial dysfunction than with something like inhaled fibers. They mean that schizophrenia is inherited; the possibility that familial dysfunction plays a role is precisely what they are at pains to deny.

9. The etiological relevance of family dysfunction to schizophrenia, let alone to other psychological disorders, is well-established. A review of three recent major studies concludes that "variations in the rates of schizophrenia are predictable in part from prior estimates of disturbances in the intrafamilial environment" (M. J. Goldstein, "The Family and Psychopathology," p. 289).

10. See my article on this subject, "Suffer the Restless Children."

11. This impression comes from interviews I have conducted with a number of prominent specialists in the field as well as from a review of more than a hundred journal articles and chapters on the subject. Moreover, in a survey of nearly five hundred primary care physicians published in 1983, the majority said they believed organic causes of hyperactivity were usually primary (F. C. Bennett and R. Sherman, "Management of Childhood 'Hyperactivity' by Primary Care Physicians," p. 90).

12. G. Coles, *The Learning Mystique*, pp. xv, 133.

13. Searles's findings are described in B. Bower, "Alcoholism's Elusive Genes," pp. 74–75. The same article quotes the anthropologist Dwight B. Heath as saying, "No one is genetically predestined to become an alcoholic. Even if the genetic missing link were eventually found, the interaction of various environmental factors is certainly crucial if alcoholism is to occur in an individual" (p. 79).

14. See L. J. Kamin, "Is Crime in the Genes?" and "Are There Genes for Crime?"

15. E. Currie, *Confronting Crime*, pp. 24–25.

16. A. Tellegen et al., "Personality Similarity in Twins Reared Apart and Together," p. 1036.

17. M. W. Lear, "The Cheapskate Ploy," p. 56. Ellipses and emphasis in original.

18. L. Van Gelder, "His Rabbit's Voice." There is no shortage of similar examples. To boost the response rate in a government survey of driving habits, a state bureaucrat decided to offer a chance at a cash prize to encourage participation. This, he told a reporter, was because "it's human nature" to want to win money (Associated Press, "Traffic Survey Offers a Prize").

19. A. Landers, "Parental Guilt Trip." That was in 1976. In 1988 she was still at it. A woman complained that her adopted son is a poor student and a pot

smoker while her other children are well-adjusted. "We are sure that there is nothing we could have done to make Bobby 'turn out right,' " she wrote. "The answer is, as you pointed out, 'genes.' " Absolutely, replied the advice columnist: "While many adopted children turn out well, some do not, and we now know that it may have nothing to do with poor parenting. This is not to say that environment counts for nothing, but we now know it is less significant than we thought" (A. Landers, "Role of Genetics Often Overlooked").

20. The epigraph is from Plomin, "Environment and Genes," pp. 105, 110. "More and more," he told an interviewer in 1989, "I find myself standing up before funding committees and the public to say, 'Hey, wait a minute everybody, hold on. It's not *all* genetic.' " This comment appeared toward the end of a *New York Times Magazine* article that exemplifies precisely the sort of hyperbolic hereditarianism Plomin seems to have in mind. The writer passes off as scientific fact such sweeping claims as this: "The core of many behaviors and most personality traits—the determinants of whether we're shy or extroverted, even the kinds of jokes we find funny and the kinds of people we like—seem largely embedded in the coils of chromosomes that our parents pass to us at conception" (D. Franklin, "What a Child Is Given," pp. 49, 36).

21. H. Gardner, *Frames of Mind,* p. 316.

22. C. B. MacPherson, *The Political Theory of Possessive Individualism,* pp. 22, 27. "Even Hobbes's physiological postulates are about the physiology of socialized men," he adds (p. 69). Similarly, even if one finds plausible the bleak scenario portrayed in *Lord of the Flies,* more light is shed on the way its characters were socialized than on the nature with which they were born.

23. *Playboy* article quoted in B. Beckwith, "He-Man, She-Woman," p. 47. Human nature also has been invoked to explain the abuse of steroids. A former Olympic athlete, now awaiting sentencing for his part in a steroid trafficking ring, commented not long ago: "People died in the space shuttle, but it didn't stop science. To stop would be contrary to man's nature" (quoted in M. Janofsky and P. Alfano, "Victory at Any Cost," p. C13).

24. For example, see R. A. Knox, "Interest Grows in Serotonin-Violence Link."

25. J. Kagan, *Unstable Ideas,* p. 9.

26. E. Fromm, *To Have or to Be?* p. 100. He continues, "To the members of many different societies of both past and present, the concept of innate human selfishness and laziness would appear as fantastic as the reverse sounds to us."

27. See my *No Contest,* pp. 14–15, 190–92.

28. N. Pastore, *The Nature-Nurture Controversy,* p. 179.

29. Lewontin, Rose, and Kamin, *Not in Our Genes,* p. 238.

30. A. H. Maslow, *The Psychology of Science,* pp. 15–16.

31. L. W. Hoffman, "The Changing Genetics/Socialization Balance," p. 128.

32. See, for example, M. W. Lear, "Redefining Anxiety."

33. See S. Malitz and H. A. Sackheim, eds., *ECT: Clinical and Basic Research Issues.*

34. See Grace Lichtenstein's *New York Times* article, "Fund Backs Controversial Study of 'Racial Betterment' "; and Barry Mehler, "The New Eugenics," pp. 25–26. A *Washington Post* article, too, notes that "The Pioneer Fund . . . has financed research into 'racial betterment' by scientists seeking to prove that blacks are genetically inferior to whites" (T. B. Edsall and D. A. Vise, "CBS Fight a Litmus Test for Conservatives," p. A16).

35. It is in Rushton's work that the link between a hereditarian orientation and outright racism turns up even more explicitly—and, because of his mainstream credentials, even more disturbingly. When he claimed a few years ago to have demonstrated the heritability of altruism and aggression, he was taken seriously because of his many publications on prosocial behavior and on genetic factors in personality. But alert journal readers have lately come to realize just what informs his hereditarian thinking. In 1985, Rushton published a paper that cited "evolutionary mechanisms" to explain why "Mongoloids are more behaviourally restrained than Caucasoids who, in turn, are more so than Negroids" ("Differential K Theory and Race Differences in E and N," p. 770). Two years later, he elaborated by offering the claim that whites "manifest less precocity and more [sexual] restraint than blacks" due to "the presence of genetic and evolutionary influences." The "larger penises and shorter menstrual cycles of Africans, for example, are likely a result of evolutionary selection pressures. Even permissive attitudes are found to have a genetic component." The idea that blacks are naturally more promiscuous is "not counterintuitive," Rushton added coyly. The primary substantiation for this "study"—the money for which came from the Pioneer Fund—was the 1898 diary of a French Army Surgeon and an article that appeared in *Penthouse Forum,* a pornographic magazine. Rushton's article appeared, presumably after passing peer review, in the *Journal of Research in Personality* (Rushton and A. F. Bogaert, "Race Differences in Sexual Behavior: Testing an Evolutionary Hypothesis," pp. 538, 543, 545). It reads as a tasteless joke, but any doubt concerning its seriousness was laid to rest in late 1988, when he published yet another paper, this one resurrecting the canard that brain size is correlated with intelligence and claiming that blacks have smaller brains than whites. Blacks' lower scores on IQ tests are not due to cultural factors, he asserts. (This article, "Race Differences in Behaviour," like the one from 1985, was published in *Personality and Individual Differences,* a journal edited by Hans Eysenck and featuring Arthur Jensen on its editorial board.)

36. Personal communication, January 1988. Goldstein has written that popular articles about aggression are typically characterized by these themes: "1) That the causes of human violence exist within the individual. 2) . . . that if psychiatrists, psychologists, and biologists were only clever enough, they could identify the genetic or personality factors that give rise to violent behavior. 3) Given the 'fact' that the causes of violence reside within the individual's skin, it

is assumed to be at least theoretically possible to identify potential offenders before they ever commit an offence by using some sort of bio-genetic or psychological screening procedure" ("Beliefs about Human Aggression," p. 16).

37. Personal communication with David Adams, January 1988.

38. "The Violent Mind," written and directed by Martin Freeth, was the ninth and final episode of *The Mind,* and was aired on PBS in December 1988. An advertisement for the episode that appeared in the *New York Times* announced: "We are all heirs to a savage inheritance. Deep inside the brain are primitive wellsprings of rage and aggression that evolution and custom help us to control" (December 7, 1988, p. C30). Jerome Kagan noticed the same sort of ideology behind a made-for-TV movie about incest that aired several years ago: "The most profound assumption, which was made explicit after the father's molesting of his daughter had been discovered, is that humans are vulnerable to such overpowering, animal-like impulses that no person can be held totally responsible for his or her behavior when passion grows strong" (*Unstable Ideas,* p. 7).

39. B. L. Benderly, *The Myth of Two Minds,* pp. 2–3.

40. M. McLoughlin et al., "Men vs. Women," esp. p. 54.

41. R. Fox, "Introduction," p. 7. Fox is by no means the only writer with this view. In *Sociobiology and the Law,* John Beckstrom refers to "innate preferences unadulterated by cultural influence" (p. 10). It would also be, I hasten to add, an oversimplification to adopt the shibboleth that Fox identifies: man is as culture does.

42. See, however, note 8 of this chapter. Also, Melvin Konner, an anthropologist generally associated with sociobiology, remarks on the functional irrelevance of genetic accounts of changes in human behavior. Observing that in the course of a single century there has been a drastic increase in literacy and a drastic decline in the birth rate, he writes: "To the question, How could these two changes in the phenotype of the species occur in only one hundred years? the genes have nothing to say. That question can only be answered in terms of the conventional and rapidly developing knowledge of behavioral and social science: the laws of learning, the laws of cognition, the laws of social psychology, the laws of economics, the laws of culture change. That the genes underline all these laws is a high-minded, useless sociobiological truism; for this question, that truism will help us not at all" (*The Tangled Wing,* p. 405).

43. John Cairns, Julie Overbaugh, and Stephan Miller, "The Origin of Mutants."

44. See, for example, D. Yankelovich and W. Barrett, *Ego and Instinct,* pp. 360–61.

45. See D. M. Gordon, "Caste and Change in Social Insects."

46. P. R. Billings and J. Beckwith, "Genetics and Human Behavior," p. 12. The Amish are mentioned here because it was a study of this population that convinced many researchers of a genetic role in MDI. More broadly, many people do not realize that, even apart from the impact of the environment, most charac-

teristics are the product of interaction among multiple genes. Never mind complex behaviors or temperamental features—even the color of one's eyes is not due to a single gene.

47. For example, see Lewontin, Rose, and Kamin, *Not in Our Genes,* pp. 10, 267. Gould, too, not only cites culture and upbringing but also emphasizes that "the intangibles that we call 'free will' determine how we restrict our behaviors from the wide spectrum—extreme altruism to extreme selfishness—that our genes permit" ("So Cleverly Kind an Animal," p. 266).

48. See, for instance, the final chapter of R. Dawkins, *The Selfish Gene.*

49. The first example is from Lewontin, Rose, and Kamin, *Not in Our Genes,* p. 255. The second is from David Adams.

50. E. O. Wilson, "Human Decency Is Animal," p. 48.

51. Richard Lewontin makes this point frequently. See, for example, his "Sleight of Hand," p. 24.

52. J. Klama, *Aggression,* pp. 136, 151.

53. On testosterone, see p. 27 and note 78 of this chapter. On serotonin, see a discussion of research by Michael Raleigh and his colleagues in Knox, "Interest Grows in Serotonin-Violence Link," p. 30.

54. The analogy is Leon Kamin's, as quoted in L. Krueger, "The Rise of the New Psychiatry," p. 52.

55. M. R. Rosenzweig, E. L. Bennett, and M. C. Diamond, "Brain Changes in Response to Experience." "There can now be no doubt that many aspects of brain anatomy and brain chemistry are changed by experience," they wrote (p. 27).

56. Israel Rosenfield has summarized Edelman's theory in the final part of his book *The Invention of Memory.* The quotation is from p. 177. Studies with the visual system of cats, meanwhile, suggest that parts of the brain's "structure and function remain plastic for some time, particularly in the cerebral cortex. . . . Experience—sights, smells, tastes, sounds, touch and posture—activates and, with time, reinforces specific neural pathways while others fall into disuse . . . [so] each individual person, in spite of being formed by inexorable genetic processes, is also the unique product of experience" (C. Aoki and P. Siekevitz, "Plasticity in Brain Development," pp. 56, 64).

57. This is true for a range of species, from mice to human beings. See various articles by M. K. McClintock, including "Menstrual Synchrony and Suppression."

58. The analogy, by Agata Mendel, is quoted by Ruth Hubbard in "The Theory and Practice of Genetic Reductionism," p. 73.

59. Dawkins, *The Selfish Gene,* p. 3.

60. R. B. Cairns, "An Evolutionary and Developmental Perspective on Aggressive Patterns," pp. 83–84.

61. C. Geertz, "Blurred Genres," p. 167. For critiques of sociobiology, I would particularly recommend Marshall Sahlins's early (1976) work from an

anthropologist's perspective, *The Use and Abuse of Biology;* Philip Kitcher's exhaustive and meticulous book, *Vaulting Ambition;* and the chapter on sociobiology in Lewontin, Rose, and Kamin, *Not in Our Genes.* On Wilson in particular, there is Stuart Hampshire's review, "The Illusion of Sociobiology." On Dawkins, readers might consult Gunther Stent's "You Can Take the Ethics out of Altruism but You Can't Take the Altruism out of Ethics" and Mary Midgley's trenchant review, "Gene-juggling."

62. W. D. Hamilton, "Innate Social Aptitudes of Man," p. 134.

63. Dawkins, *The Selfish Gene,* p. 202.

64. I am not being facetious here. A study published in *Science* found that panhandlers are more successful when they are nicely dressed, and concluded that this is a function of the evolutionary advantages of reciprocal food sharing, presumably because contributors unconsciously assume that street people in neater clothes are more likely to return the favor one day (J. S. Lockard, L. L. McDonald, D. A. Clifford, and R. Martinez, "Panhandling"). An anthropologist, meanwhile, speculated that the popularity of fast food "probably harks back to an eating strategy our primate relatives adopted over 50 million years ago" (H. Fisher, "A Primitive Prescription for Equality").

65. B. Schwartz, *The Battle for Human Nature,* pp. 190–91.

66. Sahlins, *The Use and Abuse of Biology,* chap. 3. See also my *No Contest,* pp. 23–24, and the references there.

67. M. T. Ghiselin, *The Economy of Nature and the Evolution of Sex,* pp. 34–35.

68. *Business Week,* "A Genetic Defense of the Free Market," p. 100.

69. See, for example, D. Barash, *The Hare and the Tortoise.* Kitcher comments that sociobiologists' claims to the effect that society has pushed us to adopt some maladaptive behaviors are curious because they suggest "that our nature is sufficiently plastic to allow society to foist off on us values that lead us to contravene our fitness . . . [raising the question of] how the tendency to indoctrinability (allegedly produced by evolution) fits with the confident claims about limits on our social behavior" (*Vaulting Ambition,* p. 406).

70. For example, see A. Fausto-Sterling, *Myths of Gender;* Benderly, *The Myth of Two Minds;* and R. Bleier, *Science and Gender.*

71. N. Chodorow, *The Reproduction of Mothering,* p. 30.

72. The research is summarized in G. F. Melson and A. Fogel, "Learning to Care."

73. Anke Ehrhardt puts it this way: "If boys show, on the average, a stronger propensity towards physically active play than girls, we should not and cannot extrapolate or conclude that girls are more passive, more dependent, have less initiative, less leadership behavior, or are generally less assertive" than boys ("Biology Is Not Destiny," p. 13). See also Bleier, *Science and Gender,* p. 95.

74. E. M. Cummings et al., "Early Organization of Altruism and Aggression," p. 179. Different measures—for example, self-report, aggression-anxiety scores, and teacher ratings—produced different findings about gender differ-

ences in another study of aggression, this one of older children conducted by researchers at UCLA (N. D. Feshbach and S. Feshbach, "Affective Processes and Academic Achievement," p. 1340).

75. A. Frodi, J. Macaulay, and P. R. Thome, "Are Women Always Less Aggressive Than Men?" p. 655. A later research review found that men were more aggressive than women overall, but by less than one-third of a standard deviation (A. H. Eagly and V. J. Steffen, "Gender and Aggressive Behavior").

76. For example, in the *New York Times Magazine* (Melvin Konner, "The Aggressors"); and *The Atlantic* (Winifred Gallagher, "Sex and Hormones").

77. Ehrhardt, "Biology Is Not Destiny," pp. 12–13.

78. Fausto-Sterling, *Myths of Gender,* p. 127. Studies at the Yerkes Primate Center in Georgia have shown that "the recent social experience of a male [monkey] influences his circulating level of androgen." Hormones rise and fall depending on a monkey's position in the hierarchy of a group into which he has been placed. (I. S. Bernstein, T. P. Gordon, and R. M. Rose, "The Interaction of Hormones, Behavior, and Social Context in Nonhuman Primates." The quotation is from p. 558.)

79. See Bleier, *Science and Gender,* pp. 96–100. Moreover, testosterone levels are subject to appreciable fluctuation in an individual male, making causal links even more difficult to draw.

80. C. de Lacoste-Utamsing and R. L. Holloway, "Sexual Dimorphism in the Human Corpus Callosum."

81. D. Wahlsten, "Bias and Sampling Error in Sex Difference Research."

82. See M. C. Linn and J. S. Hyde, "Gender, Mathematics, and Science," for a review of several meta-analyses on the topic.

83. C. Sprafkin et al., "Sex-Differentiated Play," pp. 171–79.

84. C. P. Benbow and J. C. Stanley, "Sex Differences in Mathematical Ability."

85. For example, J. Beckwith, "Gender and Math Performance"; J. Beckwith and J. Durkin, "Girls, Boys, and Math"; Bleier, *Science and Gender,* pp. 104–105; and a series of responses following Benbow's paper in *Behavioral and Brain Sciences* (1988): 2, particularly those by Bleier, Bloom, Chipman, Kenrick, Kornbrot, Newcombe and Baenninger, and Wahlsten.

86. The study, described by Gila Hanna at a meeting of the American Association for the Advancement of Science, was reported in R. A. Knox, "Study: Boys, Girls about Equal in Learning Math." A new meta-analysis of one hundred studies involving some four million subjects reveals that girls actually have a slight edge in math during the elementary- and middle-school years; the advantage shifts to boys only in high school, when students have more latitude in selecting their courses. Moreover, gender differences are smaller in more recent studies and minuscule in tests of the general population (J. S. Hyde, E. Fennema, and S. J. Lamon, "Gender Differences in Mathematics Performance.")

87. As of early 1989, the data from these studies, conducted by Doreen Kimura, a psychologist, and Elizabeth Hampson, a graduate student, were not widely available for review. The prominent news coverage of the research was based exclusively on an oral presentation given at a conference of the Society for Neuroscience in November 1988. Apart from descriptions in the popular press, I have been able to obtain only two written accounts of the research: a three-page journal article published several months before the conference (E. Hampson and D. Kimura, "Reciprocal Effects of Hormonal Fluctuations on Human Motor and Perceptual-Spatial Skills") and an unpublished synopsis of the conference presentation that was distributed afterward (D. Kimura, "Hormonal Influences on Cognitive/Motor Function in Post-menopausal Women"). These two sources suggest several grave problems with the methodology, which were not mentioned in the breathless newspaper accounts.

First, no measures of hormone levels appeared to have been taken in the study; women were simply defined as being in the low estrogen condition when they were menstruating, and in the high condition when they were between periods. It is entirely possible, then, that one subject's low level was actually higher than another's high level, undermining any conclusions about the relation of hormone to performance.

Second, the subjects apparently were not blind to the study's purpose—a serious problem in any behavioral research, but a vitiating flaw here in light of other research, which has documented widespread and erroneous assumptions about the psychological effects of menstrual periods.

Third, verbal skills were operationalized as the speed with which subjects could repeat "a box of mixed biscuits in a biscuit mixer" five times—a measure ludicrously irrelevant to any ability used in the real world. (Studies of more significant tasks, particularly those involving problem-solving abilities, generally find no systematic changes with the menstrual cycle. (See B. Sommers, "Cognitive Behavior and the Menstrual Cycle.")

Finally, the subjects in one of the key studies were older women who received hormone replacement therapy. When each subject was compared with herself (with and without the estrogen), the results were inconclusive. The findings that made the front page of the *New York Times* were based on a comparison of ten estrogen women and ten nonestrogen women—much too small a sample to support the assumption that the hormone actually caused the effect.

88. T. H. Maugh II, "Studies Tie Sex Hormones to Women's Level of Skills," p. 1.

89. J. Z. Rubin, F. J. Provenzano, and Z. Luria, "The Eye of the Beholder."

90. J. Condry and S. Condry, "Sex Differences."

91. Reported in D. Goleman, "Sex Roles Reign Powerful as Ever in the Emotions," p. C13.

92. See J. H. Block, "Another Look at Sex Differentiation in the Socializa-

tion Behaviors of Mothers and Fathers." Even with animals, interestingly, sex-based differences may result from nurture as well as nature. Mother rats, for example, spend more time licking their newborn male offspring than their female offspring (C. L. Moore and G. A. Morelli, "Mother Rats Interact Differently with Male and Female Offspring").

93. J. Greenberg, "Inheriting Mental Illness," p. 12. To take another measure, Greenberg quotes Seymour Kety, whose name has become synonymous with twin studies, as reporting that there was no history of the disorder at all in the biological families of half of the schizophrenic adoptees he investigated. Nor is this fact restricted to schizophrenia. Nongenetic factors account for the majority of the variance with respect to most human behavior.

94. See, for example, the research reviewed in A. Bass, "When Siblings Are Unlike Peas in a Pod," p. 26.

95. For example, see Lewontin, Rose, and Kamin, *Not in Our Genes,* p. 115. This pattern continues into adulthood. A survey of nearly 13,000 Swedish twin pairs found that about half of the MZ's saw each other almost every day, while this was true of only one-third of the DZ's (B. Floderus-Myrhed, N. Pedersen, and I. Rasmuson, "Assessment of Heritability for Personality").

96. R. J. Rose and J. Kaprio, "Frequency of Social Contact and Intrapair Resemblance of Adult Monozygotic Cotwins," p. 316.

97. Plomin, "Environment and Genes," p. 109.

98. Lewontin, Rose, and Kamin, *Not in Our Genes,* pp. 218–19.

99. Billings and Beckwith, "Genetics and Human Behavior," p. 5.

100. Personal communication, September 1988. For further criticism of adoption studies, see Lewontin, Rose, and Kamin, *Not in Our Genes,* pp. 220–28. Also see T. Lidz, S. Blatt, and B. Cook, "Critique of the Danish-American Studies of the Adopted-Away Offspring of Schizophrenic Parents"; and T. Lidz and S. Blatt, "Critique of the Danish-American Studies of the Biological and Adoptive Relatives of Adoptees Who Became Schizophrenic."

101. Hoffman, "The Changing Genetics/Socialization Balance," p. 138.

102. Ibid., p. 144.

103. M. W. Feldman and R. C. Lewontin write that "if natural selection has long been in operation on a character, the additive genetic variance for the character should be small" ("The Heritability Hang-up," p. 1167).

104. See the comments of Sandra Scarr quoted in W. H. Angoff, "The Nature-Nurture Debate, Aptitudes, and Group Differences," pp. 714–15. Scarr also has noted that differences within a particular group may be highly heritable even as between-group differences are entirely environmental. On this point, also see Lewontin, Rose, and Kamin, *Not in Our Genes,* pp. 116–18.

105. Gould, "Similarities between the Sexes."

106. R. C. Lewontin, "The Analysis of Variance and the Analysis of Causes," p. 406.

CHAPTER 2

1. D. L. Kanter and P. H. Mirvis, *The Cynical Americans,* esp. pp. 8–10.

2. Cicero, quoted in J. J. O'Connor, "Pop Culture as Insults and Threatened Violence."

3. H. A. Hornstein et al., "Effects of Knowledge about Remote Social Events on Prosocial Behavior, Social Conception, and Mood"; and E. LaKind and H. A. Hornstein, "The Effect of Mood and Social Outlook on Hypothetical Juridic Decisions." The latter study ascertained that the broadcasts indeed affected social outlook rather than just mood. An earlier and somewhat weaker study found that college students who were sympathetic to the views of President John F. Kennedy developed a less favorable outlook on human nature—although only temporarily—after he was assassinated (L. S. Wrightsman and F. C. Noble, "Reactions to the President's Assassination and Changes in Philosophies of Human Nature").

4. H. A. Hornstein, *Cruelty and Kindness,* p. 126.

5. G. Gerbner et al., "Television's Mean World," pp. 10, 12.

6. F. Dostoyevsky, *The Possessed,* p. 19.

7. M. A. Wallach and L. Wallach, *Psychology's Sanction for Selfishness,* p. 25.

8. T. M. Amabile and A. H. Glazebrook, "A Negativity Bias in Interpersonal Evaluation," p. 2.

9. For a delightfully provocative critique of doubt as the default condition of the scholar, see W. Booth, *Modern Dogma and the Rhetoric of Assent.*

10. Amabile and Glazebrook, "A Negativity Bias in Interpersonal Evaluation."

11. T. M. Amabile, "Brilliant but Cruel." The quotation is from p. 151.

12. R. May, *The Meaning of Anxiety,* p. 128.

13. L. Eisenberg, "The *Human* Nature of Human Nature," p. 124.

14. B. Schwartz, *The Battle for Human Nature,* p. 250.

15. J. Kagan, *Unstable Ideas,* p. 9.

16. H. Schulweis, foreword to *The Altruistic Personality,* p. xi.

17. S. Freud, *The Interpretation of Dreams,* p. 283; S. Freud, *Civilization and Its Discontents,* p. 69. The idea of a distinct death instinct to account for this aggression was, of course, devised late in Freud's career and repudiated even by many of his most slavish devotees. But the ingredients of what seem to constitute a secular variant of Original Sin were present in his work long before that conceptual twist was added.

18. K. Lorenz, *On Aggression,* p. 236.

19. R. Dawkins, *The Selfish Gene,* p. ix.

20. The comment is offered by Sam McCracken (personal communication, June 1988), a contributor to such publications as *Commentary* and *The National Review.*

21. See R. May, "The Problem of Evil."

22. For example, Erich Fromm has written: "Man's nature cannot be defined in terms of a specific quality, such as love, hate, reason, good or evil, but only in terms of fundamental *contradictions* that characterize human existence and have their root in the biological dichotomy between missing instincts and self-awareness" (*The Anatomy of Human Destructiveness,* pp. 254–55).

23. What Sartre stresses is not only that no fixed human nature exists but that the ideas of good and evil are defined by us; there is no transcendent meaning to these terms against which we can be meaningfully compared.

24. A. Smith, *The Theory of Moral Sentiments,* p. 9. In fact, the economist Amartya Sen argues that "Smith did not assign a generally superior role to the pursuit of self-interest in any of his writings. . . . The professor of moral philosophy and the pioneer economist did not, in fact, lead a life of spectacular schizophrenia. Indeed, it is precisely the narrowing of the broad Smithian view of human beings, in modern economies, that can be seen as one of the major deficiencies of contemporary economic theory" (A. Sen, *On Ethics and Economics,* pp. 25, 28).

25. The case for this reading of Hobbes is made by Bernard Gert in "Hobbes and Psychological Egoism": "Though Hobbes's political theory requires that all men be concerned with their own self-interest, especially their own preservation, it does not require that they cannot be concerned with anything else. Nothing in Hobbes's political theory requires that men not have friends for whom they are willing to make some sacrifice. . . . [The theory] is not psychological egoism. What Hobbes does deny is an undifferentiated natural benevolence" (p. 512).

26. H. Spencer, *The Principles of Ethics,* vol. 1. Quotations are from pp. 233, 241; see also pp. 278–85.

27. Michael and Lise Wallach contend, with considerable justification, that "Freud's wish to unmask illusion and combat hypocrisy may have led him to a more extreme position in most of his pronouncements about the nature of human beings than the facts justify" (*Psychology's Sanction for Selfishness,* p. 50).

28. S. Freud, *Introductory Lectures on Psychoanalysis,* pp. 146–47.

29. R. A. Baron, *Human Aggression,* p. 269.

30. A. H. Maslow, *The Farther Reaches of Human Nature,* pp. 208–9.

31. E. Fromm, *The Anatomy of Human Destructiveness,* pp. 174–75.

32. This point is made by Ashley Montagu in *The Nature of Human Aggression,* p. 97.

33. The Klama authors *(Aggression)* put this point strikingly by asking what we could conclude even if it were shown that aggression of one sort or another had been selected for—which is to say, that it were an evolved adaptation. Such a concession "would not tell us: (1) whether such aggression is to be found in all, some, or even any contemporary human societies; (2) whether, given that it occurs, it is functional in any particular cultural environment other than the one in which it evolved; (3) whether, given that it occurs, learning is or is not involved

in its development; or (4) whether, how, when, or why it could or should be changed" (p. 46).

34. The University of Missouri sociologist Donald Granberg has conducted several surveys of this kind and reviewed some done by others. Seventy percent of a sample of about three hundred undergraduates agreed with the sentence, "The roots of war are in man's basic nature" (D. Granberg, "War Expectancy and the Evaluation of a Specific War," p. 547). In other polls, 63 percent of under-graduates, 62 percent of high school juniors, and 58 percent of adults agreed that "Human nature being what it is, there will always be war" (D. Granberg, "Pathways to Peace," table 2–1; the survey of undergraduates was also published in "War Expectancy: Some Further Studies," p. 12).

35. Rousseau quoted in M. Sahlins, *The Use and Abuse of Biology*, p. 9. Sahlins adds: "To attribute any or all human wars, dominance hierarchies, or the like to human aggressiveness is a kind of bargain made with reality in which an under-standing of the phenomenon is gained at the cost of everything we know about it" (p. 15).

36. S. Keen, *Faces of the Enemy*, p. 178.

37. R. Leakey and R. Lewin, *Origins*, p. 223. Likewise, Arthur Koestler wrote that soldiers "are motivated not by aggression, but by *devotion*" ("The Limits of Man and His Predicament," p. 52).

38. Malraux paraphrased in H. R. Lottman, *Albert Camus*, p. 304.

39. Orwell, "Homage to Catalonia," p. 35.

40. In order to be able to kill the evil emperor Caligula, Camus's Cherea says, "I have silenced in my heart all that might be akin to him" (*Caligula*, p. 56). Likewise, the heroic revolutionary who plans to kill the Grand Duke from a few feet away is determined that he "shall not see him . . . with God's help, my hatred will surge up just in time, and blind me" so he can commit the murder (*The Just Assassins*, in *Caligula and Three Other Plays*, pp. 248–49).

41. See, for example, J. C. Savitsky and T. Eby, "Emotion Awareness and Antisocial Behavior," p. 482. In Stanley Milgram's famous experiments, the willingness to carry out orders and administer electric shocks to a stranger was "significantly reduced as the victim was rendered more immediate to the subject." Specifically, 35 percent refused to carry out the instructions when the victim was remote, 37.5 percent said no when the victim's voice was audible, 60 percent refused when the victim was in the same room, and 70 percent rejected the experimenter's orders when it was necessary to force the victim's hand onto the electrical device (S. Milgram, *Obedience to Authority*, pp. 34–36).

42. S. L. A. Marshall, *Men against Fire*, pp. 54, 50.

43. Ibid., p. 57.

44. Ibid., pp. 78–79; see also p. 59.

45. In so doing, he offended a great many other military men, some of whom have lately taken to charging that Marshall's data were fraudulent. Two veterans in particular, one a retired FBI official and the other a military historian

for the U.S. Army, have pointed out inconsistencies in Marshall's claims or doubted the likelihood of his having conducted interviews in the way he said he did. These charges were reviewed sympathetically in a recent article that closes with a proud affirmation that "ordinary people eventually discover, quite by themselves, the knack of skillful killing." (The author also, however, acknowledges that "a fair number of people had always had an impressionistic sense of the phenomenon" of refusal to fire that Marshall described.) I have not investigated Marshall's methodology and thus cannot comment knowledgeably about whether his critics' charges are completely, partially, or not at all credible. Readers may want to read his book and the article summarizing the criticisms and form their own opinions. (F. Smoler, "The Secret of the Soldiers Who Didn't Shoot." Quotations appear on pp. 45 and 37. Also see R. Halloran, "General's Grandson Says Gunfire Thesis Is Backed," for a response to the charges.)

46. Klama, *Aggression*, pp. 7, 152. Leon Eisenberg makes much the same point: "The mere observation in divergent species of similar behavioral outcomes that fit the generic label 'attack' justifies no conclusion about an underlying aggressive instinct, without detailed study of the conditions evoking, and the mechanisms governing, the behavior of each. Such 'explanations' reify a descriptive label that has been indiscriminately applied to markedly different levels of behavioral organization, as though naming were the same as explaining" ("The *Human* Nature of Human Nature," p. 125).

47. K. E. Moyer, *Violence and Aggression*, p. 100. Emphasis his. For an animal behaviorist's perspective, see the writings of John Paul Scott.

48. For a discussion of nonaggressive societies, see the essays in A. Montagu, ed., *Learning Non-Aggression*.

49. See the discussion and sources cited in my *No Contest*, pp. 144–47. Carol Tavris has nicely disposed of the catharsis model as it pertains to anger in chapter 5 ("Getting It Out of Your System") of her book, *Anger*. And Jerome Kagan writes: "Is it basic to human nature to express anger or to suppress it? The answer seems to be 'Neither.' The consequences of suppression of anger are a function of the social context in which the child is adapting" (p. 26).

50. Montagu, *The Nature of Human Aggression*, p. 225.

51. S. Schachter and J. E. Singer, "Cognitive, Social and Physiological Determinants of Emotional State."

52. See D. Adams, "The Use and Misuse of Aggression Research," p. 533; and Montagu, *The Nature of Human Aggression*, esp. pp. 57, 62, 82. Montagu quotes Richard G. van Gelder as follows: "There is no more reason to believe that man fights wars because fish or beavers are territorial than to think that man can fly because bats have wings" (p. 266).

53. See J. P. Scott, "The Biological Basis of Warfare"; and M. K. Roper, "A Survey of the Evidence for Intrahuman Killing in the Pleistocene," p. 427.

54. See B. E. Ginsburg and B. F. Carter, "The Behaviors and the Genetics of Aggression," p. 69. See also chapter 5 of Klama, *Aggression*.

55. R. B. Cairns, D. J. MacCombie, and K. E. Hood, "A Developmental-Genetic Analysis of Aggressive Behavior in Mice," pp. 87, 89.

56. See my *No Contest*, pp. 19–24. Still more testimony in support of this view is offered in chapter 4 of R. Augros and G. Stanciu, *The New Biology*.

57. F. de Waal, *Peacemaking among Primates*.

58. See Roper, "A Survey of the Evidence for Intrahuman Killing in the Pleistocene."

59. R. Eisler, *The Chalice and the Blade*. For most of the hundreds of thousands of years of human history, she argues, "in most European and Near Eastern societies the emphasis was on technologies that support and enhance the quality of life. . . . The fall of Crete approximately three thousand years ago can be said to mark the end of an era. . . . It is not human nature but a dominator model of society that in our age of high technology inexorably drives us toward nuclear war" (pp. 42, 56, 159).

60. Eisenberg, "The *Human* Nature of Human Nature," p. 127.

61. For example, see H. G. Gough, "A Sociological Theory of Psychopathy."

62. For example, see K. A. Dodge, "Social Information-Processing Variables in the Development of Aggression and Altruism in Children," esp. pp. 290–93.

63. R. Plomin, T. T. Foch, and D. C. Rowe, "Bobo Clown Aggression in Childhood."

64. An early review of the research can be found in W. C. Becker, "Consequences of Different Kinds of Parental Discipline," esp. pp. 177–89. Researchers at the University of Illinois found a correlation between boys' aggressiveness and their parents' use of physical punishment in 1960. When they tracked down their subjects in the early 1980s, the boys had grown up and raised aggressive children of their own (L. D. Eron et al., "Aggression and Its Correlates over 22 Years").

65. For example, see C. Howes and R. Eldredge, "Responses of Abused, Neglected, and Non-Maltreated Children to the Behaviors of Their Peers."

66. E. Staub, "A Conception of the Determinants and Development of Altruism and Aggression," p. 137.

67. H. C. Kelman, "Violence without Moral Restraint," p. 38.

68. Ibid., pp. 38–52.

69. P. G. Zimbardo, "The Human Choice," p. 304.

70. This idea arguably comes to us from Nietzsche by way of Alfred Adler. Among recent writings that present variations on this theme are Rollo May's *Power and Innocence*, Arno Gruen's *The Betrayal of the Self*, Alice Miller's *For Your Own Good*, and Andrew Bard Schmookler's *Out of Weakness*. The threat of powerlessness may also help to explain the appeal of believing that human nature is fundamentally violent and egoistic: short of actually sticking a knife in someone's ribs, one can share in the heady sensation of power by attributing a self-regarding savagery to one's most basic nature.

71. Obviously the death penalty does not cause the great majority of violent crimes. But a careful study of New York State from 1907 to 1963 supported the idea that just such a "brutalizing effect" exists and calculated that each execution was causally linked to at least two additional homicides (W. J. Bowers and G. L. Pierce, "Deterrence or Brutalization").

72. Granberg, *Pathways to Peace*, chap. 2, p. 20.

73. This estimate is actually based on the more conservative of two sources. In a report to a U.S. congressional subcommittee in 1975, the Foreign Affairs Division of the Congressional Research Service, a branch of the Library of Congress, listed 191 "instances of [the] use of United States Armed Forces abroad" between 1798 and that year, all but 39 of them since 1850. (Since 1975, of course, the tradition of intervening and invading has continued.) Under a much wider definition of using the "armed forces as a political instrument," Barry Blechman and his colleagues at the Brookings Institute counted 215 such incidents just between 1946 and 1975, as enumerated in their book, *Force without War*. Virtually all instances of U.S. intervention around the globe have been described by the government as defensive in nature—not surprising, given that every aggressive nation in history has described its incursions this way.

74. R. Wahlstrom, "The Psychological Basis for Peace Education."

75. D. Adams and S. Bosch, "The Myth That War Is Intrinsic to Human Nature Discourages Action for Peace by Young People."

76. Granberg, "War Expectancy and the Evaluation of a Specific War."

77. C. W. Mills, *The Causes of World War Three*, p. 90 and passim.

CHAPTER 3

1. For a very brief history of prosocial research, including a pictorial representation of the explosion of studies in the field from 1964 to 1980, see chapter 1 of M. Smithson, P. R. Amato, and P. Pearce, *Dimensions of Helping Behaviour*.

2. Apart from the fact that actions with different costs obviously will not be viewed as interchangeable—compare, for example, the decision to let another shopper ahead of you in line and to donate one of your kidneys—some, though not all, research has cast doubt on the practice of lumping together helping, sharing, and caring under one rubric.

A small study of elementary school children by J. Larrieu and P. Mussen ("Some Personality and Motivational Correlates of Children's Prosocial Behavior") found that these three were "relatively independent domains," particularly for boys. Other research has pointed in the same direction for both sexes: M. Radke-Yarrow and C. Zahn-Waxler ("Dimensions and Correlates of Prosocial Behavior in Young Children") found a moderate correlation between preschoolers' sharing and comforting, but no relationship between either of these activities and helping. N. Eisenberg-Berg and M. Hand ("The Relationship of Preschoolers' Reasoning about Prosocial Moral Conflicts to Prosocial Behavior") combined helping and comforting into a single score and found that it was unrelated to the presence of sharing. One study (C. L. Richman et al., "Factors Related to Helping Behavior in Preschool-Age Children") even found helping and comforting to be negatively related.

Marian Radke-Yarrow and her colleagues at the National Institute of Mental Health list several prosocial behaviors and argue, in effect, that there is no reason they *should* occur together given that they "require different sensitivities, motives, and skills; interact with different personal attributes; and probably have different antecedents." (M. Radke-Yarrow, C. Zahn-Waxler, and M. Chapman, "Children's Prosocial Dispositions and Behavior," p. 477.) There is no particular reason we should expect, for example, that altruistically and nonaltruistically motivated prosocial behaviors would be highly correlated.

Beyond the question of whether two prosocial studies chosen at random can be meaningfully compared is the matter of whether either one of them really tells us anything meaningful. The target behaviors in much of the research include donating play money that children have just won in a game, picking up spilled paper clips, or signing up to be a subject in someone else's experiment—none of which seems terribly informative about the brighter side of human nature. Yarrow and her co-workers have been among the most penetrating critics of the field's methodology: "It is apparent that a very narrow band of actions has been manipulated or observed in research. Many of the indices are trivial, without reality in children's experiences with others, and generally without appreciable affective or serious dimensions. Rarely is prosocial behavior evaluated in terms other than frequency . . . [and there is a] heavy emphasis upon a materialistic, impersonal interchange of relatively trivial commodities as the criterion of prosocial actions. (Ibid., pp. 529, 478. Also see D. Krebs and F. Van Hesteren, "The Development of Altruism," p. 3.) These comments address research with children, but seem to apply to prosocial research in general. The writers also note that in the countless studies where children are asked to donate some of their game winnings to "the poor" or to some other abstract group of absent children, there is reason to doubt whether the young subjects fully grasp the category and thus the nature of the request (p. 477).

Readers may leaf through the studies and judge for themselves whether such measures of prosocial inclination are unavoidable given the subject matter, or are the result of poorly conceived experimental designs and, more generally, the sort of reductive empiricism that turns human goodness into Mean Number of Plastic Tokens Deposited into Box Labeled "For Charity." Furthermore, it is not clear whether the practical consequence of these unsatisfactory methodologies is that the depth of our inclination to help is given short shrift or rather that we have *over*estimated our prosocial character by making it too easy to do good. The latter is the implication of a recent critique by Joseph Adelson. Most measures of helping, he argues, constitute "a thin form of altruism, at best. Ought we not expect altruism to embody a painful deprivation or a genuinely hazardous choice, and if so can we contrive an experiment to reproduce those deprivations or hazards?" ("The Psychology of Altruism," p. 40) In any case, it seems clear that we are obliged to proceed cautiously in making use of the research about helping, sharing, and caring.

3. Polls from 1986 are cited in V. A. Hodgkinson, *Motivations for Giving and Volunteering*, pp. 21–22. "Even in a decade when analysts are concerned about the enormous materialism and selfishness of American society, giving as a percentage of total personal wealth has increased steadily for nearly a decade" (p. ii). Not only do twenty million American families give five percent or more of their income to charity, but eighty million people spent a total of nearly fifteen billion hours on volunteer work in 1988 (B. O'Connell, "Already, 1,000 Points of Light").

4. S. H. Schwartz, "Elicitation of Moral Obligation and Self-Sacrificing Behavior." Specifically, 59 percent of the sample of 144 blood donors agreed to be on call to give some of their bone marrow to whomever needed it; another 24 percent said they would probably donate to a specific patient whose situation had just been described to them. It may be that blood donors represent an atypical subset of the population, but the difference between these two sorts of donation was very clear to the subjects, many of whom asked for time to think about the request before acceding to it. The experimenter found the widespread willingness to help "quite unexpected."

5. Stern quoted in Radke-Yarrow, Zahn-Waxler, and Chapman, "Children's Prosocial Dispositions and Behavior," p. 479.

6. L. Bender, "Genesis of Hostility in Children," p. 243.

7. W. Damon, *The Moral Child*, p. 13. Marian Radke-Yarrow and her associates note that whereas "two decades ago . . . the prosocial data themselves had little basic impact on conceptions of children or of child development," today specialists have come to take a radically different view of children in light of repeated demonstrations "that sharing, cooperating, helping, feeling empathy, and caring for others are as much a part of children's behavioral repertoires as are other kinds of social interactions" (Radke-Yarrow, Zahn-Waxler, and Chapman, "Children's Prosocial Dispositions and Behavior," pp. 527–28).

8. M. L. Simner, "Newborn's Response to the Cry of Another Infant"; A. Sagi and M. L. Hoffman, "Empathic Distress in the Newborn."

9. G. B. Martin and R. D. Clark III, "Distress Crying in Neonates."

10. Sagi and Hoffman, "Empathic Distress in the Newborn," p. 176.

11. M. Radke-Yarrow and C. Zahn-Waxler, "Roots, Motives, and Patterns in Children's Prosocial Behavior," p. 97.

12. Radke-Yarrow and Zahn-Waxler, "Dimensions and Correlates of Prosocial Behavior in Young Children," p. 120.

13. Ibid., p. 123.

14. See B. Latane and J. M. Darley, *The Unresponsive Bystander.*

15. M. J. Lerner, "The Justice Motive in Human Relations and the Economic Model of Man," pp. 259–60. Darley and Latane, however, maintain that the observers knew their neighbors, too, could see what was going on and that the bystander theory therefore offers an adequate account of their failure to act (see J. M. Darley and B. Latane, "Bystander Intervention in Emergencies," p. 377).

16. Darley and Latane, "Bystander Intervention in Emergencies," p. 382.

17. A. Gruen, *The Betrayal of the Self,* pp. 41–42. The critique of Latane and Darley's theory begins on p. 36.

18. H. Takooshian, S. Haber, and J. Lucido, "Who Wouldn't Help a Lost Child?"

19. On the question of cooperativeness versus competitiveness, see the work of Spencer Kagan and his associates. (Some of that work is summarized in L. L. Nelson and S. Kagan, "Competition: The Star-Spangled Scramble.")

20. T. Nagel, "Comment," pp. 66–67. Likewise, the economist Robert Frank points out that "environments that encourage repeated interactions" do not generate cooperation simply out of fear of sanctions but also because of "the opportunities they provide to discern traits of character and to foster personal ties and loyalty. These, in turn, can sustain cooperation even in situations where defection is impossible to detect (and hence impossible to retaliate against)" (*Passions within Reason,* p. 247).

21. Takooshian, Haber, and Lucido, "Who Wouldn't Help a Lost Child?" p. 68.

22. S. Milgram, "The Experience of Living in Cities," p. 1463. In fact, Milgram continues, "the cities develop new norms of noninvolvement. These are so well-defined and so deeply a part of city life that *they* constitute the norms people are reluctant to violate. Men are actually embarrassed to give up a seat on the subway to an old woman; they mumble 'I was getting off anyway,' instead of making the gesture in a straightforward and gracious way. These norms . . . are evolved in response to frequent discrete experiences of overload; they persist and become generalized modes of responding" (pp. 1463–64).

23. C. Krauthammer, "How to Save the Homeless Mentally Ill," p. 24. Another writer put it this way: "Every time someone walks away from an importuning hand, he risks becoming a little harder, a little tougher, a little less like the person he should be" (N. R. Gibbs, "Begging: To Give or Not to Give," p. 71).

24. This, according to Martin Hoffman, can be witnessed not only in discrete acts of assisting strangers, of the sort that social psychologists normally examine, but also in the personal histories of prosocial activists—those involved, for example, in the civil rights or antiwar movement. "The activists' direct, repeated contact with a disadvantaged group seemed to have had the effect of intensifying their initial empathic and sympathetic distress. The repeated contact

also seemed to diminish their intellectual remoteness and objectivity" ("Empathy and Prosocial Activism," p. 82).

25. For example, see E. Staub, *Positive Social Behavior and Morality*, vol. 1, chap. 7; and J. Karylowski, "Self-esteem, Similarity, Liking and Helping."

26. H. A. Hornstein, *Cruelty and Kindness*, p. 125.

27. Among the many sources available on the relation between positive mood and prosocial behavior, see B. S. Moore, B. Underwood, and D. L. Rosenhan, "Affect and Altruism"; A. M. Isen, "Success, Failure, Attention, and Reaction to Others"; L. Berkowitz and W. H. Connor, "Success, Failure, and Social Responsibility." A number of other studies on the subject are cited in D. L. Rosenhan, P. Salovey, and K. Hargis, "The Joys of Helping," p. 899. Various researchers have spent a good deal of time debating the precise mechanism of this effect, trying to decide whether positive moods chiefly affect emotion, cognition, or attention.

28. B. Underwood et al., "Attention, Negative Affect, and Altruism."

29. D. R. Sherrod and R. Downs, "Environmental Determinants of Altruism." Subjects who had spent only fifteen minutes performing a task in the face of distractions including raucous music in the background did half as much volunteer work—consisting of working out math problems for another researcher—as those who performed the initial task without the noise. It is questionable, however, whether a desire to leave the area for a quieter setting rather than do mathematics work is a valid indicator of reduced altruism.

30. Russell Bennett and David Kauffman's study was reported in *Psychology Today*, "Smoke Gets in the Way." As with the findings on background noise, I am inferring the presence of an unpleasant emotional state that mediates the reduction in prosocial behavior.

31. On both of these points, see D. J. Baumann, R. B. Cialdini, and D. T. Kenrick, "Altruism as Hedonism," pp. 1045 and 1039 n.1, respectively.

32. W. C. Thompson, C. L. Cowan, and D. L. Rosenhan, "Focus of Attention Mediates the Impact of Negative Affect on Altruism." Also see J. Karylowski, "Focus of Attention and Altruism," p. 148.

33. M. A. Barnett, L. M. King, and J. A. Howard, "Inducing Affect about Self or Other." Indeed, those focusing on someone else's distress were even more generous than those in the positive affect condition, suggesting that a negative mood per se does not inhibit helping behavior. It is worth noting, too, that generosity here was measured by donation of prize tokens to unknown other children who "won't have a chance to be in the study and earn" them—not by willingness to help the other child whose misfortune they had just recalled. The prosocial response generalized, in other words, to a third party.

34. C. D. Batson et al., "Critical Self-Reflection and Self-Perceived Altruism."

35. See L. Berkowitz, "Mood, Self-Awareness, and Willingness to Help."

This is also one reading of the Rosenhan, Salovey, and Hargis study, "The Joys of Helping."

36. F. X. Gibbons and R. A. Wicklund, "Self-Focused Attention and Helping Behavior." The quotation is from p. 470.

37. P. M. Oliner, "Legitimating and Implementing Prosocial Education," p. 400. The relevance of competence has also been noted by N. Eisenberg, *Altruistic Emotion, Cognition, and Behavior*, p. 207; and E. Staub, "A Conception of the Determinants and Development of Altruism and Aggression," p. 144. One set of experiments showed that children given special instructions for operating a game or opening a box were more likely to stop what they were doing and use those skills to assist someone else (L. Peterson, "Role of Donor Competence, Donor Age, and Peer Presence on Helping in an Emergency," and "Influence of Age, Task Competence, and Responsibility Focus on Children's Altruism").

38. A review of some of the research on guilt is contained in D. L. Rosenhan et al., "Emotion and Altruism," pp. 237–39.

39. C. Zahn-Waxler et al., "The Early Development of Prosocial Behavior," p. 6.

40. The subversive suggestion has been made that all trait theories rest on a foundation of sand because the cross-situation personality characteristics that people attribute to themselves are based more on perception than reality. The argument is that, interrater reliabilities aside, our behavioral consistencies are actually quite small: the person who is assertive in one situation is not terribly likely to be assertive in another. In order to describe a person's behavior with any confidence, we must take into account an indeterminate number of contextual specifics ("We know that she tends to be assertive if she's dealing with her mother and if her mother is visiting her during the holidays and if they haven't seen each other for a while and if she feels that her marriage is going well at the time . . .")—the trait becoming narrowed in the process to the point of losing all predictive utility. This sort of critique has been offered by Walter Mischel, Richard Shweder, and others, but it will be set aside here.

41. M. A. Barnett, "Empathy and Related Responses in Children," p. 156.

42. Staub, "A Conception of the Determinants and Development of Altruism and Aggression," p. 142.

43. Ibid., p. 145.

44. S. Feshbach and N. D. Feshbach, "Aggression and Altruism," pp. 200–1.

45. A. Pines and T. Solomon, "Perception of Self as a Mediator in the Dehumanization Process."

46. Some of these studies are reviewed in E. Midlarsky, "Competence and Helping," pp. 299–300. She also discusses work corroborating a positive relationship between self-esteem and helping.

47. The distinction is stressed, for example, by the Oliners, whose survey

of individuals who rescued Jews during World War II found that the willingness to rescue was positively related to internal locus of control but not at all related to self-esteem (S. P. Oliner and P. M. Oliner, *The Altruistic Personality,* pp. 177–78).

48. See Eisenberg, *Altruistic Emotion, Cognition, and Behavior,* p. 203. Conversely, where helping or sharing is regarded as suspect—or is for some other reason difficult to carry out—we would expect higher self-esteem to provide an advantage.

49. Feshbach and Feshbach, "Aggression and Altruism," pp. 207–12.

50. E. Staub, "Promoting Positive Behavior in Schools, in Other Educational Settings, and in the Home," p. 110. In chapter 6, we will see how a school-based program designed to promote prosocial behavior has corroborated this: children there have turned out to be both more caring *and* more likely to stand up for their own views than are their counterparts in other schools. Also see Eisenberg, *Altruistic Emotion, Cognition, and Behavior,* pp. 110–13, for a discussion of interpersonal problem-solving skills.

51. D. E. Barrett and M. Radke-Yarrow, "Prosocial Behavior, Social Inferential Ability, and Assertiveness in Children." The word *spontaneous* is important here: assertive children are more likely to help of their own accord, but less likely to comply with requests for assistance. (See Eisenberg, *Altruistic Emotion, Cognition, and Behavior,* pp. 100, 207; and N. Eisenberg, E. Cameron, and K. Tryon, "Prosocial Behavior in the Preschool Years," pp. 107–14.)

52. L. Stanhope, R. Q. Bell, and N. Y. Parker-Cohen, "Temperament and Helping Behavior in Preschool Children." While willingness to help an adult in a laboratory situation was strongly correlated with sociability, mothers' reports of the children's helpfulness at home was not.

53. A. P. Mannarino, "Friendship Patterns and Altruistic Behavior in Preadolescent Males."

54. P. London, "The Rescuers," pp. 247, 249.

55. Oliner and Oliner, *The Altruistic Personality,* p. 176.

56. Ibid., p. 160.

57. M. Walzer, "Socialism and the Gift Relationship," p. 436.

58. The tests in question are based on the stage theory of moral development devised by the late Lawrence Kohlberg. Findings from several studies of a correspondence between liberalism and "postconventional" reasoning on moral dilemmas (representing the most sophisticated sort, according to this framework) are reviewed in Eisenberg, *Altruistic Emotion, Cognition, and Behavior,* p. 152. For girls, scores on Eisenberg's own test of *prosocial* moral reasoning were reasonably strongly related to a questionnaire-based measure of political liberalism. The relationship for boys was not statistically significant (N. Eisenberg-Berg, "Relationship of Prosocial Moral Reasoning to Altruism, Political Liberalism, and Intelligence," p. 88).

59. Z. Rubin and L. A. Peplau, "Who Believes in a Just World?" p. 82.

60. Deuteronomy 3:6.

61. Bertrand Russell espied a pattern here: "The more intense has been the religion of any period and the more profound has been the dogmatic belief, the greater has been the cruelty and the worse has been the state of affairs" (*Why I Am Not a Christian*, p. 20).

62. G. W. Allport and J. M. Ross, "Personal Religious Orientation and Prejudice," p. 432. Those findings began in the 1940s, but Allport and Ross qualify them in two ways: first, people who attend church frequently tend to be less prejudiced than those who seldom attend; and, second, the *style* of one's religiosity appears to play a role. Specifically, those committed to the intrinsic value of their beliefs were more tolerant of minorities than those who were primarily interested in what they could get out of religion for themselves (an "extrinsic" orientation). Those labeled as "indiscriminately proreligious" were the least tolerant of all (p. 441).

63. C. Y. Glock, B. B. Ringer, and E. R. Babbie, *To Comfort and to Challenge*, pp. 182–83. The authors go on to observe that "in some cases a negative relationship appears" between church involvement and charity.

64. R. W. Friedrichs, "Alter versus Ego," p. 505.

65. V. B. Cline and J. M. Richards, Jr., "A Factor-Analytic Study of Religious Belief and Behaviors," p. 577.

66. L. V. Annis, "Emergency Helping and Religious Behavior."

67. R. E. Smith, G. Wheeler, and E. Diener, "Faith without Works."

68. S. Georgianna, "Is a Religious Neighborhood a Good Neighborhood?"

69. Oliner and Oliner, *The Altruistic Personality*, p. 156.

70. Faced with the failure to find a relationship between theism and helping behavior, it has been suggested, following Allport's distinction between extrinsic and intrinsic orientations, that what matters is not how religious one is but how one is religious. C. Daniel Batson, for example, has added a third category to Allport's schema: a "quest" orientation, which is characterized by an open-ended theological search, more a process of questioning than an assertion of certitude.

The fact is that none of these styles of religiosity has ever been shown to be reliably related to the likelihood of helping people in need. Batson argues, however, that there is a connection between these versions of belief and the *motivation* for helping. In one study, he and his collaborators made it difficult for subjects to qualify for the privilege of helping someone in need, the rationale being that people motivated by internal reward or avoidance of guilt might volunteer to help but then not try very hard to qualify. It turned out that of the subjects who volunteered, those characterized by the quest orientation tended to work harder than other volunteers to earn the chance to actually help. In Batson's framework, their motives were more truly altruistic. However, those who scored high on the quest measure were not any more likely than others to have volunteered in the first place (C. D. Batson et al., "Religious Prosocial Motivation").

It also should be kept in mind that intrinsic, extrinsic, and quest orientations may well be confounded with other personality traits. Even if it developed that someone displaying one of these approaches was unusually responsive to others' needs, it would not be at all clear that religion per se had anything to do with this. In fact, the quest orientation is defined so that anyone, including an atheist, will score high if he or she continues to struggle with the big questions about human existence (Batson, personal communication, January 1989).

71. P. Senneker and C. Hendrick, "Androgyny and Helping Behavior."

72. See, for example, the studies reviewed in D. Bar-Tal, *Prosocial Behavior*, pp. 61–62.

73. This, as its authors are the first to note, is the central limitation in A. H. Eagly and M. Crowley's meta-analysis of 172 studies on the subject, which found greater helping on the part of men ("Gender and Helping Behavior," esp. pp. 286, 300).

74. H. A. Hornstein et al., "Effects of Knowledge about Remote Social Events on Prosocial Behavior, Social Conception, and Mood," p. 1042.

75. In chapter 4, I will show that physiological measures of empathy do not reveal any such gender differences; only self-report measures do. Nevertheless, the fact that women are more inclined to see themselves that way, to have internalized norms of empathy and caring, may itself be relevant to a search for generalizations about helping behavior. On guilt, see A. Frodi, J. Macaulay, and P. R. Thome, "Are Women Always Less Aggressive Than Men?" pp. 644–45; and E. M. Cummings et al., "Early Organization of Altruism and Aggression," p. 184.

76. "Women are expected to care for the personal and emotional needs of others, to deliver routine forms of personal service, and, more generally, to facilitate the progress of others towards their goals. The demand for women to serve others in these ways is especially strong within the family and applies to some extent in other close relationships, such as friendships. Research on gender stereotypes provides evidence that norms fostering this nurturant and caring helpfulness are associated with the female gender role. In stereotype studies . . . women have typically been rated more favorably than men, not only on helpfulness, but also on kindness, compassion, and the ability to devote oneself completely to others. Furthermore, such attributes are often rated as more desirable in women than men" (Eagly and Crowley, "Gender and Helping Behavior," p. 284).

77. D. M. Tice and R. F. Baumeister, "Masculinity Inhibits Helping in Emergencies." The quotation appears on p. 424.

78. Here, for instance, is Jean Baker Miller: for men, "to cooperate, to share, means somehow to lose something, or at best, altruistically, to give something away. . . . We have created a situation in which men's allowing themselves in a primary way to be attuned to the needs of others and to serve others threatens them with being like a woman. To be like a woman is almost to be nothing. . . . Men are forced to turn off those naturally responsive parts of themselves" (*Toward a New Psychology of Women*, pp. 42, 70, 71).

79. Eisenberg-Berg and Hand, "The Relationship of Preschoolers' Reasoning about Prosocial Moral Conflicts to Prosocial Behavior," p. 360.

80. Darley and Latane, "Bystander Intervention in Emergencies," p. 381.

81. L. Peterson, "Influence of Age, Task Competence, and Responsibility Focus on Children's Altruism."

82. Radke-Yarrow, Zahn-Waxler, and Chapman, "Children's Prosocial Dispositions and Behavior," pp. 518–23. "Children may manifest facial expressions and ritualized verbal expressions that are not in themselves altruistic but which cause others to see them in an altruistic light. It might be revealing to study boys' and girls' rescue and helping behaviors when the same prosocial acts are labeled differently—as bravery in one condition and as compassion in another condition" (p. 522).

83. For one example, see a recent study of undergraduates by Eisenberg and her co-workers. Femininity scores on the Personal Attributes Questionnaire were related to the *amount* of helping to which subjects agreed—that is, the number of hours they volunteered to help a woman whose children had been injured in a car accident. However, (1) the correlation was not particularly impressive ($r = .26, p < .023$), (2) the relationship was only with the amount of help promised by those who had agreed to volunteer; no relationship at all turned up between femininity and the actual decision to help, (3) only intention to help, rather than actual helping, was assessed, and (4) the situation was not an emergency and thus, in Eisenberg's words, "did not require quick, instrumental action. . . . Therefore, one would not have expected instrumentality [reflected in measures of masculinity] to be positively related to our index of helping" (N. Eisenberg et al., "Gender-Related Traits and Helping in a Nonemergency Situation"; quotation from p. 617).

84. Latane and Darley, *The Unresponsive Bystander*, pp. 119–20.

85. Oliner and Oliner, *The Altruistic Personality*, pp. 123, 127, 142, 222.

86. Ibid., pp. 135–38.

87. Not all students of the field have been Johnny-come-latelies to this approach. Ervin Staub has long talked about and attempted to operationalize a "prosocial orientation" said to be related to an inclination to help irrespective of situational factors.

88. C. D. Batson et al., "Where Is the Altruism in the Altruistic Personality?"

89. N. Eisenberg et al., "The Role of Sympathy and Altruistic Personality Traits in Helping."

90. Of course, it is also true that some children "who progress equally in complex and effective prosocial intervention manifest prosocial behavior that is without apparent strong emotional underpinnings. They appear to be approaching the distress 'cognitively'—by inspecting, exploring, asking questions" (Radke-Yarrow and Zahn-Waxler, "Roots, Motives, and Patterns in Children's Prosocial Behavior," p. 92).

91. A review by Yarrow and her colleagues turned up some studies that found significant associations "in the low to moderate range (+.20 to +.40)" and others with "almost no consistency across measures" (Radke-Yarrow, Zahn-Waxler, and Chapman, "Children's Prosocial Dispositions and Behavior," p. 526). In one study conducted by Yarrow herself, helping scores across settings were not related (Radke-Yarrow and Zahn-Waxler, "Dimensions and Correlates of Prosocial Behavior in Young Children," p. 121). Recall, too, that even relatively stable temperamental features, such as sociability, may predict helping in the laboratory but not at home (see note 54, above).

92. See D. Romer, C. L. Gruder, and T. Lizzadro, "A Person-Situation Approach to Altruistic Behavior."

93. The type of prosocial behavior probably matters, too. Short-term, spontaneous acts of helping, such as are required in emergencies, may vary less with disposition than do lengthier commitments to assist others.

94. Adelson, "The Psychology of Altruism," p. 42.

95. C. Zahn-Waxler, "Conclusions," p. 308.

96. E. G. Clary and J. Miller, "Socialization and Situational Influences on Sustained Altruism." The quotation appears on pp. 1365–66.

97. Among the sources for what follows in the text are these writings: M. L. Hoffman, "Altruistic Behavior and the Parent-Child Relationship"; C. J. Zahn-Waxler, M. R. Radke-Yarrow, and R. A. King, "Child Rearing and Children's Prosocial Inclinations toward Victims of Distress"; and R. R. Sears, E. E. Maccoby, and H. Levin, *Patterns of Child Rearing.* See also the summaries of research presented in Damon, *The Moral Child,* chap. 4; P. Mussen and N. Eisenberg, *The Roots of Prosocial Behavior in Children,* chap. 6. On the destructive effects of physical punishment in particular, see W. C. Becker, "Consequences of Different Kinds of Parental Discipline"; M. M. Lefkowitz, L. O. Walder, and L. D. Eron, "Punishment, Identification, and Aggression," and the follow-up investigation with the same subjects, L. D. Eron et al., "Aggression and Its Correlates over 22 Years."

98. A number of the contributors to a recent anthology, *Altruism and Aggression,* edited by C. Zahn-Waxler, E. M. Cummings, and R. Ianotti, address the relationship between these two sorts of behaviors. See especially pp. 8–9, 167–69, 191–92, and 213. Also see Radke-Yarrow, Zahn-Waxler, and Chapman, "Children's Prosocial Dispositions and Behavior," p. 523.

99. See, for example, E. Staub, "A Conception of the Determinants and Development of Altruism and Aggression," p. 153.

100. The concept of "secure attachment" is derived from the work of John Bowlby and Mary Ainsworth. Operationally defined, a securely attached infant seems glad to see, and eager to reestablish contact with, his parent after a brief separation. Probably the most widely cited report on the relationship between secure attachment and later prosocial behavior is E. Waters, J. Wippman, and L. A. Sroufe, "Attachment, Positive Affect, and Competence in the Peer Group," which describes two studies, neither of which is especially large, but both of which

seem reasonably conclusive. See also L. A. Sroufe, "Infant-Caregiver Attachment and Patterns of Adaptation in Preschool," p. 63; C. Zahn-Waxler, E. M. Cummings, and R. Iannotti, "Altruism and Aggression," p. 11; and Staub, "A Conception of the Determinants and Development of Altruism and Aggression," pp. 149–50. The idea that an infant with a reliable connection to a loving caretaker will grow up to be more autonomous has important consequences for prosocial behavior. Autonomy—not to be confused with reactive isolation—begets the sort of assertiveness that allows one to freely help and care for others. It is also associated with higher levels of moral reasoning (Eisenberg, *Altruistic Emotion, Cognition, and Behavior,* p. 161).

101. Interesting treatments of the relationship between nurturance and prosocial behavior include B. K. Bryant, "Mental Health, Temperament, Family, and Friends"; Barnett, "Empathy and Related Responses in Children," esp. pp. 149–53; M. Radke-Yarrow, P. M. Scott, and C. Zahn-Waxler, "Learning Concern for Others"; Radke-Yarrow, Zahn-Waxler, and Chapman, "Children's Prosocial Dispositions and Behavior," pp. 504–9; and various writings of Martin Hoffman, Ervin Staub, and Norma Feshbach. Both Hoffman and Staub also have done pioneering work on the importance of communicating prosocial values to children and the virtue of explaining rather than just enforcing norms; these topics are explored in the following section.

102. J. J. Rousseau, *Emile,* p. 213.

103. Hoess quoted in A. Miller, *For Your Own Good,* pp. 67–68.

104. In a guide for parents, Adele Faber and Elaine Mazlish emphasize some of these themes in suggesting how children can be encouraged to share their toys. "*Making* children share . . . only makes them clutch their possessions more tightly. Forced sharing undermines goodwill." Instead, they propose that sharing be encouraged as follows: "1. By putting the children in charge of the sharing ('Kids, I bought one bottle of bubble soap for everyone. What's the best way to share it?') 2. By pointing out the advantages of sharing. ('If you give her half of your red crayon, and she gives you half of her blue crayon, you'll both be able to make purple.') 3. By allowing time for inner process. ('Lucy will let you know when she's ready to share.') 4. By showing appreciation for sharing when it occurs spontaneously. ('Thank you for giving me a bite of your cookie. It was delicious.') 5. By modeling sharing yourself. ('Now I want to give you a bite of my cookie')" (*Siblings without Rivalry,* pp. 173, 177–78).

105. Oliner and Oliner, *The Altruistic Personality,* pp. 162, 179–83. The quotation appears on pp. 182–83.

106. J. H. Block, N. Haan, and M. B. Smith, "Socialization Correlates of Student Activism," esp. pp. 169, 175–76. Another, much smaller study may also be of interest. High school girls who seemed prosocially oriented were sorted on the basis of a questionnaire into "endocentric" and "exocentric" groups depending on whether an opportunity to help was construed as "a challenge to the self and an opportunity to verify one's moral assets" or was associated with a con-

scious focus on the needs of the person being helped. Significantly, differences in how these girls were raised were sharper than the differences between all subjects who were prosocially oriented and those who were not. The mothers of self-oriented (endocentric) helpers were more likely to have used love withdrawal as a disciplinary measure, while the mothers of other-oriented (exocentric) helpers more often used other-oriented induction, pointing out the consequences of the child's behavior for someone else (Karylowski, "Focus of Attention and Altruism," esp. pp. 142, 146).

107. London, "The Rescuers," p. 247.

108. D. Rosenhan, "The Natural Socialization of Altruistic Autonomy," p. 262.

109. On modeling, see J. H. Bryan and N. H. Walbek, "Preaching and Practicing Generosity"; J. H. Bryan and P. London, "Altruistic Behavior by Children"; Hoffman, "Altruistic Behavior and the Parent-Child Relationship"; and Radke-Yarrow, Scott, and Zahn-Waxler, "Learning Concern for Others."

110. When an adult exhorts children to donate by describing how doing so would make the poor recipients happier—the "empathic preaching" condition—the children's generosity is significantly higher. The comparison here is with other sorts of exhortation (such as announcing that it is "good to donate") rather than with modeling (N. Eisenberg-Berg and E. Geisheker, "Content of Preachings and Power of the Model/Preacher").

111. See Staub, *Positive Social Behavior and Morality, vol. 2,* and many of his later writings.

112. J. E. Grusec and T. Dix, "The Socialization of Prosocial Behavior," p. 220.

113. U. S. Naidu, *Altruism in Children,* esp. pp. 61, 104–110. The study was of 270 boys, ages seven to eleven. It is possible, however, that prosocial tendencies were confounded with attitudes toward authority since the donations were made in the presence of the experimenter.

114. See, for example, N. B. Graves and T. D. Graves, "The Impact of Modernization on the Personality of a Polynesian People," and others of their writings.

115. See my *No Contest,* chaps. 3 and 5, respectively.

116. D. W. Johnson et al., "Effects of Cooperative versus Individualized Instruction on Student Prosocial Behavior, Attitudes toward Learning, and Achievement."

117. T. Graves, review of "The Effects of Cooperative Games on Preschool Children's Prosocial Behavior."

118. See, for example, the research cited in D. W. Johnson and R. T. Johnson, "The Socialization and Achievement Crisis," p. 137 and in their *Cooperation and Competition,* pp. 67–69. Also see E. Aronson and D. Bridgeman, "Jigsaw Groups and the Desegregated Classroom," p. 443.

119. M. A. Barnett, K. A. Matthews, and C. B. Corbin, "The Effect of Competitive and Cooperative Instructional Sets on Children's Generosity," p. 93.

120. M. A. Barnett and J. H. Bryan, "Effects of Competition with Outcome Feedback on Children's Helping Behavior." The detrimental effect of competition is not limited to children. A study in which undergraduates played the roles of corporate managers discovered that those who had been instructed to compete against other subjects were less able to take the perspective of these other mock managers and understand their positions on issues facing the company (D. Tjosvold, "Effects of Departments' Interdependence on Organizational Decision Making").

121. Barnett, Matthews, and Corbin, "The Effect of Competitive and Cooperative Instructional Sets on Children's Generosity."

122. J. T. Lanzetta and B. G. Englis, "Expectations of Cooperation and Competition and Their Effects on Observers' Vicarious Emotional Responses."

123. E. Rutherford and P. Mussen, "Generosity in Nursery School Boys," p. 763.

124. The effect of boys' competitiveness was reported in M. A. Barnett, K. A. Matthews, and J. A. Howard, "Relationship between Competitiveness and Empathy in 6- and 7-Year-Olds." The effect of fathers' competitiveness was reported in N. D. Feshbach, "Studies of Empathic Behavior in Children," p. 36.

125. Grusec and Dix, "The Socialization of Prosocial Behavior," pp. 226–33.

126. See the research cited in Radke-Yarrow, Zahn-Waxler, and Chapman, "Children's Prosocial Dispositions and Behavior," pp. 499–500; and Grusec and Dix, "The Socialization of Prosocial Behavior," p. 232.

127. This mother is quoted in J. Segal, "Compassionate Kids," p. 110.

128. Barnett, "Empathy and Related Responses in Children," p. 158.

129. W. M. Landes and R. A. Posner, "Altruism in Law and Economics," p. 420.

130. Radke-Yarrow is quoted in M. Pines, "Good Samaritans at Age Two?" p. 73. In fact, the extent to which a child has learned to prefer this institutionalized version of altruism to direct contact with real human beings is taken as an index of his or her reasoning ability. The most popular intelligence test used with children, the WISC-R, contains the following question: "Why is it usually better to give money to a well-known charity rather than to a street beggar?"

CHAPTER 4

1. R. L. Selman, "Social-Cognitive Understanding," p. 307.

2. G. H. Mead, *Mind, Self, and Society,* p. 141n.

3. For example, see D. W. Johnson and F. P. Johnson, *Joining Together,* p. 244.

4. L. Kohlberg, *The Philosophy of Moral Development,* pp. 141–45. Quotation appears on p. 144.

5. D. W. Johnson, "Affective Perspective Taking and Cooperative Predisposition." More broadly, Mead argued that the cooperative processes that define any society rely on this skill.

6. See D. Krebs and C. Russell, "Role-Taking and Altruism," p. 148; and M. E. Ford, "The Construct Validity of Egocentrism."

7. Analogously, Daniel Stern argues that physical and sensory relatedness to—which incorporates the notion of being distinct from—another person is, for the infant, a precondition of sharing subjective experiences (*The Interpersonal World of the Infant,* p. 125).

8. J. H. Flavell, *Cognitive Development,* pp. 139, 140. Also see Krebs and Russell, "Role-Taking and Altruism," p. 143. Flavell goes on to sketch different levels of sophistication with respect to affective perspective taking: at first a child may be able to recognize only that someone else feels good or bad, whereas he eventually will distinguish between different ways of feeling bad, such as anger, sadness, fear, and so on (p. 140).

9. J. Strayer, "Affective and Cognitive Perspectives on Empathy," especially pp. 222, 232, 238.

10. M. Buber, *The Knowledge of Man,* p. 70.

11. J. H. Flavell, *The Development of Role-Taking and Communication Skills in Children,* pp. 208–11.

12. See R. L. Selman, "Toward a Structural Analysis of Developing Interpersonal Relations Concepts," esp. pp. 159–67, "Social-Cognitive Understanding," esp. pp. 302–7, and *The Growth of Interpersonal Understanding,* pp. 37–40. The age estimates are taken from the last source since it is the most recent of the three.

13. See, for example, C. U. Shantz, "Social Cognition," pp. 511–12; M. L. Hoffman, "Interaction of Affect and Cognition in Empathy," p. 109; and Ford, "The Construct Validity of Egocentrism," p. 1184. One of the key challenges to the Piagetian timetable came from Helene Borke, who showed that by age three children could correctly point to a picture of a happy face to indicate how a character in a story would feel in a pleasant situation. If the task used by psychologists to measure a child's awareness is made too complicated, Borke pointed out, the child will be unable to communicate her understanding ("Interpersonal Perception of Young Children"). However, Borke's conclusion has been criticized on the grounds that the children may have picked the correct emotion by virtue of knowing how most people feel—or how they, themselves, feel—in a given situation (M. J. Chandler and S. Greenspan, "Ersatz Egocentrism"). Neither of these bases for arriving at the correct response constitutes genuine perspective taking as the concept is normally understood, but, as Carolyn Shantz points out, "The important fact remains that significant increases in understanding others' emotions and situations that elicit emotions occur between the ages of 3 and 5" (p. 517).

14. J. Piaget, *The Moral Judgment of the Child,* p. 251.

15. W. R. Looft, "Egocentrism and Social Interaction across the Life Span," p. 74.

16. Shantz, "Social Cognition," p. 509.

17. Ibid.

18. The last, provocative suggestion is offered in passing by Ashley Montagu. He refers to "processes of culturalization which emphasize egocentricity" (*On Being Human,* p. 83).

19. K. Horney, *Neurosis and Human Growth,* p. 48.

20. For example, see H. G. Gough, "A Sociological Theory of Psychopathy"; and, more recently, J. C. Gibbs, "Social Processes in Delinquency," esp. p. 305.

21. R. Firth, "Ethical Absolutism and the Ideal Observer."

22. Mead, *Mind, Self, and Society,* pp. 154–64.

23. T. Nagel, *The Possibility of Altruism,* p. 3.

24. J. Rawls, *A Theory of Justice,* p. 12 and passim.

25. As may already be obvious, taking the collective other's and the hypothetical other's perspective are not unrelated. As one developmental psychologist has observed, "the capacity to take the role of another is related to the ability to create the notion of a continuing social other which retains its properties from one social perception to the next" (R. Kegan, *The Evolving Self,* p. 54).

26. J. Piaget quoted in Looft, "Egocentrism and Social Interaction across the Life Span," p. 82.

27. I am indebted to Fred Hapgood for this example.

28. N. Rescher, *Unselfishness,* pp. 100–101.

29. E. Keen, *A Primer in Phenomenological Psychology,* p. 49.

30. C. Gilligan and G. Wiggins, "The Origins of Morality in Early Childhood Relationships," p. 125. Indeed, even in his later work, Kohlberg conceived of the highest stage of perspective taking as a process of "temporarily separating the actual identities of persons from their claims and interests in order to assess what could be the relative merits of those claims and interests from the point of view of any person implicated in the dilemma" (L. Kohlberg, D. Boyd, and C. Levine, "The Return of Stage 6," manuscript p. 14).

31. Buber, *The Knowledge of Man,* p. 81.

32. That gang member was interviewed by Leon Bing. Their conversation was reprinted as "Reflections of a Gangbanger."

33. T. Nagel, "Comment," p. 64; K. Baier, *The Moral Point of View,* p. 202.

34. A. Smith, *The Theory of Moral Sentiments,* p. 317. Smith's point is that empathy ("sympathy") is not egoistic since it "does not arise even from the imagination of any thing that has befallen, or that relates to myself, in my own proper person and character, but which is entirely occupied about what relates to you." (Interestingly, he opens this book by seeming to rule out the possibility of imagining the other in her situation: "As we have no immediate experience of

what other men feel, we can form no idea of the manner in which they are affected, but by conceiving of what we ourselves should feel in the like situation" [p. 9].)

35. M. Scheler, *The Nature of Sympathy*, pp. 39–40.

36. Shaw quoted in P. Singer, "The Hypothalamus and the Impartial Perspective," p. 85.

37. N. Noddings, *Caring*, pp. 14, 24. Also see J. V. Jordan's discussion of "contextual empathy" ("Clarity in Connection," p. 7).

38. In fact, Scheler went so far as to argue that "direct reference to the other person, as such, or to the *individual uniqueness* of his sorrow or joy . . . can hardly happen indeed, unless it is based on love" (*The Nature of Sympathy*, p. 40; also see pp. 142–43).

39. M. Buber, *Between Man and Man*, pp. 19–22, 175.

40. Buber, *The Knowledge of Man*, p. 74.

41. For more, see L. Wispe, "History of the Concept of Empathy."

42. In *Group Psychology and the Analysis of the Ego*, Freud said that empathy "plays the largest part in our understanding of what is inherently foreign to our ego in other people" (p. 40) and is "the mechanism by means of which we are asked to take up any attitude at all towards another mental life" (p. 42 n.2). Freud also referred to empathy in his analysis of humor (*Jokes and Their Relation to the Unconscious*, pp. 186, 195–97).

43. For example, see N. D. Feshbach, "Sex Differences in Empathy and Social Behavior in Children," pp. 319–20.

44. H. Kohut quoted in G. S. Reed, "The Antithetical Meaning of the Term 'Empathy' in Psychoanalytic Discourse," p. 13.

45. "To sense the client's private world as if it were your own, but without ever losing the 'as if' quality—this is empathy," Rogers wrote in *On Becoming a Person* (p. 284). Also see N. D. Feshbach, "Studies of Empathic Behavior in Children," p. 5.

46. "The German word *Einfühlung* refers to the ability of one person to come to know first-hand, so to speak, the experience of another. . . . [The] common translation of empathy as 'feeling with' emphasizes affective resonance to the exclusion of inference, judgment, and other aspects of reasoning thought which are equally important to the concept of *Einfühlung*. In other words, 'empathy' has led to a confusion of 'feeling with' with the much broader concept of *Einfühlung* or 'feeling into' " (M. F. Basch, "Empathic Understanding," p. 110).

47. See, for example, Feshbach, "Sex Differences in Empathy and Social Behavior in Children," p. 320.

48. M. L. Hoffman, "Empathy, Social Cognition, and Moral Action."

49. See R. J. Gruen and G. Mendelsohn, "Emotional Responses to Affective Displays in Others." Sympathy for someone else's situation was found to be a function of "the fit between the observer's habitual ways of perceiving and acting and the nature of the situation in which the other is observed," whereas empathy does not seem to depend on this relation. "The pattern of variables that predict

sympathy across [different] conditions does not also consistently predict empathy" (pp. 613–14). See also note 86 below.

50. For Dan Batson, for example, the term "does not mean feeling the same emotion one imagines the person in need is feeling, nor does it mean feeling the emotion one would if suffering the other's plight. Instead, it is a more other-oriented emotional response elicited by and congruent with the perceived welfare of someone else" ("Prosocial Motivation," p. 93; also see C. D. Batson and J. S. Coke, "Empathy," p. 170). Batson's idiosyncratic—though, he insists, not completely aberrant—use of the term complicates matters because he is one of the leading researchers in the field. For a general review of the confusion among psychologists and a proposed set of definitions, see L. Wispe, "The Distinction between Sympathy and Empathy."

51. While the empathizer "is sensitive to the full range and depth of the other's affective state or situation . . . the sympathizer, in contrast, is more preoccupied with his or her own feelings in response to the other" (A. P. Goldstein and G. Y. Michaels, *Empathy,* p. 8).

52. The need to move beyond sympathy is stressed by Gilligan and Wiggins, who point out that the term connotes a certain distance: there is an absence of connection implied if one chooses "to stand apart and look *at* the other, feeling sympathy *for* her or him" as opposed to *"participat[ing]* in another's feelings . . . signifying an attitude of engagement rather than an attitude of judgment or observation" ("The Origins of Morality in Early Childhood Relationships," p. 122).

53. In effect, Scheler expressed more admiration for sympathy than for empathy. In *"genuine* fellow-feeling," he said, "we are able to *savour* [the other's] joy without thereby needing to get into a joyful mood ourselves" (*The Nature of Sympathy,* p. 42).

54. L. Binswanger, "Insanity as Life-Historical Phenomenon and as Mental Disease," p. 226.

55. Noddings, *Caring,* p. 30. Also see Reed, "The Antithetical Meaning of the Term 'Empathy' in Psychoanalytic Discourse," pp. 16–19. There is something of this idea in Hume's use of *sympathy,* too.

56. Wispe, "The Distinction between Sympathy and Empathy," p. 318.

57. See Reed, "The Antithetical Meaning of 'Empathy' in Psychoanalytic Discourse," pp. 16–17.

58. S. P. Oliner and P. M. Oliner, *The Altruistic Personality,* p. 221.

59. E. Wiesel, *The Town beyond the Wall,* p. 103.

60. Buber, *Between Man and Man,* pp. 96–97.

61. J. Aronfreed, "The Socialization of Altruistic and Sympathetic Behavior."

62. H. S. Sullivan, "The Illusion of Personal Individuality," p. 326.

63. H. S. Sullivan, *The Interpersonal Theory of Psychiatry,* p. 41.

64. One commentator describes Hoffman's theory as "a reformulation of

the analytic view in conditioning terms" (R. A. Thompson, "Empathy and Emotional Understanding," pp. 120–21).

65. Ibid., p. 136.

66. M. L. Hoffman, "The Contribution of Empathy to Justice and Moral Judgment," p. 51. Readers may find Hoffman's description of what he takes to be the four stages of empathy in almost any of his writings on the general topic.

67. M. Radke-Yarrow, C. Zahn-Waxler, and M. Chapman, "Children's Prosocial Dispositions and Behavior," p. 481.

68. H. Bengtsson and L. Johnson, "Cognitions Related to Empathy in Five- to Eleven-Year-Old Children."

69. Hoffman, "Interaction of Affect and Cognition in Empathy," pp. 121–22.

70. Kohut quoted in Reed, "The Antithetical Meaning of 'Empathy' in Psychoanalytic Discourse," p. 15.

71. Kohut quoted in J. V. Jordan, "Empathy and Self Boundaries," p. 11.

72. Sullivan, *The Interpersonal Theory of Psychiatry,* p. 32.

73. Hoffman, "Interaction of Affect and Cognition in Empathy," p. 107, and "Is Altruism Part of Human Nature?"

74. F. H. Sawyier, "A Conceptual Analysis of Empathy," p. 43.

75. D. Hume, *An Enquiry Concerning the Principles of Morals,* excerpts from which are reprinted as "Morality, Self-Love, and Benevolence," pp. 43, 46–47n.

76. See N. Eisenberg and J. Strayer, eds., *Empathy and Its Development,* pp. 351–85.

77. J. Strayer and N. Eisenberg, "Empathy Viewed in Context," p. 397. To make matters worse, the various measures are "generally not consistently related to one another in the literature, especially past early childhood" (N. Eisenberg et al., "Relation of Sympathy and Personal Distress to Prosocial Behavior," p. 63).

78. For one illustration of how a dispositional inclination to take the perspectives of others can interact with an instruction to do just that and can affect emotional reactions, see M. H. Davis et al., "Emotional Reactions to Dramatic Film Stimuli."

79. M. A. Barnett, "Empathy and Related Responses in Children," p. 149.

80. M. Kundera, *The Unbearable Lightness of Being,* p. 31. In Arthur Koestler's novel *Darkness at Noon,* we read of what amounts to involuntary perspective taking: "He tried to hold on to the hatred he had for a few minutes felt for the officer with the scar; he thought it might stiffen him for the coming struggle. Instead, he fell once more under the familiar and fatal constraint to put himself in the position of his opponent, and to see the scene through the other's eyes" (p. 17).

81. A. Camus, *The Rebel,* pp. 16–17.

82. P. A. Miller and N. Eisenberg, "The Relation of Empathy to Aggressive and Externalizing/Antisocial Behavior," p. 326. Some teachers found that swas-

tikas began appearing on school walls after they taught a lesson about the Holocaust. According to one educator, "Kids who grow up in an atmosphere of violence translate it into terms of their experience and simply use it as another means of expression of hostility and violence. They didn't see what was wrong with public expression of hatred or violence against a group you dislike" (Bonnie Gurewitsch quoted in J. Berger, "Once Rarely Explored, the Holocaust Gains Momentum as a School Topic").

83. E. Hartmann, *The Nightmare,* chap. 6.

84. "Perception of similarity increases the disposition to imagine how one would feel in another's place" (D. Krebs, "Empathy and Altruism," p. 1143).

85. Basch, "Empathic Understanding," p. 120.

86. Nevertheless, at least one study has found that the tendency to empathize is less variable across situations than the tendency to sympathize or to put oneself in the place of another (Gruen and Mendelsohn, "Emotional Responses to Affective Displays in Others").

87. A. Miller, *For Your Own Good,* p. 258.

88. Buber, *The Knowledge of Man,* p. 80.

89. "Feeling that our own needs are sufficiently satisfied . . . we can afford to empathize with the dysphoria of others" (Strayer, "Affective and Cognitive Perspectives on Empathy," p. 229).

90. N. Chodorow, *The Reproduction of Mothering,* p. 167.

91. See C. Gilligan, *In a Different Voice.*

92. D. Krebs and B. Sturrup, "Role-Taking Ability and Altruistic Behaviour in Elementary School Children," p. 96. In a review of fourteen studies with twenty-two samples, all but two of them with children, no significant gender differences in perspective taking were found in eighteen of them; boys had the advantage in the remaining four (M. L. Hoffman, "Sex Differences in Empathy and Related Behaviors," p. 717).

93. J. A. Hall, "Gender Effects in Decoding Nonverbal Cues." In a later review of the research, Eisenberg and a colleague qualify this finding as follows: "Although women appear to be more skilled than men at decoding visual, overt nonverbal cues, there seem to be relatively few consistent sex differences in children's affective role taking (including decoding) abilities. Girls do seem to be better than boys at decoding auditory cues; however, there is relatively little evidence that girls and boys differ in ability to decode visual nonverbal cues or in performance on traditional affective role taking tasks. Moreover, with increasing age, males tend to become more skilled than females at decoding deceptive or covert cues" (N. Eisenberg and R. Lennon, "Sex Differences in Empathy and Related Capacities," p. 122). Another researcher found that one's position of dominance is a better predictor of sensitivity to other people's emotional states than one's gender is. People in subordinate roles need to pay careful attention to the leader's state of mind—and it happens that men are more likely to be the leaders in our culture (S. E. Snodgrass, "Women's Intuition").

94. N. Eisenberg et al., "Differentiation of Vicariously Induced Emotional Reactions in Children," p. 245.

95. Feshbach, "Sex Differences in Empathy and Social Behavior in Children." These findings were complicated by different patterns of empathic response depending on whether the response was to a pleasant or unpleasant affect. Eisenberg, too, found that sympathetic reactions were more strongly associated with prosocial behavior in the case of girls (N. Eisenberg, H. McCreath, and R. Ahn, "Vicarious Emotional Responsiveness and Prosocial Behavior").

96. B. K. Bryant, "Mental Health, Temperament, Family, and Friends," p. 253.

97. Feshbach found a "quite modest difference" ("Sex Differences in Empathy and Social Behavior in Children," p. 328), for example, while a larger difference turned up in a recent study of fourth-graders (J. Larrieu and P. Mussen, "Some Personality and Motivational Correlates of Children's Prosocial Behavior").

98. Hoffman, "Sex Differences in Empathy and Related Behaviors."

99. Eisenberg and Lennon, "Sex Differences in Empathy and Related Capacities," pp. 125–26.

100. Ibid., p. 109; and Feshbach, "Studies of Empathic Behavior in Children," pp. 24–25. The measure, developed by Feshbach, involves telling a story to children (sometimes illustrated with pictures) and then asking them to describe their own emotional state or to point to a picture of the corresponding facial expression.

101. R. Lennon and N. Eisenberg, "Gender and Age Differences in Empathy and Sympathy," p. 203.

102. Bryant, "Mental Health, Temperament, Family, and Friends," p. 248. Mothers' assessment of their children's mental health was related to the children's reported level of empathy—but not, interestingly, to the children's skill at social perspective taking.

103. For example, Robert Hare, in a book on the subject, writes, "Most clinical descriptions of the psychopath make some sort of reference to his egocentricity, lack of empathy, and inability to form warm, emotional relationships with others—characteristics that lead him to treat others as objects instead of as persons and prevent him from experiencing guilt and remorse for having done so" (*Psychopathy*, p. 7). Also see Gibbs, "Social Processes in Delinquency," pp. 303–4; and W. Damon, *The Moral Child*, pp. 17–18.

104. N. D. Feshbach and S. Feshbach, "The Relationship between Empathy and Aggression in Two Age Groups." This relationship was not found for younger children.

105. Miller and Eisenberg, "The Relation of Empathy to Aggressive and Externalizing/Antisocial Behavior," p. 339.

106. Hoffman, "Is Altruism Part of Human Nature?" pp. 128–35.

107. N. Eisenberg and P. A. Miller, "The Relation of Empathy to Prosocial and Related Behaviors."

108. Ibid., p. 114. Also see Eisenberg, McCreath, and Ahn, "Vicarious Emotional Responsiveness and Prosocial Behavior."

109. N. Eisenberg and P. Miller, "Empathy, Sympathy, and Altruism," p. 298. Empathy with positive emotion, according to Feshbach, "can foster an egocentric antisocial orientation" ("Sex Differences in Empathy and Social Behavior in Children," p. 331) and does not prove consistent across time for a given individual (N. D. Feshbach and S. Feshbach, "Affective Processes and Academic Achievement," p. 1339).

110. M. L. Hoffman, "Development of Prosocial Motivation," p. 294. See also Eisenberg and Miller, "The Relation of Empathy to Prosocial and Related Behaviors," p. 108; and S. Feshbach and N. D. Feshbach, "Aggression and Altruism," p. 195.

111. Eisenberg and Miller, "The Relation of Empathy to Prosocial and Related Behaviors," pp. 114–15. However, it may be that personal distress is related to helping in the case of emergencies (p. 103). Also see N. Eisenberg and R. A. Fabes, "Examining the Altruism-Empathy Hypothesis."

112. Z. Rubin and L. A. Peplau, "Who Believes in a Just World?" pp. 73–74, 85.

113. Piaget, *The Moral Judgment of the Child,* p. 229. Likewise, another psychologist writes that "moral anger can be an alternative to or escape from empathic distress at the victim's plight, a way of drowning it out" (D. Wright, *The Psychology of Moral Behaviour,* p. 195).

114. M. Chapman et al., "Empathy and Responsibility in the Motivation of Children's Helping," p. 145.

115. "Rescuers were not only more empathic toward others' pain than nonrescuers, but they were also more likely to get and stay more involved because of their general sense of responsibility and tendency to make commitments" (Oliner and Oliner, *The Altruistic Personality,* pp. 174–75).

116. For evidence of the link between experimental induction of empathy and prosocial behavior, see Eisenberg and Miller, "The Relation of Empathy to Prosocial and Related Behaviors," pp. 110–11; and C. D. Batson et al., "Negative-State Relief and the Empathy-Altruism Hypothesis."

117. M. L. Hoffman, "Empathy and Prosocial Activism."

118. This point is raised periodically by both Feshbach and Hoffman. Likewise, Dennis Krebs points out that the fact that higher levels of moral reasoning are often associated with prosocial behavior does not prove that these reasoning skills are called into play in any given situation. "Nobody has established that any subject in any experiment has engaged in moral reasoning or perspective-taking from which they've derived a moral behavior. Yes, they're correlated, and yes, we

can safely say there's some connection, but we can't say [someone bases his or her] moral decision on these processes" (D. Krebs, personal communication, April 1988).

119. Eisenberg and Miller, "The Relation of Empathy to Prosocial and Related Behaviors," p. 114.

120. Johnson was quoted by J. Boswell, who was quoted by F. C. Sharp, who was quoted by R. D. Milo, "Introduction," pp. 16–17. This same general point was made by N. Eisenberg, *Altruistic Emotion, Cognition, and Behavior,* p. 46.

121. S. E. Hobfoll, "Personal Characteristics of the College Volunteer." Unfortunately, the extremely brief published description of this experiment does not specify the measure of empathy and does not indicate what difference (if any) in empathy scores was found between the subgroup of students who volunteered for tutoring and the subgroup who tutored as part of a course requirement. Also, the empathy scores for the control group are not given.

122. Nagel, "Comment," p. 64.

123. In one very small study of second- and third-graders ($N = 24$), perspective-taking ability was correlated with observers' judgments of the children's prosocial activities over the course of several weeks (Krebs and Sturrup, "Role-Taking Ability and Altruistic Behaviour"). Compared with a control group, kindergarten boys in a second experiment who completed a role-taking exercise were more likely to donate candy to "a poor child," while the girls were more likely to assist a child who was hurt, distressed, or needed help. Boys did not help more and girls did not donate more as a result of the intervention (E. Staub, "The Use of Role Playing and Induction in Children's Learning of Helping and Sharing Behavior"). In still another study, both kindergarten and third-grade boys who were trained at perspective taking donated more candies to "a poor boy" than those who were not trained. Interestingly, perspective-taking and empathy scores were negatively correlated for the younger children (R. J. Iannotti, "Effect of Role-Taking Experiences on Role Taking, Empathy, Altruism, and Aggression").

124. B. Underwood and B. Moore, "Perspective-Taking and Altruism."

125. Krebs and Russell, "Role-Taking and Altruism," p. 161. With certain kinds of helping, perspective taking may simply be a skill that facilitates the intervention. Just as mechanical aptitude would likely increase the probability of helping a stranded motorist, so a good perspective taker may be inclined to volunteer as a counselor (see E. G. Clary and L. Orenstein, "The Amount and Effectiveness of Help").

126. For example, see C. Zahn-Waxler, M. Radke-Yarrow, and J. Brady-Smith, "Perspective-taking and Prosocial Behavior." No affective perspective taking was involved here, however.

127. L. A. Kurdek, "Relationship between Cognitive Perspective Taking and Teachers' Ratings of Children's Classroom Behavior in Grades One through Four"; and L. LeMare and D. Krebs, "Perspective-Taking and Styles of (Pro) Social Behavior in Elementary School Children."

128. For example, see W. J. Froming, L. Allen, and R. Jensen, "Altruism, Role-Taking, and Self-Awareness," p. 1228; Krebs and Russell, "Role-Taking and Altruism," p. 160; E. Staub, "Promoting Positive Behavior in Schools, in Other Educational Settings, and in the Home," p. 112; and Damon, *The Moral Child*, p. 93.

129. For example, see Flavell, *The Development of Role-Taking and Communication Skills in Children*, pp. 45–46.

130. L. A. Sroufe, "Infant-Caregiver Attachment and Patterns of Adaptation in Preschool," p. 63. Also see Radke-Yarrow, Zahn-Waxler, and Chapman, "Children's Prosocial Dispositions and Behavior," p. 489; B. Spiecker, "Psychopathy"; J. C. Savitsky and T. Eby, "Emotion Awareness and Antisocial Behavior," pp. 480–81; Strayer, "Affective and Cognitive Perspectives on Empathy," p. 225; Eisenberg, *Altruistic Emotion, Cognition, and Behavior*, p. 106.

131. B. Williams, *Ethics and the Limits of Philosophy*, p. 91. Scheler, too, has noted that cruelty consists not in insensitivity to others' suffering but in taking pleasure from it. And a cruel individual "owes his awareness of the pain and sorrow he causes entirely to a capacity for visualizing feeling!" (*The Nature of Sympathy*, p. 14).

132. N. D. Feshbach, "Empathy Training," p. 238.

133. Flavell, *Cognitive Development*, pp. 139–40.

134. Hoffman, "Interaction of Affect and Cognition in Empathy," pp. 104–6. Also see N. Eisenberg and J. Strayer, "Critical Issues in the Study of Empathy," p. 9; and Thompson, "Empathy and Emotional Understanding," p. 124.

135. Mead, *Mind, Self, and Society*, p. 366.

136. "Taking another's perspective increases emotional reactions to that person's pleasure or pain" (C. D. Batson, J. Fultz, and P. A. Schoenrade, "Adults' Emotional Reactions to the Distress of Others," p. 172).

137. Stern, *The Interpersonal World of the Infant*, p. 145.

138. Selman is quoted in L. Kutner, "Empathy Must Be Learned, Just Like Any Other Skill."

139. For a careful treatment of the topic, see J. B. Bavelas et al., "Motor Mimicry as Primitive Empathy."

140. The late psychologist Sidney Jourard once wrote about how he had confessed to a colleague one morning that he was depressed, whereupon "a glaze came over her eyes. I felt myself transmuted from 'Sid' into a 'client.' Her face assumed an expression that was supposed to be warmth, and she said, 'You feel pretty rotten, don't you Sid.' That ended the dialogue as far as I was concerned" (*The Transparent Self*, p. 13). As a student, I had a similar experience with an instructor who happened to be a psychiatrist. I sought him out before class one day to raise a concern about something concerning the mechanics of the course. "I can see you're angry," he said, nodding. As best as I can recall, I hadn't been angry—up until then, that is. It wasn't merely that his response seemed reflexive or unperceptive, I reflected later. Rather, it referred only to what he believed was

my mood, effectively brushing aside the content of what I had expressed. His exclusively affective focus felt dismissive, even infantilizing, rather than empathic or understanding.

141. Ervin Staub calls this false empathy ("Commentary on Part I," p. 105).

142. E. Stotland, "Exploratory Investigations of Empathy," pp. 288–97.

143. Buber, *The Knowledge of Man,* p. 70.

144. "I would not call such maturational failures or defects 'pseudoempathy' since what is in question here are defenses like projection . . . [which] involve processes different from those used to establish empathic communication and should not be thought of as related to empathic transformation of affective communication" (Basch, "Empathic Understanding," p. 120). An early study of college freshmen found a strong negative relationship between empathy and projection (−.65), but the measures of the two qualities were crude at best, empathy having been operationalized as expressing the belief that "others" have a certain trait when this judgment agrees with what most people say about themselves (R. D. Norman and P. Ainsworth, "The Relationships among Projection, Empathy, Reality, and Adjustment, Operationally Defined").

145. See, for instance, R. D. Laing's earlier work on family dynamics, or some of the object relations theorists. Nancy Chodorow describes a case study of Enid Balint's in which "the 'empathy' of the patient's mother was a false empathy . . . probably a distorted projection of what the mother thought her infant daughter's needs should be. As her daughter grew, and was able to express wants and needs, the mother systematically ignored these expressions and gave feedback not to her actual behavior but rather to what she had in the first place projected onto her child. . . . '[The daughter] felt that she was unrecognized, that she was empty of herself, that she had to live in a void' " (*The Reproduction of Mothering,* pp. 100–1).

146. Hoffman, "Interaction of Affect and Cognition in Empathy," pp. 119–20.

147. Just as Gilligan and Wiggins resist the idea of perspective taking based on an interpretation that excludes assuming the point of view of the concrete other, so do they repudiate *empathy* on the grounds that the word implies "an identity of feelings—that self and other feel the same" (Gilligan and Wiggins, "The Origins of Morality in Early Childhood Relationships," p. 122). There is no reason to limit our understanding of the word in this way.

148. Scheler, *The Nature of Sympathy,* p. 47.

149. Buber, *The Knowledge of Man,* pp. 96, 79.

CHAPTER 5

1. K. Marx, *Capital,* vol. 1, p. 645.

2. For a description of the systematic dehumanization wrought by apart-

heid, a process very much like what I have been describing, see S. Haas, "The Psychology of Apartheid." Haas quotes a black South African priest who recounts how he once "worked in a restaurant where staff meals for blacks were served without utensils. I was expected to eat with my hands a bowl of rice covered in gravy. . . . [When I] protested that I wanted at least a spoon, I was fired. But what about those who ate that food with their hands? They began to believe in their own inhumanity" (p. 3).

3. The idea that we "attempt to believe that people in general deserve their fate either by virtue of their actions or because of their intrinsic personal worth"—the so-called Just World phenomenon—is relevant here. See, for example, M. J. Lerner, "The Desire for Justice and Reactions to Victims" (quotation appears on p. 226).

4. P. G. Zimbardo, "The Human Choice," p. 298.

5. S. P. Oliner and P. M. Oliner, *The Altruistic Personality,* p. 146.

6. For example, see V. W. Bernard, P. Ottenberg, and F. Redl, "Dehumanization," pp. 109–10; H. C. Kelman, "Violence without Moral Restraint," p. 50; N. Struch and S. H. Schwartz, "Intergroup Aggression," p. 365.

7. Subjects were willing to administer more severe shocks to people described as "an animalistic, rotten bunch" than to those who were described positively or not described at all. The shocks were used by subjects to punish people for failure to learn, but when the shocks they thought they were giving did not eliminate errors, "aggression was precipitously escalated to extreme levels with dehumanized performers." Subjects apparently absolved themselves of blame, switched off their consciences, and became even more aggressive. "The uniformly low aggressiveness at the outset and the differential escalation of punitiveness under different feedback conditions indicate that the dehumanizing procedures produced their effects by divesting the victims of their humanness rather than through social sanctioning of punitive actions" (A. Bandura, B. Underwood, and M. E. Fromson, "Disinhibition of Aggression"; quotations from pp. 258, 265, 267).

8. D. A. Kaplan, "Haunting Chronicle of a Death Foretold," p. H38. Of course, a viewer who supported capital punishment might well be unmoved by the plight of a person who had been sentenced to die, but this only sets the problem back a step. How does one arrive at a frame of mind such that one not only approves of killing criminals, but persists in this ideological commitment despite witnessing its concrete consequences—that is, a real human being talking about the fact that he will not exist in a few weeks? And what is the relationship between this indifference to a human and this profusion of pity for a rabbit?

9. Coppola quoted in R. Lindsey, "Promises to Keep," p. 23.

10. J. C. Savitsky and T. Eby, "Emotion Awareness and Antisocial Behavior," p. 475. Likewise, Bandura and his colleagues write: "Designations of others in terms that humanize them can serve as an effective corrective against aggres-

sion" (Bandura, Underwood, and Fromson, "Disinhibition of Aggression," p. 267).

11. V. Woolf, *To the Lighthouse,* pp. 128–29.

12. N. Humphrey, "An Immodest Proposal," p. 36.

13. D. A. Wilder, "Social Categorization," p. 317.

14. See H. Solomon et al., "Anonymity and Helping."

15. See R. M. Dawes, J. McTavish, and H. Shaklee, "Behavior, Communication, and Assumptions about Other People's Behavior in a Commons Dilemma Situation." Other such studies are mentioned in R. H. Frank, *Passions within Reason,* p. 224.

16. Lorraine Rosenblatt, director of a posttrial mediation program in Quincy, Mass., describes the process this way: "Most of the time, when they are given the opportunity to talk about what happened, they begin to recognize one another as human beings—the offender, too. I have very few victim-offender meetings in which people don't apologize . . . [and] when the individual victim says, 'Where are you living?' and the kid says they live in a shelter and after 45 days they can't live there anymore, [the victim] can understand why the kid doesn't think too much about grabbing their TV if the back door's open" (quoted in C. Robb, "Is Vengeance Ours?" p. 52).

17. H. A. Hornstein, *Cruelty and Kindness,* p. 148. The capacity for abstract thought also means that physical proximity is not required for "barriers of *they,*" he adds.

18. D. Aderman, S. S. Brehm, and L. B. Katz, "Empathic Observation of an Innocent Victim." "It would appear that empathizing [i.e., perspective taking] observers consider compassion the only just response to undeserved suffering," the authors concluded (p. 345).

19. M. Scheler, *The Nature of Sympathy,* p. 98. Also see Alfred Adler's discussion of *Gemeinschaftsgefühl* in *The Individual Psychology of Alfred Adler,* pp. 133–42.

20. Zimbardo, "The Human Choice," p. 297.

21. The systematic dehumanization of the Vietnamese by the U.S. invasion forces—including the use of insect imagery—is noted in R. J. Lifton, "Existential Evil." Also see Mark Baker's account of the war: "A GI was real. But if a gook got killed, it was like me going out here and stepping on a roach." (Quoted in S. Keen, *Faces of the Enemy,* p. 125. On this same page is another horrifying photograph—this one of a group of Thai children enjoying the sight of a left-wing youth being massacred.)

22. Keen, *Faces of the Enemy,* pp. 24–25.

23. Wilder, "Social Categorization," p. 316.

24. The instructor, Robert Franke, who teaches at the University of Arkansas at Little Rock, is quoted by Studs Terkel, who is in turn quoted in C. E. Claffey, "Terkel at 76," p. B78.

25. J. Viorst, "A Palestinian, a Jew, a Sense of Humanity," p. 27. By contrast, the inability to take a different perspective is captured in a journalist's

account of a group of fundamentalist Jews who have moved into the West Bank, which Israel occupies. Asked to imagine what life might be like for the Palestinians, these people "were not able, even for a little while, to shift their point of view; they did not allow themselves even a split second of empathy and uncommitted participation in the lives of those whose fates are intertwined and interwoven so much with theirs. Like fossils, they did not succeed in freeing themselves from those very bonds which they are unwilling to admit exist" (D. Grossman, *The Yellow Wind,* p. 39).

26. Himmler's speech is quoted in A. Miller, *For Your Own Good,* p. 79.

27. In their 1978 parody of a small-town newspaper ("The Dacron Republican-Democrat"), the writers of the *National Lampoon* satirized just this sort of parochialism. One of the paper's front-page stories begins as follows: "Possible tragedy has marred the vacation plans of Miss Frances Bundle and her mother Olive as volcanos destroyed Japan early today."

28. M. Deutsch, *The Resolution of Conflict,* p. 83.

29. See the studies cited in my *No Contest,* pp. 48–49, 152–53.

30. J. M. Rabbie and J. H. C. de Brey, "The Anticipation of Intergroup Cooperation and Competition under Private and Public Conditions." Quotation appears on p. 243.

31. J. M. Rabbie et al., "Differential Power and Effects of Expected Competitive and Cooperative Intergroup Interaction on Intragroup and Outgroup Attitudes." Quotation appears on p. 55.

32. J. W. Julian, D. W. Bishop, and F. E. Fielder, "Quasi-Therapeutic Effects of Intergroup Competition," p. 325.

33. See, for example, R. M. Dawes, A. J. C. van de Kragt, and J. M. Orbell, "Cooperation for the Benefit of Us."

34. Hornstein, *Cruelty and Kindness,* p. 18. See also pp. 41–42.

35. N. D. Feshbach, "Studies of Empathic Behavior in Children," p. 20.

36. H. E. Mitchell and D. Byrne, "The Defendant's Dilemma."

37. C. H. Cooley, *Social Organization,* p. 113.

38. P. Singer, *The Expanding Circle,* p. 134. Singer, an Australian philosopher, stresses that the circle expands as a function of our capacity to reason rather than because of what he disdainfully refers to as "altruistic sentiments"—a distinction we will encounter again in the final chapter. The moral circle also encompasses animals, according to Singer, who is best known for his defense of animal rights. He would undoubtedly have little patience for my suggestion that widespread concern for animals may be an earmark of a dehumanizing society.

39. L. Eisenberg, "The *Human* Nature of Human Nature," p. 127. Also see Hornstein, *Cruelty and Kindness,* esp. pp. 96, 113–14, 150; and R. Gorney, *The Human Agenda.*

40. G. H. Mead, *Mind, Self, and Society,* pp. 136, 171.

41. "My concrete relations with the Other . . . are wholly governed by my attitudes with respect to the object which I am for the Other. . . . It is therefore

useless for human-reality to seek to get out of this dilemma: one must either transcend the Other or allow oneself to be transcended by him. The essence of the relations between consciousness is not the *Mitsein* [being-with]; it is conflict" (J.-P. Sartre, *Being and Nothingness,* pp. 473, 555). Needless to say, I do not follow Sartre to this verdict.

42. Kelman, "Violence without Moral Restraint," p. 51. Also see Bernard, Ottenberg, and Redl, "Dehumanization," pp. 103–4.

43. "Under conditions specified as deindividuating, these sweet, normally mild-mannered college girls shocked another girl almost every time they had an opportunity to do so, sometimes for as long as they were allowed, and it did not matter whether or not that fellow student was a nice girl who didn't deserve to be hurt. In addition, there was no agent of coercion present to force the girls to act like killers. . . . Conditions which induce feelings of remoteness lead to lowered self-consciousness, less embarrassment, and reduced inhibition about punishing the victim" (Zimbardo, "The Human Choice," p. 270).

44. Zimbardo is quoted in Hornstein, *Cruelty and Kindness,* p. 140. Also recall the findings described in chapter 3 concerning the relationship between prosocial behavior and both self-esteem and internal locus of control.

45. Miller, *For Your Own Good,* p. 115.

46. "The broader the range of affective arousal and tolerance of feelings in oneself, the more potential empathic responsiveness may occur to the other. As there is a narrowing of which affects are appropriate for the self, there also may be a curtailment of empathic responsiveness, a loss of the immediate, pressing reactivity to another's inner state" (J. V. Jordan, "Empathy and Self Boundaries," p. 5; see also p. 9). Directed introspection also has been found to enhance perspective taking in children. See A. P. Goldstein and G. Y. Michaels, *Empathy,* p. 30.

47. This is the title of a 1969 record album by The Firesign Theatre.

48. Even the common assumption that fusion is experienced in infancy has been challenged. Daniel Stern argues that infants "never experience a period of total self/other undifferentiation. There is no confusion between self and other in the beginning or at any point during infancy. . . . In fact, the subjective experiences of union with another can occur only after a sense of a core self and a core other exists. Union experiences are thus viewed as the successful result of actively organizing the experience of self-being-with-another, rather than as the product of a passive failure of the ability to differentiate self from other" (D. Stern, *The Interpersonal World of the Infant,* p. 10).

49. M. Buber, *The Knowledge of Man,* p. 62.

50. Ibid., pp. 107–8, 100.

51. M. Buber, *Between Man and Man,* pp. 97, 175.

52. M. L. Hoffman, "Interaction of Affect and Cognition in Empathy," p. 130.

53. M. L. Hoffman, "Developmental Synthesis of Affect and Cognition and Its Implications for Altruistic Motivation," p. 610.

54. N. D. Feshbach, "Sex Differences in Empathy and Social Behavior in Children," p. 330.

55. "True altruistic feelings based on genuine sympathy will reach a mature level only if the altruistic person is capable of avoiding over-identification which is identical with the loss of the self, and is able to maintain helpfulness based on difference rather than fusion" (R. Ekstein, "Psychoanalysis and Education for the Facilitation of Positive Human Qualities," p. 80).

56. "A continuous sense of one's own feelings must, in other words, be one factor that keeps the normal person from losing himself in his empathic imaginings of another's feelings" (D. Shapiro, *Neurotic Styles*, p. 91).

57. "Although empathy is an essential source of human connection, and connecting identities can be beneficial in many ways, losing identities can be disastrous" (E. Staub, "Commentary on Part I," p. 114).

58. "In being with the other, I do not lose myself. I retain my own identity and am aware of my own reactions to him and his world" (M. Mayeroff, *On Caring*, p. 42).

59. C. Gilligan and G. Wiggins, "The Origins of Morality in Early Childhood Relationships," pp. 120, 123.

60. Jordan, "Empathy and Self Boundaries," pp. 3–5.

61. C. Gilligan, personal communication, March 1989.

62. Bernard, Ottenberg, and Redl, "Dehumanization," pp. 106, 109. They continue: "The greater our reliance on dehumanization as a mechanism for coping with life, the less readily can the new facts of our existence be integrated into our full psychic functioning since so many of its vital components, such as empathy, have been shunted aside, stifled, or obscured" (p. 111).

63. A. Camus, *Resistance, Rebellion, and Death*, p. 30.

64. One newspaper columnist writes: "Hatred is such an odd thing, the one emotion I cannot seem to make myself feel secondhand. I cannot empathize with the people who have let it sear their souls, color their every thought, shape their behavior so that they waste precious time stalking other human beings who are, essentially, cut from the same cloth as they are" (A. Quindlen, "The Dimming of Prejudice Also Fans Its Flames").

65. B. Bettelheim, "Their Specialty Was Murder," p. 62.

66. See, for example, G. Allport, *The Nature of Prejudice*, pp. 407–8.

67. Cooley, *Social Organization*, p. 15. Also see Lauren Wispe: "It might be hard to muster sympathy for a murderer, but one could empathize with that person in order to try to understand him or her, while still disapproving of his or her actions" ("The Distinction between Sympathy and Empathy," p. 319).

68. Miller, *For Your Own Good*, p. 143.

69. L. N. Henderson, "Legality and Empathy," p. 1585.

70. M. Minow, "Justice Engendered," pp. 58, 60, 72.

71. B. Barber, *Strong Democracy,* pp. 175, 189. Also see J. Mansbridge, *Beyond Adversary Democracy,* p. 272.

72. Mead, *Mind, Self, and Society,* p. 327.

73. R. K. White, *Fearful Warriors,* p. 160.

74. Robert Scheer, personal communication, November 1982.

75. Plous and Lifton are quoted in D. Colburn, "No More 'Evil Empire,' " p. 7.

76. M. Lazar, "Not My Problem," p. 435.

77. Buber, *Between Man and Man,* p. 11.

78. This assessment is echoed in P. A. Miller and N. Eisenberg, "The Relation of Empathy to Aggressive and Externalizing/Antisocial Behavior," p. 333.

79. See N. Eisenberg and P. A. Miller, "The Relation of Empathy to Prosocial and Related Behaviors," pp. 110–11.

80. M. J. Chandler, "Egocentrism and Antisocial Behavior." The quotation is from p. 328. However, the mean number of delinquent offenses in experimental, placebo, and control conditions ranges only from 1.0 to 2.1 at follow-up. Chandler concedes, moreover, that the subjects may have been atypically unsuccessful at crime from the beginning since, after all, they would not have been in the study if they had not been caught. Likewise, it is possible that the perspective-taking skills they learned helped them to avoid detection rather than to change their behavior.

CHAPTER 6

1. P. M. Oliner, "Legitimating and Implementing Prosocial Education," pp. 391, 395–96.

2. N. D. Feshbach and S. Feshbach, "Affective Processes and Academic Achievement." "Empathy may be conceived of as a coping skill that the young girl uses in adapting to the school environment" (p. 1346).

3. See my *No Contest,* pp. 46–64.

4. B. Spiecker, "Psychopathy," p. 103.

5. N. D. Feshbach, "Empathy Training," pp. 244–45.

6. N. D. Feshbach et al., *Learning to Care.*

7. N. D. Feshbach and S. Feshbach, "Empathy Training and the Regulation of Aggression," pp. 406–7; Feshbach et al., *Learning to Care,* p. 4.

8. For reviews of research on the various models of cooperative learning, see the contributions in R. Slavin et al., eds., *Learning to Cooperate, Cooperating to Learn;* D. W. Johnson and R. T. Johnson, *Cooperation and Competition;* R. E. Slavin, *Cooperative Learning;* and the newsletter of the International Association for the Study of Cooperation in Education (edited by Nancy and Ted Graves, 136 Liberty

St., Santa Cruz, CA 95060). On the question of how students come to regard their classmates in cooperative (as opposed to competitive and independent) learning situations, see D. W. Johnson, R. T. Johnson, and G. Maruyama, "Interdependence and Interpersonal Attraction among Heterogeneous and Homogeneous Individuals."

9. See K. Smith, D. W. Johnson, and R. T. Johnson, "Can Conflict Be Constructive?"; and D. Tjosvold and D. W. Johnson, "The Effects of Controversy on Cognitive Perspective-Taking." Within Piaget's framework, conflict is an important factor in moving past egocentrism (see W. R. Looft, "Egocentrism and Social Interaction across the Life Span," pp. 75–76).

10. This mirrors Ervin Staub's emphasis on learning by doing—specifically, learning prosocial attitudes by having a chance to try them out (*Positive Social Behavior and Morality*, vol. 2).

11. See E. B. Fiske, "When Johnny Can't Read His Sixth-Grade Book, an Eighth-Grader Might Be Able to Help."

12. A. Bizman et al., "Effects of the Age Structure of the Kindergarten on Altruistic Behavior."

13. See F. C. Power, A. Higgins, and L. Kohlberg, *Lawrence Kohlberg's Approach to Moral Education.*

14. For a review of the scant and unsatisfying research supporting the effectiveness of Assertive Discipline, see G. F. Render, J. N. M. Padilla, and H. M. Krank, "What Research Really Shows about Assertive Discipline."

15. Another classroom management issue is raised by Carolyn Zahn-Waxler. She cautions that a teacher who routinely and efficiently takes care of a child in distress in order to preserve order in the classroom may unwittingly be teaching two lessons: "(1) that people do not react emotionally to upset in others and (2) that if someone is hurt, someone else who is in charge will handle it" ("Conclusions," p. 310).

16. The account that follows of how the project functions, how it is perceived by participants and interested observers, and how well it seems to be working appeared in a different form in my article, "P Is for Prosocial Teaching." It is based on interviews, firsthand observation, and several reports prepared by the CDP staff. Among the latter are: V. Battistich et al., "The Child Development Project"; D. Solomon et al., "Cooperative Learning as Part of a Comprehensive Classroom Program Designed to Promote Prosocial Development"; V. Battistich et al., "Effects of an Elementary School Program to Enhance Prosocial Behavior on Children's Cognitive Social Problem-Solving Skills and Strategies"; and D. Solomon et al., "Enhancing Children's Prosocial Behavior in the Classroom."

17. Eric Schaps is director of the CDP, Marilyn Watson is program director, and Daniel Solomon is director of research.

18. The Child Development Project has compiled a bibliography of children's literature that promotes prosocial values, "Good Books for Good Kids."

19. Solomon et al., "Cooperative Learning as Part of a Comprehensive Classroom Program Designed to Promote Prosocial Development."

20. M. Watson et al., "The Child Development Project."

21. "A child's sense of self can be preserved even in the face of serious misbehavior if the teacher attributes the best possible motive to the child consistent with the facts, while simultaneously stopping or even punishing the action. . . . Many teachers believe that children are self-centered, manipulative, and lazy, and that when they misbehave it is because they are not trying hard, or are seeking attention, testing limits, or challenging authority. If one sees children this way, the logical way to prevent or respond to misbehavior is to use threat or punishment, and the logical way to get children to behave well is to use rewards. We try to help teachers see children as not just self-interested but also as prosocially oriented. If one sees children as interested in learning, and as wanting to please and to be fair and kind, then the logical response to misbehavior is to find out why the child wasn't able to do the right thing, and to provide the necessary help. The logical approach to getting children to behave well is to be sure they know what is expected, have the skills required, and can see that it is a reasonable, fair, responsible, or kind thing to do" (ibid.).

22. Of the 350 or so children in the cohort when the project began, about 165 remained to be tested and observed after five years.

23. For more specific information on the results after five years, see the research reports listed in note 16. Refreshingly, the CDP staff seems to take pains to qualify, and to avoid exaggerating the significance of, its findings.

CHAPTER 7

1. Kai Nielsen, for example, defines psychological egoism as "the view that for every individual all of his voluntary acts are acts which are done to further or protect what he believes to be in his own interest or will promote or protect what he judges to be his own greatest good. He is concerned to help others when and only when helping them or being concerned about them will, in his judgment, further his own interests. The thing that is always decisive in moving anyone to action is the belief that what he is about to do will promote his own good. It is the ultimate motivating force or onsetting factor for all voluntary actions. . . . What the psychological egoist is committed to denying is that people ever voluntarily act to promote the interests of others as an *end* in itself or that one ever acts disinterestedly, i.e. acts in such a way that he has the same regard for himself as he has for others" ("The Voices of Egoism," pp. 84–85).

2. Alasdair MacIntyre emphasizes the recency of questions about altruism and egoism, pointing to the significance of their absence from the works of Plato and Aristotle and arguing that "it is only when Hobbes detaches the doctrines of natural law from their Aristotelian framework . . . present[ing] a completely

individualist picture of human nature . . . that the problem emerges in a sharp form" ("Egoism and Altruism," pp. 462–63).

3. J. Butler, *The Analogy of Religion,* p. 496.

4. J. S. Mill, "Three Essays on Religion," p. 394. He continued: "Whether there ever was a person in whom . . . natural benevolence was a more powerful attribute than selfishness in any of its forms, may remain undecided. That such cases are extremely rare, every one must admit" (p. 395).

5. B. Schwartz, *The Battle for Human Nature,* p. 148.

6. E. O. Wilson, *Sociobiology,* p. 3.

7. See S. C. Kolm, "Altruism and Efficiency," p. 19. Darwin was not un-aware of either the existence of widespread prosocial behaviors in many species, or of the challenge this posed for his theory.

8. R. Dawkins, *The Selfish Gene,* p. 3.

9. W. D. Hamilton, "Innate Social Aptitudes of Man," p. 151. Just in case we failed to get the message about the true meaning of altruism, Trivers proceeds to talk about a wide variety of human emotions and institutions as if their very existence could be explained in terms of the evolved practice of individuals' tricking others into helping them without having to reciprocate. In his article, "The Evolution of Reciprocal Altruism," he discusses "friendship, moralistic aggression, guilt, sympathy, and gratitude" under the heading "Subtle Cheating" (p. 50). Likewise, from a recent book by one C. R. Badcock: "Indeed, given the central importance of reciprocal altruism in human social interaction, it seems highly likely that the prime motivating factor behind general altruistic moraliza-tion and the advocacy of allegedly 'pure' altruism is a desire to cheat by demand-ing altruistic sacrifices on the part of some without compensating reciprocity by others" (*The Problem of Altruism,* p. 138). In *The Selfish Gene,* meanwhile, Dawkins suggests that even the human capacity for rational thought "evolved as a mecha-nism of ever more devious cheating" (p. 202). And Richard Alexander explains with a straight face that consciousness is "a game of life in which the participants are trying to comprehend what is in one another's minds before, and more effectively than, it can be done in reverse," while self-awareness is designed "largely for seeing ourselves as others see us and then altering others' views of ourselves so as to serve our own rather than their interests when there are conflicts" (*The Biology of Moral Systems,* pp. 113, 253). Of course, the whole theory of reciprocal altruism as applied to human beings—to say nothing of the role of sympathy and guilt as outgrowths of cheating—is based on nothing more than fanciful speculation.

10. Trivers, "The Evolution of Reciprocal Altruism," p. 35.

11. E. O. Wilson, *On Human Nature,* p. 164. A similar model is offered by Badcock. Human altruism is said to reduce to three sorts: inclusive-fitness, recip-rocal, or "induced." (In the last type, A forces B to sacrifice himself in order that A may benefit.) Before long, Badcock is quoting Frederick Hayek and Milton Friedman, making explicit the devotion to laissez-faire capitalism that has all

along guided his attempt to define real altruism out of existence (see *The Problem of Altruism*).

12. D. Barash, *The Whisperings Within,* p. 167.

13. M. T. Ghiselin, *The Economy of Nature and the Evolution of Sex,* p. 247. And there is more of this: "No hint of genuine charity ameliorates our vision of society, once sentimentalism has been laid aside. What passes for cooperation turns out to be a mixture of opportunism and exploitation."

14. Alexander, *The Biology of Moral Systems,* pp. 139, 253.

15. P. Kitcher, *Vaulting Ambition,* p. 403.

16. Edgeworth is quoted in A. Sen, "Rational Fools," p. 1.

17. Mueller is quoted in A. Etzioni, *The Moral Dimension,* pp. 56–57.

18. Smith may not have been as blind as some of his followers in this respect; he understood that economic self-interest did not (and, indeed, should not) define the whole of human existence. So, at any rate, argues Amartya Sen (*On Ethics and Economics,* pp. 22–28).

19. W. M. Landes and R. A. Posner, "Altruism in Law and Economics," pp. 417, 419, 418.

20. O. M. Amos, Jr., "Empirical Analysis of Motives Underlying Individual Contributions to Charity," p. 46.

21. H. Margolis, *Selfishness, Altruism, and Rationality,* pp. 11–12. Margolis tries to claim that because economists fail to ask motivational questions, the notion of self-interest is broadened to include more than selfish behavior per se. This, however, is hardly a virtue. It means that selfish and altruistic acts are lumped together under a concept (self-interest) that is either highly misleading or else tautological; the reality of altruistic motivation is either denied or swept aside.

22. University of Chicago economist Lester Telser is quoted in R. H. Frank, *Passions within Reason,* p. 75n.

23. P. Blau, *Exchange and Power in Social Life,* pp. 17, 260.

24. This summary of Homans's views is contained in D. Wright, *The Psychology of Moral Behaviour,* p. 131.

25. A. W. Gouldner, "The Norm of Reciprocity," pp. 171, 173.

26. B. Barber, *Strong Democracy,* p. 113. Likewise, Naomi Scheman writes: "Classical liberal social theory gets off the ground with the observation that individuals so defined are in need of being enticed—or threatened—into enduring and stable association with one another" ("Individualism and the Objects of Psychology," p. 231). The primary concern of both Barber and Scheman is not the egoistic but the individualistic premises of Liberalism, to which I will return later. The view of human nature that undergirds most Western political thought not only conceives us as separate entities (who may or may not choose to associate) but as egoistic individuals (whose decision to associate will be based exclusively on self-interest).

27. Frank, *Passions within Reason,* p. 21. See also my discussion of cynicism in chapter 2.

28. M. A. Wallach and L. Wallach, *Psychology's Sanction for Selfishness,* p. 204.

29. R. Ekstein, "Psychoanalysis, Sympathy, and Altruism," p. 168. Likewise the Wallachs: "Although many aspects of Freud's theory have been subjected to serious criticism and are accepted now, when at all, largely in revised form, most students of Freud seem to have continued taking for granted the basic egoism or selfishness that the theory assumes" (*Psychology's Sanction for Selfishness,* p. 31). One exception was an analyst named Otto Sperling who argued for the existence of "social-mindedness," which he saw as a "highly sublimated form of love" for society or the underprivileged that cannot be reduced to narcissism or masochism ("A Psychoanalytic Study of Social-Mindedness").

30. S. Freud, *The Interpretation of Dreams,* pp. 284, 301.

31. Freud is quoted in Wallach and Wallach, *Psychology's Sanction for Selfishness,* p. 42.

32. Freud is quoted in Ekstein, "Psychoanalysis, Sympathy, and Altruism," p. 169.

33. A. Freud, *The Ego and the Mechanisms of Defense,* pp. 122–34, especially pp. 133–34. In a footnote she adds: "It remains an open question whether there is such a thing as a genuinely altruistic relation to one's fellowmen, in which the gratification of one's own instinct plays no part at all, even in some displaced and sublimated form." She then proceeds to mention a few other pathological explanations that might provide an answer to this "open question" (p. 134 n4).

34. Freud is quoted in Wallach and Wallach, *Psychology's Sanction for Selfishness,* p. 44.

35. J. B. Miller, *Toward a New Psychology of Women,* p. 63.

36. R. N. Bellah et al., *Habits of the Heart,* pp. 129, 139.

37. A. Bloom, *The Closing of the American Mind,* p. 178.

38. D. C. McClelland, "Some Reflections on the Two Psychologies of Love," pp. 335, 339. Here the psychologists have learned well from conservative economists. Gary Becker, for example, wrote: "An efficient marriage market develops 'shadow' prices to guide participants to marriages that will maximize their expected well-being" (quoted in Frank, *Passions within Reason,* p. 185).

39. E. Walster, G. W. Walster, and E. Berscheid, *Equity,* p. 7.

40. L. Berkowitz, "Mood, Self-Awareness, and Willingness to Help," p. 722.

41. R. B. Cialdini et al., "Empathy-Based Helping," p. 750.

42. C. D. Batson, "Prosocial Motivation," p. 66. Batson, as we shall see in the next chapter, is one of the very few researchers to take seriously the possibility of altruistic motivation. But it seems that not many writers have even noticed the profound egoistic bias of work on prosocial behavior. To the short list that includes Batson and the Wallachs, we must, however, add Melvin J. Lerner, who

observed that "there is no well recognized theory of prosocial or altruistic behavior that does not reflect [the assumption] . . . that a profit-maximizing, cost-accounting homunculus guides the person's acts" ("The Justice Motive in Human Relations and the Economic Model of Man," p. 251).

43. For instance, one psychologist writes: "The rewarding consequences for the individual may not be obvious, and the forms they take are often subtle and obscure." Sometimes we have to dig a little to realize that "altruism may be a form of power-seeking . . . or [that] we help others in order to create in them an obligation to ourselves" or even that "a mother's selfless care of her baby is amply repaid by the increased status, importance and attention accorded her, especially when he becomes intensely and exclusively attached to her." Only at the very end of his chapter on altruism does this author, like Anna Freud before him, relent and ask whether there might be more to the story: "Some people act altruistically, not for any of the reasons listed, but because the logic of a situation demands it. They dispassionately assess a situation, conclude that the rational and fitting solution to the problem requires from them an action of a certain sort, and then go ahead and do it. . . . This kind of altruism has been almost entirely neglected by psychologists—indeed certain of the theories they have adopted seem to imply that it could not exist; but though in daily life it is frequently unobtrusive and taken for granted, it does exist, and we cannot ignore it." Notice that in this afterthought the only altruism conceded to be real is based on rational and dispassionate judgment. There is no acknowledgment of the possibility of empathy-based altruism. (Wright, *The Psychology of Moral Behaviour,* pp. 127, 140–41, 132, 150–51.)

44. J. M. Darley and B. Latane, "Bystander Intervention in Emergencies," p. 382.

45. W. C. Thompson, C. L. Cowan, and D. L. Rosenhan, "Focus of Attention Mediates the Impact of Negative Affect on Altruism," p. 298. Emphasis added.

46. D. Rosenhan, "The Natural Socialization of Altruistic Autonomy," p. 253.

47. E. Staub, *Positive Social Behavior and Morality,* vol. 1, p. 7. It is more difficult to determine the extent to which one of the other leading theorists in the field, Martin Hoffman, is ultimately an egoist. On the one hand, he sees empathy, rather than an overt quest for self-reward, as the principal mediator of prosocial behavior. On the other hand, he sometimes describes empathy in terms consistent with egoistic theorists like Cialdini: "The consequences to observers of helping someone in distress corresponded closely to the consequences of acting to relieve their own distress." On the one hand, he explicitly points to elements of empathy as being altruistic. On the other hand, those elements—the fact that empathy is based on someone else's problem and is associated with trying to solve that problem—do not seem to constitute altruism as the term is normally defined, nor to rule out egoistic explanations. Hoffman ultimately proposes empathy as

a bridge *between* egoistic and altruistic motives. At times, he seems to mean by this last view merely that empathy benefits both the self and the other, while at other times he emphasizes that empathy precipitates a shift from egoistic to altruistic motives. (M. L. Hoffman, "Is Altruism Part of Human Nature?" esp. pp. 127, 133–34; "Interaction of Affect and Cognition in Empathy," pp. 116–17; and "The Development of Empathy," p. 55. For another discussion of Hoffman's mixed signals on this issue, see Batson, "Prosocial Motivation," pp. 72–74, 81.)

48. D. Krebs and K. Denton, "Moral Justification," p. 26. The prescription that follows from this assessment is as follows: "Rather than waging a futile battle against self-interest, perhaps we should . . . [help people to understand the personal] gains associated with high-level moral systems" (pp. 57–58). It is not clear to me that this view predominates among developmentalists specializing in moral reasoning.

49. "The significance of [ethical] egoism philosophically is not as an alternative conception of right but as a challenge to any such conception" (J. Rawls, *A Theory of Justice,* p. 136).

50. Nielsen, "The Voices of Egoism," p. 83. Taken to its logical conclusion, the doctrine self-destructs, he argues. "If, where interests conflict, we are simply told that each person is always to act to satisfy his own interests, we have no way rationally to adjudicate conflicts of interest. We in effect tell the people who are in conflict to go on conflicting" (p. 104; see also p. 99). Thomas Nagel makes the point that a consistent egoism "would have to show itself not only in the lack of direct concern for others but also in an inability to regard one's own concerns as being of interest to anyone else, except instrumentally or contingently upon the operation of some sentiment. An egoist who needs help, before concluding that anyone else has reason to assist him, must be able to answer the question 'What's it to him?' He is precluded from feeling resentment" if other people leave him to suffer (*The Possibility of Altruism,* pp. 84–85).

51. That ethical egoism is not confined to this corner of psychology was underscored when Robert Perloff, newly elected president of the 67,000-member American Psychological Association, declared in his 1986 presidential address that he was a "proud and unabashed advocate of self-interest" ("Self-Interest and Personal Responsibility Redux," p. 3).

52. M. F. Belenky et al., *Women's Ways of Knowing,* p. 77.

53. It is assumed in our culture that " 'mankind' is basically self-seeking, competitive, aggressive, and destructive. Such a theory overlooks the fact that millions of people (most of them women) have spent millions of hours for hundreds of years giving their utmost to millions of others. . . . Self-interest, we say, is basic. But it is not *the* basic element. It is just one possibility. . . . Our image of human possibilities is built on what men have done and what men have said is possible" (Miller, *Toward a New Psychology of Women,* pp. 69, 71).

54. A recent edition of *Books in Print* leaves little doubt about what is being written on the topic; among the available titles are the following: *You Can*

Stop Feeling Guilty, Guilt: Letting Go, Free from Guilt, Freedom from Guilt, Goodbye to Guilt.

55. Schwartz, *The Battle for Human Nature,* pp. 216, 233. Likewise, Melvin Lerner writes that as a result of our economic system, "we begin to see ourselves and others in instrumental terms. We view ourselves as a collection of wants and of resources that can be developed, exploited, or exchanged with others in order to meet those wants. We interact with others in ways that are designed to optimize our use of these resources—we want to get the most out of our time, efforts, talents. And we assume everyone does that" ("The Justice Motive in Human Relations," p. 252). Also see Amitai Etzioni: "If it is true that people do seek to balance their pleasures with moral considerations, and if they are taught, to the contrary, that they are 'really' only out to maximize their pleasure (and all that follows, that people behave morally only as long as it pays, and so on), there is likely to be a negative, anti-moral effect" (*The Moral Dimension,* p. 251).

56. Wilson, *On Human Nature,* p. 172.

57. A. Rand, *The Virtue of Selfishness,* p. 34.

58. A. Camus, *The Plague,* p. 124 (p. 120 in some editions).

59. G. C. Thomas, C. D. Batson, and J. S. Coke, "Do Good Samaritans Discourage Helpfulness?" "Further, subjects exposed to highly helpful models were less likely to attribute their [own] helping to intrinsic feelings of sympathy, concern, and compassion, although their belief in the importance of helping did not diminish. . . . Exposure to paragons of helpfulness may undermine the intrinsic motivation to help" (p. 199). This study also suggests a limit to the effectiveness of modeling as a means of encouraging prosocial behavior.

60. M. Radke-Yarrow, P. M. Scott, and C. Zahn-Waxler, "Learning Concern for Others," p. 241.

61. J. M. Ratcliffe, Introduction to *The Good Samaritan and the Law,* p. xii. This anthology, based on papers presented at a conference, is an interesting, if somewhat dated, treatment of the topic. But as of the late 1970s, it was still the case that "neither our tort nor our criminal law concerns itself with the good that one does not do, but rather attempts merely to forbid the doing of harm" (J. Kaplan, "A Legal Look at Prosocial Behavior," p. 292). It might be argued that taking steps to mandate prosocial behavior would, apart from its other virtues or drawbacks, constitute an admission that people in that society are not inclined to take such action without the threat of sanctions. Perhaps the law *should* be silent on such matters. But feminist legal scholars have argued that a legal system like ours, set up without any duty to rescue, is "devoid of care and responsiveness to the safety of others. . . . That someone, a human being, a part of us, is drowning and will die without some affirmative action . . . seems more urgent . . . than any possible infringement of individual autonomy by the imposition of an affirmative duty" (L. Bender, "A Lawyer's Primer on Feminist Theory and Tort," pp. 36, 34). Moreover, one participant in the earlier conference emphasized: "There is no neutrality. If the law does not encourage rescue, it is sure to discourage it. If it

does not compensate, it will indirectly penalize. If the rescuer who suffers injury or incurs expense or simply expends his skill goes without compensation, the law, so far as it influences conduct at all, is discouraging rescue" (A. M. Honore, "Law, Morals, and Rescue," p. 232).

62. In the late nineteenth century, the word *altruism* was used, apparently without pejorative connotation, as a catch-all term to promote the agendas of progressives, utopian thinkers, and other reformists. This is the gist of an article by Louis J. Budd published in the 1950s ("Altruism Arrives in America").

63. N. R. Gibbs, "Begging: To Give or Not to Give," p. 71.

64. J. Kagan, *Unstable Ideas,* p. 283. Unfortunately, the only human motivation Kagan identifies to show that self-interest does not reign supreme is "the continuous wish to affirm the evaluative self's virtue" (p. 280). This would seem more a variant of self-interest than a genuine alternative to it, suggesting that even some critics of egoism are reluctant to talk seriously about genuine altruism.

65. Plato, *The Republic,* p. 52.

66. E. R. Growald and A. Luks, "Beyond Self," p. 53.

67. W. E. Leary, "U.S. Urged to Fight Infant Mortality."

68. M. Freudenheim, "Employers Act to Stop Family Violence," p. A1.

69. J. Berger, "Price of Illiteracy Translates into Poverty and Humiliation," p. A1.

70. The authors of an economics textbook that challenges egoistic assumptions have noticed this, too. "The appeal for social programs is usually made on self-interest grounds, no doubt under the influence of conventional economists and their belief that there is only self-interest. So it is stated that welfare leads to less crime, less political unrest, is cheaper in the long run, and so forth" (M. A. Lutz and K. Lux, *Humanistic Economics,* p. 249).

71. On one of his albums, the comedian Robert Klein paused from his parody of late-night television public service announcements to make a serious point: "I look forward to the day," he said, "when they will not ask private citizens for donations to do what should be done by all of our treasure." Now some people who support the idea of private charity—as well as some conservatives who are opposed on principle to anything smacking of income redistribution—have opposed a more munificent welfare policy on the grounds that it might discourage volunteerism. I find this reasoning unpersuasive, but it is important that any discussion of the matter begin by acknowledging the reality of widespread hunger and homelessness. The United States has, by any measure, one of the least generous welfare states in the Western world. Our programs are either appallingly deficient (e.g., public housing) or else simply absent (e.g., national health insurance), and the evidence of misery all around us (e.g., infant mortality, property crimes) is exactly what one would expect as a result. The first priority of elected officials, it would seem, is to take care of these problems with the public funds available to them rather than to think up strategies for promoting private charity. There is research to suggest that government support for such programs

does not cause anything like a dollar-for-dollar reduction in private donations. (Two studies by Burtran Abrams and Mark Schmitz are cited in Frank, *Passions within Reason,* p. 223.) But even if fewer citizens did donate to private relief efforts because there was less need for these efforts, what would we have lost? I have seen no evidence to support the hypothesis that prosocial behavior on the part of individuals would decline because they were no longer compelled to do the government's work for it. Indeed, it is not my impression that Swedes are less caring and generous people than Americans—a conclusion that would seem to follow from this way of thinking. If anything, we would expect that a magnanimous public policy would model generosity for private citizens. Conversely, a government that looks the other way while people go hungry models indifference, just as a government that invades other countries and kills its criminals models violence.

72. Lisbeth Schorr's comments described in N. McCain, "Fighting Poverty," p. 27.

73. On the perils of extrinsic incentives, see the work of Edward Deci, much of it summarized in E. L. Deci and R. M. Ryan, *Intrinsic Motivation and Self-Determination in Human Behavior;* Mark Lepper (notably the readings in *The Hidden Costs of Reward,* which he co-edited); and Teresa Amabile, who has demonstrated in numerous studies the destructive effects of external incentives on creativity (e.g., "Motivation and Creativity" and Amabile, B. A. Hennessey, and B. S. Grossman, "Social Influences on Creativity").

74. C. L. Smith et al., "Children's Causal Attributions Regarding Help Giving."

75. J. E. Grusec et al., "Modeling, Direct Instruction, and Attributions."

76. J. E. Grusec and E. Redler, "Attribution, Reinforcement, and Altruism," pp. 526–29.

77. R. A. Fabes et al., "Effects of Rewards on Children's Prosocial Motivation."

78. C. D. Batson et al., "Buying Kindness." The quotation is from p. 90.

79. M. Zuckerman, M. M. Lazzaro, and D. Waldgeir, "Undermining Effects of the Foot-in-the-Door Technique with Extrinsic Rewards."

80. D. L. Paulhus, D. R. Shaffer, and L. L. Downing, "Effects of Making Blood Donor Motives Salient upon Donor Retention."

81. A. Strenta and W. Dejong, "The Effect of a Prosocial Label on Helping Behavior."

82. R. M. Titmuss, *The Gift Relationship.* Titmuss's 1967 survey of nearly four thousand blood donors in England persuaded him that "the commercialization of blood and donor relationships represses the expression of altruism" (p. 245). It also increases social and medical costs in the long run, creating more shortages, administrative difficulties, and an inequitable redistribution of blood from the poor to the rich—all problems he observed in the United States. Since

the early 1970s, however, almost all blood in the United States has come from volunteer donors.

83. P. M. Oliner, "Legitimating and Implementing Prosocial Education," p. 399. Orthodox behaviorism sees humans as mere responders to the pulls of reinforcements, while the evidence reviewed above suggests that intrinsic interest can be a far more powerful motivator than rewards are. But just as we do not automatically seek rewards, neither is our intrinsic motivation automatically destroyed by them. Two psychologists suggest that people in the helping professions, who are paid for prosocial behavior, may not stand idly by and allow their altruistic motivation to be undermined. Instead, they may actively look for other, unpaid opportunities to be helpful (E. G. Clary and T. J. Thieman, "Self Perceptions of Helpfulness").

CHAPTER 8

1. Santayana quoted in H. M. Schulweis, Foreword to *The Altruistic Personality*, pp. ix–x.

2. J. Feinberg, "Psychological Egoism," pp. 490–91.

3. J. J. Rousseau, *Emile*, pp. 213–14.

4. E. Fromm, *Man for Himself*, pp. 134–35. Just as the absence of self-love may—paradoxically, as it seems at first—produce selfishness, so the absence of self-awareness in the child may explain egocentricity. Thus, writes Piaget: "The self is at the center of reality to begin with for the very reason that it is not aware of itself" (*Six Psychological Studies*, p. 13).

5. On this point, see, for example, P. W. Taylor, *Principles of Ethics*, pp. 42–43.

6. The tendentious syllogism runs as follows, says Fromm: "Self-interest is a biologically given striving anchored in human nature; self-interest equals greed; ergo: greed is rooted in human nature—and not a character-conditioned human passion. Q.E.D." (*The Anatomy of Human Destructiveness*, p. 237).

7. G. Allport, *Becoming*, p. 45.

8. R. D. Milo, Introduction to *Egoism and Altruism*, p. 2.

9. Because of this distinction, one is puzzled to encounter a definition of *altruism* such as the following: "Self-sacrificial acts intended to benefit others regardless of material or social outcomes for the actor" (S. H. Schwartz and J. A. Howard, "Internalized Values as Motivators of Altruism," p. 229). It would seem that *either* an act requires self-sacrifice in order to be labeled altruistic *or* personal outcome is irrelevant to its qualifying for the label. Unless some words are being used in an idiosyncratic way here, it is difficult to understand how both conditions can obtain. I am arguing for a definition in which no self-sacrifice is required, such as that offered by Christopher Jencks: people behave altruistically, he wrote,

"when they feel and act as if the long-term welfare of others is important *independent* of its effects on their own welfare" ("Varieties of Altruism," p. 53). Also see L. A. Blum, *Friendship, Altruism, and Morality*, pp. 9–10, 76.

10. M. Midgley, "Gene-juggling," p. 444. Midgley goes on to say that "one's own feelings are the inducement" for the altruistic act, which seems to me a description not only unrelated to what precedes it and unnecessary for a positive definition, but inimical to the idea of distinguishing altruism from egoism as a motive for carrying out prosocial acts.

11. R. M. Lemos, "Psychological Egoism," p. 540. A criticism of Lemos's paper published the following year in the same journal began by admitting that he was "correct in believing that [egoism] is hardly more than a dead issue nowadays, at least among philosophers" (D. C. Hodges, "Psychological Egoism," p. 246).

12. N. J. Brown, "Psychological Egoism Revisited," p. 293. Precisely the same point about egoism's seeming persuasive only to freshmen was made by Bernard Gert: "It is unusual to find psychological egoists at all. The only ones I have met are beginning students of philosophy" ("Hobbes and Psychological Egoism," p. 506 n.18).

13. Milo, *Egoism and Altruism*, esp. pp. 4–7.

14. Chesterton quoted in Feinberg, "Psychological Egoism," p. 498.

15. See, for example, the findings reported—and other research reviewed—in G. M. Williamson and M. S. Clark, "Providing Help and Desired Relationship Type as Determinants of Changes in Moods and Self-Evaluations." Also see the self-reports of kidney donors, described in C. H. Fellner and J. R. Marshall, "Kidney Donors Revisited," p. 359.

16. N. Rescher, *Unselfishness*, p. 13.

17. Evidence for this proposition is sketchy. College students (N = 16) who did volunteer work in a psychiatric hospital scored as being more accepting of themselves than those who did not volunteer (M. King, L. O. Walder, and S. Pavey, "Personality Change as a Function of Volunteer Experience in a Psychiatric Hospital"); an earlier study had found a similar increase in self-confidence, but it did not include a control group (K. E. Scheibe, "College Students Spend Eight Weeks in Mental Hospital"). The idea that prosocial behavior "strengthens [one's] sense of personal worth and power" was endorsed by Jerome Frank (*Persuasion and Healing*, p. 278). The Oliners argued that, at least for people with a strong sense of attachment to, and responsibility for, others, taking part in helping activities leads to a positive self-evaluation (S. P. Oliner and P. M. Oliner, *The Altruistic Personality*, p. 251). Finally, Norma Feshbach found that training in perspective taking was associated with a more positive self-concept among children (N. D. Feshbach, "Learning to Care," p. 269).

18. Frank writes: "The model suggests an intelligible answer to the pressing question of 'What's in it [i.e., moral behavior] for me?'" acknowledging later: "For the model to work, satisfaction from doing the right thing must *not* be

premised on the fact that material gains may later follow; rather, it must be *intrinsic* to the act itself. . . . Moral sentiments do not lead to material advantage unless they are heartfelt" (*Passions within Reason,* pp. 19, 253). The entire thesis turns, then, on the existence of some undefined but extremely elaborate mechanism of self-deception whose existence (let alone workings) is never demonstrated. Having quite convincingly shown that non-self-interested behavior exists, Frank asserts that it is only apparently or superficially non-self-interested, arguing in effect that if people act honestly or helpfully, the most economical explanation must surely be long-term self-interest. I would suggest that this explanation is more economics-based than economical. (See my review of the book, "Altruism within Egoism.")

19. Mill wrote in his autobiography: "Those only are happy . . . who have their minds fixed on some object other than their own happiness; on the happiness of others, on the improvement of mankind, even on some act or pursuit, followed not as a means but as itself an ideal end. Aiming thus at something else, they find happiness by the way" (quoted in M. A. Lutz and K. Lux, *Humanistic Economics,* p. 41).

20. H. Spencer, *The Principles of Ethics,* pp. 241, 279. "Surely," Bishop Butler wrote 150 years earlier, "that character we call selfish is not the most promising for happiness" (J. Butler, *The Analogy of Religion,* p. 488).

21. I am aware of only one attempt to document this impression—a rather silly survey of about two hundred college students that was conducted in the late 1950s but only published in 1982. Each student was asked to list the ten people he or she knew best, to decide whether these people were happy or unhappy, and then to classify them as selfish or unselfish. Of the nearly two thousand names generated, fewer than four percent were judged to be both happy and selfish. (Thirty-seven percent were selfish but not happy, 42 percent were happy but not selfish, and the remainder were neither.) "Selfish people are, by definition, those whose activities are devoted to *bringing themselves happiness.* Yet, at least as judged by others, these selfish people are far *less* likely to be happy than those whose efforts are devoted to making others happy. . . . Conclusion: Do unto others as you would have them do unto you (p < .001)" (B. Rimland, "The Altruism Paradox," quotation on p. 522).

22. Taylor, *Principles of Ethics,* p. 40. Also see Arthur Caplan: "The claim that none of our actions is really motivated by our conscious thoughts and motives is held to be a *reductio* of the entire enterprise of ethics since such a thesis is merely a shabbily disguised version of hard causal determinism rather than an empirical theory about the proper characterization of human nature and motivation" ("Sociobiology, Human Nature and Psychological Egoism," p. 30).

23. R. P. Wolff, *The Poverty of Liberalism,* p. 174n. Essentially the same point has been made by K. Nielsen, "The Voices of Egoism," p. 93; D. Collard, *Altruism and Economy,* p. 6; and Feinberg, "Psychological Egoism," p. 492.

24. See S. Holmes, "The Secret History of Self-Interest."

25. Sidgwick quoted in A. Sen, "Rational Fools," p. 20.

26. See R. W. Perrett, "Egoism, Altruism, and Intentionalism in Buddhist Ethics," esp. pp. 74–77. Likewise, Christopher Jencks writes: "The mechanisms that make us take account of the welfare of our future selves are, I think, much the same as the mechanisms that make us take account of others" ("Varieties of Altruism," p. 55).

27. P. Passell, "Why It Pays to Be Generous."

28. In prisoners' dilemma, two players separately and simultaneously decide whether to "cooperate" or "defect," and their decisions, taken together, determine the reward. Under one scoring system, A gets five points if she defects but B cooperates, three points if both cooperate, one point if both defect, and no points if she cooperates while B defects. (The actual point value is less important than the relationships between the payoffs in each condition.) From A's solitary perspective, in other words, it makes sense to defect either way—to cut her losses if B defects and to maximize her gains if B cooperates. B, of course, reasons identically. But *both* players do better if both cooperate rather than trying to stick it to the other. Since the game turns on the importance of transcending the individual's point of view, I follow political scientist Jane Mansbridge (who, in turn, follows Michael Taylor) in referring to it as prisoners' (rather than prisoner's) dilemma (J. Mansbridge, "On the Relation of Altruism and Self-Interest," p. 323n3).

29. Rescher, *Unselfishness*, pp. 40, 39 (emphasis omitted). What determines whether an action is rational is whether appropriate means are chosen for reaching a goal, not whether the goal is self-serving. (See A. Etzioni, *The Moral Dimension*, p. 146; and R. Brandt, "Rationality, Egoism, and Morality," esp. p. 685.) Sen writes: "A consistent chooser can have any degree of egoism that we care to specify. . . . The exclusion of any consideration other than self-interest seems to impose a wholly arbitrary limitation on the notion of rationality" ("Rational Fools," pp. 7, 20).

30. Frank, *Passions within Reason*, p. 236.

31. K. Nielsen, "Egoism in Ethics," p. 502. Also see Taylor, *Principles of Ethics*, p. 34. In a later paper, Nielsen notes that this incompatibility between the two sorts of egoism is true only of a strong version of psychological egoism (one specifying that we can do no other than to try to benefit ourselves). The problem vanishes with a weaker version (one specifying that we *do* try to benefit ourselves). (Nielsen, "The Voices of Egoism," pp. 86–87.)

32. R. W. K. Paterson, "Psychological Egoism," pp. 97, 100–1.

33. Dawkins makes a point of saying that his "definitions of altruism and selfishness are *behavioural*, not subjective. I am not concerned here with the psychology of motives" (*The Selfish Gene*, p. 4).

34. This point was made by Dawkins in a 1979 lecture and is paraphrased in C. D. Batson, "Sociobiology and the Role of Religion in Promoting Prosocial Behavior," p. 1381.

35. For a discussion of this question, see B. C. R. Bertram, "Problems with

Altruism," esp. p. 256; M. A. Simon, "Biology, Sociobiology, and the Understanding of Human Social Behavior," p. 300; P. Kitcher, *Vaulting Ambition,* p. 399ff. Darwin, too, wrestled with the question of whether animals' behavior could properly be called moral (see *The Descent of Man,* pp. 112–13). Jerome Kagan has written that "comparing the behavior of bees in a hive with that of a volunteer in a hospital comes close to meeting the criterion for metaphor" (*Unstable Ideas,* p. 51).

36. M. Sahlins, *The Use and Abuse of Biology,* p. 57.

37. "Can we maintain that the ultimate criterion in human value-based selection is genetic continuity—that the most appropriate ethics is that which best assures the survival of genes like one's own? To do so we would have to suppose that all instances of religious, political, and intellectual martyrdom—all self-sacrificing acts committed in disregard for continuity of genes like one's own—are aberrations destined for oblivion. Yet such acts have been highly revered, and the values underlying them transmitted in particular cultures. . . . Nothing we know of human evolution indicates that we are obliged to perpetuate our genes, or that our ethical behavior evolves so as to assure their perpetuation" (A. W. Ravin, "Natural Selection and Human Choice," pp. 30–31).

38. Kitcher, *Vaulting Ambition,* p. 402.

39. R. L. Trivers, "The Evolution of Reciprocal Altruism," p. 36.

40. Sahlins, *The Use and Abuse of Biology,* p. 87.

41. Trivers, "The Evolution of Reciprocal Altruism," p. 52. He continues in this vein, apparently playing it by ear: "In a system of strong multiparty interactions it is possible that in some situations individuals are selected to demonstrate generalized altruistic tendencies and that their main concern when they have harmed another is to show that they are genuinely altruistic, which they best do by acting altruistic without any apparent ulterior motive" (p. 53).

42. R. Alexander, *The Biology of Moral Systems,* pp. 38, 93.

43. Ibid., p. 120.

44. Ibid., pp. 152, 160.

45. Ibid., pp. 106, 113, 102.

46. Ibid., p. 121.

47. Melvin Konner has pointed out that even with other species, "the non-genetic sources of variation in behavior may be so large as to swamp any effects of the genes." In a useful thought experiment, he stipulates the existence of a gene-directed hormone in birds that increases self-sacrificing behavior but shows how random mutations and environmental changes (such as food availability and climate) could easily overwhelm the impact of the hypothetical genetic influence (*The Tangled Wing,* pp. 402–4).

48. G. W. Allport, *Pattern and Growth in Personality,* esp. pp. 226–44. With respect to moral values, see N. Eisenberg, *Altruistic Emotion, Cognition, and Behavior,* p. 117.

49. P. Singer, *The Expanding Circle,* pp. 47–48.

50. M. L. Hoffman, "Is Altruism Part of Human Nature?"

51. Darwin, *The Descent of Man,* esp. pp. 99–111, 121–29, 136.

52. J. Panksepp, "The Psychobiology of Prosocial Behaviors," p. 20. For a refreshingly nonreductive treatment of the possible biological basis of empathy, see L. Brothers, "A Biological Perspective on Empathy."

53. K. A. Matthews et al., " 'Principles in His Nature Which Interest Him in the Fortune of Others. . . .' "

54. J. P. Rushton et al., "Altruism and Aggression."

55. See Sen, "Rational Fools"; S. C. Kolm, "Altruism and Efficiency"; G. Davidson and P. Davidson, *Economics for a Civilized Society;* Etzioni, *The Moral Dimension;* M. S. McPherson, "Limits on Self-Seeking"; B. Schwartz, *The Battle for Human Nature,* esp. chap. 6; Lutz and Lux, *Humanistic Economics;* and Collard, *Altruism and Economy.* All have been published since the late 1970s. For a useful review of recent writings challenging the self-interest model in several of the social sciences, see pp. 16–19 in J. Mansbridge, "The Rise and Fall of Self-Interest in the Explanation of Political Life." See also my "Altruism within Egoism."

56. After listing some critical works, Sen reminds his readers that "the assumption of purely self-interested behaviour remains the standard one in economics, providing the behavioural foundation of standard economic theory and policy analysis, and the basis of much of what is taught to students of economics" (*On Ethics and Economics,* p. 17 n.12). And, from another source: "In spite of the protests . . . modern economic science still embraces self-interest as the heart and soul of Economic Man" (Lutz and Lux, *Humanistic Economics,* p. 99).

57. Kolm, "Altruism and Efficiency," pp. 18–36.

58. Sen noted that "work motivation problems . . . lie outside the economics of rewards and punishments; and one reason why economists seem to have little to contribute in this area is the neglect in traditional economic theory of this whole issue of commitment [that is, altruistic considerations] and the social relations surrounding it" ("Rational Fools," p. 13). See also, in this connection, my discussion in the preceding chapter of the ineffectiveness of rewards as motivators.

59. McPherson, "Limits on Self-Seeking," pp. 84, 76–77. Referring to Adam Smith's proposition that benefits to everyone accrue from self-interested rather than altruistic actions, Etzioni observes: "If there [are] no fundamental differences between 'self-love' and love for others, Smith's whole thesis vanishes. . . . It thus seems, on grounds of sound conceptualization, that the quest for self-satisfactions, and seeking to serve others (the public included) out of a sense of moral obligation, are best kept apart" (*The Moral Dimension,* p. 29).

60. Five sources to this effect are cited in V. A. Hodgkinson, *Motivations for Giving and Volunteering,* chap. 2, manuscript pp. 81–83.

61. A. Lodge, "Taxes and Charity." When a particular person suddenly has more money, he or she may donate more to charity, but this does not mean that the fraction of the population with more to give away—i.e., the affluent—donate

a greater proportion of their income than do those with fewer resources. On the contrary. "The combined giving of corporations and foundations is only 10 percent of all that is contributed; 90 percent comes from individuals. . . . [Of those individuals,] people with incomes under $10,000 give 2.8 percent of what they have, and those at $10,000 to $30,000 give 2.5 percent. At the other end of the scale, people with incomes of $50,000 to $75,000 give 1.5 percent; $75,000 to $100,000 give 1.7 percent; and $100,000 or more, 2.1 percent. One-half of what is contributed comes from families with incomes under $30,000" (B. O'Connell, "Already, 1,000 Points of Light").

62. D. T. Miller, "Personal Deserving versus Justice for Others."

63. M. J. Lerner, "The Justice Motive in Human Relations and the Economic Model of Man," p. 254. Lerner proposes that research apparently supporting traditional self-interest assumptions—notably the literature on equity theory in social psychology—seems to measure not what the subjects themselves actually prefer but the sorts of thinking they "believe are operative in the business world," particularly inasmuch as they are often asked to role-play businesspeople in these experiments. Moreover, Lerner has shown that the average subject assumes that "others" are more preoccupied with self-interest than people actually are (pp. 267, 270).

64. G. R. Orren, "Beyond Self-Interest," p. 24. He continues: "The longer one studies politics or participates in public affairs, the less it seems that our understanding of human behavior is advanced by the economic model of individual consumers competing fiercely for possessions and profit or the pluralist conception of political life as a clash of irreconcilable interests. The impoverished language and premises of self-interest can neither articulate nor explain powerful human sentiments like compassion, loyalty, affection, and duty" (pp. 26–27).

65. Research by David Sears, which has appeared in a number of articles and chapters, provides evidence for this. See, for example, D. O. Sears and C. L. Funk, "Self-Interest in Americans' Political Opinions."

66. T. R. Tyler, "Justice, Self-Interest, and the Legitimacy of Legal and Political Authority," p. 174.

67. Even without appealing to altruistic motivation, the idea that people will try to avoid participating in collective action is misconceived, as Albert O. Hirschman observed. Such participation, like other instances of striving toward a goal, should not properly be counted as a cost; the very process is part of what brings fulfillment. Such a "melting of the cost into the pleasure segment," a "fusion of striving and attaining," is common in public-regarding activities—a fact that neoclassical economists often fail to acknowledge. As evidence of the poverty of Olson's theory, Hirschman recalls that the impossibility of collective action for large groups was being proclaimed "at the precise moment when the Western world was about to be all but engulfed by an unprecedented wave of public movements, marches, protests, strikes, and ideologies. . . . Once [these events] had safely run their course, the many people who found them deeply upsetting

could go back to *The Logic of Collective Action* and find in it good and reassuring reasons why those collective actions of the sixties should never have happened in the first place, were perhaps less real than they seemed, and would be most unlikely ever to recur" (*Shifting Involvements,* pp. 78–79, 86–89).

68. G. Marwell, "Altruism and the Problem of Collective Action," pp. 210–11.

69. G. Marwell and R. E. Ames, "Economists Free Ride, Does Anyone Else?" pp. 306–309.

70. The tragedy of the commons was laid out by Garrett Hardin: from the perspective of each cattle farmer with access to a public pasture, it is sensible to keep adding animals to his herd. But the same reasoning that makes this decision seem sensible to one individual will make it seem sensible to all individuals. Each will pursue his self-interest, the grass will be depleted, and everyone will lose. Hardin uses the parable to argue for mandatory birth control ("The Tragedy of the Commons").

71. This finding is substantiated by research described in R. M. Dawes, A. J. C. van de Kragt, and J. M. Orbell, "Cooperation for the Benefit of Us." It is conceivable—although Dawes himself disputes this interpretation (personal communication, March 1989)—that allowing subjects to chat and come to know each other promotes cooperative decisions less because a group identity has been formed than because it reduces anonymity and encourages each individual to see every other individual as a subject, a real human being whose interests are salient and compelling.

72. A. Downs, *An Economic Theory of Democracy,* quoted in Mansbridge, "The Rise and Fall of Self-Interest in the Explanation of Political Life."

73. S. B. Dreman and C. W. Greenbaum, "Altruism or Reciprocity," pp. 66–67.

74. M. S. Clark and J. Mills, "Interpersonal Attraction in Exchange and Communal Relationships," p. 23.

75. L. Hyde, *The Gift,* p. 9.

76. Dreman and Greenbaum, "Altruism or Reciprocity," pp. 64, 66.

77. J. Youniss, "Development in Reciprocity through Friendship," pp. 95–101. Quotation is from p. 101.

78. J. Suls, S. Witenberg, and D. Gutkin, "Evaluating Reciprocal and Nonreciprocal Prosocial Behavior."

79. D. Romer, C. L. Gruder, and T. Lizzadro, "A Person-Situation Approach to Altruistic Behavior." This does not mean that altruistic helpers will be no more generous than egoistic helpers across all situations, though. The authors suggest that the reluctance of altruists to help in a quid pro quo arrangement depends on there being no pressing need for assistance. As the need becomes more extreme, as in emergency situations, "altruists should become more likely to help and the effect of compensation should decline" (p. 1008).

80. E. Staub and L. Sherk, "Need for Approval, Children's Sharing Behav-

ior, and Reciprocity in Sharing," p. 250. The difference did not reach statistical significance, however.

81. Clark and Mills, "Interpersonal Attraction in Exchange and Communal Relationships."

82. M. S. Clark, "Record Keeping in Two Types of Relationships."

83. M. S. Clark et al., "Recipient's Mood, Relationship Type, and Helping."

84. B. I. Murstein, M. Cerreto, and M. G. MacDonald, "A Theory and Investigation of the Effect of Exchange-Orientation on Marriage and Friendship." The negative correlation was considerably stronger for men than for women. The same article reports a study of college friendships in which a positive relation was found between exchange orientation and friendship intensity among college students, but the friendships in question were relatively short, superficial, and situation-determined.

85. M. J. Lerner and J. R. Meindl, "Justice and Altruism," p. 220.

86. N. Eisenberg-Berg and C. Neal, "Children's Moral Reasoning about Their Own Spontaneous Prosocial Behavior." Eisenberg observes that such appeals to authority or punishment (which were completely absent here) are what one would expect if the children were at Kohlberg's first stage of moral reasoning (p. 229), and that the apparently altruistic needs-oriented explanations have often—and presumably unfairly—been coded as Stage 2, i.e., as an immature, "preconventional" way of thinking about moral problems (N. Eisenberg-Berg and M. Hand, "The Relationship of Preschoolers' Reasoning about Prosocial Moral Conflicts to Prosocial Behavior," p. 362).

87. R. M. Titmuss, *The Gift Relationship*, pp. 237–38.

88. P. P. Hallie, *Lest Innocent Blood Be Shed*, pp. 284–86.

89. A. Camus, *The Plague*, pp. 120, 154, 238 (pp. 117, 150, 231 in some editions). The last remark occurs in the context of one of the novel's most memorable exchanges. Rieux's friend Tarrou expresses a desire to be a saint in a world without God, prompting Rieux to say that he is interested only in being a man. "Yes," Tarrou replies, "we're both after the same thing, but I'm less ambitious" (p. 238).

90. Oliner and Oliner, *The Altruistic Personality*, pp. 113, 228.

91. The foregoing facts are noted in ibid., pp. 1, 6, 81, 85, 108, 127.

92. Staub and Sherk: "In general, children with a strong need for approval may be inhibited and inactive in social situations, especially novel or ambiguous ones. This would limit their prosocial behavior, because helping others or sharing with others often involves initiation of action" ("Need for Approval, Children's Sharing Behavior, and Reciprocity in Sharing," p. 251). Other studies to the same effect are cited in Hoffman, "Is Altruism Part of Human Nature?", p. 126.

93. L. Berkowitz and L. R. Daniels, "Responsibility and Dependency." Notice how this finding challenges the helping-as-reciprocity view as well as the hypothesis that prosocial behavior is motivated by a search for approval.

94. C. D. Batson, *The Altruism Question*, chap. 7, manuscript p. 183.

95. C. D. Batson, "Prosocial Motivation," pp. 93, 96.

96. The story is recounted by John Aubrey and cited in A. MacIntyre, "Egoism and Altruism," p. 463. A very similar anecdote has been told about Abraham Lincoln.

97. I. M. Piliavin, J. Rodin, and J. A. Piliavin, "Good Samaritanism," p. 298. Some years later the Piliavins qualified this by conceding that on occasion "the motive for helping has a sympathetic rather than a selfish tone." The model, however, remains fundamentally egoistic (J. A. Piliavin et al., "Responsive Bystanders," p. 286).

98. C. D. Batson, J. Fultz, and P. A. Schoenrade, "Adults' Emotional Reactions to the Distress of Others"; Batson, "Prosocial Motivation," esp. pp. 96–103; and other writings.

99. N. Eisenberg et al., "Differentiation of Personal Distress and Sympathy in Children and Adults."

100. This and similar experiments are described in Batson, "Prosocial Motivation," pp. 106–9.

101. C. D. Batson et al., "Five Studies Testing Two New Egoistic Alternatives to the Empathy-Altruism Hypothesis," pp. 54–58.

102. Ibid., p. 69.

103. For example, see R. B. Cialdini et al., "Empathy-Based Helping."

104. See C. D. Batson et al., "Negative-State Relief and the Empathy-Altruism Hypothesis," pp. 922–23.

105. Ibid.

106. D. A. Schroeder et al., "Empathic Concern and Helping Behavior."

107. N. Eisenberg et al., "Differentiation of Vicariously Induced Emotional Reactions in Children"; and "Differentiation of Personal Distress and Sympathy in Children and Adults." It is true, as Eisenberg subsequently admits, that heart rate deceleration "could also reflect an outward orientation unaccompanied by sympathy" (N. Eisenberg et al., "Relation of Sympathy and Personal Distress to Prosocial Behavior," p. 56).

108. N. Eisenberg, H. McCreath, and R. Ahn, "Vicarious Emotional Responsiveness and Prosocial Behavior." More recently, Eisenberg has shown that dispositional sympathy (similar to Batson's empathy) does indeed predict helping in a way that seems to support the existence of genuine altruism (N. Eisenberg et al., "The Role of Sympathy and Altruistic Personality Traits in Helping").

109. P. A. Schoenrade et al., "Attachment, Accountability, and Motivation to Benefit Another Not in Distress."

110. Batson, "Prosocial Motivation," pp. 94, 109.

111. M. A. Wallach and L. Wallach, "How Psychology Sanctions the Cult of the Self," pp. 51–52.

112. Collard, *Altruism and Economy*, p. 69.

CHAPTER 9

1. Arthur Koestler, for example, asserts that "homicide for *un*selfish reasons, at the risk of one's own life, is the dominant phenomenon in history. . . . The trouble with our species is not an excess of aggression, but an excess of devotion. . . . The egotism of the group feeds on the altruism of its members" ("The Limits of Man and His Predicament," pp. 51–53). I think Andrew Bard Schmookler is right when he rejoins that altruism is hardly the dominant phenomenon in such situations (see his *Out of Weakness,* p. 223). Not only must the term be stretched until it includes group loyalty, but altruism is particuarly unfriendly to the ideas of competition and out-groups.

2. Dennis Krebs prefers to talk about gradations of altruism rather than reserving the term for only one motivational pattern. See D. Krebs and F. Van Hesteren, "The Development of Altruism."

3. "Because the ultimate goal [for the principled helper] is to uphold or express the moral principle, it would not be appropriate to call the motivation . . . either egoistic or altruistic. . . . If one's ultimate goal is to uphold a moral principle such as justice, then neither self nor other benefit is at issue, even though one's actions to uphold the principle may benefit self, other, or both" (C. D. Batson, "Personal Values, Moral Principles, and a Three-Path Model of Prosocial Motivation," p. 225).

4. N. Eisenberg and P. A. Miller, "The Relation of Empathy to Prosocial and Related Behaviors," pp. 111–13.

5. T. Nagel, *The Possibility of Altruism,* p. 80n.

6. H. Melville, "Bartleby," p. 79.

7. Z. Rubin and L. A. Peplau, "Belief in a Just World and Reactions to Another's Lot," p. 74. See also N. Eisenberg, *Altruistic Emotion, Cognition, and Behavior,* pp. 110, 197.

8. D. Aderman, S. S. Brehm, and L. B. Katz, "Empathic Observation of an Innocent Victim."

9. Eisenberg, *Altruistic Emotion, Cognition, and Behavior,* p. 110.

10. S. Kelman, "Why Public Ideas Matter," p. 37.

11. M. Radke-Yarrow, C. Zahn-Waxler, and M. Chapman, "Children's Prosocial Dispositions and Behavior," p. 478.

12. Paul Schervish, personal communication, September 1988.

13. Everett Sanderson, quoted in W. R. Young, " 'There's a Girl on the Tracks!' " p. 95.

14. Bruce Dobbs, quoted in L. Wheeler, "Runner Pulls Man from Car in River," p. B2.

15. E. E. Sampson, "Psychology and the American Ideal," p. 770.

16. I have in mind Alasdair MacIntyre's assertion that in the course of working with others, "questions of benevolence or altruism simply do not arise,

any more than questions of self-interest do. In my social life I cannot but be involved in reciprocal relationships, in which it may certainly be conceded that the price I have to pay for self-seeking behavior is a loss of certain kinds of relationships. But if I want to lead a certain kind of life, with relationships of trust, friendship, and cooperation with others, then my wanting their good and my wanting my good are not two independent, discriminable desires. It is not even that I have two separate motives, self-interest and benevolence, for doing the same action. I have one motive, a desire to live in a certain way, which cannot be characterized as a desire for my good rather than that of others. For the good that I recognize and pursue is not mine particularly, except in the sense that I recognize and pursue it" ("Egoism and Altruism," p. 466). In some respects, MacIntyre's formulation is tantalizingly similar to the phenomenon I am attempting to describe. But his last two sentences reflect a different point of departure: not "us" but "it," not our relationship but a conception of the Good to which both of us are related. It is the pursuit of a transcendent moral imperative, rather than the existence of a bond between two individuals, that melts the distinction between egoism and altruism in his conception.

17. For example, the opposition "between egoism and altruism . . . does not figure in Buddhist ethics because the Buddhist account of the self defuses the whole question" by virtue of holding that the self is not "a uniform substance that persists through time, but a cluster of past, present and future 'selves' connected to each other by ties of various degrees" (R. W. Perrett, "Egoism, Altruism and Intentionalism in Buddhist Ethics," pp. 71, 73).

18. For example, see A. H. Maslow, *Toward a Psychology of Being*, pp. 139–40 ("Regarding selfishness and unselfishness as contradictory and mutually exclusive is itself characteristic of a lower level of personality development. . . . How could selfish hedonism be opposed to altruism, when selfishness became selfishly pleasurable" for self-actualizing subjects?); N. Noddings, *Caring*, p. 99 ("Since I am defined in relation, I do not sacrifice myself when I move toward the other as one-caring. Caring is, thus, both self-serving and other-serving"); D. Krebs and F. Van Hesteren, "The Development of Altruism," pp. 30–31 ("At high levels of development, it is more the case that the distinction between selfishness and unselfishness disappears than that the focus becomes exclusively other-oriented"); and A. P. Goldstein and G. Y. Michaels, *Empathy*, p. 170 ("It can even be argued that the concept of altruism, which has often been linked theoretically to empathy, starts to become meaningless in the context of parent empathy, because helping one's child often feels like helping one's self").

19. L. A. Blum, *Friendship, Altruism, and Morality*, p. 76. This, of course, is not to say that every friendship—or even every act in the closest friendship—can be so described. Prescriptively, too, Blum argues that parents ought to emphasize more than the "us" motive. The ideal, he says, is to raise children who, first, derive pleasure from helping others; second, are willing to help even when doing

so is not pleasurable; and third, develop relationships in which their pleasure and the other's are interchangeable (personal communication, January 1988).

20. C. Gilligan, *In a Different Voice*, p. 74. Elsewhere she has described her account of a morality of care as an attempt "to capture the experience of attachment or interdependence, which overrides the traditional contrast between egoism and altruism" ("Remapping the Moral Domain," p. 241).

21. M. Heidegger, *Being and Time*, p. 162. "Being-with" is the awkward, though literal, translation of the German *Mitsein*, for which there is no precise English equivalent.

22. N. D. Feshbach and S. Feshbach, "Empathy Training and the Regulation of Aggression," p. 411. See also J. V. Jordan, "Empathy and Self Boundaries," p. 2: "Empathy is . . . the process through which one's experienced sense of basic connection and similarity to other humans is established. . . . Without empathy, there is no intimacy, no real attainment of an appreciation of the paradox of separateness within connection."

23. H. S. Sullivan, *Conceptions of Modern Psychiatry*, pp. 55–56. Emphasis in original.

24. J. Ortega y Gasset, *Man and People*, pp. 39, 46.

25. C. B. MacPherson, *The Political Theory of Possessive Individualism*, p. 3.

26. K. Marx, "On the Jewish Question," pp. 42–43. For more on the "classic liberal mistake of conceiving the relationship among men as purely instrumental or accidental, rather than as intrinsic and essential," see R. P. Wolff, *The Poverty of Liberalism*, esp. chap. 5.

27. P. Marin, "The New Narcissism," pp. 45–46.

28. Sampson, "Psychology and the American Ideal," p. 780. Also see R. Hogan, "Theoretical Egocentrism and the Problem of Compliance"; and J. T. Spence, "Achievement American Style." Sampson makes a special point of challenging psychologists who think they have brought the discipline to a new and higher dimension by virtue of transcending dichotomies such as masculinity versus femininity. These "dialectical syntheses," he points out, are generally located in the usual place—that is, within the individual. For example, "androgyny as a sign of good health thereby reflects an individualistic social arrangement in which persons wish to be self-contained and self-sufficient in order to be successful" (p. 774).

29. L. Dumont, *Essays on Individualism*, pp. 262–63.

30. P. Slater, *The Pursuit of Loneliness*, p. 26.

31. R. N. Bellah et al., *Habits of the Heart*, passim.

32. Paul Wachtel has called attention to the false dichotomy of individualism versus helpless dependence. See *The Poverty of Affluence*, pp. 139–40.

33. J. W. Meyer, "Myths of Socialization and of Personality," p. 211.

34. N. Chodorow, "Beyond Drive Theory," p. 286.

35. Marin, "The New Narcissism," p. 50. Brewster Smith also questioned "how truly humanistic is the 'transpersonal' frontier of humanistic psychology

when it loses sight of the finite humanness of everyday life in the pursuit of the ineffable" ("Humanism and Behaviorism in Psychology," p. 29).

36. "Reference to our modern notions of the 'person' or 'self' is inescapably part of any inquiry into other such notions. For . . . there is an individualist mode of thought, distinctive of modern Western cultures, which, though we may criticise it in part or in whole, we cannot escape. It indelibly marks every interpretation we give of other modes of thought and every attempt we make to revise our own" (S. Lukes, "Conclusion," p. 298).

37. C. Geertz, "From the Native's Point of View," p. 59. Also see the work of Marcel Mauss, with whom Dumont studied, such as his essay, "A Category of the Human Mind"; and many of the essays in T. C. Heller, M. Sosna, and D. E. Wellbery, eds., *Reconstructing Individualism*.

38. Still, even Sartre devoted some 250 pages in his *Being and Nothingness* to an exploration of the question of "Being-with-Others," and his ethics were founded on the idea that each person must act as if he were responsible for all people. See my essay "Existentialism Here and Now," esp. pp. 387–88.

39. Heidegger, *Being and Time*, pp. 156–57.

40. "We are what we are only through the community of mutually conscious understandings. There can be no man who is a man for himself alone, as a mere individual" (K. Jaspers, *Reason and Existenz*, p. 77).

41. "Yet this *I* seems always to be posited as being in confrontation with a *thou*, for whom in turn I myself am a *thou*. And it is in function of this dialogue and in relation to it that a *he* or *it* can be defined, that is, an independent world or at least a world that is—doubtless by a fiction—treated as independent. . . . By a striking coincidence, I discovered the particular reality of the 'Thou' at approximately the same time Buber was writing his book" (G. Marcel quoted in M. Friedman, *The Worlds of Existentialism*, pp. 209, 213).

42. See especially his treatment of metaphysical and political revolt in *The Rebel:* "Man's solidarity is founded upon rebellion, and rebellion, in its turn, can only find its justification in this solidarity. . . . In absurdist experience, suffering is individual. But from the moment when a movement of rebellion begins, suffering is seen as a collective experience. Therefore the first progressive step for a mind overwhelmed by the strangeness of things is to realize that this feeling of strangeness is shared with all men and that human reality, in its entirety, suffers from the distance which separates it from the rest of the universe. . . . I rebel—therefore we exist" (p. 22).

43. K. Marx, *The Economic and Philosophic Manuscripts of 1844*, p. 137. His last phrase is questionable because in our culture we seem to lack consciousness of ourselves as social beings.

44. M. Midgley, "Sex and Personal Identity," p. 51. She continues: "In spite of its force and nobility, it contains a deep strain of falsity, not just because the reasons why it was not applied to one half of the human race were not honestly looked at, but because the supposed independence of the male was itself false.

It was parasitical, taking for granted the love and service of non-autonomous females (and indeed often of the less enlightened males as well). It pretended to be universal when it was not."

45. N. Scheman, "Individualism and the Objects of Psychology," p. 226.

46. See, for example, Chodorow, "Beyond Drive Theory," pp. 306–11; and her "Toward a Relational Individualism," esp. pp. 200–7.

47. H. S. Sullivan, "The Illusion of Personal Individuality," p. 329.

48. Even in as individualistic a society as has ever existed, "we discover who we are face to face and side by side with others in work, love, and learning. All of our activity goes on in relationships, groups, associations, and communities ordered by institutional structures and interpreted by cultural patterns of meaning. Our individualism is itself one such pattern" (Bellah et al., *Habits of the Heart,* p. 84).

49. See Ortega y Gasset, *Man and People,* pp. 166–70.

50. L. Thomas, *The Lives of a Cell,* pp. 2, 167.

51. Psychoanalyst Joan Riviere is quoted in Chodorow, "Toward a Relational Individualism," pp. 202–3.

52. J. Youniss, "Development in Reciprocity through Friendship," p. 104; see also pp. 95–96.

53. The October 1987 crash "seemed to many analysts to have had its beginnings in failure of international cooperation. Angered by West German central bankers' decision to permit interest rates there to rise, US Treasury Secretary James Baker threatened Sunday [the day before the crash] to let the dollar resume its fall against the yen and the mark" (D. Warsh, "A Financial World in Dark until It Finds Bottom Line").

54. S. Gordon, "The Crisis in Caring," p. 58.

55. L. Goldmann, *Immanuel Kant,* p. 198. As Larry Blum points out, the fact that utilitarianism appears to be concerned with universal happiness even while being anchored in individualism suggests that Goldmann's remark may pertain primarily to Kantian thinking rather than expressing a universal truth.

56. I. Kant, *Critique of Practical Reason,* abridged and reprinted as "Morality and the Duty of Love toward Other Men," p. 62.

57. I. Kant, *Foundations of the Metaphysics of Morals,* abridged and reprinted as "The Foundation of Morals," pp. 346–47.

58. See I. Kant, *The Doctrine of Virtue,* a section of which appears as part of "Morality and the Duty of Love toward Other Men," pp. 74–75.

59. S. Freud, *Civilization and Its Discontents,* p. 59.

60. Nagel, *The Possibility of Altruism,* pp. 3, 144.

61. See Blum, *Friendship, Altruism, and Morality,* See also D. B. Wong, *Moral Relativity,* p. 186: "Capriciousness is not an intrinsic feature of the altruistic emotions, any more than inconsistency is an intrinsic feature of practical reason."

62. Nagel, *The Possibility of Altruism,* p. 79.

63. Blum, *Friendship, Altruism, and Morality,* pp. 9–10.

64. Noddings, *Caring,* p. 3.

65. D. Hume, *A Treatise of Human Nature.* Quotations appear in book 2, pt. 3, sec. 3, and book 3, pt. 3, sec. 6, respectively (pp. 415 and 618 in this edition).

66. The Oliners found that the majority of those who rescued Jews from the Nazis were motivated neither by principles such as justice *nor* by empathy and a feeling of direct concern for the victims. Those in this third group helped primarily because they felt an identification with a social reference group, such as their family or community, that expected or appreciated prosocial behavior (S. P. Oliner and P. M. Oliner, *The Altruistic Personality,* esp. pp. 199, 210). The key question for these "normocentric" individuals—which probably should be considered only a sociological category and not a third model for morality—is not whether the act was intrinsically right so much as whether it was approved by key people. With respect to motive, conformity also is very different from caring (for the victim) (see, for example, S. Feshbach and N. D. Feshbach, "Aggression and Altruism," p. 214). It leads to prosocial consequences only as long as the reference group values such behavior and thus would seem to be inherently less reliable than either principled or empathic helping.

67. E. Staub, "A Conception of the Determinants and Development of Altruism and Aggression," p. 138.

68. Oliner and Oliner, *The Altruistic Personality,* p. 257.

69. Hoess quoted in R. M. Dawes, "Plato vs. Russell," p. 21.

70. The philosopher Nicholas Rescher, for example, says that if one is interested, "one's care for the other's welfare (or pleasure) proceeds with an eye to one's own overall welfare-interests as well, so that another's welfare (or happiness) is at least in part a determining factor for one's own." By contrast, someone with disinterested concern—defining the latter word so as to avoid a contradiction in terms—"cares for the other's welfare solely for its own sake, without reference to repercussions for oneself and one's own interests" (*Unselfishness,* pp. 9–10).

71. See C. D. Batson et al., "Religious Prosocial Motivation," p. 883. Blum stops just short of making this point explicit (*Friendship, Altruism, and Morality,* p. 120). Batson does not argue that principled helping is precisely egoistic but that it appears to stand somewhere outside the altruism/egoism dichotomy (personal communication, January 1989). For a model that equates altruism with an affirmation of moral values (but that does not respond directly to this sort of objection), see S. H. Schwartz and J. A. Howard, "Internalized Values as Motivators of Altruism."

72. D. Hume, *A Treatise of Human Nature,* book 3, pt. 1, sec. 1 (pp. 469–70 in this edition).

73. Noddings, *Caring,* p. 93. Her emphasis.

74. L.A. Blum, *Friendship, Altruism, and Morality,* p. 124. Also see pp. 125, 154, 185.

75. See L. Kohlberg, "Conscience as Principled Responsibility," p. 10.

Dennis Krebs has made a similar point, but unfortunately he goes on to claim that empathy has no moral force at all and that self-interest ultimately accounts for the decisions we make about whose perspective to take.

76. S. P. Oliner and P. M. Oliner, *The Altruistic Personality,* p. 174. Staub, too, has insisted that something like responsibility must be added to the virtue of empathic response; the resulting "prosocial orientation [is] a more reliable source of positive behavior than empathic capacity" alone ("A Conception of the Determinants and Development of Altruism and Aggression," p. 143). Recall that this feeling of responsibility, rather than empathy alone, has been empirically associated with children's willingness to help (p. 126).

77. Rescher, *Unselfishness,* p. 8.

78. J. S. Mill, "Three Essays on Religion," p. 394.

79. D. Hume, *An Enquiry Concerning the Principles of Morals,* abridged and reprinted as "Morality, Self-Love, and Benevolence," pp. 43–44.

80. M. L. Hoffman, "Empathy, Social Cognition, and Moral Action." Also see his "Development of Prosocial Motivation," p. 310. Hoffman points out that cognitive morality, too, can be biased.

81. Noddings offers other examples, but her solution in each case is to reject principles. A woman not only will not but *should* not sacrifice her own child to save the life of ten other children, she writes (*Caring,* p. 44).

82. V. W. Bernard, P. Ottenberg, and F. Redl, "Dehumanization," pp. 110–11.

83. The Oliners, for example, endorse an "ethic of care" which stipulates that "the interests of individuals may be subordinated to the greater good" (*The Altruistic Personality,* p. 217).

84. A. Camus, *The Plague,* p. 86 (p. 83 in some editions). More prosaically, consider the case of a Louisville, Kentucky, police officer who was suspended for turning in traffic tickets with fictitious names to disguise the fact that he could not bring himself to give tickets to real people. As he put it, "I had a conscience. I had a heart. I started seeing the human beings behind the driver's wheels" (D. Johnson, "Police Looking Closer at Unarresting Officer"). Now this sort of compassion and perspective taking is surely laudable in itself—and may even seem heroic to people who feel they have been ticketed unnecessarily. But if we believe that ticketing unsafe drivers can save lives in the long run, then this police officer is guilty of letting his compassion supersede a morally appropriate capacity for abstraction.

85. W. Barrett, *Irrational Man,* pp. 270–71.

86. Oliner and Oliner, *The Altruistic Personality,* p. 221.

87. M. L. Hoffman, "The Contribution of Empathy to Justice and Moral Judgment," p. 72.

88. For example, see J. Strayer, "Affective and Cognitive Perspectives on Empathy," p. 228; Noddings, *Caring,* p. 57; and C. Jencks, "Varieties of Altruism," pp. 59–60.

89. On the one hand, Piaget argued that "sympathy . . . has of itself nothing moral in the eyes of conscience. To be sensitive alone is not to be good. . . . Before this sympathy can acquire a moral character there must be a common law, a system of rules." On the other hand, he exclaimed: "How much more precious is a little humanity than all the rules in the world" (J. Piaget, *The Moral Judgment of the Child*, pp. 389, 191). Kohlberg's protegés argue fiercely that, notwithstanding Carol Gilligan's critique of his one-sided devotion to abstract principles, his framework actually incorporated the idea of care. Indeed, his later work does seem to reflect more than a passing interest in this direction. In a paper published in Germany in 1986, he and two colleagues discussed "benevolence or 'active sympathy' for others" as characteristic of Stage 6 moral reasoning. This benevolence "presupposes and expresses one's identification and empathic connection with others . . . [and it is] logically and psychologically prior to what we are calling justice" (L. Kohlberg, D. Boyd, and C. Levine, "The Return of Stage 6," ms. pp. 3, 6). On the relation between care and justice, also see J. Kagan, *The Nature of the Child*, pp. 118–24; and W. Damon, *The Moral Child*, p. 102.

90. John Noonan is quoted in L. N. Henderson, "Legality and Empathy," p. 1574.

91. C. Gilligan and G. Wiggins, "The Origins of Morality in Early Childhood Relationships," p. 118. My emphasis.

92. Rescher, *Unselfishness*, pp. 102–3.

93. M. Buber, *Between Man and Man*, pp. 35–36.

References

ADAMS, DAVID. "The Use and Misuse of Aggression Research." In *Multidisciplinary Approaches to Aggression Research,* edited by Paul F. Brain and David Benton. Amsterdam: Elsevier/North-Holland Biomedical Press, 1981.

ADAMS, DAVID, and SARAH BOSCH. "The Myth That War Is Intrinsic to Human Nature Discourages Action for Peace by Young People." In *Essays on Violence,* edited by J. Martin Ramirez, Robert A. Hinde, and Jo Groebel. Seville, Spain: Publicaciones de la Universidad de Sevilla, 1987.

ADELSON, JOSEPH. "The Psychology of Altruism." *Commentary,* November 1988, 40–44.

ADERMAN, DAVID, SHARON S. BREHM, and LAWRENCE B. KATZ. "Empathic Observation of an Innocent Victim: The Just World Revisited." *Journal of Personality and Social Psychology* 29 (1974): 342–47.

ADLER, ALFRED. *The Individual Psychology of Alfred Adler,* edited by Heinz L. Ansbacher and Rowena R. Ansbacher. New York: Harper and Row, 1964.

ALEXANDER, RICHARD D. *The Biology of Moral Systems.* Hawthorne, N.Y.: Aldine de Gruyter, 1987.

ALLPORT, GORDON W. *Becoming: Basic Considerations for a Psychology of Personality.* New Haven, Conn.: Yale University Press, 1955.

———. *The Nature of Prejudice.* Garden City, N.Y.: Anchor Books, 1958.

———. *Pattern and Growth in Personality.* New York: Holt, Rinehart and Winston, 1937.

ALLPORT, GORDON W., and J. MICHAEL ROSS. "Personal Religious Orientation and Prejudice." *Journal of Personality and Social Psychology* 5 (1967): 432–43.

AMABILE, TERESA M. "Brilliant but Cruel: Perceptions of Negative Evaluators." *Journal of Experimental Social Psychology* 19 (1983): 146–56.

———. "Motivation and Creativity: Effects of Motivational Orientation on Creative Writers." *Journal of Personality and Social Psychology* 48 (1985): 393–99.

AMABILE, TERESA M., and ANN H. GLAZEBROOK. "A Negativity Bias in Interpersonal Evaluation." *Journal of Experimental Social Psychology* 18 (1981): 1–22.

AMABILE, TERESA M., BETH ANN HENNESSEY, and BARBARA S. GROSSMAN. "Social Influences on Creativity: The Effects of Contracted-for Reward." *Journal of Personality and Social Psychology* 50 (1986): 14–23.

AMOS, ORLEY M., JR. "Empirical Analysis of Motives Underlying Individual Contributions to Charity." *Atlantic Economic Journal* 10 (1982): 45–52.

ANGOFF, WILLIAM H. "The Nature-Nurture Debate, Aptitudes, and Group Differences." *American Psychologist* 43 (1988): 713–20.

ANNIS, LAWRENCE V. "Emergency Helping and Religious Behavior." *Psychological Reports* 39 (1976): 151–58.

AOKI, CHIYE, and PHILIP SIEKEVITZ. "Plasticity in Brain Development." *Scientific American,* December 1988, 56–64.

ARISTOTLE. *Aristotle,* edited by Philip Wheelwright. Indianapolis: Bobbs-Merrill, 1951.

ARONFREED, JUSTIN. "The Socialization of Altruistic and Sympathetic Behavior: Some Theoretical and Experimental Analyses." In *Altruism and Helping Behavior,* edited by J. Macaulay and L. Berkowitz. New York: Academic Press, 1970.

ARONSON, ELLIOT, and DIANE BRIDGEMAN. "Jigsaw Groups and the Desegregated Classroom: In Pursuit of Common Goals." *Personality and Social Psychology Bulletin* 5 (1979): 438–46.

ASSOCIATED PRESS. "Traffic Survey Offers a Prize." *New York Times,* 13 November 1988, 58.

AUGROS, ROBERT, and GEORGE STANCIU. *The New Biology: Discovering the Wisdom in Nature.* Boston: Shambhala, 1988.

BADCOCK, C. R. *The Problem of Altruism: Freudian-Darwinian Solutions.* Oxford, England: Basil Blackwell, 1986.

BAIER, KURT. *The Moral Point of View: A Rational Basis of Ethics.* Ithaca, N.Y.: Cornell University Press, 1958.

BANDURA, ALBERT, BILL UNDERWOOD, and MICHAEL E. FROMSON. "Disinhibition of Aggression." *Journal of Research in Personality* 9 (1975): 253–69.

BAR-TAL, DANIEL. *Prosocial Behavior: Theory and Research.* Washington, D.C.: Hemisphere, 1976.

BARASH, DAVID. *The Hare and the Tortoise: Biology, Culture, and Human Nature.* New York: Viking, 1986.

———. *The Whisperings Within.* New York: Harper and Row, 1979.

BARBER, BENJAMIN R. *Strong Democracy: Participatory Politics for a New Age.* Berkeley: University of California Press, 1984.

BARNETT, MARK A. "Empathy and Related Responses in Children." In *Empathy and Its Development,* edited by Nancy Eisenberg and Janet Strayer. Cambridge, England: Cambridge University Press, 1987.

BARNETT, MARK A., and JAMES H. BRYAN. "Effects of Competition with Outcome Feedback on Children's Helping Behavior." *Developmental Psychology* 10 (1974): 838–42.

BARNETT, MARK A., LAURA M. KING, and JEFFREY A. HOWARD. "Inducing Affect about Self or Other: Effects on Generosity in Children." *Developmental Psychology* 15 (1979): 164–67.

BARNETT, MARK A., KAREN A. MATTHEWS, and CHARLES B. CORBIN. "The Effect of Competitive and Cooperative Instructional Sets on Children's Generosity." *Personality and Social Psychology Bulletin* 5 (1979): 91–94.

BARNETT, MARK A., KAREN A. MATTHEWS, and JEFFREY A. HOWARD. "Relationship between Competitiveness and Empathy in 6- and 7-Year-Olds." *Developmental Psychology* 15 (1979): 221–22.

BARON, ROBERT A. *Human Aggression.* New York: Plenum, 1977.

BARRETT, DAVID E., and MARIAN RADKE-YARROW. "Prosocial Behavior, Social Inferential Ability, and Assertiveness in Children." *Child Development* 48 (1977): 475–81.

BARRETT, WILLIAM. *Irrational Man: A Study in Existential Philosophy.* Garden City, N.Y.: Anchor Books, 1962.

BASCH, MICHAEL FRANZ. "Empathic Understanding." *Journal of the American Psychoanalytic Association* 31 (1983): 101–26.

BASS, ALISON. "When Siblings Are *Un*like Peas in a Pod." *Boston Globe,* 30 January 1980, 25–26.

BATSON, C. DANIEL. *The Altruism Question.* Forthcoming.

———. "Personal Values, Moral Principles, and a Three-Path Model of Prosocial Motivation." In *Social and Moral Values: Individual and Societal Perspectives,* edited by Nancy Eisenberg, Janusz Reykowski, and Ervin Staub. Hillsdale, N.J.: Lawrence Erlbaum, 1989.

———. "Prosocial Motivation: Is It Ever Truly Altruistic?" In *Advances in Experimental Social Psychology,* vol. 20, edited by Leonard Berkowitz. San Diego: Academic Press, 1987.

———. "Sociobiology and the Role of Religion in Promoting Prosocial Behavior: An Alternative View." *Journal of Personality and Social Psychology* 45 (1983): 1380–85.

BATSON, C. DANIEL, JUDY G. BATSON, CARI A. GRIFFITT, SERGIO BARRIENTOS, J. RANDALL BRANDT, PETER SPRENGELMEYER, and MICHAEL J. BAYLY. "Negative-State Relief and the Empathy-Altruism Hypothesis." *Journal of Personality and Social Psychology* 56 (1989): 922–33.

BATSON, C. DANIEL, MICHELLE H. BOLEN, JULIE A. CROSS, and HELEN E. NEURINGER-BENEFIEL. "Where Is the Altruism in the Altruistic Personality?" *Journal of Personality and Social Psychology* 50 (1986): 212–20.

BATSON, C. DANIEL, and JAY S. COKE. "Empathy: A Source of Altruistic Motivation for Helping?" In *Altruism and Helping Behavior: Social, Personality, and Developmental Perspectives,* edited by J. Philippe Rushton and Richard M. Sorrentino. Hillsdale, N.J.: Lawrence Erlbaum, 1981.

BATSON, C. DANIEL, JAY S. COKE, M. L. JASNOSKI, and MICHAEL HANSON. "Buying Kindness: Effect of an Extrinsic Incentive for Helping on Perceived Altruism." *Personality and Social Psychology Bulletin* 4 (1978): 86–91.

BATSON, C. DANIEL, JANINE L. DYCK, J. RANDALL BRANDT, JUDY G. BATSON, ANNE L. POWELL, M. ROSALIE McMASTER, and CARI GRIFFITT. "Five Studies Testing Two New Egoistic Alternatives to the Empathy-Altruism Hypothesis." *Journal of Personality and Social Psychology* 55 (1988): 52–77.

BATSON, C. DANIEL, JIM FULTZ, and PATRICIA A. SCHOENRADE. "Adults' Emotional Reactions to the Distress of Others." In *Empathy and Its Development,* edited by Nancy Eisenberg and Janet Strayer. Cambridge, England: Cambridge University Press, 1987.

BATSON, C. DANIEL, JIM FULTZ, PATRICIA A. SCHOENRADE, and ALAN PADUANO. "Critical Self-Reflection and Self-Perceived Altruism: When Self-Reward Fails." *Journal of Personality and Social Psychology* 53 (1987): 594–602.

BATSON, C. DANIEL, KATHRYN C. OLESON, JOY L. WEEKS, SEAN P. HEALY, PENNY J. REEVES, PATRICK JENNINGS, and THOMAS BROWN. "Religious Prosocial Motivation: Is It Altruistic or Egoistic?" *Journal of Personality and Social Psychology* 57 (1989): 873–84.

BATTISTICH, VICTOR, DANIEL SOLOMON, MARILYN WATSON, and ERIC SCHAPS. "Effects of an Elementary School Program to Enhance Prosocial Behavior on Children's Cognitive Social Problem-Solving Skills and Strategies." *Journal of Applied Developmental Psychology* 10 (1989): 147–69.

BATTISTICH, VICTOR, MARILYN WATSON, DANIEL SOLOMON, ERIC SCHAPS, and JUDITH SOLOMON. "The Child Development Project: A Comprehensive Program for the Development of Prosocial Character." In *Moral Behavior and Development: Advances in Theory, Research, and Applications,* edited by William M. Kurtines and Jacob L. Gewirtz. Hillsdale, N.J.: Lawrence Erlbaum, 1989.

BAUMANN, DONALD J., ROBERT B. CIALDINI, and DOUGLAS T. KENRICK. "Altruism as Hedonism: Helping and Self-Gratification as Equivalent Responses." *Journal of Personality and Social Psychology* 40 (1981): 1039–46.

BAVELAS, JANET BEAVIN, ALEX BLACK, CHARLES R. LEMERY, and JENNIFER MULLETT. "Motor Mimicry as Primitive Empathy." In *Empathy and Its Development,* edited by Nancy Eisenberg and Janet Strayer. Cambridge, England: Cambridge University Press, 1987.

BECKER, WESLEY C. "Consequences of Different Kinds of Parental Discipline." In *Review of Child Development Research,* vol. 1, edited by Martin L. Hoffman and Lois Wladis Hoffman. New York: Russell Sage Foundation, 1964.

BECKSTROM, JOHN H. *Sociobiology and the Law.* Urbana: University of Illinois Press, 1985.

BECKWITH, BARBARA. "He-Man, She-Woman: *Playboy* and *Cosmo* Groove on Genes." *Columbia Journalism Review,* January/February 1984, 46–47.

BECKWITH, JON. "Gender and Math Performance: Does Biology Have Implications for Educational Policy?" *Boston University Journal of Education* 165 (1983): 158–74.

BECKWITH, JON, and JOHN DURKIN. "Girls, Boys, and Math." *Science for the People,* September/October 1981, 6–9, 32–35.

BELENKY, MARY FIELD, BLYTHE McVICKER CLINCHY, NANCY RULE GOLDBERGER, and JILL MATTUCK TARULE. *Women's Ways of Knowing: The Development of Self, Voice, and Mind.* New York: Basic Books, 1986.

BELLAH, ROBERT N., RICHARD MADSEN, WILLIAM M. SULLIVAN, ANN SWIDLER, and STEVEN M. TIPTON. *Habits of the Heart: Individualism and Commitment in American Life.* Berkeley: University of California Press, 1985.

BENBOW, CAMILLA PERSSON, and JULIAN C. STANLEY. "Sex Differences in Mathematical Ability: Fact or Artifact?" *Science,* 12 December 1980, 1262–63.

BENDER, LAURETTA. "Genesis of Hostility in Children." *American Journal of Psychiatry* 105 (1948): 241–45.

BENDER, LESLIE. "A Lawyer's Primer on Feminist Theory and Tort." *Journal of Legal Education* 38 (1988): 3–37.

BENDERLY, BERYL LIEFF. *The Myth of Two Minds: What Gender Means and Doesn't Mean.* New York: Doubleday, 1987.

BENGTSSON, HANS, and LENA JOHNSON. "Cognitions Related to Empathy in Five- to Eleven-Year-Old Children." *Child Development* 58 (1987): 1001–12.

BENNETT, FORREST C., and ROBERTA SHERMAN. "Management of Childhood 'Hyperactivity' by Primary Care Physicians." *Developmental and Behavioral Pediatrics* 4 (1983): 88–93.

BERGER, JOSEPH. "Once Rarely Explored, the Holocaust Gains Momentum as a School Topic." *New York Times,* 3 October 1988, A16.

———. "Price of Illiteracy Translates into Poverty and Humiliation." *New York Times,* 6 September 1988, A1.

BERKOWITZ, LEONARD. "Mood, Self-Awareness, and Willingness to Help." *Journal of Personality and Social Psychology* 52 (1987): 721–29.

BERKOWITZ, LEONARD, and WILLIAM H. CONNOR. "Success, Failure, and Social Responsibility." *Journal of Personality and Social Psychology* 4 (1966): 664–69.

BERKOWITZ, LEONARD, and LOUISE R. DANIELS. "Responsibility and Dependency." *Journal of Abnormal and Social Psychology* 66 (1963): 429–36.

BERNARD, VIOLA W., PERRY OTTENBERG, and FRITZ REDL. "Dehumanization." In *Sanctions for Evil,* edited by Nevitt Sanford, Craig Comstock, et al. San Francisco: Jossey-Bass, 1971.

BERNSTEIN, IRWIN S., THOMAS P. GORDON, and ROBERT M. ROSE. "The Interaction of Hormones, Behavior, and Social Context in Nonhuman Primates." In *Hormones and Aggressive Behavior,* edited by Bruce B. Svare. New York: Plenum, 1983.

BERTRAM, BRIAN C. R. "Problems with Altruism." In *Current Problems in Sociobiology,* edited by King's College Sociobiology Group, Cambridge. Cambridge, England: Cambridge University Press, 1982.

BETTELHEIM, BRUNO. "Their Specialty Was Murder." Review of *The Nazi Doctors,* by Robert Jay Lifton. *New York Times Book Review,* 5 October 1986, 1, 61–62.

BILLINGS, PAUL R., and JONATHAN BECKWITH. "Genetics and Human Behavior: Past and Future." Photocopy.

BING, LEON. "Reflections of a Gangbanger." *Harper's,* August 1988, 26, 28.

BINSWANGER, LUDWIG. "Insanity as Life-Historical Phenomenon and as Mental Disease: The Case of Ilse." 1945. Reprinted in *Existence: A New Dimension in Psychiatry and Psychology,* edited by Rollo May, Ernest Angel, and Henri F. Ellenberger. New York: Simon and Schuster, 1958.

BIRNS, BEVERLY. "The Emergence and Socialization of Sex Differences in the Earliest Years." *Merrill-Palmer Quarterly* 22 (1976): 229–54.

BIZMAN, AHARON, YOEL YINON, ESTHER MIVTZARI, and RIVKA SHAVIT. "Effects of the Age Structure of the Kindergarten on Altruistic Behavior." *Journal of School Psychology* 16 (1978): 154–59.

BLAU, PETER M. *Exchange and Power in Social Life.* New York: John Wiley, 1964.

BLECHMAN, BARRY M., and STEPHEN S. KAPLAN. *Force without War: U.S. Armed Forces as a Political Instrument.* Washington, D.C.: Brookings Institution, 1978.

BLEIER, RUTH. *Science and Gender: A Critique of Biology and Its Theories on Women.* New York: Pergamon Press, 1984.

BLOCK, JEANNE H. "Another Look at Sex Differentiation in the Socialization Behaviors of Mothers and Fathers." In *The Psychology of Women: Future Directions in Research,* edited by Julia A. Sherman and Florence L. Denmark. New York: Psychological Dimensions, 1978.

BLOCK, JEANNE H., NORMA HAAN, and M. BREWSTER SMITH. "Socialization Correlates of Student Activism." *Journal of Social Issues* 25 (1969): 143–77.

BLOOM, ALLAN. *The Closing of the American Mind: How Higher Education Has Failed Democracy and Impoverished the Souls of Today's Students.* New York: Simon and Schuster, 1987.

BLUM, LAWRENCE A. *Friendship, Altruism, and Morality.* London: Routledge and Kegan Paul, 1980.

BOOTH, WAYNE C. *Modern Dogma and the Rhetoric of Assent.* Chicago: University of Chicago Press, 1974.

BORKE, HELENE. "Interpersonal Perception of Young Children: Egocentrism or Empathy?" *Developmental Psychology* 5 (1971): 263–69.

BOWER, BRUCE. "Alcoholism's Elusive Genes." *Science News,* 30 July 1988, 74–79.

BOWERS, WILLIAM J., and GLENN L. PIERCE. "Deterrence or Brutalization: What Is the Effect of Executions?" *Crime and Delinquency,* October 1980, 453–84.

BRANDT, RICHARD. "Rationality, Egoism, and Morality." *Journal of Philosophy* 69 (1972): 681–97.

BROTHERS, LESLIE. "A Biological Perspective on Empathy." *American Journal of Psychiatry* 146 (1989): 10–19.

BROWN, NORMAN J. "Psychological Egoism Revisited." *Philosophy* 54 (1979): 293–309.

BRYAN, JAMES H., and PERRY LONDON. "Altruistic Behavior by Children." *Psychological Bulletin* 73 (1970): 200–211.

BRYAN, JAMES H., and NANCY HODGES WALBEK. "Preaching and Practicing Generosity: Children's Actions and Reactions." *Child Development* 41 (1970): 329–53.

BRYANT, BRENDA K. "Mental Health, Temperament, Family, and Friends: Perspectives on Children's Empathy and Social Perspective Taking." In *Empathy and Its Development*, edited by Nancy Eisenberg and Janet Strayer. Cambridge, England: Cambridge University Press, 1987.

BUBER, MARTIN. *Between Man and Man.* Translated by Ronald Gregor Smith. 1947. Reprint. New York: Macmillan, 1965.

———. *The Knowledge of Man: A Philosophy of the Interhuman.* Translated by Maurice Friedman and Ronald Gregor Smith. New York: Harper and Row, 1965.

BUDD, LOUIS J. "Altruism Arrives in America." *American Quarterly* 8 (1956): 40–52.

Business Week. "A Genetic Defense of the Free Market." 10 April 1978, 100, 104.

BUTLER, JOSEPH. *The Analogy of Religion.* London: Henry G. Bohn, 1860.

CAIRNS, JOHN, JULIE OVERBAUGH, and STEPHAN MILLER. "The Origin of Mutants." *Nature,* 8 September 1988, 142–45.

CAIRNS, ROBERT B. "An Evolutionary and Developmental Perspective on Aggressive Patterns." In *Altruism and Aggression: Biological and Social Origins,* edited by Carolyn Zahn-Waxler, E. Mark Cummings, and Ronald Iannotti. Cambridge, England: Cambridge University Press, 1986.

CAIRNS, ROBERT B., DENNIS J. MacCOMBIE, and KATHRYN E. HOOD. "A Developmental-Genetic Analysis of Aggressive Behavior in Mice: 1. Behavioral Outcomes." *Journal of Comparative Psychology* 97 (1983): 69–89.

CAMUS, ALBERT. *Caligula and Three Other Plays.* Translated by Stuart Gilbert. New York: Vintage, 1958.

———. *The Plague.* Translated by Stuart Gilbert. 1947. New York: Vintage, 1972.

———. *The Rebel.* Translated by Anthony Bower. New York: Vintage, 1956.

———. *Resistance, Rebellion, and Death.* 1960. Translated by Justin O'Brien. New York: Vintage, 1974.

CAPLAN, ARTHUR L. "Sociobiology, Human Nature, and Psychological Egoism." *Journal of Social and Biological Structures* 2 (1979): 27–38.

CHANDLER, MICHAEL J. "Egocentrism and Antisocial Behavior: The Assessment and Training of Social Perspective-Taking Skills." *Developmental Psychology* 9 (1973): 326–32.

CHANDLER, MICHAEL J., and STEPHEN GREENSPAN. "Ersatz Egocentrism: A Reply to H. Borke." *Developmental Psychology* 7 (1972): 104–6.

CHAPMAN, MICHAEL, CAROLYN ZAHN-WAXLER, GERI COOPERMAN, and RONALD IANNOTTI. "Empathy and Responsibility in the Motivation of Children's Helping." *Developmental Psychology* 23 (1987): 140–45.

CHODOROW, NANCY. "Beyond Drive Theory: Object Relations and the Limits of Radical Individualism." *Theory and Society* 14 (1985): 271–319.

———. *The Reproduction of Mothering: Psychoanalysis and the Sociology of Gender.* Berkeley: University of California Press, 1978.

————. "Toward a Relational Individualism: The Mediation of Self through Psychoanalysis." In *Reconstructing Individualism: Autonomy, Individuality, and the Self in Western Thought,* edited by Thomas C. Heller, Morton Sosna, and David E. Wellbery. Stanford, Calif.: Stanford University Press, 1986.

CIALDINI, ROBERT B., MARK SCHALLER, DONALD HOULIHAN, KEVIN ARPS, JIM FULTZ, and ARTHUR L. BEAMAN. "Empathy-Based Helping: Is It Selflessly or Selfishly Motivated?" *Journal of Personality and Social Psychology* 52 (1987): 749–58.

CLAFFEY, CHARLES E. "Terkel at 76." *Boston Globe,* 9 October 1988, B77–78.

CLARK, MARGARET S. "Record Keeping in Two Types of Relationships." *Journal of Personality and Social Psychology* 47 (1984): 549–57.

CLARK, MARGARET S., and JUDSON MILLS. "Interpersonal Attraction in Exchange and Communal Relationships." *Journal of Personality and Social Psychology* 37 (1979): 12–24.

CLARK, MARGARET S., ROBERT OULETTE, MARTHA C. POWELL, and SANDRA MILBERG. "Recipient's Mood, Relationship Type, and Helping." *Journal of Personality and Social Psychology* 53 (1987): 94–103.

CLARY, E. GIL, and JUDE MILLER. "Socialization and Situational Influences on Sustained Altruism." *Child Development* 57 (1986): 1358–69.

CLARY, E. GIL, and LESLIE ORENSTEIN."The Amount and Effectiveness of Help: The Relationship of Motives and Abilities to Helping Behavior." *Personality and Social Psychology Bulletin,* in press.

CLARY, E. GIL, and THOMAS J. THIEMAN. "Self-Perceptions of Helpfulness: Different Meanings for Different People?" Paper presented at the annual meeting of the American Psychological Association, Atlanta, Ga., August 1988.

CLINE, VICTOR B., and JAMES M. RICHARDS, JR. "A Factor-Analytic Study of Religious Belief and Behavior." *Journal of Personality and Social Psychology* 1 (1965): 569–78.

COLBURN, DON. "No More 'Evil Empire.'" *Washington Post Health,* 7 June 1988, 7.

COLES, GERALD. *The Learning Mystique: A Critical Look at "Learning Disabilities."* New York: Pantheon, 1987.

COLLARD, DAVID. *Altruism and Economy: A Study in Non-selfish Economics.* New York: Oxford University Press, 1978.

CONDRY, JOHN, and SANDRA CONDRY. "Sex Differences: A Study of the Eye of the Beholder." *Child Development* 47 (1976): 812–19.

COOLEY, CHARLES HORTON. *Social Organization: A Study of the Larger Mind.* New York: Scribner's, 1909.

CUMMINGS, E. MARK, BARBARA HOLLENBECK, RONALD IANNOTTI, MARIAN RADKE-YARROW, and CAROLYN ZAHN-WAXLER. "Early Organization of Altruism and Aggression: Developmental Patterns and Individual Differences." In *Altruism and Aggression: Biological and Social Origins,* edited by Carolyn Zahn-Waxler, E.

Mark Cummings, and Ronald Iannotti. Cambridge, England: Cambridge University Press, 1986.

CURRIE, ELLIOTT. *Confronting Crime: An American Challenge.* New York: Pantheon, 1985.

DAMON, WILLIAM. *The Moral Child: Nurturing Children's Natural Moral Growth.* New York: Free Press, 1988.

DARLEY, JOHN, and BIBB LATANE. "Bystander Intervention in Emergencies: Diffusion of Responsibility." *Journal of Personality and Social Psychology* 8 (1968): 377–83.

DARWIN, CHARLES. *The Descent of Man and Selection in Relation to Sex.* 2d ed. New York: D. Appleton, 1907.

DAVIDSON, GREG, and PAUL DAVIDSON. *Economics for a Civilized Society.* New York: Norton, 1988.

DAVIS, MARK H., JAY G. HULL, RICHARD D. YOUNG, and GREGORY G. WARREN. "Emotional Reactions to Dramatic Film Stimuli: The Influence of Cognitive and Emotional Empathy." *Journal of Personality and Social Psychology* 52 (1987): 126–33.

DAWES, ROBYN M. "Plato vs. Russell: Hoess and the Relevance of Cognitive Psychology." *Religious Humanism* 22 (1988): 20–26.

DAWES, ROBYN M., ALPHONS J. C. VAN DE KRAGT, and JOHN M. ORBELL. "Cooperation for the Benefit of Us—Not Me or My Conscience." In *Beyond Self-Interest,* edited by Jane Mansbridge. Chicago: University of Chicago Press, 1990.

DAWES, ROBYN M., JEANNE MCTAVISH, and HARRIET SHAKLEE. "Behavior, Communication, and Assumptions About Other People's Behavior in a Commons Dilemma Situation." *Journal of Personality and Social Psychology* 35 (1977): 1–11.

DAWKINS, RICHARD. *The Selfish Gene.* New York: Oxford University Press, 1976.

DECI, EDWARD L., and RICHARD M. RYAN. *Intrinsic Motivation and Self-Determination in Human Behavior.* New York: Plenum, 1985.

DEUTSCH, MORTON. *The Resolution of Conflict: Constructive and Destructive Processes.* New Haven, Conn.: Yale University Press, 1973.

DODGE, KENNETH A. "Social Information-Processing Variables in the Development of Aggression and Altruism in Children." In *Altruism and Aggression: Biological and Social Origins,* edited by Carolyn Zahn-Waxler, E. Mark Cummings, and Ronald Iannotti. Cambridge, England: Cambridge University Press, 1986.

DOSTOYEVSKY, FYODOR. *The Possessed.* Translated by Andrew R. MacAndrew. New York: New American Library, 1962.

DREMAN, S. B., and CHARLES W. GREENBAUM. "Altruism or Reciprocity: Sharing Behavior in Israeli Kindergarten Children." *Child Development* 44 (1973): 61–68.

DUMONT, LOUIS. *Essays on Individualism: Modern Ideology in Anthropological Perspective.* Chicago: University of Chicago Press, 1986.

EAGLY, ALICE H., and MAUREEN CROWLEY. "Gender and Helping Behavior: A Meta-Analytic Review of the Social Psychological Literature." *Psychological Bulletin* 100 (1986): 283–308.

EAGLY, ALICE H., and VALERIE J. STEFFEN. "Gender and Aggressive Behavior: A Meta-Analytic Review of the Social Psychological Literature." *Psychological Bulletin* 100 (1986): 309–30.

EDSALL, THOMAS B., and DAVID A. VISE. "CBS Fight a Litmus Test for Conservatives." *Washington Post,* 31 March 1985, A1, A16.

EHRHARDT, ANKE A. "Biology Is Not Destiny." *Science for the People,* July/August 1986, 12–13.

EISENBERG, LEON. "The *Human* Nature of Human Nature." *Science,* 14 April 1972, 123–28.

EISENBERG, NANCY. *Altruistic Emotion, Cognition, and Behavior.* Hillsdale, N.J.: Lawrence Erlbaum, 1986.

———. "Relationship of Prosocial Moral Reasoning to Altruism, Political Liberalism, and Intelligence." *Developmental Psychology* 15 (1979): 87–89.

EISENBERG, NANCY, ELLEN CAMERON, and KELLY TRYON. "Prosocial Behavior in the Preschool Years: Methodological and Conceptual Issues." In *Development and Maintenance of Prosocial Behavior: International Perspectives on Positive Morality,* edited by Ervin Staub, Daniel Bar-Tal, Jerzy Karylowski, and Janusz Reykowski. New York: Plenum, 1984.

EISENBERG, NANCY, and RICHARD A. FABES. "Examining the Altruism-Empathy Hypothesis with Physiological and Somatic Indices." Paper presented at the annual meeting of the Society of Experimental Social Psychology, Charlottesville, Va., October 1987.

EISENBERG, NANCY, RICHARD A. FABES, DENISE BUSTAMANTE, ROBIN M. MATHY, PAUL A. MILLER, and ERNEST LINDHOLM. "Differentiation of Vicariously Induced Emotional Reactions in Children." *Developmental Psychology* 24 (1988): 237–46.

EISENBERG, NANCY, RICHARD A. FABES, PAUL A. MILLER, JIM FULTZ, RITA SHELL, ROBIN M. MATHY, and RAY R. RENO. "Relation of Sympathy and Personal Distress to Prosocial Behavior: A Multimethod Study." *Journal of Personality and Social Psychology* 57 (1989): 55–66.

EISENBERG-BERG, NANCY, and ELIZABETH GEISHEKER. "Content of Preachings and Power of the Model/Preacher: The Effect on Children's Generosity." *Developmental Psychology* 15 (1979): 168–75.

EISENBERG-BERG, NANCY, and MICHAEL HAND. "The Relationship of Preschoolers' Reasoning about Prosocial Moral Conflicts to Prosocial Behavior." *Child Development* 50 (1979): 356–63.

EISENBERG, NANCY, and RANDY LENNON. "Sex Differences in Empathy and Related Capacities." *Psychological Bulletin* 94 (1983): 100–131.

EISENBERG, NANCY, HEATHER McCREATH, and RANDALL AHN. "Vicarious Emotional Responsiveness and Prosocial Behavior: Their Interrelations in

Young Children." *Personality and Social Psychology Bulletin* 14 (1988): 298–311.

EISENBERG, NANCY, and PAUL A. MILLER. "Empathy, Sympathy, and Altruism: Empirical and Conceptual Links." In *Empathy and Its Development*, edited by Nancy Eisenberg and Janet Strayer. Cambridge, England: Cambridge University Press, 1987.

———. "The Relation of Empathy to Prosocial and Related Behaviors." *Psychological Bulletin* 101 (1987): 91–119.

EISENBERG, NANCY, PAUL A. MILLER, MARK SCHALLER, RICHARD A. FABES, JIM FULTZ, RITA SHELL, and CINDY L. SHEA. "The Role of Sympathy and Altruistic Personality Traits in Helping: A Reexamination." *Journal of Personality* 57 (1989): 41–67.

EISENBERG-BERG, NANCY, and CYNTHIA NEAL. "Children's Moral Reasoning about Their Own Spontaneous Prosocial Behavior." *Developmental Psychology* 15 (1979): 228–29.

EISENBERG, NANCY, MARK SCHALLER, RICHARD A. FABES, DENISE BUSTAMANTE, ROBIN M. MATHY, RITA SHELL, and KELLY RHODES. "Differentiation of Personal Distress and Sympathy in Children and Adults." *Developmental Psychology* 24 (1988): 766–75.

EISENBERG, NANCY, MARK SCHALLER, PAUL A. MILLER, JIM FULTZ, RICHARD A. FABES, and RITA SHELL. "Gender-Related Traits and Helping in a Nonemergency Situation." *Sex Roles* 19 (1988): 605–18.

EISENBERG, NANCY, and JANET STRAYER. "Critical Issues in the Study of Empathy." In *Empathy and Its Development*, edited by Nancy Eisenberg and Janet Strayer. Cambridge, England: Cambridge University Press, 1987.

EISENBERG, NANCY, and JANET STRAYER, EDS. *Empathy and Its Development.* Cambridge, England: Cambridge University Press, 1987.

EISLER, RIANE. *The Chalice and the Blade: Our History, Our Future.* San Francisco: Harper and Row, 1987.

EKSTEIN, RUDOLF. "Psychoanalysis and Education for the Facilitation of Positive Human Qualities." *Journal of Social Issues* 28 (1972): 71–85.

———. "Psychoanalysis, Sympathy, and Altruism." In *Altruism, Sympathy, and Helping: Psychological and Social Principles*, edited by Lauren Wispe. New York: Academic Press, 1978.

ERON, LEONARD D., L. ROWELL HUESMANN, ERIC DUBOW, RICHARD ROMANOFF, and PATTY WARNICK YARMEL. "Aggression and Its Correlates over 22 Years." In *Childhood Aggression and Violence*, edited by David H. Crowell, Ian M. Evans, and Clifford R. O'Donnell. New York: Plenum, 1987.

ETZIONI, AMITAI. *The Moral Dimension: Toward a New Economics.* New York: Free Press, 1988.

FABER, ADELE, and ELAINE MAZLISH. *Siblings without Rivalry.* New York: Norton, 1987.

FABES, RICHARD A., JIM FULTZ, NANCY EISENBERG, TRACI MAY-PLUMLEE, and F.

Scott Christopher. "Effects of Rewards on Children's Prosocial Motivation: A Socialization Study." *Developmental Psychology* 25 (1989): 509–15.

Fausto-Sterling, Anne. *Myths of Gender: Biological Theories about Women and Men.* New York: Basic Books, 1985.

Feinberg, Joel. "Psychological Egoism." In *Reason and Responsibility: Readings in Some Basic Problems of Philosophy,* edited by Joel Feinberg. 2d ed. Encino, Calif.: Dickenson, 1971.

Feldman, M. W., and R. C. Lewontin. "The Heritability Hang-up." *Science,* 19 December 1975, 1163–68.

Fellner, Carl H., and Marshall, John R. "Kidney Donors Revisited." In *Altruism and Helping Behavior: Social, Personality, and Developmental Perspectives,* edited by J. Philippe Rushton and Richard M. Sorrentino. Hillsdale, N.J.: Lawrence Erlbaum, 1981.

Feshbach, Norma Deitch. "Empathy Training: A Field Study in Affective Education." In *Aggression and Behavior Change: Biological and Social Processes,* edited by Seymour Feshbach and Adam Fraczek. New York: Praeger, 1979.

———. "Learning to Care: A Positive Approach to Child Training and Discipline." *Journal of Clinical Child Psychology* 12 (1983): 266–71.

———. "Sex Differences in Empathy and Social Behavior in Children." In *The Development of Prosocial Behavior,* edited by Nancy Eisenberg. New York: Academic Press, 1982.

———. "Studies of Empathic Behavior in Children." In *Progress in Experimental Personality Research,* vol. 8, edited by Brendan A. Maher. New York: Academic Press, 1978.

Feshbach, Norma Deitch, and Seymour Feshbach. "Affective Processes and Academic Achievement." *Child Development* 58 (1987): 1335–47.

———. "Empathy Training and the Regulation of Aggression." *Academic Psychology Bulletin* 4 (1982): 399–413.

———. "The Relationship Between Empathy and Aggression in Two Age Groups." *Developmental Psychology* 1 (1969): 102–7.

Feshbach, Norma Deitch, Seymour Feshbach, Mary Fauvre, and Michael Ballard-Campbell. *Learning to Care: Classroom Activities for Social and Affective Development.* Glenview, Ill.: Scott, Foresman, 1983.

Feshbach, Seymour, and Norma Deitch Feshbach. "Aggression and Altruism: A Personality Perspective." In *Altruism and Aggression: Biological and Social Origins,* edited by Carolyn Zahn-Waxler, E. Mark Cummings, and Ronald Iannotti. Cambridge, England: Cambridge University Press, 1986.

Firth, Roderick. "Ethical Absolutism and the Ideal Observer." 1952. Reprinted in *Readings in Ethical Theory,* edited by Wilfrid Sellars and John Hospers. Englewood Cliffs, N.J.: Prentice-Hall, 1970.

Fisher, Helen. "A Primitive Prescription for Equality." *U.S. News and World Report,* 8 August 1988, 57.

FISKE, EDWARD B. "When Johnny Can't Read His Sixth-Grade Book, an Eighth-Grader Might Be Able to Help." *New York Times,* 30 November 1988, B14.

FLAVELL, JOHN H. *Cognitive Development.* 2d ed. Englewood Cliffs, N.J.: Prentice-Hall, 1985.

———. *The Development of Role-Taking and Communication Skills in Children.* New York: John Wiley, 1968.

FLODERUS-MYRHED, BIRGITTA, NANCY PEDERSEN, and INGRID RASMUSON. "Assessment of Heritability for Personality, Based on a Short-Form of the Eysenck Personality Inventory: A Study of 12,898 Twin Pairs." *Behavior Genetics* 10 (1980): 153–62.

FORD, MARTIN E. "The Construct Validity of Egocentrism." *Psychological Bulletin* 86 (1979): 1169–88.

FOREIGN AFFAIRS DIVISION, CONGRESSIONAL RESEARCH SERVICE, LIBRARY OF CONGRESS. *Background Information on the Use of U.S. Armed Forces in Foreign Countries.* Washington, D.C.: Government Printing Office, 1975.

FOX, ROBIN. "Introduction." In *Biosocial Anthropology,* edited by Robin Fox. New York: John Wiley, 1975.

FRANK, JEROME D. *Persuasion and Healing: A Comparative Study of Psychotherapy.* Rev. ed. New York: Schocken, 1974.

FRANK, ROBERT H. *Passions within Reason: The Strategic Role of the Emotions.* New York: Norton, 1988.

FRANKLIN, DEBORAH. "What a Child Is Given." *New York Times Magazine,* 3 September 1989, 36–49.

FREUD, ANNA. *The Ego and the Mechanisms of Defense.* 1937. Reprint. Rev. ed. Translated by Cecil Baines. New York: International Universities Press, 1966.

FREUD, SIGMUND. *Civilization and Its Discontents.* Translated and edited by James Strachey. New York: Norton, 1961.

———. *Group Psychology and the Analysis of the Ego.* 1921. Reprint. Translated by James Strachey. New York: Norton, 1959.

———. *The Interpretation of Dreams.* Translated and edited by James Strachey. New York: Avon Discus, 1965.

———. *Introductory Lectures on Psychoanalysis.* Translated and edited by James Strachey. New York: Norton, 1966.

———. *Jokes and Their Relation to the Unconscious.* Translated by James Strachey. New York: Norton, 1960.

FREUDENHEIM, MILT. "Employers Act to Stop Family Violence." *New York Times,* 23 August 1988, A1.

FRIEDMAN, MAURICE, ed. *The Worlds of Existentialism: A Critical Reader.* New York: Random House, 1964.

FRIEDRICHS, ROBERT W. "Alter versus Ego: An Exploratory Assessment of Altruism." *American Sociological Review* 25 (1960): 496–508.

FRODI, ANN, JACQUELINE MACAULAY, and PAULINE ROPERT THOME. "Are Women

Always Less Aggressive Than Men?: A Review of the Experimental Literature." *Psychological Bulletin* 84 (1977): 634–60.

FROMING, WILLIAM J., LETICIA ALLEN, and RICHARD JENSEN. "Altruism, Role-Taking, and Self-Awareness: The Acquisition of Norms Governing Altruistic Behavior." *Child Development* 56 (1985): 1223–28.

FROMM, ERICH. *The Anatomy of Human Destructiveness.* New York: Fawcett Crest, 1975.

———. *Man for Himself: An Inquiry into the Psychology of Ethics.* Greenwich, Conn.: Fawcett, 1947.

———. *To Have or to Be?* New York: Harper and Row, 1976.

GALLAGHER, WINIFRED. "Sex and Hormones." *The Atlantic,* March 1988, 77–82.

GARDNER, HOWARD. *Frames of Mind: The Theory of Multiple Intelligences.* New York: Basic Books, 1983.

GEERTZ, CLIFFORD. "Blurred Genres: The Refiguration of Social Thought." *American Scholar,* Spring 1980, 165–79.

———. "From the Native's Point of View: On the Nature of Anthropological Understanding." In *Local Knowledge.* New York: Basic Books, 1983.

GELDER, LINDSAY VAN. "His Rabbit's Voice." *New York Times,* 24 June 1988, C8.

GEORGIANNA, SHARON. "Is a Religious Neighborhood a Good Neighborhood?" *Humboldt Journal of Social Relations* 11 (1984): 1–16.

GERBNER, GEORGE, LARRY GROSS, NANCY SIGNORIELLI, and MICHAEL MORGAN. "Television's Mean World: Violence Profile No. 14–15." Annenberg School of Communications, University of Pennsylvania. September 1986. Mimeograph.

GERT, BERNARD. "Hobbes and Psychological Egoism." *Journal of the History of Ideas* 28 (1967): 503–20.

GHISELIN, MICHAEL T. *The Economy of Nature and the Evolution of Sex.* Berkeley: University of California Press, 1974.

GIBBONS, FREDERICK X., and ROBERT A. WICKLUND. "Self-Focused Attention and Helping Behavior." *Journal of Personality and Social Psychology* 43 (1982): 462–74.

GIBBS, JOHN C. "Social Processes in Delinquency: The Need to Facilitate Empathy as Well as Sociomoral Delinquency." In *Moral Development through Social Interaction,* edited by William M. Kurtines and Jacob L. Gewirtz. New York: John Wiley, 1987.

GIBBS, NANCY R. "Begging: To Give or Not to Give." *Time,* 5 September 1988, 68–74.

GILLIGAN, CAROL. *In a Different Voice: Psychological Theory and Women's Development.* Cambridge, Mass.: Harvard University Press, 1982.

———. "Remapping the Moral Domain: New Images of the Self in Relationship." In *Reconstructing Individualism: Autonomy, Individuality, and the Self in Western Thought,* edited by Thomas C. Heller, Morton Sosna, and David E. Wellbery. Stanford, Calif.: Stanford University Press, 1986.

GILLIGAN, CAROL, and GRANT WIGGINS. "The Origins of Morality in Early Child-
hood Relationships." In *Mapping the Moral Domain,* edited by Carol Gilligan,
Janie Victoria Ward, and Jill McLean Taylor. Cambridge, Mass.: Harvard
University Press, 1988.

GINSBURG, BENSON E. "Developmental Genetics of Behavioral Capacities: The
Nature-Nurture Problem Re-evaluated." *Merrill-Palmer Quarterly* 17 (1971):
187–202.

GINSBURG, BENSON E., and BONNIE F. CARTER. "The Behaviors and the Genetics
of Aggression." In *Essays on Violence,* edited by J. Martin Ramirez, Robert A.
Hinde, and Jo Groebel. Seville, Spain: Publicaciones de la Universidad de
Sevilla, 1987.

GLOCK, CHARLES Y., BENJAMIN B. RINGER, and EARL R. BABBIE. *To Comfort and to
Challenge.* Berkeley: University of California Press, 1967.

GOLDMANN, LUCIEN. *Immanuel Kant.* Translated by Robert Black. London: NLB,
1971.

GOLDSTEIN, ARNOLD P., and GERALD Y. MICHAELS. *Empathy: Development, Training,
and Consequences.* Hillsdale, N.J.: Lawrence Erlbaum, 1985.

GOLDSTEIN, JEFFREY H. "Beliefs about Human Aggression." In *Aggression and War:
Their Social And Biological Bases,* edited by Jo Groebel and Robert A. Hinde.
Cambridge, England: Cambridge University Press, 1988.

GOLDSTEIN, MICHAEL J. "The Family and Psychopathology." *Annual Review of
Psychology* 39 (1988): 283–99.

GOLEMAN, DANIEL. "Sex Roles Reign Powerful as Ever in the Emotions." *New York
Times,* 23 August 1988, C1, C13.

GORDON, D. M. "Caste and Change in Social Insects." In *Oxford Surveys in Evolutionary Biology,* vol. 8, edited by P. H. Harvey and L. Partridge. Oxford:
Oxford University Press, in press.

GORDON, SUZANNE. "The Crisis in Caring." *Boston Globe Magazine,* 10 July 1988.

GORNEY, RODERIC. *The Human Agenda.* New York: Simon and Schuster, 1972.

GOUGH, HARRISON G. "A Sociological Theory of Psychopathy." *American Journal
of Sociology* 53 (1948): 359–66.

GOULD, STEPHEN JAY. "Similarities between the Sexes." Review of *Science and
Gender,* by Ruth Bleier. *New York Times Book Review,* 12 August 1984, 7.

———. "So Cleverly Kind an Animal." In *Ever Since Darwin.* New York: Norton,
1977.

GOULDNER, ALVIN W. "The Norm of Reciprocity: A Preliminary Statement."
American Sociological Review 25 (1960): 161–78.

GRANBERG, DONALD. *Pathways to Peace.* Photocopy.

———. "War Expectancy and the Evaluation of a Specific War." *Conflict Resolution*
13 (1969): 546–49.

———. "War Expectancy: Some Further Studies." *International Journal of Group
Tensions* 5 (1975): 8–25.

GRAVES, NANCY B., and THEODORE D. GRAVES. "The Impact of Modernization on the Personality of a Polynesian People." *Human Organization* 37 (1978): 115–35.

GRAVES, TED. Review of "The Effects of Cooperative Games on Preschool Children's Prosocial Behavior," by Remedios A. Armendi. *International Association for the Study of Cooperation in Education Newsletter,* September 1988, 18.

GREENBERG, JOEL. "Inheriting Mental Illness: Nature and Nurture." *Science News,* 5 January 1980, 10–12.

GROSSMAN, DAVID. *The Yellow Wind.* Translated by Haim Watzman. New York: Farrar, Straus and Giroux, 1988.

GROWALD, EILEEN ROCKEFELLER, and ALLAN LUKS. "Beyond Self." *American Health,* March 1988, 51–53.

GRUEN, ARNO. *The Betrayal of the Self: The Fear of Autonomy in Men and Women.* Translated by Hildegarde and Hunter Hannum. New York: Grove Press, 1988.

GRUEN, RAND J., and GERALD MENDELSOHN. "Emotional Responses to Affective Displays in Others: The Distinction between Empathy and Sympathy." *Journal of Personality and Social Psychology* 51 (1986): 609–14.

GRUSEC, JOAN E., and THEODORE DIX. "The Socialization of Prosocial Behavior: Theory and Reality." In *Altruism and Aggression: Biological and Social Origins,* edited by Carolyn Zahn-Waxler, E. Mark Cummings, and Ronald Iannotti. Cambridge, England: Cambridge University Press, 1986.

GRUSEC, JOAN E., LEON KUCZYNSKI, J. PHILIPPE RUSHTON, and ZITA M. SIMUTI. "Modeling, Direct Instruction, and Attributions: Effects on Altruism." *Developmental Psychology* 14 (1978): 51–57.

GRUSEC, JOAN E., and ERICA REDLER. "Attribution, Reinforcement, and Altruism: A Developmental Analysis." *Developmental Psychology* 16 (1980): 525–34.

HAAS, SCOTT. "The Psychology of Apartheid." Photocopy. Cambridge, Mass.

HALL, JUDITH A. "Gender Effects in Decoding Nonverbal Cues." *Psychological Bulletin* 85 (1978): 845–57.

HALLIE, PHILIP P. *Lest Innocent Blood Be Shed: The Story of the Village of Le Chambon and How Goodness Happened There.* New York: Harper Colophon, 1979.

HALLORAN, RICHARD. "General's Grandson Says Gunfire Thesis Is Backed." *New York Times,* 3 July 1989, 10.

HAMILTON, W. D. "Innate Social Aptitudes of Man: An Approach from Evolutionary Genetics." In *Biosocial Anthropology,* edited by Robin Fox. New York: John Wiley, 1975.

HAMPSHIRE, STUART. "The Illusion of Sociobiology." Review of *On Human Nature,* by Edward O. Wilson. *New York Review of Books,* 12 October 1978, 64–69.

HAMPSON, ELIZABETH, and DOREEN KIMURA. "Reciprocal Effects of Hormonal Fluctuations on Human Motor and Perceptual-Spatial Skills." *Behavioral Neuroscience* 102 (1988): 456–59.

HARDIN, GARRETT. "The Tragedy of the Commons." *Science*, 13 December 1968, 1243–48.

HARE, ROBERT D. *Psychopathy: Theory and Research.* New York: John Wiley, 1970.

HARTMANN, ERNEST. *The Nightmare: The Psychology and Biology of Terrifying Dreams.* New York: Basic Books, 1984.

HEIDEGGER, MARTIN. *Being and Time.* Translated by John Macquarrie and Edward Robinson. New York: Harper and Row, 1962.

HELLER, THOMAS C., MORTON SOSNA, and DAVID E. WELLBERY, eds. *Reconstructing Individualism: Autonomy, Individuality, and the Self in Western Thought.* Stanford, Calif.: Stanford University Press, 1986.

HENDERSON, LYNNE N. "Legality and Empathy." *Michigan Law Review* 85 (1987): 1574–1653.

HIRSCHMAN, ALBERT O. *Shifting Involvements: Private Interest and Public Action.* Princeton, N.J.: Princeton University Press, 1982.

HOBFOLL, STEVAN E. "Personal Characteristics of the College Volunteer." *American Journal of Community Psychology* 8 (1980): 503–6.

HODGES, DONALD CLARK. "Psychological Egoism: A Note on Professor Lemos' Discussion." *Philosophy and Phenomenological Research* 22 (1961): 246–48.

HODGKINSON, VIRGINIA A. *Motivations for Giving and Volunteering: A Selected Review of the Literature.* New York: Foundation Center, forthcoming.

HOFFMAN, LOIS WLADIS. "The Changing Genetics/Socialization Balance." *Journal of Social Issues* 41 (1985): 127–48.

HOFFMAN, MARTIN L. "Altruistic Behavior and the Parent-Child Relationship." *Journal of Personality and Social Psychology* 31 (1975): 937–43.

———. "The Contribution of Empathy to Justice and Moral Development." In *Empathy and Its Development,* edited by Nancy Eisenberg and Janet Strayer. Cambridge, England: Cambridge University Press, 1987.

———. "The Development of Empathy." In *Altruism and Helping Behavior: Social, Personality, and Developmental Perspectives,* edited by J. Philippe Rushton and Richard M. Sorrentino. Hillsdale, N.J.: Lawrence Erlbaum, 1981.

———. "Development of Prosocial Motivation: Empathy and Guilt." In *The Development of Prosocial Behavior,* edited by Nancy Eisenberg. New York: Academic Press, 1982.

———. "Developmental Synthesis of Affect and Cognition and Its Implications for Altruistic Motivation." *Developmental Psychology* 11 (1975): 607–22.

———. "Empathy and Prosocial Activism." In *Social and Moral Values: Individual and Societal Perspectives,* edited by Nancy Eisenberg, Janusz Reykowski, and Ervin Staub. Hillsdale, N.J.: Lawrence Erlbaum, 1989.

———. "Empathy, Social Cognition, and Moral Action." In *Moral Behavior and Development: Advances in Theory, Research, and Applications,* edited by William M. Kurtines and Jacob L. Gewirtz. Hillsdale, N.J.: Lawrence Erlbaum, 1989.

———. "Interaction of Affect and Cognition in Empathy." In *Emotions, Cognition, and Behavior,* edited by Carroll E. Izard, Jerome Kagan, and Robert B. Zajonc. Cambridge, England: Cambridge University Press, 1984.

———. "Is Altruism Part of Human Nature?" *Journal of Personality and Social Psychology* 40 (1981): 121–37.

———. "Sex Differences in Empathy and Related Behaviors." *Psychological Bulletin* 84 (1977): 712–22.

HOGAN, ROBERT. "Theoretical Egocentrism and the Problem of Compliance." *American Psychologist* 30 (1975): 533–40.

HOLMES, STEPHEN. "The Secret History of Self-Interest." In *Beyond Self-Interest,* edited by Jane Mansbridge. Chicago: University of Chicago Press, 1990.

HONORE, ANTONY M. "Law, Morals, and Rescue." In *The Good Samaritan and the Law,* edited by James M. Ratcliffe. 1966. Reprint. Gloucester, Mass.: Peter Smith, 1981.

HORNEY, KAREN. *Neurosis and Human Growth: The Struggle toward Self-Realization.* New York: Norton, 1950.

HORNSTEIN, HARVEY A. *Cruelty and Kindness: A New Look at Aggression and Altruism.* Englewood Cliffs, N.J.: Prentice-Hall, 1976.

HORNSTEIN, HARVEY A., ELIZABETH LaKIND, GLADYS FRANKEL, and STELLA MANNE. "Effects of Knowledge about Remote Social Events on Prosocial Behavior, Social Conception, and Mood." *Journal of Personality and Social Psychology* 32 (1975): 1038–46.

HOWES, CAROLLEE, and ROBERT ELDREDGE. "Responses of Abused, Neglected, and Non-Maltreated Children to the Behaviors of Their Peers." *Journal of Applied Developmental Psychology* 6 (1985): 261–70.

HUBBARD, RUTH. "The Theory and Practice of Genetic Reductionism: From Mendel's Laws to Genetic Engineering." In *Towards a Liberatory Biology,* edited by Steven Rose. London: Allison and Busby, 1982.

HUME, DAVID. "Morality, Self-Love, and Benevolence." 1751. In *Egoism and Altruism,* edited by Ronald D. Milo. Belmont, Calif.: Wadsworth, 1973.

———. *A Treatise of Human Nature.* Oxford: Clarendon Press, 1888.

HUMPHREY, NICHOLAS. "An Immodest Proposal." In *In a Dark Time,* edited by Robert Jay Lifton and Nicholas Humphrey. Cambridge, Mass.: Harvard University Press, 1984.

HYDE, JANET SHIBLEY, ELIZABETH FENNEMA, and SUSAN J. LAMON. "Gender Differences in Mathematics Performance: A Meta-Analysis." *Psychological Bulletin,* in press.

HYDE, JANET SHIBLEY, and MARCIA C. LINN. "Gender Differences in Verbal Ability: A Meta-Analysis." *Psychological Bulletin* 104 (1988): 53–69.

HYDE, LEWIS. *The Gift: Imagination and the Erotic Life of Property.* New York: Vintage, 1983.

IANNOTTI, RONALD J. "Effect of Role-Taking Experiences on Role Taking, Empathy, Altruism, and Aggression." *Developmental Psychology* 14 (1978): 119–24.

ISEN, ALICE M. "Success, Failure, Attention, and Reaction to Others: The Warm Glow of Success." *Journal of Personality and Social Psychology* 15 (1970): 294–301.

JANOFSKY, MICHAEL, and PETER ALFANO. "Victory at Any Cost: Drug Pressure Growing." *New York Times,* 21 November 1988, A1, C13.

JASPERS, KARL. *Reason and Existenz.* Translated by William Earle. New York: Noonday Press, 1955.

JENCKS, CHRISTOPHER. "Varieties of Altruism." In *Beyond Self-Interest,* edited by Jane Mansbridge. Chicago: University of Chicago Press, 1990.

JOHNSON, DAVID W. "Affective Perspective Taking and Cooperative Predisposition." *Developmental Psychology* 11 (1975): 869–70.

JOHNSON, DAVID W., and FRANK P. JOHNSON. *Joining Together: Group Theory and Group Skills.* 3d ed. Englewood Cliffs, N.J.: Prentice-Hall, 1987.

JOHNSON, DAVID W., and ROGER T. JOHNSON. *Cooperation and Competition.* Edina, Minn.: Interaction Book Co., 1989.

———. "The Socialization and Achievement Crisis: Are Cooperative Learning Experiences the Solution?" In *Applied Social Psychology Annual 4,* edited by L. Bickman. Beverly Hills, Calif.: Sage, 1983.

JOHNSON, DAVID W., ROGER T. JOHNSON, JEANETTE JOHNSON, and DOUGLAS ANDERSON. "Effects of Cooperative versus Individualized Instruction on Student Prosocial Behavior, Attitudes toward Learning, and Achievement." *Journal of Educational Psychology* 68 (1976): 446–52.

JOHNSON, DAVID W., ROGER T. JOHNSON, and GEOFFREY MARUYAMA. "Interdependence and Interpersonal Attraction among Heterogeneous and Homogeneous Individuals: A Theoretical Formulation and a Meta-analysis of the Research." *Review of Educational Research* 53 (1983): 5–54.

JOHNSON, DIRK. "Police Looking Closer at Unarresting Officer." *New York Times,* 12 August 1988, A8.

JORDAN, JUDITH V. "Clarity in Connection: Empathic Knowing, Desire and Sexuality." Stone Center for Developmental Services and Studies, no. 29. Wellesley, Mass. 1987.

———. "Empathy and Self Boundaries." Stone Center for Developmental Services and Studies, no. 16. Wellesley, Mass. 1984.

JOURARD, SIDNEY M. *The Transparent Self.* Rev. ed. New York: D. Van Nostrand, 1971.

JULIAN, JAMES W., DOYLE W. BISHOP, and FRED E. FIEDLER. "Quasi-Therapeutic Effects of Intergroup Competition." *Journal of Personality and Social Psychology* 3 (1966): 321–27.

KAGAN, JEROME. *The Nature of the Child.* New York: Basic Books, 1984.

———. *Unstable Ideas: Temperament, Cognition, and Self.* Cambridge, Mass.: Harvard University Press, 1989.

KAMIN, LEON. "Are There Genes for Crime?" *Science for the People,* July/August 1986, 8–10.

————. "Is Crime in the Genes? The Answer May Depend on Who Chooses What Evidence." Review of *Crime and Human Nature,* by James Q. Wilson and Richard J. Herrnstein. *Scientific American,* February 1986, 22–27.

KANT, IMMANUEL. "The Foundation of Morals." In *Ethics and Metaethics: Readings in Ethical Philosophy,* edited by Raziel Abelson. New York: St. Martin's Press, 1963.

————. "Morality and the Duty of Love toward Other Men." In *Egoism and Altruism,* edited by Ronald D. Milo. Belmont, Calif.: Wadsworth, 1973.

KANTER, DONALD L. and PHILIP H. MIRVIS. *The Cynical Americans: Living and Working in an Age of Discontent and Disillusion.* San Fancisco: Jossey-Bass, 1989.

KAPLAN, DAVID A. "Haunting Chronicle of a Death Foretold." *New York Times,* 22 May 1988, 38H.

KAPLAN, JOHN. "A Legal Look at Prosocial Behavior: What Can Happen If One Tries to Help or Fails to Help Another." In *Altruism, Sympathy, and Helping: Psychological and Social Principles,* edited by Lauren Wispe. New York: Academic Press, 1978.

KARYLOWSKI, JERZY. "Focus of Attention and Altruism: Endocentric and Exocentric Sources of Altruistic Behavior." In *Development and Maintenance of Prosocial Behavior: International Perspectives on Positive Morality,* edited by Ervin Staub, Daniel Bar-Tal, Jerzy Karylowski, and Janusz Reykowski. New York: Plenum, 1984.

————. "Self-esteem, Similarity, Liking and Helping." *Personality and Social Psychology Bulletin* 2 (1976): 71–74.

KEEN, ERNEST. *A Primer in Phenomenological Psychology.* New York: Holt, Rinehart and Winston, 1975.

KEEN, SAM. *Faces of the Enemy: Reflections of the Hostile Imagination.* San Francisco: Harper and Row, 1986.

KEGAN, ROBERT. *The Evolving Self: Problem and Process in Human Development.* Cambridge, Mass.: Harvard University Press, 1982.

KELMAN, HERBERT C. "Violence without Moral Restraint: Reflections on the Dehumanization of Victims and Victimizers." *Journal of Social Issues* 29 (1973): 25–61.

KELMAN, STEVEN. "Why Public Ideas Matter." In *The Power of Public Ideas,* edited by Robert B. Reich. Cambridge, Mass.: Ballinger, 1988.

KIMURA, DOREEN. "Hormonal Influences on Cognitive/Motor Function in Postmenopausal Women: The Effect of Hormone Replacement Therapy." Photocopy. London, Ontario. 1988.

KING, MARK, LEOPOLD O. WALDER, and STANLEY PAVEY. "Personality Change as a Function of Volunteer Experience in a Psychiatric Hospital." *Journal of Consulting and Clinical Psychology* 35 (1970): 423–25.

KITCHER, PHILIP. *Vaulting Ambition: Sociobiology and the Quest for Human Nature.* Cambridge, Mass.: MIT Press, 1985.

KLAMA, JOHN, ed. [pseudonym for John Durant, Peter Klopfer, and Susan

Oyama]. *Aggression: The Myth of the Beast Within.* New York: John Wiley, 1988.

KNOX, RICHARD A. "Interest Grows in Serotonin-Violence Link." *Boston Globe,* 12 December 1988, 29–30.

———. "Study: Boys, Girls about Equal in Learning Math." *Boston Globe,* 14 February 1988, 49.

KOESTLER, ARTHUR. *Darkness at Noon.* Translated by Daphne Hardy. 1941. New York: Bantam, 1966.

———. "The Limits of Man and His Predicament." In *The Limits of Human Nature,* edited by Jonathan Benthall. London: Allen Lane, 1973.

KOHLBERG, LAWRENCE. "Conscience as Principled Responsibility." In *Conscience: An Interdisciplinary View,* edited by G. Zecha and P. Weingartner. Dordrecht, Holland: D. Reidel, 1987.

———. *The Philosophy of Moral Development: Moral Stages and the Idea of Justice.* Vol. 1 of *Essays on Moral Development.* San Francisco: Harper and Row, 1981.

KOHLBERG, LAWRENCE, DWIGHT BOYD, and CHARLES LEVINE. "The Return of Stage 6: Its Principle and Moral Point of View." In *Zur Bestimmung der Moral Philosophische und sozialwissenschaftliche Beitrage zur Moralforschung,* edited by W. Edelstein and G. Nunner-Winkler. Frankfurt: Suhrkamp Verlag, 1986.

KOHN, ALFIE. "Altruism within Egoism." Review of *Passions within Reason: The Strategic Role of the Emotions,* by Robert H. Frank. *The Nation,* 29 May 1989, 742–44.

———. "Existentialism Here and Now." *The Georgia Review* 38 (1984): 381–97.

———. *No Contest: The Case against Competition.* Boston: Houghton Mifflin, 1986.

———. "P Is for Prosocial Teaching." *Boston Globe Magazine,* 6 November 1988, 24–25, 61–71.

———. "Suffer the Restless Children." *The Atlantic,* November 1989, 90–100.

KOLM, SERGE-CHRISTOPHE. "Altruism and Efficiency." *Ethics* 94 (1983): 18–65.

KONNER, MELVIN. "The Aggressors." *New York Times Magazine,* 14 August 1988, 33–34.

———. *The Tangled Wing.* New York: Harper and Row, 1982.

KOSHLAND, DANIEL E., JR. "Nature, Nurture, and Behavior." *Science,* 20 March 1987, 1445.

KRAUTHAMMER, CHARLES. "How to Save the Homeless Mentally Ill." *New Republic,* 8 February 1988, 22–25.

KREBS, DENNIS. "Empathy and Altruism." *Journal of Personality and Social Psychology* 32 (1975): 1134–46.

KREBS, DENNIS, and KATHY DENTON. "Moral Justification: In the Service of Self." In *From Moral Action to Judgment and Back: The Relationships between Action and Stage,* edited by Michael L. Commons, Maria A. Broderick, Jacob L. Gewirtz, and Lawrence Kohlberg. In preparation.

KREBS, DENNIS, and CRISTINE RUSSELL. "Role-Taking and Altruism: When You Put Yourself in the Shoes of Another, Will They Take You to Their Owner's

Aid?" In *Altruism and Helping Behavior: Social, Personality, and Developmental Perspectives,* edited by J. Philippe Rushton and Richard M. Sorrentino. Hillsdale, N.J.: Lawrence Erlbaum, 1981.

KREBS, DENNIS, and BERT STURRUP. "Role-Taking Ability and Altruistic Behaviour in Elementary School Children." *Journal of Moral Education* 11 (1982): 94–100.

KREBS, DENNIS, and FRANK VAN HESTEREN. "The Development of Altruism." Photocopy.

KRUEGER, LESLEY. "The Rise of the New Psychiatry." *Maclean's,* 15 February 1982, 45–53.

KUNDERA, MILAN. *The Unbearable Lightness of Being.* Translated by Michael Henry Heim. New York: Harper and Row, 1984.

KURDEK, LAWRENCE A. "Relationship between Cognitive Perspective Taking and Teachers' Ratings of Children's Classroom Behavior in Grades One through Four." *Journal of Genetic Psychology* 132 (1978): 21–27.

KUTNER, LAWRENCE. "Empathy Must Be Learned, Just Like Any Other Skill." *New York Times,* 17 March 1988, C8.

LACOSTE-UTAMSING, CHRISTINE DE, and RALPH L. HOLLOWAY. "Sexual Dimorphism in the Human Corpus Callosum." *Science,* 25 June 1982, 1431–32.

LAKIND, ELIZABETH, and HARVEY A. HORNSTEIN. "The Effect of Mood and Social Outlook on Hypothetical Juridic Decisions." *Journal of Applied Social Psychology* 9 (1979): 548–59.

LANDERS, ANN. "Parental Guilt Trip." *Boston Globe,* 27 July 1976, 17.

———. "Role of Genetics Often Overlooked." *Boston Globe,* 23 May 1988, 12.

LANDES, WILLIAM M., and RICHARD A. POSNER. "Altruism in Law and Economics." *American Economic Review* 68 (1978): 417–21.

LANZETTA, JOHN T., and BASIL G. ENGLIS. "Expectations of Cooperation and Competition and Their Effects on Observers' Vicarious Emotional Responses." *Journal of Personality and Social Psychology* 56 (1989): 543–54.

LARRIEU, JULIE, and PAUL MUSSEN. "Some Personality and Motivational Correlates of Children's Prosocial Behavior." *Journal of Genetic Psychology* 147 (1986): 529–42.

LATANE, BIBB, and JOHN DARLEY. *The Unresponsive Bystander: Why Doesn't He Help?* New York: Appleton-Century-Crofts, 1970.

LAZAR, MICHAEL. "Not My Problem." *New York Times,* 30 September 1988, A35.

LEAKEY, RICHARD, and ROGER LEWIN. *Origins.* New York: Dutton, 1978.

LEAR, MARTHA WEINMAN. "The Cheapskate Ploy." *New York Times Magazine,* 30 October 1988, 54, 56.

———. "Redefining Anxiety." *New York Times Magazine,* 31 July 1988, 30–31.

LEARY, WARREN E. "U.S. Urged to Fight Infant Mortality." *New York Times,* 5 August 1988, D17.

LEFKOWITZ, MONROE M., LEOPOLD O. WALDER, and LEONARD D. ERON. "Punishment, Identification, and Aggression." *Merrill-Palmer Quarterly* 9 (1963): 159–74.

LeMARE, LUCY, and DENNIS KREBS. "Perspective-Taking and Styles of (Pro) Social Behavior in Elementary School Children." *Academic Psychology Bulletin* 5 (1983): 289–97.

LEMOS, RAMON M. "Psychological Egoism." *Philosophy and Phenomenological Research* 20 (1960): 540–46.

LENNON, RANDY, and NANCY EISENBERG. "Gender and Age Differences in Empathy and Sympathy." In *Empathy and Its Development*, edited by Nancy Eisenberg and Janet Strayer. Cambridge, England: Cambridge University Press, 1987.

LEPPER, MARK R., and DAVID GREENE, eds. *The Hidden Costs of Rewards.* Hillsdale, N.J.: Lawrence Erlbaum, 1978.

LERNER, MELVIN J. "The Desire for Justice and Reactions to Victims." In *Altruism and Helping Behavior*, edited by J. Macaulay and L. Berkowitz. New York: Academic Press, 1970.

———. "The Justice Motive in Human Relations and the Economic Model of Man: A Radical Analysis of Facts and Fictions." In *Cooperation and Helping Behavior: Theories and Research*, edited by Valerian J. Derlega and Janusz Grzelak. New York: Academic Press, 1982.

LERNER, MELVIN J., and JAMES R. MEINDL. "Justice and Altruism." In *Altruism and Helping Behavior: Social, Personality, and Developmental Perspectives*, edited by J. Philippe Rushton and Richard M. Sorrentino. Hillsdale, N.J.: Lawrence Erlbaum, 1981.

LEWONTIN, RICHARD C. "The Analysis of Variance and the Analysis of Causes." *American Journal of Human Genetics* 26 (1974): 400–411.

———. "Sleight of Hand." Review of *Genes, Mind, and Culture: The Coevolutionary Process*, by Charles J. Lumsden and Edward O. Wilson. *The Sciences*, July/August 1981, 23–26.

LEWONTIN, RICHARD C., STEVEN ROSE, and LEON KAMIN. *Not in Our Genes.* New York: Pantheon, 1984.

LICHTENSTEIN, GRACE. "Fund Backs Controversial Study of 'Racial Betterment.' " *New York Times,* 11 December 1977, 76.

LIDZ, THEODORE, and SIDNEY BLATT. "Critique of the Danish-American Studies of the Biological and Adoptive Relatives of Adoptees Who Became Schizophrenic." *American Journal of Psychiatry* 140 (1983): 426–35.

LIDZ, THEODORE, SIDNEY BLATT, and BARRY COOK. "Critique of the Danish-American Studies of the Adopted-Away Offspring of Schizophrenic Parents." *American Journal of Psychiatry* 138 (1981): 1063–68.

LIFTON, ROBERT JAY. "Existential Evil." In *Sanctions for Evil*, edited by Nevitt Sanford, Craig Comstock, et al. San Francisco: Jossey-Bass, 1971.

LINDSEY, ROBERT. "Promises to Keep." *New York Times Magazine,* 24 July 1988.

LINN, MARCIA C., and JANET S. HYDE. "Gender, Mathematics, and Science." *Educational Researcher,* in press.

LOCKARD, J. S., L. L. McDONALD, D. A. CLIFFORD, and R. MARTINEZ. "Panhandling: Sharing of Resources." *Science,* 30 January 1976, 406–7.

LODGE, ARTHUR. "Taxes and Charity." *Journal of Accountancy,* May 1988, 146.

LONDON, PERRY. "The Rescuers: Motivational Hypotheses about Christians Who Saved Jews from the Nazis." In *Altruism and Helping Behavior,* edited by J. Macaulay and L. Berkowitz. New York: Academic Press, 1970.

LOOFT, WILLIAM R. "Egocentrism and Social Interaction across the Life Span." *Psychological Bulletin* 78 (1972): 73–92.

LORENZ, KONRAD. *On Aggression.* Translated by Marjorie Kerr Wilson. New York: Harcourt Brace Jovanovich, 1966.

LOTTMAN, HERBERT R. *Albert Camus.* New York: George Braziller, 1980.

LUKES, STEVEN. "Conclusion." In *The Category of the Person: Anthropology, Philosophy, History,* edited by Michael Carrithers, Steven Collins, and Steven Lukes. Cambridge, England: Cambridge University Press, 1985.

LUTZ, MARK A., and KENNETH LUX. *Humanistic Economics: The New Challenge.* New York: Bootstrap Press, 1988.

MACINTYRE, ALASDAIR. "Egoism and Altruism." In *Encyclopedia of Philosophy,* edited by Paul Edwards. New York: Macmillan, 1967.

MACPHERSON, C. B. *The Political Theory of Possessive Individualism: Hobbes to Locke.* New York: Oxford University Press, 1962.

MALITZ, SIDNEY, and HAROLD A. SACKHEIM, eds. *ECT: Clinical and Basic Research Issues.* Annals of the New York Academy of Sciences, vol. 462. New York: New York Academy of Sciences, 1986.

MANNARINO, ANTHONY P. "Friendship Patterns and Altruistic Behavior in Preadolescent Males." *Developmental Psychology* 12 (1976): 555–56.

MANSBRIDGE, JANE. *Beyond Adversary Democracy.* Chicago: University of Chicago Press, 1983.

———. "The Rise and Fall of Self-Interest in the Explanation of Political Life." In *Beyond Self-Interest,* edited by Jane Mansbridge. Chicago: University of Chicago Press, 1990.

———. "On the Relation of Altruism and Self-Interest." In *Beyond Self-Interest,* edited by Jane Mansbridge. Chicago: University of Chicago Press, 1990.

MARCEL, GABRIEL. *Man against Mass Society.* 1951. Reprint. Translated by G. S. Fraser. South Bend, Ind.: Gateway, 1978.

MARGOLIS, HOWARD. *Selfishness, Altruism, and Rationality.* Cambridge, England: Cambridge University Press, 1982.

MARIN, PETER. "The New Narcissism." *Harper's,* October 1975, 45–56.

MARSHALL, S. L. A. *Men against Fire.* New York: William Morrow, 1947.

MARTIN, GRACE B., and RUSSELL D. CLARK III. "Distress Crying in Neonates: Species and Peer Specificity." *Developmental Psychology* 18 (1982): 3–9.

MARWELL, GERALD. "Altruism and the Problem of Collective Action." In *Coopera-

tion and Helping Behavior: Theories and Research, edited by Valerian J. Derlega and Janusz Grzelak. New York: Academic Press, 1982.

MARWELL, GERALD, and RUTH E. AMES. "Economists Free Ride, Does Anyone Else?" *Journal of Public Economics* 15 (1981): 295–310.

MARX, KARL. *Capital.* Vol. 1, *A Critical Analysis of Capitalist Production.* 1887. Reprint. Translated by Samuel Moore and Edward Aveling. New York: International, 1967.

———. *The Economic and Philosophic Manuscripts of 1844.* Translated by Martin Milligan. New York: International, 1964.

———. "On the Jewish Question." In *The Marx-Engels Reader,* edited by Robert C. Tucker. 2d ed. New York: Norton, 1978.

MASLOW, ABRAHAM H. *The Farther Reaches of Human Nature.* New York: Penguin, 1976.

———. *The Psychology of Science: A Reconnaissance.* Chicago: Henry Regnery, 1966.

———. *Toward a Psychology of Being.* 2d ed. New York: D. Van Nostrand, 1968.

MATTHEWS, KAREN A., C. DANIEL BATSON, JOSEPH HORN, and RAY H. ROSENMAN. "'Principles in His Nature Which Interest Him in the Fortune of Others . . .': The Heritability of Empathic Concern for Others." *Journal of Personality* 49 (1981): 237–47.

MAUGH, THOMAS H. II. "Studies Tie Sex Hormones to Women's Level of Skills." *Los Angeles Times,* 17 November 1988, 1, 33.

MAUSS, MARCEL. "A Category of the Human Mind: The Notion of Person; the Notion of Self." 1938. Reprinted in *The Category of the Person: Anthropology, Philosophy, History,* edited by Michael Carrithers, Steven Collins, and Steven Lukes. Cambridge, England: Cambridge University Press, 1985.

MAY, ROLLO. *The Meaning of Anxiety.* Rev. ed. New York: Norton, 1977.

———. *Power and Innocence: A Search for the Sources of Violence.* New York: Norton, 1972.

———. "The Problem of Evil: An Open Letter to Carl Rogers." *Journal of Humanistic Psychology* 22 (1982): 10–21.

MAYEROFF, MILTON. *On Caring.* New York: Harper and Row, 1971.

McCAIN, NINA. "Fighting Poverty: Finding What Works." *Boston Globe,* 8 November 1988, 25, 27.

McCLELLAND, DAVID C. "Some Reflections on the Two Psychologies of Love." *Journal of Personality* 54 (1986): 334–53.

McCLINTOCK, MARTHA K. "Menstrual Synchrony and Suppression." *Nature,* 22 January 1971, 244–45.

McLOUGHLIN, MERRILL. "Men vs. Women." *U.S. News and World Report,* 8 August 1988, 50–56.

McPHERSON, MICHAEL S. "Limits on Self-Seeking: The Role of Morality in Economic Life." In *Neoclassical Political Economy,* edited by David C. Colander. Cambridge, Mass.: Ballinger, 1984.

MEAD, GEORGE HERBERT. *Mind, Self, and Society from the Standpoint of a Social Behav-*

iorist. Vol. 1 of *Works of George Herbert Mead,* edited by Charles W. Morris. Chicago: University of Chicago Press, 1934.

MEHLER, BARRY. "The New Eugenics: Academic Racism in the U.S. Today." In *Biology as Destiny: Scientific Fact or Social Bias?,* edited by the Science for the People Sociobiology Study Group. Cambridge, Mass.: Science for the People, 1984.

MELSON, GAIL F., and ALAN FOGEL. "Learning to Care." *Psychology Today,* January 1988, 39–45.

MELVILLE, HERMAN. "Bartleby." In *Billy Budd, Sailor and Other Stories.* Middlesex, England: Penguin, 1967.

MENCIUS. *Mencius,* edited and translated by W.A.C.H. Dobson. Toronto: University of Toronto Press, 1963.

MEYER, JOHN W. "Myths of Socialization and of Personality." In *Reconstructing Individualism: Autonomy, Individuality, and the Self in Western Thought,* edited by Thomas C. Heller, Morton Sosna, and David E. Wellbery. Stanford, Calif.: Stanford University Press, 1986.

MIDGLEY, MARY. "Gene-juggling." *Philosophy* 54 (1979): 439–58.

———. "Sex and Personal Identity." *Encounter,* June 1984, 50–55.

MIDLARSKY, ELIZABETH. "Competence and Helping: Notes toward a Model." In *Development and Maintenance of Prosocial Behavior: International Perspectives on Positive Morality,* edited by Ervin Staub, Daniel Bar-Tal, Jerzy Karylowski, and Janusz Reykowski. New York: Plenum, 1984.

MILGRAM, STANLEY. "The Experience of Living in Cities." *Science,* 13 March 1970, 1461–68.

———. *Obedience to Authority.* New York: Harper Colophon, 1975.

MILL, JOHN STUART. "Three Essays on Religion." In *Essays on Ethics, Religion, and Society.* Vol. 10 of *Collected Works of John Stuart Mill,* edited by J. M. Robson. Toronto: University of Toronto Press, 1969.

MILLER, ALICE. *For Your Own Good: Hidden Cruelty in Child-Rearing and the Roots of Violence.* New York: Farrar, Straus and Giroux, 1984.

MILLER, DALE T. "Personal Deserving versus Justice for Others: An Exploration of the Justice Motive." *Journal of Experimental Social Psychology* 13 (1977): 1–13.

MILLER, JEAN BAKER. *Toward a New Psychology of Women.* Boston: Beacon, 1976.

MILLER, PAUL A., and NANCY EISENBERG. "The Relation of Empathy to Aggressive and Externalizing/Antisocial Behavior." *Psychological Bulletin* 103 (1988): 324–44.

MILLS, C. WRIGHT. *The Causes of World War Three.* Armonk, N.Y.: M. E. Sharpe, 1960.

MILO, RONALD D. Introduction to *Egoism and Altruism,* edited by Ronald D. Milo. Belmont, Calif.: Wadsworth, 1973.

MINOW, MARTHA. "Justice Engendered." *Harvard Law Review* 101 (1987): 10–95.

MITCHELL, HERMAN E., and DONN BYRNE. "The Defendant's Dilemma: Effects of

Jurors' Attitudes and Authoritarianism on Judicial Decisions." *Journal of Personality and Social Psychology* 25 (1973): 123–29.

MONTAGU, ASHLEY. *On Being Human.* New York: Hawthorn, 1966.

———. *The Nature of Human Aggression.* Oxford: Oxford University Press, 1976.

MONTAGU, ASHLEY, ed. *Learning Non-Aggression: The Experience of Non-Literate Societies.* New York: Oxford University Press, 1978.

MOORE, BERT S., BILL UNDERWOOD, and D. L. ROSENHAN. "Affect and Altruism." *Developmental Psychology* 8 (1973): 99–104.

MOORE, CELIA L., and GILDA A. MORELLI. "Mother Rats Interact Differently with Male and Female Offspring." *Journal of Comparative and Physiological Psychology* 93 (1979): 677–84.

MOYER, K. E. *Violence and Aggression: A Physiological Perspective.* New York: Paragon House, 1987.

MURSTEIN, BERNARD I., MARY CERRETO, and MARCIA G. MACDONALD. "A Theory and Investigation of the Effect of Exchange-Orientation on Marriage and Friendship." *Journal of Marriage and the Family* 39 (1977): 543–48.

MUSSEN, PAUL, and NANCY EISENBERG. *The Roots of Prosocial Behavior in Children.* Cambridge, England: Cambridge University Press, 1989.

NAGEL, THOMAS. "Comment." In *Altruism, Morality, and Economic Theory,* edited by Edmund S. Phelps. New York: Russell Sage Foundation, 1975.

———. *The Possibility of Altruism.* 1970. Reprint. Princeton, N.J.: Princeton University Press, 1978.

NAIDU, USHA SIDANA. *Altruism in Children: A Cross-Sectional Study of Boys in a Welfare Residential Institution.* Bombay, India: Tata Institute of Social Sciences, 1980.

NELSON, LINDEN L., and SPENCER KAGAN. "Competition: The Star-Spangled Scramble." *Psychology Today,* September 1972, 53–56, 90–91.

NIELSEN, KAI. "Egoism in Ethics." *Philosophy and Phenomenological Research* 19 (1959): 502–10.

———. "The Voices of Egoism." *Philosophical Studies* 30 (1984): 83–107.

NODDINGS, NEL. *Caring: A Feminine Approach to Ethics and Moral Education.* Berkeley: University of California Press, 1984.

NORMAN, RALPH D., and PATRICIA AINSWORTH. "The Relationships among Projection, Empathy, Reality, and Adjustment, Operationally Defined." *Journal of Consulting Psychology* 18 (1954): 53–58.

O'CONNELL, BRIAN. "Already, 1,000 Points of Light." *New York Times,* 25 January 1989, A23.

O'CONNOR, JOHN J. "Pop Culture as Insults and Threatened Violence." *New York Times,* 14 March 1989, C22.

OLINER, PEARL M. "Legitimating and Implementing Prosocial Education." *Humboldt Journal of Social Relations* 13 (1985–86): 391–410.

OLINER, SAMUEL P., and PEARL M. OLINER. *The Altruistic Personality: Rescuers of Jews in Nazi Europe.* New York: Free Press, 1988.

ORREN, GARY R. "Beyond Self-Interest." In *The Power of Public Ideas,* edited by Robert B. Reich. Cambridge, Mass.: Ballinger, 1988.

ORTEGA Y GASSET, JOSÉ. *Man and People.* Translated by Willard R. Trask. New York: Norton, 1957.

ORWELL, GEORGE. "Homage to Catalonia." Excerpted in *In a Dark Time,* edited by Robert Jay Lifton and Nicholas Humphrey. Cambridge, Mass.: Harvard University Press, 1984.

PANKSEPP, JAAK. "The Psychobiology of Prosocial Behaviors: Separation Distress, Play, and Altruism." In *Altruism and Aggression: Biological and Social Origins,* edited by Carolyn Zahn-Waxler, E. Mark Cummings, and Ronald Iannotti. Cambridge, England: Cambridge University Press, 1986.

PASSELL, PETER. "Why It Pays to Be Generous." *New York Times,* 25 January 1989, D2.

PASTORE, NICHOLAS. *The Nature-Nurture Controversy.* New York: King's Crown Press, 1949.

PATERSON, R. W. K. "Psychological Egoism." *Ratio* 6 (1964): 92–103.

PAULHUS, DELROY L., DAVID R. SHAFFER, and LESLIE L. DOWNING. "Effects of Making Blood Donor Motives Salient upon Donor Retention: A Field Experiment." *Personality and Social Psychology Bulletin* 3 (1977): 99–102.

PERLOFF, ROBERT. "Self-Interest and Personal Responsibility Redux." *American Psychologist* 42 (1987): 3–11.

PERRETT, ROY W. "Egoism, Altruism, and Intentionalism in Buddhist Ethics." *Journal of Indian Philosophy* 15 (1987): 71–85.

PETERSON, LIZETTE. "Influence of Age, Task Competence, and Responsibility Focus on Children's Altruism." *Developmental Psychology* 19 (1983): 141–48.

———. "Role of Donor Competence, Donor Age, and Peer Presence on Helping in an Emergency." *Developmental Psychology* 19 (1983): 873–80.

PIAGET, JEAN. *The Moral Judgment of the Child.* Translated by Marjorie Gabain. New York: Free Press, 1965.

———. *Six Psychological Studies.* Translated by Anita Tenzer. New York: Vintage, 1968.

PILIAVIN, IRVING M., JUDITH RODIN, and JANE ALLYN PILIAVIN. "Good Samaritanism: An Underground Phenomenon?" *Journal of Personality and Social Psychology* 13 (1969): 289–99.

PILIAVIN, JANE ALLYN, JOHN F. DOVIDIO, SAMUEL L. GAERTNER, and RUSSELL D. CLARK III. "Responsive Bystanders: The Process of Intervention." In *Cooperation and Helping Behavior: Theories and Research,* edited by Valerian J. Derlega and Janusz Grzelak. New York: Academic Press, 1982.

PINES, AYALA, and TRUDY SOLOMON. "Perception of Self as a Mediator in the Dehumanization Process." *Personality and Social Psychology Bulletin* 3 (1977): 219–23.

PINES, MAYA. "Good Samaritans at Age Two?" *Psychology Today,* June 1979, 66–74.

PLATO. *The Republic of Plato.* Translated by Francis MacDonald Cornford. London: Oxford University Press, 1941.

PLOMIN, ROBERT. "Environment and Genes: Determinants of Behavior." *American Psychologist* 44 (1989): 105–11.

PLOMIN, ROBERT, TERRYL T. FOCH, and DAVID C. ROWE. "Bobo Clown Aggression in Childhood: Environment, Not Genes." *Journal of Research in Personality* 15 (1981): 331–42.

POWER, F. CLARK, ANN HIGGINS, and LAWRENCE KOHLBERG. *Lawrence Kohlberg's Approach to Moral Education.* New York: Columbia University Press, 1989.

PSYCHOLOGY TODAY. "Smoke Gets in the Way." November 1988, 8.

QUINDLEN, ANNA. "The Dimming of Prejudice Also Fans Its Flames." *New York Times,* 22 September 1988, C2.

RABBIE, JACOB M., FRITS BENOIST, HENK OOSTERBAAN, and LIEUWE VISSER. "Differential Power and Effects of Expected Competitive and Cooperative Intergroup Interaction on Intragroup and Outgroup Attitudes." *Journal of Personality and Social Psychology* 30 (1974): 46–56.

RABBIE, JACOB M., and J. H. C. DE BREY. "The Anticipation of Intergroup Cooperation and Competition under Private and Public Conditions." *International Journal of Group Tensions* 1 (1971): 230–51.

RADKE-YARROW, MARIAN, PHYLLIS M. SCOTT, and CAROLYN ZAHN-WAXLER. "Learning Concern for Others." *Developmental Psychology* 8 (1973): 240–60.

RADKE-YARROW, MARIAN, and CAROLYN ZAHN-WAXLER. "Dimensions and Correlates of Prosocial Behavior in Young Children." *Child Development* 47 (1976): 118–25.

———. "Roots, Motives, and Patterns in Children's Prosocial Behavior." In *Development and Maintenance of Prosocial Behavior: International Perspectives on Positive Morality,* edited by Ervin Staub, Daniel Bar-Tal, Jerzy Karylowski, and Janusz Reykowski. New York: Plenum, 1984.

RADKE-YARROW, MARIAN, CAROLYN ZAHN-WAXLER, and MICHAEL CHAPMAN. "Children's Prosocial Dispositions and Behavior." In *Handbook of Child Psychology,* vol. 4, edited by Paul H. Mussen. 4th ed. New York: John Wiley, 1983.

RAND, AYN. *The Virtue of Selfishness: A New Concept of Egoism.* New York: Signet, 1964.

RATCLIFFE, JAMES M. Introduction to *The Good Samaritan and the Law,* edited by James M. Ratcliffe. 1966. Reprint. Gloucester, Mass.: Peter Smith, 1981.

RAVIN, ARNOLD W. "Natural Selection and Human Choice." *Hastings Center Report,* December 1980, 30–31.

RAWLS, JOHN. *A Theory of Justice.* Cambridge, Mass.: Harvard University Press, 1971.

REED, GAIL S. "The Antithetical Meaning of the Term 'Empathy' in Psychoanalytic Discourse." In *Empathy I,* edited by Joseph Lichtenberg, Melvin Bornstein, and Donald Silver. Hillsdale, N.J.: Lawrence Erlbaum, 1984.

RENDER, GARY F., JE NELL M. PADILLA, and H. MARK KRANK. "What Research

Really Shows about Assertive Discipline." *Educational Leadership,* March 1989, 72–75.

RESCHER, NICHOLAS. *Unselfishness: The Role of the Vicarious Affects in Moral Philosophy and Social Theory.* Pittsburgh: University of Pittsburgh Press, 1975.

RICHMAN, CHARLES L., CAROLYN BERRY, MONNIE BITTLE, and KIM HIMAN. "Factors Related to Helping Behavior in Preschool-Age Children." *Journal of Applied Developmental Psychology* 9 (1988): 151–65.

RIMLAND, BERNARD. "The Altruism Paradox." *Psychological Reports* 51 (1982): 521–22.

ROBB, CHRISTINA. "Is Vengeance Ours?: A New Look at the 'Instinctual' Need to Get Even." *Boston Globe Magazine,* 16 April 1989.

ROGERS, CARL R. *On Becoming a Person: A Therapist's View of Psychotherapy.* Boston: Houghton Mifflin, 1961.

ROMER, DANIEL, CHARLES L. GRUDER, and TERRI LIZZADRO. "A Person-Situation Approach to Altruistic Behavior." *Journal of Personality and Social Psychology* 51 (1986): 1001–12.

ROPER, MARILYN KEYES. "A Survey of the Evidence for Intrahuman Killing in the Pleistocene." *Current Anthropology* 10 (1969): 427–48.

ROSE, RICHARD J., and JAAKKO KAPRIO. "Frequency of Social Contact and Intrapair Resemblance of Adult Monozygotic Cotwins—Or Does Shared Experience Influence Personality After All?" *Behavior Genetics* 18 (1988): 309–28.

ROSENFIELD, ISRAEL. *The Invention of Memory: A New View of the Brain.* New York: Basic Books, 1988.

ROSENHAN, DAVID. "The Natural Socialization of Altruistic Autonomy." In *Altruism and Helping Behavior,* edited by J. Macaulay and L. Berkowitz. New York: Academic Press, 1970.

ROSENHAN, DAVID, PETER SALOVEY, and KENNETH HARGIS. "The Joys of Helping: Focus of Attention Mediates the Impact of Positive Affect on Alruism." *Journal of Personality and Social Psychology* 40 (1981): 899–905.

ROSENHAN, DAVID, PETER SALOVEY, JERZY KARYLOWSKI, and KENNETH HARGIS. "Emotion and Altruism." In *Altruism and Helping Behavior: Social, Personality, and Developmental Perspectives,* edited by J. Philippe Rushton and Richard M. Sorrentino. Hillsdale, N.J.: Lawrence Erlbaum, 1981.

ROSENZWEIG, MARK R., EDWARD L. BENNETT, and MARIAN CLEEVES DIAMOND. "Brain Changes in Response to Experience." *Scientific American,* February 1972, 22–29.

ROUSSEAU, JEAN JACQUES. *Emile.* Translated by Allan Bloom. New York: Basic Books, 1979.

RUBIN, JEFFREY Z., FRANK J. PROVENZANO, and ZELLA LURIA. "The Eye of the Beholder: Parents' Views on Sex of Newborns." *American Journal of Orthopsychiatry* 44 (1974): 512–19.

RUBIN, ZICK, and ANNE PEPLAU. "Belief in a Just World and Reactions to Another's Lot: A Study of Participants in the National Draft Lottery." *Journal of Social Issues* 29 (1973): 73–93.

———. "Who Believes in a Just World?" *Journal of Social Issues* 31 (1975): 65–89.

RUSHTON, J. PHILIPPE. "Differential K Theory and Race Differences in E and N." *Personality and Individual Differences* 6 (1985): 769–70.

———. "Race Differences in Behaviour: A Review and Evolutionary Analysis." *Personality and Individual Differences* 9 (1988): 1009–24.

RUSHTON, J. PHILIPPE, and ANTHONY F. BOGAERT. "Race Differences in Sexual Behavior: Testing an Evolutionary Hypothesis." *Journal of Research in Personality* 21 (1987): 529–51.

RUSHTON, J. PHILIPPE, DAVID W. FULKER, MICHAEL C. NEALE, DAVID K. B. NIAS, and HANS J. EYSENCK. "Altruism and Aggression: The Heritability of Individual Differences." *Journal of Personality and Social Psychology* 50 (1986): 1192–98.

RUSSELL, BERTRAND. *Why I Am Not a Christian.* New York: Simon and Schuster, 1957.

RUTHERFORD, ELDRED, and PAUL MUSSEN. "Generosity in Nursery School Boys." *Child Development* 39 (1968): 755–65.

SAGI, ABRAHAM, and MARTIN L. HOFFMAN. "Empathic Distress in the Newborn." *Developmental Psychology* 12 (1976): 175–76.

SAHLINS, MARSHALL. *The Use and Abuse of Biology: An Anthropological Critique of Sociobiology.* Ann Arbor: University of Michigan Press, 1976.

SAMPSON, EDWARD E. "Psychology and the American Ideal." *Journal of Personality and Social Psychology* 35 (1977): 767–82.

SARTRE, JEAN-PAUL. *Being and Nothingness: A Phenomenological Essay on Ontology.* Translated by Hazel E. Barnes. New York: Washington Square Press, 1966.

SAVITSKY, JEFFREY C., and THOMAS EBY. "Emotion Awareness and Antisocial Behavior." In *Emotions in Personality and Psychopathology,* edited by Carroll E. Izard. New York: Plenum, 1979.

SAWYIER, FAY HORTON. "A Conceptual Analysis of Empathy." *Annual of Psychoanalysis* 3 (1975): 37–47.

SCHACHTER, S., and J. E. SINGER. "Cognitive, Social, and Physiological Determinants of Emotional State." *Psychological Review* 69 (1962): 379–99.

SCHEIBE, KARL E. "College Students Spend Eight Weeks in Mental Hospital: A Case Report." *Psychotherapy: Theory, Research, and Practice* 2 (1965): 117–20.

SCHELER, MAX. *The Nature of Sympathy.* Translated by Peter Heath. London: Routledge and Kegan Paul, 1954.

SCHEMAN, NAOMI. "Individualism and the Objects of Psychology." In *Discovering Reality,* edited by Sandra Harding and Merrill B. Hintikka. Dordrecht, Holland: D. Reidel, 1983.

SCHMOOKLER, ANDREW BARD. *Out of Weakness: Healing the Wounds That Drive Us to War.* New York: Bantam, 1988.

SCHOENRADE, PATRICIA A., C. DANIEL BATSON, J. RANDALL BRANDT, and ROBERT E. LOUD, JR. "Attachment, Accountability, and Motivation to Benefit Another Not in Distress." *Journal of Personality and Social Psychology* 51 (1986): 557–63.

SCHROEDER, DAVID A., JOHN F. DOVIDIO, MARK E. SIBICKY, LINDA L. MATTHEWS, and JUDITH L. ALLEN. "Empathic Concern and Helping Behavior: Egoism or Altruism?" *Journal of Experimental Social Psychology* 24 (1988): 333–53.

SCHULWEIS, HAROLD M. Foreword to *The Altruistic Personality: Rescuers of Jews in Nazi Europe,* by Samuel P. Oliner and Pearl M. Oliner. New York: Free Press, 1988.

SCHWARTZ, BARRY. *The Battle for Human Nature: Science, Morality, and Modern Life.* New York: Norton, 1986.

SCHWARTZ, SHALOM H. "Elicitation of Moral Obligation and Self-Sacrificing Behavior." *Journal of Personality and Social Psychology* 15 (1970): 283–93.

SCHWARTZ, SHALOM H., and JUDITH A. HOWARD. "Internalized Values as Motivators of Altruism." In *Development and Maintenance of Prosocial Behavior: International Perspectives on Positive Morality,* edited by Ervin Staub, Daniel Bar-Tal, Jerzy Karylowski, and Janusz Reykowski. New York: Plenum, 1984.

SCOTT, J. PAUL. "The Biological Basis of Warfare." In *Essays on Violence,* edited by J. Martin Ramirez, Robert A. Hinde, and Jo Groebel. Seville, Spain: Publicaciones de la Universidad de Sevilla, 1987.

SEARS, DAVID O., and CAROLYN L. FUNK. "Self-Interest in Americans' Political Opinions." In *Beyond Self-Interest,* edited by Jane Mansbridge. Chicago: University of Chicago Press, 1990.

SEARS, ROBERT R., ELEANOR E. MACCOBY, and HARRY LEVIN. *Patterns of Child Rearing.* Evanston, Ill.: Row, Peterson, 1957.

SEGAL, JULIUS. "Compassionate Kids." *Parents,* September 1988, 104–10.

SELMAN, ROBERT L. *The Growth of Interpersonal Understanding: Developmental and Clinical Analyses.* New York: Academic Press, 1980.

———. "Social-Cognitive Understanding: A Guide to Educational and Clinical Practice." In *Moral Development and Behavior,* edited by Thomas Lickona. New York: Holt, Rinehart and Winston, 1976.

———. "Toward a Structural Analysis of Developing Interpersonal Relations Concepts: Research with Normal and Disturbed Preadolescent Boys." In *Tenth Annual Minnesota Symposium on Child Psychology,* edited by A. Pick. Minneapolis: University of Minnesota, 1976.

SEN, AMARTYA. *On Ethics and Economics.* Oxford, England: Basil Blackwell, 1987.

———. "Rational Fools: A Critique of the Behavioural Foundations of Economic Theory." In *Scientific Models and Man,* edited by Henry Harris. Oxford, England: Clarendon Press, 1979.

SENNEKER, PHYLLIS, and CLYDE HENDRICK. "Androgyny and Helping Behavior." *Journal of Personality and Social Psychology* 45 (1983): 916–25.

SHANTZ, CAROLYN UHLINGER. "Social Cognition." In *Handbook of Child Psychology,* vol. 3, edited by Paul H. Mussen. 4th ed. New York: John Wiley, 1983.

SHAPIRO, DAVID. *Neurotic Styles.* New York: Basic Books, 1965.

SHERROD, DRURY R., and ROBIN DOWNS. "Environmental Determinants of Altruism: The Effects of Stimulus Overload and Perceived Control on Helping." *Journal of Experimental Social Psychology* 10 (1974): 468–79.

SIMNER, MARVIN L. "Newborn's Response to the Cry of Another Infant." *Developmental Psychology* 5 (1971): 136–50.

SIMON, MICHAEL A. "Biology, Sociobiology, and the Understanding of Human Social Behavior." In *Sociobiology Examined,* edited by Ashley Montagu. New York: Oxford University Press, 1980.

SINGER, PETER. *The Expanding Circle: Ethics and Sociobiology.* New York: Farrar, Straus and Giroux, 1981.

———. "The Hypothalamus and the Impartial Perspective." *Behavioral and Brain Sciences* 10 (1987): 84–85.

SLATER, PHILIP. *The Pursuit of Loneliness: American Culture at the Breaking Point.* Boston: Beacon, 1970.

SLAVIN, ROBERT. *Cooperative Learning.* New York: Longman, 1983.

SLAVIN, ROBERT, SHLOMO SHARAN, SPENCER KAGAN, RACHEL HERTZ LAZAROWITZ, CLARK WEBB, and RICHARD SCHMUCK, eds. *Learning to Cooperate, Cooperating to Learn.* New York: Plenum, 1985.

SMITH, ADAM. *The Theory of Moral Sentiments.* 1759. Reprint. Edited by D. D. Raphael and A. L. Macfie. Oxford: Clarendon, 1976.

SMITH, CATHLEEN L., DONNA M. GELFAND, DONALD P. HARTMANN, and MARJORIE E. Y. PARTLOW. "Children's Causal Attributions Regarding Help Giving." *Child Development* 50 (1979): 203–10.

SMITH, KARL, DAVID W. JOHNSON, and ROGER T. JOHNSON. "Can Conflict Be Constructive? Controversy versus Concurrence Seeking in Learning Groups." *Journal of Educational Psychology* 73 (1981): 651–63.

SMITH, M. BREWSTER. "Humanism and Behaviorism in Psychology: Theory and Practice." *Journal of Humanistic Psychology* 18 (1978): 27–36.

SMITH, RONALD E., GREGORY WHEELER, and EDWARD DIENER. "Faith without Works: Jesus People, Resistance to Temptation, and Altruism." *Journal of Applied Social Psychology* 5 (1975): 320–30.

SMITHSON, MICHAEL, PAUL R. AMATO, and PHILIP PEARCE. *Dimensions of Helping Behaviour.* Oxford, England: Pergamon Press, 1983.

SMOLER, FREDRIC. "The Secret of the Soldiers Who Didn't Shoot." *American Heritage,* March 1989, 37–45.

SNODGRASS, SARA E. "Women's Intuition: The Effect of Subordinate Role on Interpersonal Sensitivity." *Journal of Personality and Social Psychology* 49 (1985): 146–55.

SOLOMON, DANIEL, MARILYN WATSON, KEVIN L. DELUCCHI, ERIC SCHAPS, and VICTOR BATTISTICH. "Enhancing Children's Prosocial Behavior in the Classroom." *American Educational Research Journal* 25 (1988): 527–54.

SOLOMON, DANIEL, MARILYN WATSON, ERIC SCHAPS, VICTOR BATTISTICH, and JU-

DITH SOLOMON. "Cooperative Learning as Part of a Comprehensive Classroom Program Designed to Promote Prosocial Development." In *Cooperative
Learning: Theory and Research,* edited by Shlomo Sharan. New York: Praeger,
in press.

SOLOMON, HENRY, LINDA ZENER SOLOMON, MARIA M. ARNONE, BONNIE J. MAUR,
ROSINA M. REDA, and ESTHER O. ROTHER. "Anonymity and Helping." *Journal
of Social Psychology* 113 (1981): 37–43.

SOMMER, BARBARA. "Cognitive Behavior and the Menstrual Cycle." In *Behavior
and the Menstrual Cycle,* edited by Richard C. Friedman. New York: Marcel
Dekker, 1982.

SPENCE, JANET T. "Achievement American Style: The Rewards and Costs of
Individualism." *American Psychologist* 40 (1985): 1285–95.

SPENCER, HERBERT. *The Principles of Ethics.* Vol. 1. 1897. Reprint. Indianapolis:
Liberty Classics, 1978.

SPERLING, OTTO E. "A Psychoanalytic Study of Social-Mindedness." *Psychoanalytic
Quarterly* 24 (1955): 256–69.

SPIECKER, BEN. "Psychopathy: The Incapacity to Have Moral Emotions." *Journal
of Moral Education* 17 (1988): 98–104.

SPRAFKIN, CAROL, LISA A. SERBIN, CAROL DENIER, and JANE M. CONNOR. "Sex-
Differentiated Play: Cognitive Consequences and Early Interventions." In
Social and Cognitive Skills: Sex Roles and Children's Play, edited by Marsha B. Liss.
New York: Academic Press, 1983.

SROUFE, L. ALAN. "Infant-Caregiver Attachment and Patterns of Adaptation in
Preschool." In *Minnesota Symposia on Child Psychology,* vol. 16, edited by Mar-
ion Perlmutter. Hillsdale, N.J.: Lawrence Erlbaum, 1983.

STANHOPE, LINDA, RICHARD Q. BELL, and NINA Y. PARKER-COHEN. "Temperament
and Helping Behavior in Preschool Children." *Developmental Psychology* 23
(1987): 347–53.

STAUB, ERVIN. "Commentary on Part I." In *Empathy and Its Development,* edited by
Nancy Eisenberg and Janet Strayer. Cambridge, England: Cambridge University Press, 1987.

———. "A Conception of the Determinants and Development of Altruism and
Aggression: Motives, the Self, and the Environment." In *Altruism and Aggression: Biological and Social Origins,* edited by Carolyn Zahn-Waxler, E. Mark
Cummings, and Ronald Iannotti. Cambridge, England: Cambridge University Press, 1986.

———. *Positive Social Behavior and Morality.* 2 vols. New York: Academic Press,
1978–79.

———. "Promoting Positive Behavior in Schools, in Other Educational Settings,
and in the Home." In *Altruism and Helping Behavior: Social, Personality, and
Developmental Perspectives,* edited by J. Philippe Rushton and Richard M. Sorrentino. Hillsdale, N.J.: Lawrence Erlbaum, 1981.

———. "The Use of Role Playing and Induction in Children's Learning of Helping and Sharing Behavior." *Child Development* 42 (1971): 805–16.

STAUB, ERVIN, and LINDA SHERK. "Need for Approval, Children's Sharing Behavior, and Reciprocity in Sharing." *Child Development* 41 (1970): 243–52.

STENT, GUNTHER S. "You Can Take the Ethics out of Altruism but You Can't Take the Alruism out of Ethics." Review of *The Selfish Gene,* by Richard Dawkins. *Hastings Center Report,* December 1977, 33–36.

STERN, DANIEL N. *The Interpersonal World of the Infant: A View from Psychoanalysis and Developmental Psychology.* New York: Basic Books, 1985.

STOTLAND, EZRA. "Exploratory Investigations of Empathy." In *Advances in Experimental Social Psychology,* vol. 4, edited by Leonard Berkowitz. New York: Academic Press, 1969.

STRAYER, JANET. "Affective and Cognitive Perspectives on Empathy." In *Empathy and Its Development,* edited by Nancy Eisenberg and Janet Strayer. Cambridge, England: Cambridge University Press, 1987.

STRAYER, JANET, and NANCY EISENBERG. "Empathy Viewed in Context." In *Empathy and Its Development,* edited by Nancy Eisenberg and Janet Strayer. Cambridge, England: Cambridge University Press, 1987.

STRENTA, ANGELO, and WILLIAM DEJONG. "The Effect of a Prosocial Label on Helping Behavior." *Social Psychology Quarterly* 44 (1981): 142–47.

STRUCH, NAOMI, and SHALOM H. SCHWARTZ. "Intergroup Aggression: Its Predictors and Distinctness from In-Group Bias." *Journal of Personality and Social Psychology* 56 (1989): 364–73.

SULLIVAN, HARRY STACK. *Conceptions of Modern Psychiatry.* New York: Norton, 1953.

———. "The Illusion of Personal Individuality." *Psychiatry* 13 (1950): 317–32.

———. *The Interpersonal Theory of Psychiatry.* New York: Norton, 1953.

SULS, JERRY, SUSAN WITENBERG, and DANIEL GUTKIN. "Evaluating Reciprocal and Nonreciprocal Prosocial Behavior: Developmental Changes." *Personality and Social Psychology Bulletin* 7 (1981): 25–31.

TAKOOSHIAN, HAROLD, SANDRA HABER, and DAVID J. LUCIDO. "Who Wouldn't Help a Lost Child?" *Psychology Today,* February 1977, 67–68, 88.

TAVRIS, CAROL. *Anger: The Misunderstood Emotion.* New York: Simon and Schuster, 1982.

TAYLOR, PAUL W. *Principles of Ethics: An Introduction.* Encino, Calif.: Dickenson, 1975.

TELLEGEN, AUKE, THOMAS J. BOUCHARD, JR., KIMERLY J. WILCOX, NANCY L. SEGAL, DAVID T. LYKKEN, and STEPHEN RICH. "Personality Similarity in Twins Reared Apart and Together." *Journal of Personality and Social Psychology* 54 (1988): 1031–39.

THOMAS, GEORGE C., C. DANIEL BATSON, and JAY S. COKE. "Do Good Samaritans Discourage Helpfulness? Self-Perceived Altruism after Exposure to Highly Helpful Others." *Journal of Personality and Social Psychology* 40 (1981): 194–200.

THOMAS, LEWIS. *The Lives of a Cell: Notes of a Biology Watcher.* New York: Bantam, 1975.

THOMPSON, ROSS A. "Empathy and Emotional Understanding: The Early Development of Empathy." In *Empathy and Its Development,* edited by Nancy Eisenberg and Janet Strayer. Cambridge, England: Cambridge University Press, 1987.

THOMPSON, WILLIAM C., CLAUDIA L. COWAN, and DAVID L. ROSENHAN. "Focus of Attention Mediates the Impact of Negative Affect on Altruism." *Journal of Personality and Social Psychology* 38 (1980): 291–300.

TICE, DIANNE M., and ROY F. BAUMEISTER. "Masculinity Inhibits Helping in Emergencies: Personality Does Predict the Bystander Effect." *Journal of Personality and Social Psychology* 49 (1985): 420–28.

TITMUSS, RICHARD M. *The Gift Relationship: From Human Blood to Social Policy.* New York: Pantheon, 1971.

TJOSVOLD, DEAN. "Effects of Departments' Interdependence on Organizational Decision Making." *Psychological Reports* 53 (1983): 851–57.

TJOSVOLD, DEAN, and DAVID W. JOHNSON. "The Effects of Controversy on Cognitive Perspective-Taking." *Journal of Educational Psychology* 69 (1977): 679–85.

TORREY, E. FULLER. *Surviving Schizophrenia: A Family Manual.* New York: Harper and Row, 1983.

TRIVERS, ROBERT L. "The Evolution of Reciprocal Altruism." *Quarterly Review of Biology* 46 (1971): 35–57.

TYLER, TOM R. "Justice, Self-Interest, and the Legitimacy of Legal and Political Authority." In *Beyond Self-Interest,* edited by Jane Mansbridge. Chicago: University of Chicago Press, 1990.

UNDERWOOD, BILL, JAMES F. BERENSON, RONALD J. BERENSON, KENNETH K. CHENG, DAYNA WILSON, JAMES KULIK, BERT S. MOORE, and GARY WENZEL. "Attention, Negative Affect, and Altruism: An Ecological Validation." *Personality and Social Psychology Bulletin* 3 (1977): 54–58.

UNDERWOOD, BILL, and BERT MOORE. "Perspective-Taking and Altruism." *Psychological Bulletin* 91 (1982): 143–73.

VIORST, JUDITH. "A Palestinian, a Jew, a Sense of Humanity." *New York Times,* 9 July 1988, 27.

DE WAAL, FRANS. *Peacemaking among Primates.* Cambridge, Mass.: Harvard University Press, 1989.

WACHTEL, PAUL L. *The Poverty of Affluence: A Psychological Portrait of the American Way of Life.* New York: Free Press, 1983.

WAHLSTEN, DOUGLAS. "Bias and Sampling Error in Sex Difference Research." *Behavioral and Brain Sciences* 11 (1988): 214.

WAHLSTROM, RIITTA. "The Psychological Basis for Peace Education." University of Joensuu, Finland. Photocopy.

WALLACH, MICHAEL A., and LISE WALLACH. "How Psychology Sanctions the Cult of the Self." *Washington Monthly,* February 1985, 46–56.

———. *Psychology's Sanction for Selfishness: The Error of Egoism in Theory and Therapy.* San Francisco: W. H. Freeman, 1983.

WALSTER, ELAINE, G. WILLIAM WALSTER, and ELLEN BERSCHEID. *Equity: Theory and Research.* Boston: Allyn and Bacon, 1978.

WALZER, MICHAEL. "Socialism and the Gift Relationship." *Dissent,* Fall 1982, 431–41.

WARSH, DAVID. "A Financial World in Dark until It Finds Bottom Line." *Boston Globe,* 20 October 1987, 34.

WATERS, EVERETT, JUDITH WIPPMAN, and L. ALAN SROUFE. "Attachment, Positive Affect, and Competence in the Peer Group: Two Studies in Construct Validation." *Child Development* 50 (1979): 821–29.

WATSON, MARILYN, DANIEL SOLOMON, VICTOR BATTISTICH, ERIC SCHAPS, and JUDITH SOLOMON. "The Child Development Project: A Values Education Program That Combines Traditional and Developmental Approaches." In *Moral Development and Character Education: A Dialogue,* edited by Larry P. Nucci. Berkeley, Calif.: McCutchan, 1989.

WATSON, RUSSELL. "A Case of Human Error." *Newsweek,* 15 August 1988, 18.

WHEELER, LINDA. "Runner Pulls Man from Car in River." *Washington Post,* 23 December 1987, B1–2.

WHITE, RALPH K. *Fearful Warriors: A Psychological Profile of U.S.-Soviet Relations.* New York: Free Press, 1984.

WIESEL, ELIE. *The Town beyond the Wall.* Translated by Stephen Becker. New York: Avon, 1964.

WILDER, DAVID A. "Social Categorization: Implications for Creation and Reduction of Intergroup Bias." In *Advances in Experimental Social Psychology,* vol. 19, edited by Leonard Berkowitz. Orlando, Fla.: Academic Press, 1986.

WILLIAMS, BERNARD. *Ethics and the Limits of Philosophy.* Cambridge, Mass.: Harvard University Press, 1985.

WILLIAMS, ROGER R. "Nature, Nurture, and Family Predisposition." *New England Journal of Medicine,* 24 March 1988, 769–71.

WILLIAMSON, GAIL M., and MARGARET S. CLARK. "Providing Help and Desired Relationship Type as Determinants of Changes in Moods and Self-Evaluations." *Journal of Personality and Social Psychology* 56 (1989): 722–34.

WILSON, EDWARD O. "Human Decency Is Animal." *New York Times Magazine,* 12 October 1975, 38–50.

———. *On Human Nature.* New York: Bantam, 1979.

———. *Sociobiology: The New Synthesis.* Cambridge, Mass.: Harvard University Press, 1975.

WISPE, LAUREN. "The Distinction between Sympathy and Empathy: To Call Forth a Concept, a Word Is Needed." *Journal of Personality and Social Psychology* 50 (1986): 314–21.

————. "History of the Concept of Empathy." In *Empathy and Its Development,* edited by Nancy Eisenberg and Janet Strayer. Cambridge, England: Cambridge University Press, 1987.

WITELSON, SANDRA F. "The Brain Connections." *Science,* 16 August 1985, 665–68.

WOLFF, ROBERT PAUL. *The Poverty of Liberalism.* Boston: Beacon, 1968.

WONG, DAVID B. *Moral Relativity.* Berkeley: University of California Press, 1984.

WOOLF, VIRGINIA. *To the Lighthouse.* New York: Harcourt Brace Jovanovich, 1927.

WRIGHT, DEREK. *The Psychology of Moral Behaviour.* Middlesex, England: Penguin, 1971.

WRIGHTSMAN, LAWRENCE S., and FRANK C. NOBLE. "Reactions to the President's Assassination and Changes in Philosophies of Human Nature." *Psychological Reports* 16 (1965): 159–62.

YANKELOVICH, DANIEL, and WILLIAM BARRETT. *Ego and Instinct: The Psychoanalytic View of Human Nature—Revised.* New York: Vintage, 1971.

YOUNG, WARREN R. " 'There's a Girl on the Tracks!' " *Reader's Digest,* February 1977, 91–95.

YOUNISS, JAMES. "Development in Reciprocity through Friendship." In *Altruism and Aggression: Biological and Social Origins,* edited by Carolyn Zahn-Waxler, E. Mark Cummings, and Ronald Iannotti. Cambridge, England: Cambridge University Press, 1986.

ZAHN-WAXLER, CAROLYN. "Conclusions: Lessons from the Past and a Look to the Future." In *Altruism and Aggression: Biological and Social Origins,* edited by Carolyn Zahn-Waxler, E. Mark Cummings, and Ronald Iannotti. Cambridge, England: Cambridge University Press, 1986.

ZAHN-WAXLER, CAROLYN, E. MARK CUMMINGS, and RONALD IANNOTTI. "Altruism and Aggression: Problems and Progress in Research." In *Altruism and Aggression: Biological and Social Origins,* edited by Carolyn Zahn-Waxler, E. Mark Cummings, and Ronald Iannotti. Cambridge, England: Cambridge University Press, 1986.

ZAHN-WAXLER, CAROLYN, E. MARK CUMMINGS, and RONALD IANNOTTI, eds. *Altruism and Aggression: Biological and Social Origins.* Cambridge, England: Cambridge University Press, 1986.

ZAHN-WAXLER, CAROLYN, MARIAN RADKE-YARROW, and JUDY BRADY-SMITH. "Perspective-Taking and Prosocial Behavior." *Developmental Psychology* 13 (1977): 87–88.

ZAHN-WAXLER, CAROLYN, MARIAN RADKE-YARROW, and ROBERT A. KING. "Child Rearing and Children's Prosocial Inclinations toward Victims of Distress." *Child Development* 50 (1979): 319–30.

ZAHN-WAXLER, CAROLYN, MARIAN RADKE-YARROW, ELIZABETH WAGNER, and CLAUDIA PYLE. "The Early Development of Prosocial Behavior." Paper presented at the International Conference on Infant Studies, Washington, D.C., April 1988.

ZIMBARDO, PHILIP G. "The Human Choice: Individuation, Reason, and Order versus Deindividuation, Impulse, and Chaos." In *Nebraska Symposium on Motivation*, vol. 17, edited by William J. Arnold and David Levine. Lincoln: University of Nebraska Press, 1969.

ZUCKERMAN, MIRON, MICHELLE M. LAZZARO, and DIANE WALDGEIR. "Undermining Effects of the Foot-in-the-Door Technique with Extrinsic Rewards." *Journal of Applied Social Psychology* 9 (1979): 292–96.

Subject Index

Abstraction, 141, 264

Affirmative action, 146

Aggression: absence of, vs. prosocial behavior, 87; and animals, 53–54; and biochemical factors, 52–53; and catharsis, 47, 51–52; and dehumanization, 139, 141, 143–44, 151; causes of, 55–57, 139–44; claims of universality of, 45–47; discouraging, in children, 86–87, 168–69; effect of empathy on, 56, 125, 168–69; effect of proximity on, 49, 141, 285n41; gender differences in, 27–28; "human nature" explanations of, 12–13, 45–59, 269–72; reasons for belief in innateness of, 57–59; results of belief in innateness of, 58–59; as slippery concept, 50–51; treatment of, by mass media, 16–17; vs. assertiveness, 27n, 77–78; see also War

Alcoholism, 9

Altruism: attempts to find biological bases for, 217–20; based on principles vs. care, 240n, 257–60; denial of, by biologists, 23n, 183–85, 213–17; denial of, by economists, 96n, 185–87, 209n, 220–25, 323n38; denial of, by psychologists, 189–94; as distinct from "prosocial" behav-

ior, 63n, 206; evidence for existence of, 229–38; explaining doubts about existence of, 194–204; reserving term for heroes and saints, 4, 197–98, 207, 267, 329–30n9; suspiciousness of, in U.S., 64, 70–71, 96–97, 198–99, 201, 244, 256; vs. egoism (challenging dichotomy), 181, 239–47; see also Prosocial behavior; Egoism

Androgyny, 341n28

Anger: and catharsis, 286n49; moral, 126; and prosocial behavior, 74; social context of, 53

Animals: aggression of, 53–54; attitude toward, 139–40, 315n38

Apartheid, 312–13n2

Biological determinism, 6–34; and alcoholism, 9; arguments against, 18–22, 53; and crime, 9; and heritability, 32–34; and ideology, 7, 15–16, 24–25, 58, 276n35, 321–22n11; and personality, 10, 33–34; popularity of, 5, 7–11; and psychological disorders, 7–9, 12, 30–31; reasons for acceptance of, 11–17, 57–59; reductivism

Rationality *(continued)*
 ity, 257–59, 315*n*38; as harmful, 48*n*,
 265; and social interaction, 254;
 sociobiological account of, 321*n*9
Reciprocity: as social science theory,
 69, 73, 187–88, 225–28, 337*n*93;
 as sociobiological theory, 184, 215–
 17
Reductionism, 21–22, 137–38
Relationship: as context for prosocial
 action, 227–28, 237, 244–47; and
 empathy, 142, 246–47; and perspective taking, 113–14, 154, 162; vs. individualism, 250, 254; vs. principles,
 240*n*, 257–60, 266; *see also* Friendship
Religion: 79–80, 199, 295–96*n*70; *see
 also* Original Sin
Responsibility: cynicism as escape
 from, 40–42; determinism as escape
 from, 12–13, 58; diffusion of, by others' presence, 68; helping due to
 feeling of, for others, 126–27
Rewards, use of, 84, 170, 201–4, 221
Role taking, *see* Perspective taking

Sadness, 74, 125, 235–36; *see also*
 Prosocial behaviors, effect of mood
 on
Schizophrenia, 7–8, 30–31, 151
Schools and prosocial instruction,
 163–77
Secure attachment, 87–88, 298–99*n*
 100
Self-awareness: and prosocial behavior, 74–75, 125–26; sociobiological
 account of, 321*n*9
Self-centeredness, *see* Egocentricity
Self-esteem: and empathy, 76; and
 prosocial behavior, 76–77, 166, 209;
 vs. selfishness, 206

Self-interest: used as inducement for
 helping, 89, 93, 199–204, 225; vs.
 self-centeredness, 42–43, 206–7; *see
 also* Egoism
Self-love, 206–7
Selfishness, *see* Egoism
Seville Statement on aggression, 45,
 269–72
Sex differences, *see* Gender differences
Similarity: effect on empathy, 122; effect on prosocial behavior, 71–72,
 148; *see also* Humanization, from otherness and common humanness; We
 vs. they
Sociobiology: 22–25; and altruism vs.
 egoism, 23*n*, 183–85, 189, 213–17;
 political implications of, 24–25
Sociopathy, 56, 105, 112, 124–25, 128
State of nature, 12
Subject, person as: *see* Humanization
Sympathy: altruistic motive for, 84*n*,
 338*n*107; from secure attachment,
 87–88; and gender differences, 82;
 as human instinct, 219; as incor-
 porating desire to act, 241; and perspective taking, 101–2; and prosocial
 behavior, 73; vs. distress, 125, 233–
 36; vs. empathy, 115–16, 307*n*86,
 317*n*67; *see also* Empathy

Television, *see* Media, mass
Trait: as questionable concept, 293*n*
 40; vs. state, 82–85
Twin studies, 10, 29–32

United States: violence of, 7, 58, 160–
 61, 314*n*21
"Us" as motive, *see* Relationship
Utilitarianism, 211, 248, 343*n*55

Name Index

Adelson, Joseph, 84–85, 289–90n2
Aderman, David, 163
Adler, Alfred, 287n70, 314n19
Alexander, Richard, 184–85, 215–16, 321n9
Allport, Gordon, 207, 217, 295n62, 295n70
Amabile, Teresa, 38, 39, 328n73
Angyal, Andras, 254
Aristotle, 52, 239
Aronfreed, Justin, 117

Badcock, C.R., 321n9, 321–22n11
Baier, Kurt, 112
Bakan, David, 254
Balint, Enid, 312n145
Bandura, Albert, 139
Barash, David, 23, 184
Barber, Benjamin, 159, 188
Barbie, Klaus, 139
Barnett, Mark, 96
Baron, Robert A., 45
Barrett, William, 265
Batson, C. Daniel, 84n, 163, 192–93, 219, 233–37, 240n, 243, 295–96n70, 305n50, 344n71
Baumrind, Diana, 86

Becker, Gary, 24–25, 323n38
Belenky, Mary, 195
Bellah, Robert, 191, 249, 254
Benderly, Beryl Lieff, 17
Bentham, Jeremy, 248
Berkowitz, Leonard, 72, 232
Bettelheim, Bruno, 156, 157
Binswanger, Ludwig, 116
Blau, Peter, 187
Bloom, Allan, 191
Blum, Lawrence, 245–46, 258, 261, 262n, 343n55, 344n71
Borke, Helene, 302n13
Brown, Dyke, 172
Brown, Norman O., 251
Buber, Martin, 99, 102, 112, 114, 117, 119, 122, 132–33, 135, 136, 152–53, 163, 227, 253, 267
Budd, Louis, 327n62
Bush, George, 160
Butler, Joseph, 182, 331n20

Cairns, John, 18n
Cairns, Robert, 22
Camus, Albert, 35, 44, 49, 121, 155, 197, 230–31, 253, 264
Caplan, Arthur, 331n22

Chesterton, G. K., 208
Chodorow, Nancy, 26, 123, 251, 312n145
Chomsky, Noam, 161n
Cialdini, Robert, 235–36, 246, 324n47
Cicero, 37
Clark, Margaret, 227–28, 237
Clary, E. Gil, 298n96, 310n125, 329n83
Coles, Gerald, 8–9
Collard, David, 238
Cooley, Charles Horton, v, 149, 156
Coppola, Francis Ford, 140
Currie, Elliott, 9

Damon, William, 65
Daniels, Louise R., 232
Darley, John, 68, 82–83, 193, 242
Darwin, Charles, 219, 321n7, 333n35
Davidson, Greg, 220
Davidson, Paul, 220
Dawes, Robyn, 224, 247
Dawkins, Richard, 22, 23–24, 183, 213, 321n9
Deci, Edward, 328n73
Deutsch, Morton, 147n
Dix, Theodore, 92–93
Dollard, John, 56
Dostoyevsky, Fyodor, 38
Dovidio, John, 236
Downs, Thomas, 225
Dumont, Louis, 249

Edelman, Gerald, 20
Edgeworth, Francis, 185
Ehrhardt, Anke, 27
Eisenberg, Leon, 40, 55, 136, 150, 286n46
Eisenberg, Nancy, 77, 82, 84n, 124,

125, 229–30, 233–34, 236–37, 297n83
Eisler, Riane, 55
Ekstein, Rudolf, 153, 189
Etzioni, Amitai, 164, 220, 326n55, 334n59

Faber, Adele, 299n104
Fausto-Sterling, Anne, 27–28
Feinberg, Joel, 205
Feshbach, Norma, 115, 129–30, 153, 168–69, 173
Firesign Theatre, 316n47
Flavell, John, 99, 102, 103, 129, 130
Fox, Robin, 18
Frank, Robert, 188, 209n, 291n20
Freud, Anna, 190
Freud, Sigmund, 14, 43, 44, 51, 65, 115, 190, 191, 207, 257
Fromm, Erich, 13, 47, 206, 207, 253, 284n22

Gardner, Howard, 11
Geertz, Clifford, 23, 25, 252
Genovese, Kitty, 63–64, 68
Gerbner, George, 37–38
Gert, Bernard, 284n25, 330n12
Ghiselin, Michael, 24, 184
Gilligan, Carol, 99, 111–12, 123, 153, 154, 246, 266, 305n52, 312n147, 346n89
Goldilocks, 109
Goldmann, Lucien, 256
Goldstein, Jeffrey, 16, 53
Gorbachev, Mikhail, 160
Gordon, Suzanne, 254–55
Gould, Stephen Jay, 6, 24, 33, 278n47
Gouldner, Alvin, 14, 187–88
Granberg, Donald, 285n34